Belief, Imagination, and Delusion

MIND ASSOCIATION OCCASIONAL SERIES

This series consists of carefully selected volumes of significant original papers on predefined themes, normally growing out of a conference supported by a Mind Association Major Conference Grant. The Association nominates an editor or editors for each collection, and may cooperate with other bodies in promoting conferences or other scholarly activities in connection with the preparation of particular volumes.

Director, Mind Association: Daniel Whiting
Publications Officer: Eliot Michaelson

RECENTLY PUBLISHED IN THE SERIES

The Language of Ontology
Edited by J. T. M. Miller

Political Epistemology
Edited by Elizabeth Edenberg and Michael Hannon

Quine: Structure and Ontology
Edited by Frederique Janssen-Lauret

In the Light of Experience
Edited by Johan Gersel, Rasmus Thybo Jensen, Morten S. Thaning,
and Søren Overgaard

Evaluative Perception
Edited by Anna Bergqvist and Robert Cowan

Perceptual Ephemera
Edited by Thomas Crowther and Clare Mac Cumhaill

Common Sense in the Scottish Enlightenment
Edited by C. B. Bow

Art and Belief
Edited by Ema Sullivan-Bissett, Helen Bradley, and Paul Noordhof

The Actual and the Possible
Edited by Mark Sinclair

Thinking about the Emotions
Edited by Alix Cohen and Robert Stern

The Social and Political Philosophy of Mary Wollstonecraft
Edited by Sandrine Bergès and Alan Coffee

The Epistemic Life of Groups
Edited by Michael S. Brady and Miranda Fricker

Belief, Imagination, and Delusion

Edited by
EMA SULLIVAN-BISSETT

Great Clarendon Street, Oxford, OX2 6DP,
United Kingdom

Oxford University Press is a department of the University of Oxford.
It furthers the University's objective of excellence in research, scholarship,
and education by publishing worldwide. Oxford is a registered trade mark of
Oxford University Press in the UK and in certain other countries

© Oxford University Press 2024

The moral rights of the authors have been asserted

All rights reserved. No part of this publication may be reproduced, stored in
a retrieval system, or transmitted, in any form or by any means, without the
prior permission in writing of Oxford University Press, or as expressly permitted
by law, by licence or under terms agreed with the appropriate reprographics
rights organization. Enquiries concerning reproduction outside the scope of the
above should be sent to the Rights Department, Oxford University Press, at the
address above

You must not circulate this work in any other form
and you must impose this same condition on any acquirer

Published in the United States of America by Oxford University Press
198 Madison Avenue, New York, NY 10016, United States of America

British Library Cataloguing in Publication Data

Data available

Library of Congress Control Number: 2023938149

ISBN 978–0–19–887222–1

DOI: 10.1093/oso/9780198872221.001.0001

Printed and bound by
CPI Group (UK) Ltd, Croydon, CR0 4YY

Links to third party websites are provided by Oxford in good faith and
for information only. Oxford disclaims any responsibility for the materials
contained in any third party website referenced in this work.

Contents

List of Contributors	vii
1. Introduction *Ema Sullivan-Bissett*	1

PART I. LESSONS FROM DELUSION ON BELIEF AND IMAGINATION

2. Delusion and Self-Knowledge *Kengo Miyazono*	21
3. Contrast or Continuum? The Case of Belief and Imagination *Amy Kind*	42
4. Imagination, Agency, and Predictive Processing *Philip R. Corlett*	60

PART II. BELIEF AND IMAGINATION IN THE WILD

5. Religious Imaginings *Anna Ichino*	81
6. On the Place of Imagination in the Architecture of the Mind *Michael Omoge*	107
7. Believing in Stories: Delusions, Superstitions, Conspiracy Theories, and Other Fairy Tales *Neil Levy*	129

PART III. DELUSIONAL EXPERIENCE

8. The Capgras Delusion: An Interactionist Approach Revisited *Garry Young*	149
9. Cotard Syndrome: The Experience of Inexistence *Philip Gerrans*	181
10. Delusions and Everyday Life *Douglas Lavin and Lucy O'Brien*	205

vi CONTENTS

PART IV. DELUSIONS, BELIEF, AND EVIDENCE

11. Why Do You Believe That? Delusion and Epistemic Reasons 227
    Sophie Archer

12. The Paradox of Delusions: Are Deluded Individuals Resistant
    to Evidence? 240
    Nicholas Furl, Max Coltheart, and Ryan McKay

13. Irrationality and the Failures of Consciousness 266
    Paul Noordhof

Index 305

List of Contributors

Sophie Archer is a Lecturer in Philosophy at Cardiff University. Prior to this, she was The Robin Geffen Research Fellow and Tutor in Philosophy at Keble College, University of Oxford. Her primary research interests are in philosophy of mind, philosophy of psychology, and epistemology. She has worked on the problem of self-deception, on which she has published in *dialectica*, as well as on the nature of belief, on which she has published in *Philosophy and Phenomenological Research* and *Philosophical Studies*. She is currently drafting a book manuscript entitled *Belief* and is the editor of *Salience: A Philosophical Inquiry* (Routledge, 2022).

Max Coltheart is Emeritus Professor of Cognitive Science at Macquarie University and formerly Director of the Macquarie Centre for Cognitive Science. He is currently working on several topics in cognitive neuropsychiatry, especially delusional belief, and also on the methodology and philosophy of cognitive science. Macquarie University awarded him a DSc in 2001 and an Honorary LLD in 2010, and he was appointed a Member of the Order of Australia in 2010, for services to children with learning difficulties. He is a Fellow of the Australian Academy of Science, the Academy of the Social Sciences in Australia, and the British Academy.

Philip R. Corlett is an Associate Professor of Psychiatry and Psychology at Yale and a cognitive neuroscientist interested in the computations that underwrite believing, perceiving, hallucinations, and delusions. He uses functional neuroimaging and computational modelling of behaviour, drug infusions and transcranial magnetic stimulation studies to test causal hypotheses of how the brain creates the mind in health and illness.

Nicholas Furl is a Senior Lecturer in Psychology at Royal Holloway, University of London and heads the FurlLab there. He is a cognitive neuroscientist who studies how people and animals make decisions, with special interests in why people make biased decisions and how they make decisions in social contexts. He uses a variety of methods ranging from behavioural research and computational modelling to brain imaging methods including magnetic resonance imaging and magnetoencephalography.

Philip Gerrans is a Professor of Philosophy in the School of Humanities at the University of Adelaide. His main research interest is the use of psychological disorder to study the mind. He has written on developmental disorders (autism and Williams syndrome), cognitive neuropsychiatry, on moral psychopathologies (such as psychopathology) and the emotions, as well as a large monograph and associated series of papers on delusion and disorders of rationality. He is an Associate of the Swiss Centre for Affective Sciences where he collaborates with philosophers, psychologists, and neuroscientists.

Anna Ichino is an Assistant Professor at the State University of Milan. She works primarily in the philosophy of mind and philosophical psychology, with a focus on the

viii   LIST OF CONTRIBUTORS

cognitive architecture of propositional attitudes such as imagination and belief. Her articles have appeared in *Analysis, Argumenta, WIREs Cognitive Science, Philosophia, Philosophical Psychology*, and *Topoi*. For Oxford University Press she has published 'Truth and Trust in Fiction' (co-authored with Greg Currie, in *Art and Belief*, 2017), and an annotated bibliography on 'Imagination and Belief' (co-authored with Kengo Miyazono and Shen-yi Liao, in the *Oxford Bibliographies in Philosophy Series*, 2016).

Amy Kind is Russell K. Pitzer Professor of Philosophy at Claremont McKenna College, where she also serves as Director of the Gould Centre for Humanistic Studies. Her research interests lie broadly in the philosophy of mind, but most of her work centres on issues relating to imagination and to phenomenal consciousness. In addition to authoring the introductory textbooks *Philosophy of Mind: The Basics* and *Persons and Personal Identity*, she has edited or co-edited several volumes, the most recent being *Epistemic Uses of Imagination* (co-edited with Christopher Badura).

Douglas Lavin received his PhD from the University of Pittsburgh. Before joining the Philosophy Department at UCL in 2015, he was John L. Loeb Associate Professor of the Humanities (Philosophy), at Harvard University. He works in the areas of ethics, practical reason, action theory, and intersubjectivity.

Neil Levy is a Professor of Philosophy at Macquarie University (Sydney) and a Senior Research Fellow at the Oxford Uehiro Centre for Practical Ethics. He has published widely on a broad range of topics, most recently with an emphasis on social epistemology. His latest book is *Bad Beliefs: Why They Happen to Good People* (Oxford University Press, 2022).

Ryan McKay is a Professor of Psychology and PI of the Morality and Beliefs Lab (MaB-Lab) at Royal Holloway, University of London. His main research interest is human belief formation, in particular cases of apparently irrational belief (like delusions). But he also dabbles in other topics, including ritualistic behaviour, legal decision-making, and the phonetics of profanity.

Kengo Miyazono is an Associate Professor of Philosophy at Hokkaido University, Japan. His main research areas are philosophy of mind, philosophy of psychology, and philosophy of psychiatry. His recent publications include *Philosophy of Psychology: An Introduction* (Polity, 2021, with Lisa Bortolotti), *Delusions and Beliefs: A Philosophical Inquiry* (Routledge, 2018), 'Social Epistemological Conception of Delusion' (2021) *Synthese* 199: 1831–51 (with Alessandro Salice), and 'The Ethics of Delusional Belief' (2016) *Erkenntnis* 81(2): 275–96 (with Lisa Bortolotti).

Paul Noordhof is Anniversary Professor of Philosophy at the University of York. His main research interests are in the philosophy of mind, action theory, and metaphysics. His work in the philosophy of mind mainly focuses upon the nature and explanatory character of consciousness. His publications include 'The Clinical Significance of Anomalous Experience in the Explanation of Monothematic Delusion' (2021) *Synthese* (with Ema Sullivan-Bissett), 'The Essential Instability of Self-Deception' (2009) *Social Theory and Practice* 35(1): 45–71, 'Self-Deception, Interpretation and Consciousness' (2003)

Philosophy and Phenomenological Research 77(1): 75–100, and 'Believe What You Want' (2001) *Proceedings of the Aristotelian Society* 101(3): 247–65.

Lucy O'Brien is the Richard Wollheim Professor of Philosophy at University College London. Her research interests lie in the philosophy of mind and action, with a particular focus on self-consciousness and self-knowledge. She has more recently been working on self-consciousness understood in a broader setting—working on interpersonal self-consciousness, the nature of the self-conscious emotions, and self-consciousness and addiction. She is writing a book on interpersonal self-consciousness. She has published papers in a range of journals and collections, she is the author of *Self-Knowing Agents* (Oxford University Press, 2007) and co-editor, with Matthew Soteriou, of *Mental Actions* (Oxford University Press, 2009). She is co-editor, with A. W. Moore, of the journal *MIND*, and is Chair of the Royal Institute of Philosophy.

Michael Omoge is an Assistant Professor of Philosophy at the University of Alberta. His research interests intersect philosophy of mind, epistemology, metaphysics, and modality. He is currently working on topics in modality from a cognitivist perspective. Other works of his in this intersection have appeared in *South African Journal of Philosophy*, and *Epistemic Uses of Imagination* (Routledge, 2021) co-edited by Christopher Badura and Amy Kind.

Ema Sullivan-Bissett is a Reader in Philosophy at the University of Birmingham. Her research concerns the nature of belief and its connection to truth, as well as delusional belief formation and implicit bias. Her work has appeared in *European Journal of Philosophy*, *Mind & Language, Philosophical Psychology, Philosophical Studies, and Synthese*, among others. She also co-edited with Helen Bradley and Paul Noordhof the volume *Art and Belief* (Oxford University Press, 2017), and is the editor of the forthcoming *Routledge Handbook of the Philosophy of Delusion* and author of the forthcoming *Irrationality* (Cambridge University Press).

Garry Young is a Lecturer in Philosophy at Monash University. His research interests include monothematic delusions, particularly the Capgras and Cotard delusions (and the role of patient experience in the formation of the delusional belief) and embodied cognition (affordances and anti-intellectualist approaches to knowledge-how). His work has appeared in journals such as *Cognitive Neuropsychiatry, Consciousness and Cognition, Brain and Cognition, Synthese, Acta Analytica*, and *Philosophical Explorations*. He is also the author of *Philosophical Psychopathology: Philosophy Without Thought Experiments* (Routledge, 2014).

1
Introduction

Ema Sullivan-Bissett

1. Overview of the Main Themes and Questions

This volume brings together recent work on the nature of belief, imagination, and delusion, as it occurs in philosophy and psychology. Work in the philosophy of mind and epistemology employs notions of *believing* and *imagining* in its theories, whilst parallel work seeking to precisify these notions continues. Delusions are typically understood as beliefs with bizarre contents, but which often fail to function in belief-like ways. The aim of this collection is to get clearer on the nature of belief and imagination, how they relate to one another, and, in some cases to look more broadly at how these notions can be integrated into accounts of delusion formation and other mental phenomena. Recent work in the philosophy of mind and epistemology on the nature of belief and imagination allows us to formulate the issues with new precision, for example, by drawing on work concerning imagination's involvement with delusion formation (with its picking up the explanatory slack left by seemingly non-doxastic features), or by considering whether we ought to sharply distinguish imagination from belief (rather than endorse a continuum view), and if so, how to do that in a theoretically and empirically adequate way. The volume also considers questions concerning the architecture of imagination, the role of metacognitive error in our mental lives, the nature of delusional experience, and the relationship between delusion and evidence. The contributors to the volume are ideally placed to explore these issues, both individually and as a collective. Their interests span different disciplines (philosophy, psychology, cognitive science) and approaches (theoretical, empirically informed), which makes for a rich and varied collection of insights on the topics and questions which form the basis of the volume.

Characterizing the nature of *belief* is a huge task, but we can begin by pointing to some fairly uncontroversial features. Beliefs are typically thought of as related to truth in some way, secured either by belief's aim (e.g., Steglich-Petersen 2006), norm (e.g., Shah 2003; Shah and Velleman 2005), or biological function (Nolfi 2015; Sullivan-Bissett 2017, 2018, 2020). Beliefs are also taken to be responsive to evidence to at least some degree, and motivationally efficacious with respect to our behaviour. Of course, theorists take a variety of views on which of these features are essential to belief, and which merely result from the contingent circumstances

Ema Sullivan-Bissett, *Introduction* In: *Belief, Imagination, and Delusion.* Edited by: Ema Sullivan-Bissett,
Oxford University Press. © Oxford University Press 2024. DOI: 10.1093/oso/9780198872221.003.0001

2 BELIEF, IMAGINATION, AND DELUSION

of human belief formation. Some will add that belief is essentially normative, that there are constraints for forming beliefs that we *ought* to operate within. Others will be purely descriptive, and focus on belief's teleology as a way to delineate its essential nature.

Arguably, the nature of imagination is even more elusive, described in 2015 by Noël Carroll as the 'junkyard of the mind' (a scholarly blog by the same name was created in 2017 by Amy Kind, a contributor to this volume). A starting point is to contrast it with belief's characterization above: it is not connected to truth, it is not or need not be responsive to evidence (see Anna Ichino's chapter in this volume for discussion), and it is not motivationally efficacious. Whilst the first two are reasonable enough, the third is the subject of some dispute, with some philosophers arguing that imagination and belief share a motivational role (Ichino 2019; Velleman 2000). Others grant that imaginings can be efficacious in this way, but will restrict their power to certain contexts (Glüer and Wikforss 2013: 143–5; Noordhof 2001: 253; O'Brien 2005: 59, Noordhof, this volume), or will have it that belief is the practical ground for imagining having such an influence on our behaviour (Van Leeuwen 2009; cf. Ichino, this volume). An alternative approach to explicating the nature of the imagination is to turn to features generally agreed upon, rather than characterization by negation of features key to belief. We can follow Kind (2016: 1–3) in offering the following three features: first, it is a primitive mental state irreducible to other mental states (a claim critically discussed in Kind's and Michael Omoge's contributions to this volume); second, it has intentional content; and third, in common with our initial starting point of negating belief's key features, it is not connected to truth (as discussed in Kind's chapter). Imagination gains some elasticity from its thinly agreed upon nature, which might explain its being appealed to in accounts of several mental phenomena, including dreaming (Ichikawa 2009), hallucination (Allen 2015), implicit bias (Sullivan-Bissett 2019, 2023; Welpinghus 2020), mindreading (Currie and Ravenscroft 2002; Nichols and Stich 2003; Goldman 2006), practical knowledge (Hadisi 2021), self-deception (Gendler 2007), and superstitious attitudes (Ichino 2020). The chapters by Ichino and Neil Levy in the present volume add to the list of mental phenomena in which imagination has a stake, but in a way informed by several other contributions which seek to better understand the nature of belief and imagination. In this way, those interested in the nature of belief and imagination, and those interested in its role in our mental lives, are brought together in productive dialogue.

Let us turn to the volume's third area of interest: delusion. As noted, the current orthodoxy regarding the attitudinal nature of delusions has it that they are beliefs. There are, of course, other views on the market which deny this, and appeal to some other mental state as the vehicle for delusional content. Although such non-doxastic stalls are growing in number, it is still true to say that, for now, the majority of philosophers, psychologists, and cognitive scientists interested in delusion take these states to be beliefs. However, delusions do not always look like beliefs. Commonly pointed to non-doxastic features include their being irresponsive to evidence, their being circumscribed, and their not always being motivationally efficacious (see Kengo Miyazono's chapter in this volume for discussion). In her chapter, Sophie Archer provides an additional lens through which the non-doxasticist can see their preferred view: in at least some cases, people with delusions do not possess even subjective epistemic reasons which function as the basis for their attitude, and even granting that that does not rule out doxasticism, people do not grant the application of the question *why do you believe that?* to their delusional attitudes.

Two strategies suggest themselves in light of the seemingly non-doxastic character of delusions. One might take doxasticism to be plausible, and see delusions as instructive when we're thinking about the nature of belief—our accounts of the nature of belief might need adjusting in order to properly recognize all of its instances. Doxasticists have sought to do this by loosening strict conceptions of belief tying them tightly with, for example, procedural or epistemic rationality, allowing delusions to take their place along a continuum with other imperfect beliefs which can be reasonably taken to commit the same sins (Bortolotti 2010). Alternatively, one might take at face value delusions' non-doxastic presentation, and indeed look to other features of delusion which not only suggest that they are not beliefs, but also that they are better understood non-doxastically instead (see e.g., Currie 2000; Currie and Jureidini 2001; Dub 2017), or as somewhere in-between two kinds of state (Egan 2008 on 'bimagination'). By situating delusion in a more general discussion of belief and imagination, the present volume makes clearer the roles those attitudes can play in our cognitive economy, creating opportunities for a more nuanced approach to the attitudinal status of delusions. As such, new approaches to whether delusions are beliefs can be developed. In her chapter, Kind argues that delusions do not support a continuum thesis about belief and imagination, and advocates embracing *smudginess* about belief and imagination, suggesting that we might look to other contextual features to explain oddities of delusion which put pressure on its doxastic status. In contrast, Archer tightens up belief and, as noted already, defends the view that at least some people with delusions do not stand in a relationship of belief to the delusional content insofar as they fail to grant the application of the question *why do you believe that?* Levy explains why subjects with delusions acquiesce to their contents, whilst not standing in a relation of belief to them. Differently still, Douglas Lavin and Lucy O'Brien suggest moving away from the question of attitudinal status, and focusing instead on the *intentional object* of delusion.

Of course it might be thought that, if the first-order facts about how delusions behave are agreed upon, the debate simply turns on a proper understanding of the nature of belief. It is only after we settle that that we can appropriately characterize

4 BELIEF, IMAGINATION, AND DELUSION

various cognitive states as beliefs or not (Archer is very much alive to this dialectical danger in her contribution). Things are a bit more complicated in that it is not in general true that the first-order facts about the behaviour of delusions are agreed upon, and even when they are, it is possible to appeal to defeaters or excusing conditions to bridge the gap between how delusions function and how we should expect them to function if they were beliefs. One example of this comes from Kind: in her chapter she suggests that some beliefs are *disruptive* to one's cognitive network and so don't function in the way we might expect. Another way of making excuses for delusions is by appeal to the highly anomalous experiences they are often accompanied by, which might disrupt the usual behaviour of beliefs, or which can themselves be a source of evidence for the delusional content (if this is so, implications for their (ir)rationality and doxastic status may follow; see Noordhof, this volume). Of course, whether such experiences can be appealed to as presenting mitigating circumstances for the expected functioning of belief, or whether they might have the epistemic import that some argue for, may very well depend on the nature of those experiences. In their chapters Garry Young and Philip Gerrans seek to get clearer on the nature of anomalous experiences as they occur in Capgras delusion and Cotard delusion respectively. The precise nature of these experiences and their interaction with the formation of delusion will be relevant to pronouncing on the status of delusion with respect to its relationship to evidence, and more broadly, its attitudinal vehicle. In general, perhaps we shouldn't so quickly sign up to the idea that delusions do not respond to evidence (a claim which has almost reached the status of platitude but for some recent disagreement, e.g., Flores 2021). The relationship between delusion and evidence (as well as broader considerations of rationality and the doxastic status of delusion) is also explored in the volume, most notably in the contributions by Archer, Paul Noordhof, and Nick Furl, Max Coltheart, and Ryan McKay.

Overall, whilst the chapters in this book look at the nature of belief, imagination, and delusion, they also present various new approaches to common questions in these areas. I turn now to the main questions.

1.1 What Can Delusion Teach Us about the Nature of Belief and Imagination?

The first section of the book interrogates the nature of belief and imagination, drawing on the phenomenon of delusion.

One question we might ask is how it is we can distinguish, from the first-person perspective, our beliefs from our imaginings. As discussed later in the volume in Lavin and O'Brien's chapter, some (notably Currie 2000; Currie and Jureidini 2001) have appealed to metacognitive error to explain delusion as the formation of imaginative attitudes misidentified as beliefs (Levy develops a similar idea in his contribution to the volume, and Ichino appeals to this as part of her account of religious attitudes). In his chapter, Miyazono discusses the idea that in normal cases we have a metacognitive capacity that enables us to distinguish belief from imagination by observing and interpreting our behaviour. Miyazono argues that delusions put some pressure on this claim since subjects regard their delusions as beliefs in spite of the fact that they fail to play belief-like roles. In light of this Miyazono suggests that it is instead by their distinctive *phenomenal* characters that we distinguish belief from imagination, and this observation, as well as telling us something about belief, imagination, and our self-knowledge of these states, provides an important insight into the nature of delusion, specifically that subjects with delusions endorse their attitudes as beliefs because of their phenomenal character, not because of their functional role.

Related to the question concerning how it is that we distinguish belief from imagination, are the questions concerning the different powers of belief and imagination, and whether these states can be principally distinguished along any dimension. Some have argued against the idea that there is a sharp distinction to be drawn between belief and imagination, and that they are better understood as sitting on a continuum (Schellenberg 2013), or that there are states properly characterized as *in-between states* (Egan 2008). This latter view is informed, in part, by reflection on the nature of delusion, and has been argued to accommodate delusions being belief-like in some respects (i.e., *disposal to sincerely avow*), but imagination-like in others (i.e., *relative motivational inertness, evidence non-responsiveness*). A conception of these attitudes on which they are instances of in-between states is put forward as able to resolve the tensions involved in taxonomizing delusions. In her chapter, Kind argues that the case for the continuum hypothesis has not been made. She argues that it is either false that delusions do not match the functional profile of beliefs or imaginings, or the way in which they fail to match nevertheless does not support the continuum view. Instead, the functional roles of belief and imagination are a lot 'smudgier' than arguments for the continuum view would have us believe.

Another way of resisting sharp distinctions in the context of delusion comes from prediction error theories, which deny any such distinction between perception and belief. In the final chapter of this section Philip R. Corlett starts from a framework of this kind, and argues that the pathologies of blindsight and Anton's syndrome teach us that perception, imagination, and psychosis can be understood in terms of *generative adversarial networks*. Put simply, reality monitoring and conscious perception are implemented by predictive processing. Corlett's overall theoretical goal is to establish the role of agency failure for imagination in the production of delusions, from a predictive coding framework. Corlett discusses empirical work on mismatches between expectation and experience in the context of prediction error driven learning, imagining possible future states and the consequences of action choices, conditioning sensory hallucinations, and reality

6   BELIEF, IMAGINATION, AND DELUSION

testing and reality monitoring. Corlett argues that the mechanisms of generative adversarial networks are a better fit for predictive processing approaches than those which sharply distinguish perception from belief (as do some accounts of delusion formation, most notably, two-factor theories).

1.2   What Roles Do Belief and Imagination Play in Certain Other Mental Phenomena?

The second section of the book turns to belief and imagination in the wild, which is to say, how they operate in non-garden variety phenomena. The chapters here shed light on their target phenomena both by careful theorizing about the nature of belief and imagination and by drawing on work elsewhere in the volume.

In her contribution, Ichino focuses on religious attitudes. She argues for the negative thesis that such attitudes are not beliefs, and the positive thesis that they are in fact imaginings. Both of these claims are surprising in light of the fact that religious attitudes seem to exhibit many features which suggest doxasticism about them: they are responsive to evidence (in the form of religious texts and religious experiences), they are integrated into subjects' belief systems, and they are sincerely avowed. Ichino's case for her two theses is based in part on explaining away first impressions with regard to these features. She distinguishes *appealing to evidence* for religious attitudes (which subjects do) and *responding to evidence* concerning religious attitudes (which subjects do not). She draws on empirical work to show that religious attitudes are not, after all, well integrated, and although she grants that sincere avowals should be taken to express self-knowledge, that is only absent any defeaters, that is, any reasons to think those avowals are mistaken. Ichino argues that her discussion in the chapter provides such defeaters. She argues that a model of these attitudes on which they are imaginings is much better placed to explain them.

We turn next to aphantasia, with Omoge arguing that this phenomenon is instructive for theorizing about the imagination, particularly, its cognitive architecture. Omoge considers two views of the architecture of imagination: *cognitive dissent*, according to which imaginings are the by-products of other mental capacities such that imagination does not have its own psychological mechanisms, and *cognitive support*, the view that imagination does have its own cognitive architecture. Omoge argues that the phenomenon of aphantasia—understood as the inability to entertain mental imagery—can help us adjudicate between these two views of imagination's architecture. In particular, aphantasia teaches us that propositional imaginings (which are available to aphantasiacs), can function without experiential imagination, but not vice versa, and that cognitive dissent cannot explain this asymmetry. He concludes that cognitive dissenters should either endorse a stronger eliminativism (eliminating imagination as a distinct

INTRODUCTION 7

mental state and not only as having distinct cognitive architecture), or endorse cognitive support.

In the final chapter of this section, Levy considers cases of professed belief where the subject's behaviour seems to be at odds with the holding of the belief (see also discussion in Kind's chapter who prefers to frame the issue in terms of *failure of full integration*). One of his primary cases is delusions, where, for example, someone might assert that an impostor has replaced a loved one, but do none of the things one might expect from someone with a genuine belief of that kind. However, he argues that delusions are not the only attitudes which do not seem to generate behaviours in the manner of belief, and that this feature is shared by superstitious attitudes, attitudes from transportation, and conspiracy attitudes. Levy argues that we are disposed to treat satisfying narratives as representations of a way the world might be by mechanisms which evolved for helping us understand counterfactuals. If that is right, it explains why we tend to acquiesce to certain satisfying narratives, without that influencing our behaviour in the manner of belief.

1.3 What Is the Nature of Delusional Experience?

As has been noted already, delusions are often accompanied by some highly anomalous experiences. That this is so has been taken by many to be an important part of the explanation of why people form delusional beliefs. This is the empiricist approach to delusion formation, which represents the current orthodoxy. The nature of the experiences that people with delusions often undergo will be an important theoretical and empirical consideration when considering how best to understand the nature of delusions, their attitudinal status, how they interact with belief and imagination, and perhaps, how they might best be approached in therapeutic contexts. The third section of the book focuses on such themes.

In his chapter Young discusses the Capgras delusion (the delusion that one's loved one has been replaced by an impostor). This is the delusion most discussed in much of the literatures on the doxastic status of delusions and how delusions are formed, so the work here may well have more general application. Young discusses revisionist accounts which posit a sub-personal abductive inference involved in the formation of Capgras delusion and have it that the first conscious event involved in this delusion is the belief. Young argues that such accounts make a mistake when they deny the explanatory role of anomalous experience in the formation of delusion, and that by re-centring the importance of experience in delusional belief formation we come to a position with greater explanatory power.

In his chapter, Gerrans proposes an affective account of the difference in the experiences associated with Depersonalization Disorder and Cotard delusion (the

8 BELIEF, IMAGINATION, AND DELUSION

delusion that one is dead or has ceased existing). He argues against the integrated account which has it that an experience of depersonalization is the first factor in the development of Cotard delusion, and abnormal reasoning in the form of an inability to deny the experience is the second factor. Gerrans has it that Cotard delusion is better understood as a metacognitive response to a syndrome of experiences, which include (but is not exhausted by) depersonalization. With respect to the putative second factor, Gerrans argues that Cotard can be explained without appeal to reasoning failure.

The final chapter of this section represents a difference of approach with respect to starting assumptions. Lavin and O'Brien advocate moving away from the question of the attitudinal nature of delusion, to a focus instead on the object of delusion. They diagnose the difficulty of making sense of delusions as beliefs as due to a difficulty of seeing them as attitudes that aim at the truth, but argue against an imagination model on the grounds that people with delusions take them to have a reality not to be expected were they mere imaginings. Moreover, the subject's knowledge that the state of affairs which would obtain were the delusion true, is inconsistent with what she otherwise knows (or could easily know). Lavin and O'Brien turn to consider what they call *everyday expressions of delusions*, in particular the locutions often used in communicating love or grief, and argue that we should approach delusions and their expression with a similar mode of understanding as these more everyday expressions. They argue that delusions are a disrupted form of self-awareness, which concern the way in which a subject relates to and is aware of herself. The object of, at least some, delusions then is the subject's experiential relation to herself.

1.4 What Is the Relationship between Delusions, Irrationality, and Doxasticism?

The final section of the book turns to the relationship between delusions and irrationality, and whether this has implications for whether they involve belief. As we have seen, current orthodoxy has it that delusions are *beliefs*, although non-doxastic considerations concerning the functional role of delusion abound. One feature of delusion which pushes against the idea that these states are *beliefs* is that they are improperly connected to truth and evidence. Indeed, delusions are often defined as being especially irresponsive to counterevidence, with reasons given to support the uptake of a delusion taken to be poor or bizarre. The three chapters in the volume's final section discuss the nature of belief, its relationship to truth and evidence, and what that teaches us about delusion.

In her contribution, Archer argues that in at least some cases, the subject with a delusion has not even a *subjective* epistemic reason to hold the delusion. Granting for the sake of argument that there can be cases of beliefs held on the basis of no

INTRODUCTION 9

subjective epistemic reason, Archer argues that for something to be a belief, the holder has to at least grant the application of the question *why do you believe that?* Archer's appeal to an Anscombean condition on belief gives us new grounds to endorse non-doxasticism about delusion.

Furl, Coltheart, and McKay focus on two commonly ascribed ways that delusions are related to evidence. Firstly, it is commonly taken to be definitional that they are highly resistant to evidence against the delusional hypothesis. Secondly, when characterizing the reasoning abnormality taking a subject from anomalous experience to delusional belief, some have appealed to a data gathering bias, understood as a tendency to *jump to conclusions* (see e.g., Garety 1991; Garety et al. 1991), suggesting an *oversensitivity* to evidence. Embedding their discussion in the empirical evidence which bears on the relationship between delusions and evidence, Furl, Coltheart, and McKay argue that before being in a position to give an account of delusional belief, researchers need to solve the puzzle of delusions being both inflexibly reliant on prior beliefs and easily swayed by new evidence.

In the final chapter of the section and the volume, Noordhof turns to the link between belief and truth, and accounts which have sought to capture it: teleological, normative, and biological. He argues that all three approaches to the truth-link fail to explain transparency in doxastic deliberation, and our inability to believe at will (despite these accounts being formulated in part to explain such phenomena). Noordhof defends an alternative view according to which appeal to *attentive consciousness* can do the explanatory work not done by extant positions. He then turns to implications of his preferred approach for self-deceptive and delusional beliefs, the most striking of which, perhaps, is the result that self-deception can be understood as involving a greater theoretical irrationality than delusional cognition, in part because anomalous experiences function as evidence for the delusional hypothesis.

2. Concluding Remarks

As I hope the outlined questions make clear, the interaction between philosophers working on the nature of belief and imagination, and philosophers and psychologists working on delusion, is a rich one. In particular, discussion of belief and imagination has helped precisify their natures, their respective roles in our cognitive lives, both in more standard cases of self-knowledge, imaginative immersion, superstitious and religious attitudes, but also as they function in delusion. Some work has opened up new possibilities for characterizing the attitudinal status of delusion, or accounting for why delusions behave as they do. These issues concerning the nature of belief and imagining, the role they play in other mental phenomena, and their relationship in particular to delusion, are

10   BELIEF, IMAGINATION, AND DELUSION

apt to be developed further by the continuing interaction of philosophers and psychologists in this area. I hope that this volume makes more attractive continuing interaction on these topics for such researchers.

3. Synopses of Chapters

3.1 Chapter 2. Kengo Miyazono: 'Delusion and Self-Knowledge'

Miyazono focuses on how we are able to distinguish what we believe from what we imagine. Candidate accounts for how we do this have it that we are tracking either a state's functional properties, representational properties, underlying neural properties, or phenomenal properties. Miyazono uses delusion as a test case. In at least some such cases, the subject claims to *believe* the delusional content, but the delusion does not perform the functional role of belief. Miyazono defends both of these claims in his argument against the tracking functional properties account. This leads him to consider and reject two theories of self-knowledge: the boxological monitoring theory and the self-interpretation theory. The grounds on which the latter is rejected also provide reasons to reject the representational properties account of how we distinguish belief and imagining. Miyazono finishes by defending a phenomenological account which can accommodate the case of delusion.

3.2 Chapter 3. Amy Kind: 'Contrast or Continuum? The Case of Belief and Imagination'

In her contribution Kind considers two arguments for the existence of mental states intermediate between belief and imagination. She distinguishes two approaches to this claim, one which has it that in-between cases support the abandoning of the belief–imagination distinction altogether (*the cluster view*, Currie and Jureidini 2004), and another which allows for a distinction between belief and imagination, but places them on a continuum on which we can place in-between states (*the continuum view*, Egan 2008; Schellenberg 2013). Kind considers two arguments for the continuum view: (1) seamless tradition between belief and imagining (as proposed by Schellenberg in the case of imaginative immersion) and (2) functional profiles and the case of delusion having neither (as proposed by Egan). Kind replies to both of these arguments and in turn introduces the idea of *smudginess*, that is, she argues that in the case of both imagination and belief, we tolerate a smudginess with respect to the roles that they play. She concludes with some brief reflection on some methodological considerations, and suggests that we ought not to be quick to jettison our traditional categories when they seem to come under pressure, but might instead think again about the assumptions behind our taxonomizing.

3.3 Chapter 4. Philip R. Corlett: 'Imagination, Agency, and Predictive Processing'

Corlett's contribution focuses on the nature of belief and imagination as a way to examine hallucination and delusion. He argues that in doing so we can learn more about how imagination functions and that which might underwrite it, and that there is growing evidence challenging a strict distinction between belief and perception. We can be helped in our goals by imagining possible outcomes, but the mechanisms by which we do this are sensitive to noise and uncertainty and can result in perceptions and actions which fail to reflect reality. Corlett uses the idea of generative adversarial networks, whereby the generator and the critic network train one another. He suggests that this is one mechanism via which reality monitoring could be implemented by predictive coding. Corlett argues that given these generative adversarial networks are not engaged in unidirectional information flow, they are underwritten by mechanisms similar to those which underwrite predictive processing, rather than, for example, two-factor models of delusions which sharply distinguish perception from belief.

3.4 Chapter 5. Anna Ichino: 'Religious Imaginings'

Ichino draws on the case of religious attitudes to argue that the role of imaginings in our cognitive lives is larger than usually credited. She argues for two claims: (1) that religious attitudes commonly taken to be beliefs are not in fact so, and that (2) these attitudes are in fact imaginings. Ichino offers three reasons to think that religious attitudes are beliefs. First, that they are sensitive to evidence. Second, that they are coherently integrated into overall belief systems. And third, that they are expressed in sincere avowals. Her argument for claim (1) consists in part in undermining these three reasons. The anti-doxastic claim has also been defended elsewhere, for example by Van Leeuwen, whose positive account of religious attitudes is that they form a sui generis category he calls *religious credence*. Ichino argues against this view on the grounds that the considerations appealed to in support of it do not in fact justify the positing of a new mental category, and that Van Leeuwen's idea of practical setting dependence is in fact not in play in the case of either religious attitudes or imaginings. Ichino concludes by considering two forms of religious imaginings and their relationship to religious faith.

12 BELIEF, IMAGINATION, AND DELUSION

3.5 Chapter 6. Michael Omoge: 'On the Place of Imagination in the Architecture of the Mind'

In his contribution Omoge employs cognitive neuroscientific findings about perception and language on the one hand and about aphantasia on the other hand as test cases for views about the cognitive architecture of the imagination. According to the view he calls *cognitive support*, imagination is a distinct mental state with its own cognitive architecture. On the other hand, are two kinds of eliminativist. First is a view he calls *cognitive denial* which denies both that imagination is a distinct mental state and then, of course, that it has a distinct architecture. An alternative eliminativist position (*cognitive dissent*) has it that imagination is a distinct mental state but co-opts existing architecture. Omoge is interested in the debate between cognitive support and this second, weaker, eliminativist position. His broader argument is that cognitive dissent's attempt to take neural structure as definitive on matters of cognitive architecture fails. Perception and language seem indirectly connected in cognitive architecture but aphantasia tells us that propositional and experiential imagination are directly connected, and, so, the former does not share the same neural structure with the latter. He then argues that cognitive support can reconcile these findings about perception and language on the one hand, and experiential and propositional imagination on the other. Cognitive dissenters, he concludes, should become stronger eliminativists or accept that imagination has a distinct cognitive architecture.

3.6 Chapter 7. Neil Levy: 'Believing in Stories: Delusions, Superstitions, Conspiracy Theories, and Other Fairy Tales'

Levy is interested in explaining a range of cases where people claim to believe something, but where that belief seems not to be in line with their behaviour. He considers more ordinary cases where we are inclined to *say* certain things, but in which behaviours associated with believing those things do not follow, for example, superstition. Levy suggests that mechanisms which evolved for helping us understand counterfactuals dispose us to treat satisfying narratives as representations of a way the world might be. When deployed offline (in, say, the construction of fantasies or consideration of bizarre counterfactuals), these behavioural mechanisms remain poised for action. Entertaining these contents feels real enough in low-stake situations, but when stakes rise, mechanisms of epistemic vigilance kick in and prevent us from acting on these contents. Levy suggests that this account can explain why people with delusions acquiesce to the delusional content, but often fail to act on it—the subject's grip on reality means their epistemic vigilance is intact enough. In other cases, where the delusion is acted upon, Levy suggests that cultural acceptability of the particular narrative may help it reach full belief status, or impaired capacities to engage in reality monitoring might be responsible.

3.7 Chapter 8. Garry Young: 'The Capgras Delusion: An Interactionist Approach Revisited'

In his contribution, Young defends an account of the Capgras delusion which gives a central role to anomalous experience in explaining why the subject comes to believe what he does, and proposes that the maintenance of the Capgras delusion can be explained by appeal to experiential transformation. In answering the question of why the Capgras hypothesis (*my wife is an impostor*) is taken to be a candidate hypothesis by the subject following an experience of estrangement, Young argues that the strangeness of the estrangement experience makes the subject feel justified in broadening the scope of epistemic possibilities. In previous work, Young (2011) has argued against Coltheart and colleagues' (2010) model of Capgras, arguing that it is hard to see how the sudden emergence of the delusional belief could be experienced as anything other than an unbidden thought. Here he argues that a co-occurring anomalous experience of estrangement helps contextualize that unbidden thought, making it less likely to be treated as merely unbidden and more likely to be given credence. Adopting the delusional hypothesis helps transform the initial anomalous experience of estrangement into a normative sense of unfamiliarity. It is this latter thing which explains why the Capgras belief often resists revision in the face of counterevidence.

3.8 Chapter 9. Philip Gerrans: 'Cotard Syndrome: The Experience of Inexistence'

In his chapter, Gerrans is interested in mapping the relationship between Depersonalization Disorder (DPD) and Cotard delusion (the belief that *one has ceased to exist*). Gerrans argues against accounts which have it that depersonalization experience is the 'as if' version of Cotard, and seeks an alternative which explains the role of the insula in producing self-awareness, its loss in depersonalization, and its role in Cotard delusion. His account is an affective one, which distinguishes affective experience from other components of an emotional episode (including automatic and visceral reactions, action tendencies, and so on). DPD is then said to result from an unpredicted loss of the affective aspect of emotion, but this is just one part of the Cotard experience. Gerrans goes on to argue against a two-factor account of Cotard delusion according to which the Cotard subjects lacks the ability to reason about their experience due to damaged mechanisms of belief evaluation. Gerrans

14 BELIEF, IMAGINATION, AND DELUSION

objects to this view by appeal to the fact that people with Cotard (and other delusions) retain insight, and so whatever problem is introduced by brain damage ought not to be understood as one concerning the inability to reason about experience.

3.9 Chapter 10. Douglas Lavin and Lucy O'Brien: 'Delusions and Everyday Life'

Lavin and O'Brien turn their attention to the *object* of delusion, abstracting away from particular theories concerning the psychological attitudes of delusion. Their focus on a delusion's *object*, over its attitudinal nature, is partly motivated by their concern to connect, in a way that a great deal of extant discussion fails to, delusory thought with more ordinary forms of thinking present in everyday life, for example, in daydreaming or magical thinking. Lavin and O'Brien argue that many of the ways in which we think are not easily captured by a particular psychological attitude. Their key claim is that we ought not to think of delusions as encoding cognitive commitments, but as having distinctive objects.

3.10 Chapter 11. Sophie Archer: 'Why Do You Believe That? Delusion and Epistemic Reasons'

Archer presents an account of belief according to which epistemic reasons are the only ones on which beliefs can be directly formed or maintained. She turns to delusion as one version of this challenge, and argues that claims like 'A man believes *his wife is unfaithful to him* because the fifth lamp-post along on the left is unlit' are false. That is because, Archer argues, that is not and could not be the man's reason for his belief (even a subjective one), since it is not *a reason* for belief. However, even granting that the man may nevertheless believe the delusional content even without a subjective epistemic reason for doing so, Archer argues that in such cases, the agent must grant the application of the question *why do you believe that?* for the attitude to count as a belief. In the case under consideration here, that condition is not met.

3.11 Chapter 12. Nicholas Furl, Max Coltheart, and Ryan McKay: 'The Paradox of Delusions: Are Deluded Individuals Resistant to Evidence?'

Furl, Coltheart, and McKay identify what they call *the paradox of delusions*. This arises from two commonly ascribed features of delusional beliefs which appear to be in tension with one another. The first feature is that delusional beliefs are highly

INTRODUCTION 15

resistant to evidence, indeed, many have thought their incorrigibility is a necessary component of a belief's being delusional. On the other hand, delusions are also thought to be beliefs formed based on insufficient evidence, suggesting a psychology that is oversensitive to evidence. Furl, Coltheart, and McKay note that many studies have adopted a position privileging one or the other of these features. They review empirical work relevant to claims about delusions possessing these features, including evidence for subjects with delusions exhibiting: a bias against disconfirmatory evidence, better use of prior beliefs to perceive ambiguous stimuli, and over-responsiveness to evidence. They suggest that the existing research base suggests a puzzle regarding how people with delusions integrate new experience with prior beliefs, namely, how it is that they can be both inflexibly reliant on prior belief but also easily swayed by new evidence. They conclude that before we are able to provide a full account of delusional belief, researchers need to solve this puzzle.

3.12 Chapter 13. Paul Noordhof: 'Irrationality and the Failures of Consciousness'

In his chapter, Noordhof opens by considering recent approaches to the link between belief and truth, understood in terms of aims, norms, or biological functions. Such accounts have been proposed as able to explain the character of belief formation, specifically doxastic transparency and our inability to believe at will. Noordhof argues against such explanations and argues instead that the phenomena display the explanatory role of attentive consciousness, which makes manifest the attractiveness of being disposed to act upon what is presented as true. He argues that his approach has consequences for the nature of self-deception and delusion, in particular, the instability distinctive of self-deception in consciousness follows from the fact that the self-deceptive belief is not presented as true (in perception or as a result of evidence), but results from motivational factors. In contrast, the anomalous experiences associated with monothematic delusions make manifest the attractiveness of being disposed to act upon the basis of the delusional hypothesis. In the light of this, Noordhof argues that there's a sense in which self-deception constitutes the greater theoretical irrationality, and that individual differences in the capacity to consciously attend to what is presented as true explain why some subjects form delusions and others do not.

Acknowledgements

With thanks to the Arts and Humanities Research Council for funding the research of which this is a part (*Deluded by Experience*, grant no. AH/T013486/1). Thank you to Michael Rush and Paul Noordhof for comments on earlier versions of this chapter.

References

Allen, Keith. 2015. 'Hallucination and Imagination'. *Australasian Journal of Philosophy*, Vol. 92, no. 2, pp. 287–302.

Bortolotti, Lisa. 2010. *Delusions and Other Irrational Beliefs*. New York: Oxford University Press.

Coltheart, Max, Menzies, Peter, and Sutton, John. 2010. 'Abductive Inference and Delusional Belief'. *Cognitive Neuropsychiatry*, Vol. 15, no. 1, pp. 261–87.

Currie, Gregory. 2000. 'Imagination, Hallucination and Delusion'. *Mind & Language*, Vol. 15, pp. 168–83.

Currie, Gregory and Jureidini, Jon. 2001. 'Delusion, Rationality, Empathy: Commentary on Martin Davies et al.'. *Philosophy, Psychiatry, & Psychology*, Vol. 8, no. 2/3, pp. 159–62.

Currie, Gregory and Jureidini, Jon. 2004. 'Narrative and Coherence'. *Mind & Language*, Vol. 19, no. 4, pp. 409–27.

Currie, Gregory and Ravenscroft, Ian. 2002. *Recreative Minds: Imagination in Philosophy and Psychology*. New York: Oxford University Press.

Dub, Richard. 2017. 'Delusions, Acceptances, and Cognitive Feelings'. *Philosophy and Phenomenological Research*, Vol. 94, no. 1, pp. 27–60.

Egan, Andy. 2008. 'Imagination, Delusion, and Self-Deception'. In Tim Bayne and Jordi Fernández (eds.), *Delusion and Self-Deception: Affective and Motivational Influences on Belief Formation*, pp. 263–80. New York: Psychology Press.

Flores, Carolina. 2021. 'Delusional Evidence-Responsiveness'. *Synthese*, Vol. 199, no. 3/4, pp. 6299–330.

Garety, Philippa A. 1991. 'Reasoning and Delusions'. *British Journal of Psychiatry*, Vol. 159, no. 14, pp. 14–19.

Garety, Philippa, A., Hemsley, David, R., and Wessely, Sam. 1991. 'Reasoning in Deluded Schizophrenia and Paranoid Patients: Biases in Performance on a Probabilistic Inference Task'. *The Journal of Nervous and Mental Disease*, Vol. 179, no. 4, pp. 194–201.

Gendler, Tamar Szabó. 2007. 'Self-Deception as Pretense'. *Philosophical Perspectives*, Vol. 21, pp. 231–58.

Glüer, Katharin and Wikforss, Åna. 2013. 'Aiming at Truth: On the Role of Belief'. *Teorema*, Vol. 42, no. 3, pp. 137–62.

Goldman, Alvin. 2006. *Stimulating Minds: The Philosophy, Psychology, and Neuroscience of Mindreading*. New York: Oxford University Press.

Hadisi, Reza. 2021. 'Creative Imagining as Practical Knowing: An Akbariyya Account'. *Res Philosophica*, Vol. 92, no. 2, pp. 181–204.

Ichikawa, Jonathan. 2009. 'Dreaming and Imagination'. *Mind & Language*, Vol. 24, no. 1, pp. 103–21.

Ichino, Anna. 2019. 'Imagination and Belief in Action'. *Philosophia*, Vol. 47, pp. 1517–34.

Ichino, Anna. 2020. 'Superstitious Confabulations'. *Topoi*, Vol. 39, no. 1, pp. 203–17.

Kind, Amy. 2016. 'Introduction: Exploring Imagination'. In Amy Kind (ed.), *The Routledge Handbook of Philosophy of Imagination*, pp. 1–11. Abingdon: Routledge.

Nichols, Shaun and Stich, Stephen. 2003. *Mindreading: An Integrated Account of Pretence, Self-Awareness, and Understanding Other Minds*. Oxford: Clarendon Press.

Nolfi, Kate. 2015. 'How to be a Normativist about the Nature of Belief'. *Pacific Philosophical Quarterly*, Vol. 96, pp. 181–204.

Noordhof, Paul. 2001. 'Believe What You Want'. *Proceedings of the Aristotelian Society*, Vol. 101, pp. 247–65.

O'Brien, Lucy. 2005. 'Imagination and the Motivational Role of Belief'. *Analysis*, Vol. 65, no. 1, pp. 55–62.

Schellenberg, Susanna. 2013. 'Belief and Desire in Imagination and Immersion'. *Journal of Philosophy*, Vol. 110, no. 9, pp. 497–517.

Shah, Nishi. 2003. 'How Truth Governs Belief'. *The Philosophical Review*, Vol. 112, no. 4, pp. 447–82.

Shah, Nishi and Velleman, David J. 2005. 'Doxastic Deliberation'. *The Philosophical Review*, Vol. 11, no. 4, pp. 497–534.

Steglich-Petersen, Asbjorn. 2006. 'No Norm Needed: On the Aim of Belief'. *The Philosophical Quarterly*, Vol. 56, no. 225, pp. 499–516.

Sullivan-Bissett, Ema. 2017. 'Biological Function and Epistemic Normativity'. *Philosophical Explorations*, Vol. 20, no. 1, pp. 94–110.

Sullivan-Bissett, Ema. 2018. 'Explaining Doxastic Transparency: Aim, Norm, or Function?' *Synthese*, Vol. 195, pp. 3453–76.

Sullivan-Bissett, Ema. 2019. Biased by Our Imaginings'. *Mind & Language*, Vol. 34, pp. 627–47.

Sullivan-Bissett, Ema. 2020. 'We Are Like American Robins'. In Scott Stapleford and Kevin McCain (eds.), *Epistemic Duties: New Arguments, New Angles*, pp. 94–110. New York: Routledge.

Sullivan-Bissett, Ema. 2023. 'Virtually Imagining Our Biases'. *Philosophical Psychology*, Vol. 36, no. 4, pp. 860–93.

Van Leeuwen, Neil. 2009. 'The Motivational Role of Belief'. *Philosophical Papers*, Vol. 38, no. 2, pp. 219–46.

Velleman, David J. 2000. *The Possibility of Practical Reason*. Oxford: Oxford University Press.

Welpinghus, Anna. 2020. 'The Imagination Model of Implicit Bias'. *Philosophical Studies*, Vol. 177, pp. 1611–33.

Young, Garry. 2011. 'On Abductive Inference and Delusional Belief: Why There Is Still a Role for Patient Experience Within Explanations of Capgras Delusion'. *Cognitive Neuropsychiatry*, Vol. 16, no. 4, pp. 303–25.

PART I
LESSONS FROM DELUSION ON BELIEF AND IMAGINATION

2

Delusion and Self-Knowledge

Kengo Miyazono

1. Introduction

I have no difficulty in distinguishing what I believe from what I imagine. I can easily judge that "Caesar was assassinated by a group of senators" is something I believe, and that "Caesar died in his bed" is something I imagine. I seem to have a reliable metacognitive capacity to distinguish beliefs from imaginings. But how does the capacity work, exactly? How exactly do I distinguish beliefs from imaginings? How do I know that I believe, rather than imagine, that Caesar was assassinated by a group of senators? How do I know that I imagine, rather than believe, that Caesar died in his bed?[1]

This is a question about self-knowledge. It can be generalized and formulated as a question about self-knowledge of attitude-types, including not only believing and imagining but also desiring, hoping, wishing, accepting, supposing, etc. In a general form, my question is about how a person, X, can identify the particular attitude-type of X's mental state, M. We can think of several possible answers: X identifies the attitude-type of mental state M by

(1) tracking[2] functional properties of M: e.g., M is identified[3] as a belief because M plays the distinctive functional role of beliefs. (I will call this "***Tracking Function***")

(2) tracking phenomenal properties of M: e.g., M is identified as a belief because M has the distinctive phenomenology of believing. ("***Tracking Phenomenology***")

---

[1] This question makes sense even if we accept what Kind (this volume) calls the "continuum hypothesis" according to which believing and imagining are on a continuum that allows for some intermediate states. Even if the continuum hypothesis is correct, we cannot deny the fact that we actually classify some of our mental states in the category of beliefs and others in the category of imaginings. And this fact needs an explanation.

[2] Note that none of the hypotheses in the list is committed to the idea that the "tracking" is a conscious process. For example, *Tracking Brain* is not committed to the idea, which is obviously false, that people consciously tracking their neural activities.

[3] Throughout this chapter, the verb "identify" is not used as a success term. In other words, when I say that M is identified as a belief, I do not necessary mean that M is *successfully* identified as a belief (which implies that M is actually a belief).

Kengo Miyazono, *Delusion and Self-Knowledge* In: *Belief, Imagination, and Delusion.* Edited by: Ema Sullivan-Bissett, Oxford University Press. © Oxford University Press 2024. DOI: 10.1093/oso/9780198872221.003.0002

22 BELIEF, IMAGINATION, AND DELUSION

(3) tracking representational properties of M: e.g., M is identified as a belief because M has some doxastic representational content. ("*Tracking Content*")

(4) tracking underlying neural properties of M: e.g., M is identified as a belief because M has some doxastic underlying neural property. ("*Tracking Brain*")[4]

The central claim of this chapter is that delusions provide a useful test case for examining the hypotheses above. On one hand, people with delusions seem to identify their delusions as their beliefs (I will call this "*Doxastic Recognition*"). A person with the Capgras delusion, let us call him "Ken", believes that he believes that his wife has been replaced by an impostor. Ken identifies his delusion about his wife as a belief, rather than an imagining or any other mental state. On the other hand, delusions do not play the functional role of beliefs or the doxastic functional role (I will call this "*Non-Doxastic Function*"). For example, Ken's delusion about his wife fails to have belief-like effects on his mental states and behaviours. In fact, Gregory Currie (2000; Currie and Jureidini 2001; Currie and Ravenscroft 2002) suggests that delusions play the functional role of imagining, rather than the functional role of belief. Relatedly, Andy Egan (2008) suggests that delusions play the functional role of "bimagining" (i.e., an intermediate mental state that is belief-like and imagining-like at the same time).

The theory of self-knowledge needs to be able to account for these facts about delusions; it needs to be able to explain why Ken identifies his delusion as a belief despite the delusion failing to play the doxastic functional role. This requirement poses a problem for the first option in the list; i.e., *Tracking Function*. If Ken identifies his mental states by tracking their functional roles, we should expect that he does not identify his delusion about his wife as a belief. And we should expect that he identifies his delusion as an imagining (if Currie is correct that delusions play the functional role of imagining) or as an intermediate state (if Egan is correct that delusions play an intermediate functional role; see also Kind's contribution to this volume). This argument against *Tracking Function* can be formulated as follows.

Premise 1:   Ken identifies his delusion about his wife as a belief (rather than an imagining or bimagining). (*Doxastic Recognition*)

---

[4] This list of options is from Goldman (2006). This list is certainly useful, but it might not be exhaustive. There will be some other answers too, such as the transparency account of self-knowledge. But as a theory of the self-knowledge of attitude-types, the transparency account is not promising. Despite several attempts (e.g., Byrne 2018; Fernández 2013), the transparency theory has a narrow scope of application. The account is applicable mainly to belief, and at best within a very narrow range of mental state types. But then the transparency account is hopeless as a theory of the self-knowledge of attitude-types; it does not explain why I can distinguish all attitude-types from each other.

DELUSION AND SELF-KNOWLEDGE   23

Premise 2:   Ken's delusion about his wife fails to play the doxastic functional role. (*Non-Doxastic Function*)

Conclusion: Therefore, it is not the case that Ken identifies his mental states by tracking their functional roles. (The denial of *Tracking Function*)[5]

I defend *Doxastic Recognition* (Premise 1) and *Non-Doxastic Function* (Premise 2) in Sections 2 and 3, respectively. And then I argue that *Tracking Function* has to be abandoned (Conclusion) in Section 4. An implication of this is that the theories of self-knowledge that are committed to *Tracking Function*, including Peter Carruthers's (2011; see also Carruthers 2009) interpretive sensory-access theory, have to be abandoned (Section 5).[6]

In Section 6, I defend *Tracking Phenomenology* as an alternative to *Tracking Function*. I do not necessarily claim that *Tracking Phenomenology* is the only plausible alternative to *Tracking Function*, but I do claim that it is an attractive view that deserves serious philosophical attention. Unlike *Tracking Function*, *Tracking Phenomenology* is perfectly compatible with *Doxastic Recognition* and *Non-Doxastic Function*. Ken regards his delusion about his wife as a belief, rather than an imagining or an intermediate state, because, first, in general attitude-types are identified by their phenomenal characters and, second, Ken's delusion has the doxastic phenomenal character.

2. Doxastic Recognition

According to *Doxastic Recognition*, people with delusions identify their delusions as beliefs. For example, Ken identifies his delusion about his wife as a belief. This claim is overwhelmingly plausible. When we ask Ken whether he believes that his wife has been replaced by an impostor or he imagines it, he will readily deny the idea that he merely imagines it. And he will insist that he seriously believes it. For instance, David Fowler, Philippa Garety, and Elizabeth Kuipers describe a case in which a delusional person "described himself as unable to stop *believing* that the telepathic contact and his mission were real" (Fowler et al. 1995: 4 [italics added]).

---

[5] Religious attitudes can raise an analogous issue. On the one hand, as Ichino (this volume) points out, people tend to express their religious attitudes as a sincere avowal, which seems to suggest that they regard their religious attitudes as beliefs (rather than imaginings or bimaginings). On the other hand, religious attitudes might fail to play the doxastic functional role; e.g., they might lack a right kind of evidence sensitivity.

[6] Or, the defenders of *Tracking Function* might avoid the problem by excluding delusions (and perhaps other pathological mental states) from the scope of the account. However, this response is rather *ad hoc* unless there are some independent reasons to justify the exclusion. In addition, such a response makes *Tracking Function* less attractive; other things being equal, an account of self-knowledge with a narrow scope of application is less attractive than an alternative account with a broad scope of application.

24 BELIEF, IMAGINATION, AND DELUSION

Some clarifications are in order. First, I do not claim that all people with delusions readily regard their delusions as beliefs. People with delusions can get confused, lose confidence, etc. at some point. Delusional conviction can be unstable: "The conviction of many delusional patients may wax and wane, vacillating between avowal and disbelief" (Coltheart et al. 2011: 276). It is not surprising at all that people hesitate to regard their delusions as beliefs when their delusional conviction is weakened. As we will see, my argument in this chapter does not assume that *Doxastic Recognition* is true about all people with delusions.

Second, my claim that delusions are regarded as beliefs does not necessarily imply that the subjective experience of delusions is indistinguishable from the subjective experience of mundane non-delusional beliefs. For example, a delusion (especially in schizophrenia) can be experienced as an important insight into the nature of how things work, making sense of many facts that are otherwise mysterious and inexplicable. Probably such a delusion is felt to be something more than mundane beliefs Ken has about the apple on the table, the weather in London, or the assassination of Caesar. I will come back to the subjective experience of delusion in Section 5.

Third, *Doxastic Recognition* does not necessarily imply *Doxasticism about Delusions* (Bortolotti 2010; Bayne and Pacherie 2005). I claim that people with delusions regard their delusions as beliefs rather than imaginings or some intermediate states, but I do not claim (at least in this chapter) that delusions are beliefs rather than imaginings or some intermediate states as a matter of fact.[7] I will be neutral on whether *Doxasticism* is correct or not, at least in the context of this chapter.[8] My focus is not on the first order issue as to whether delusions *are beliefs* as a matter of fact, but rather on the second order issue as to whether delusions *are regarded as beliefs*.

One might try to connect the first order issue and the second order issue. For example, one might argue that if Ken regards his delusion as a belief, then we have good reason to think that his delusion is in fact a belief. After all, Ken has the first-person authority about his own mental states. If he thinks that he believes that his wife has been replaced by an impostor, then we should defer to his first-person authority and accept the conclusion that he does believe that his wife has been replaced by an impostor. But this first-person authority argument for *Doxasticism* can be challenged. For example, one can be skeptical about the first-person authority of people with psychiatric conditions because their conditions might compromise their introspective capacity. Currie (2000; Currie and Ravenscroft

---

[7] For this reason, this chapter is not committed to what Lavin and O'Brien (this volume) call the "psychological attitude" approach whose central question is whether a delusion is a belief, an imagining, or something else. I agree with Lavin and O'Brien that there are important questions about delusions that cannot be captured by the psychological attitude approach. This chapter deals with one of such questions; explaining the fact that delusions are *regarded as* beliefs.

[8] But I defended *Doxasticism* elsewhere (Miyazono 2018).

2002), for example, proposes a non-doxastic account of delusions according to which delusions are imaginings that are misidentified as beliefs due to some metacognitive errors.

3. Non-Doxastic Function

Non-Doxastic Function says that delusions do not play the doxastic functional role. In other words, the functional role of delusions is significantly different from the functional role of non-delusional beliefs.

It is widely assumed that the doxastic functional role includes some degree of (1) sensitivity to evidential inputs, (2) guidance of non-verbal actions, and (3) coherence with other beliefs as well as other mental states. *Non-Doxastic Function* is supported by numerous clinical and empirical observations that many delusions do not exhibit these features.

(1) **Insensitivity to Evidential Inputs**: Delusions typically lack belief-like sensitivity to evidential inputs. For example, Ken firmly maintains the delusion about his wife in the face of good counterevidence; e.g., when he becomes fully aware of the fact that she knows some things that only his wife knows, or the fact that trusted friends assure him that she is his real wife. The insensitivity to counterevidence is often regarded as the defining feature of delusions; e.g., DSM-5 defines delusions as being "firmly sustained despite what almost everyone else believes and despite what constitutes incontrovertible and obvious evidence to the contrary" (American Psychiatric Association 2013: 819).

(2) **Lack of Action-Guiding**: Delusions sometimes fail to guide (non-verbal) actions. Ken claims that his wife has been replaced by an impostor, but he might not exhibit relevant non-verbal actions; e.g., he does not refuse to live with the alleged impostor, he does not call the police, he does not look for his missing wife, and so on. As Tony Stone and Andrew Young note, in many cases of the Capgras delusion "one finds a curious asynchrony between the firmly stated delusional belief and actions one might reasonably expect to have followed from it", and "this failure to maintain a close co-ordination of beliefs and actions may be typical of the delusions that can follow brain injury" (Stone and Young 1997: 334).

(3) **Incoherence with Other Mental States**: Delusions are often incoherent with other mental states, such as other beliefs or emotions. Ken claims that his wife has been replaced by an impostor, but he might not exhibit relevant changes in his beliefs and emotions; e.g., he does not come to believe that his real wife is in danger, he does not become anxious about her safety, he does not feel uneasy about living with the impostor in the same house, etc. Federica Lucchelli and Hans Spinnler report a case of a person with the Capgras delusion about his wife who "never became angry or aggressive" to the alleged impostor, was "quite

pleased to see her", and "addressed her in a very gentle way" (Lucchelli and Spinnler 2007: 189).

I will be neutral on whether *Non-Doxastic Function* rules out *Doxasticism* or not. It is certainly tempting to think that if delusions do not play the doxastic functional role, then they cannot be beliefs. In fact, this seems to be a straightforward consequence of the standard functionalism in which mental states are individuated in terms of their functional roles. A mental state is a belief just in case it plays the doxastic functional role.

However, other theories of belief have different implications. For example, as I argued elsewhere (Miyazono 2018), a non-standard form of functionalism, teleofunctionalism, implies that *Non-Doxastic Function* is perfectly compatible with *Doxasticism*.[9] For the purpose of this chapter, I am neutral on whether we would adopt standard functionalism (in which case *Non-Doxastic Function* rules out *Doxasticism*) or teleo-functionalism (in which case *Non-Doxastic Function* is compatible with *Doxasticism*).

I do not argue that *Non-Doxastic Function* is true about all cases of delusion. Delusion is a very heterogeneous category. Those observations above can be seen in some cases of delusion but not in others (except for the insensitivity to evidence, which is a definitional feature of delusions). For example, some people with the Capgras delusion do act on the basis of their delusional beliefs, which can lead to violent and tragic consequences. As we will see, my argument in this chapter only assumes that *Non-Doxastic Function* is plausible at least about some cases of delusion.

Even with this qualification, *Non-Doxastic Function* is a controversial idea. Lisa Bortolotti (2010; see also Reimer 2010), for example, argues that delusions and non-delusional beliefs are on a continuum, and that the functional difference between delusions and non-delusional beliefs is just a matter of degree, not of kind. Delusions are *more insensitive* to evidential inputs than non-delusional beliefs; delusions are *less likely* to guide action than non-delusional beliefs; delusions are *more incoherent* with other mental states than non-delusional beliefs.

Since I already defended *Non-Doxastic Function* from objections elsewhere (Miyazono 2018), my defence of *Non-Doxastic Function* will be brief here. Let us focus on Bortolotti's claim that delusions and non-delusional beliefs are different only in degree, not in kind. For the sake of argument, I do not challenge this claim itself. I rather challenge the idea that if delusions and non-delusional beliefs are functionally different only in degree, then there is no significant functional difference between them. I deny the idea that a functional difference in degree between X and Y does not make a significant functional difference

---

[9] The cognitive phenomenological theory (Clutton 2018) and the normative functionalist theory (Bayne 2010) might have similar implications with regard to the compatibility between *Non-Doxastic Function* and *Doxasticism*.

between them (where "significant functional difference" between X and Y means the functional difference that is sufficient for classifying X and Y into different categories of mental states).

First, suppose that the insensitivity to evidential inputs does not constitute a significant functional difference because it is just a matter of degree. Suppose also that the lack of action-guiding and the incoherence with other mental states do not constitute a significant functional difference for the same reason. Still, it is possible that the insensitivity to evidential inputs, the lack of action-guiding, and the incoherence with other mental states make a significant difference *jointly*, even if none of them makes a significant difference *individually*.

Second, the difference in degree between X and Y could be significant enough to establish an important distinction between them. Indeed, in the standard folk-psychological classification of mental states, there are some pairs of mental state categories (e.g., believing and accepting) such that the one category differs from the other in degree, not in kind. This means that a functional difference in degree is sometimes significant enough to draw a distinction between mental state categories in the folk-psychological classification.

Third, there is a sense in which Bortolotti's claim, even if it is true, does not answer the real question. Even if delusions and beliefs are functionally different in degree, not in kind, the same thing can be true about delusions and other mental states such as imaginings; delusions and imaginings are functionally different in degree, not in kind. The real question, then, is whether the degree of difference between delusions and beliefs is smaller than the degree of difference between delusions and imaginings. Bortolotti does not give us reason to think that the former is really smaller than the latter.

4. Tracking Function Rejected

I have argued that *Doxastic Recognition* (Premise 1) and *Non-Doxastic Function* (Premise 2) are plausible. These two premises entail that *Tracking Function* is false (Conclusion). For example, Ken believes that he believes that his wife has been replaced by an impostor, and his delusion that his wife has been replaced by an impostor fails to play the doxastic functional role. These two observations about Ken entail that he does not identify the attitude-type of the delusional thought by tracking its functional role.

Please note that the argument does not presuppose that *Doxastic Recognition* is true about *all* cases of delusion. Perhaps some people with delusions do not regard their delusions as beliefs. It does not presuppose that *Non-Doxastic Function* is true about *all* cases of delusion either. Perhaps some delusions do play the doxastic functional role. The argument works as long as there are at least *some* cases of delusion in which both *Doxastic Recognition* and

28   BELIEF, IMAGINATION, AND DELUSION

Non-Doxastic Function are true. Some such cases are enough to support the argument against *Tracking Function*.

Tracking Function is an attractive idea, especially for functionalists about beliefs and other propositional attitudes. Since attitude-types are defined by the functional roles according to functionalism, it is a reasonable strategy to identify the attitude-type of a mental state by tracking its functional role. Alvin Goldman calls this idea "representational functionalism" and characterizes it as follows: "the CR [category representation; which contains the semantic information of a predicate, and is stored in the long-term memory] associated with each mental predicate M represents a distinctive set of functional properties, or functional role, FM" and "a person will ascribe a mental predicate M to himself when and only when an IR [instance representation; which represents some relevant features of a current mental state] occurs in him bearing the message: 'role FM is now instantiated'. That is, ascription occurs precisely when there is an IR that matches the functional-role content of the CR for M" (Goldman 1993: 17).[10]

Tracking Function can be associated with several theories of self-knowledge in the literature. I mention two notable examples: the boxological monitoring theory and the self-interpretation theory.[11]

(1) **Boxological Monitoring Theory**: Shaun Nichols and Stephen Stich's (2003) boxological monitoring theory presupposes the boxological representationalism according to which propositional attitudes are realized by mental representations that are stored in "boxes" (see also Omoge's contribution to this volume). For example, the belief that the university library is closed today is realized by a representation "the university library is closed today" that is stored in the Belief Box. According to Nichols and Stich, self-knowledge is achieved by a monitoring mechanism whose job is to find a representation "P" in the Belief Box, add "I believe that" to the representation, and insert the product "I believe that P" back into the Belief Box. For example, the monitoring mechanism finds "the university library is closed today" in the Belief Box, adds "I believe that" to it, and inserts the product "I believe that the university library is closed today" back into the Belief Box.

Nichols and Stich's boxological monitoring theory is likely to be committed to *Tracking Function*. As Goldman (2006) points out, the boxological monitoring

---

[10] Note, however, that this is not Goldman's own proposal; in fact he has been skeptical about this proposal (Goldman 1993, 2006). One of his objections is that functional properties cannot be introspectively detected because they are dispositional and relational. See also Currie (1998) for a related discussion.

[11] It is common in the philosophical literature to contrast the boxological monitoring theory with the self-interpretation theory, and take them to belong to opposing camps. The boxological monitoring theory presupposes a dedicated monitoring mechanism for identifying own mental states. In contrast, the self-interpretation theory (or at least the radical version of it; e.g., Carruthers 2009, 2011) denies such a dedicated mechanism. I agree that the boxological monitoring theory and the self-interpretation theory are dissimilar with respect to *the nature of the mechanism* for self-knowledge. But they are similar with respect to *the properties that are tracked by the mechanism*.

theory in itself is not very clear about how the attitude-types are identified. Why is it exactly that the monitoring mechanism adds "I believe that" rather than "I imagine that" to the representation "the university library is closed today"? The answer would be that the mechanism adds "I believe that" rather than "I imagine that" to the representation "the university library is closed today" because the representation is stored in the Belief Box. This means that the monitoring mechanism is sensitive to which box a representation is stored in. Note that the boxological terminology is a metaphor or an abbreviation. In the boxological framework, "the representation 'the university library is closed today' is in the Belief Box" is a shorthand for "the representation 'the university library is closed today' plays the doxastic functional role". Thus, if the monitoring mechanism tracks which box a representation is stored in, that means that the monitoring mechanism tracks which functional role the representation plays (which is, in effect, *Tracking Function*).

(2) **Self-Interpretation Theory**: The self-interpretation theory (Bem 1972; Gopnik 1993; Wilson 2002) can be understood as a special case of *Tracking Function*, where only the behavioural part of the functional role is tracked.

Roughly, the self-interpretation theory says that knowledge of one's own mental states is provided through the process of interpreting one's own behaviour, which is basically the same process that we rely on in knowing the mental states of others. For example, I come to know that I believe that the university library is closed today by observing and interpreting my behaving as if I believe that the university library is closed today, or as if it is the case that the university library is closed today. This process is the same in kind as the process in which I come to know that my friend, John, believes that the university library is closed today; by observing and interpreting John's behaving as if he believes that the university library is closed today, or as if it is the case that the university library is closed today. The self-interpretation theory nicely explains empirical findings that self-attribution can be a confabulation of our own behaviour (e.g., Nisbett and Wilson 1997; Gazzaniga 2000; Johansson et al. 2006).

5. Self-Interpretation Theory Rejected

This section discusses the self-interpretation theory in a greater detail. Since the self-interpretation theory is associated with *Tracking Function*, my argument raises a problem for the self-interpretation theory too. For example, Ken regards his delusion about his wife as a belief. He believes that he believes that his wife has been replaced by an impostor. In contrast, his delusion fails to have belief-like effects on his behaviour. He does not behave as if he believes that his wife has been replaced by an impostor. These facts seem to suggest that it is not the case that Ken identifies his delusion as a belief by interpreting his behaviour. After all,

30 BELIEF, IMAGINATION, AND DELUSION

his behaviour does not suggest that he believes that his wife has been replaced by an impostor.

There are, roughly, two options for the self-interpretation theorists. One option is to abandon the idea that self-interpreting is the *only* source of self-knowledge, and allow for some other sources. This option is certainly available for the self-interpretation theorists. After all, many of them hesitate to endorse the radical claim that self-interpreting is the *only* source of self-knowledge anyway. For example, Daryl Bem says that we know our mental states "partially" by interpreting own behaviour, and that self-interpretation occurs only when "internal cues are weak, ambiguous, or uninterpretable" (Bem 1972: 2). Again, Richard Nisbett and Timothy Wilson distinguish mental *contents* (such as feelings, judgements, behaviours) from mental *processes* (in which feelings, judgements, and behaviours are produced), and argue that the self-knowledge of the latter requires self-interpretation. In contrast, the former "can be known with near certainty" without self-interpretation (Nisbett and Wilson 1977: 297).

This option is certainly available for the self-interpretation theorists, but taking this option in itself does not give a satisfactory answer to our original question about how to identify attitude-types. The self-interpretation theorists can say that there are some other resources for identifying attitude-types, but this cannot be the end of the story; the nature of the "other resources" has to be clarified. What are the "other resources" exactly? Are they related to phenomenal properties, representational properties, or underlying neural properties? In short, this option does not answer our question; it only brings us back to where we were in the beginning.

Another option is to defend the idea that self-interpreting behaviour is the *only* source of self-knowledge by adopting a new understanding of "self-interpreting". According to Carruthers's interpretive sensory-access theory (Carruthers 2011; see also Carruthers 2009), which is the best example of this option, the materials for self-interpretation include not only the external behavioural cues but also inner sensory cues including inner speech and mental imagery. The interpretive sensory-access theory appears to be better equipped to meet the challenge; although external behavioural cues do not support the idea that he believes that his wife has been replaced by an impostor, Ken has access to his internal sensory cues, including inner speech and metal imagery, that might suggest that he believes that his wife has been replaced by an impostor.

In fact, Carruthers gives a similar solution to a similar challenge to the self-interpretation theory. Nichols and Stich raise the following problem for a naïve self-interpretation theory that self-knowledge is wholly dependent upon the interpretation of external behavioural cues:

> [i]t seems obvious that people can sit quietly without exhibiting any relevant behaviour and report on their current thoughts. For instance, people can answer

questions about current mental states like 'what are you thinking about?' Similarly, after silently working through a problem in their heads, people can answer subsequent questions like 'how did you figure that out?'

(Nichols and Stich 2003: 157)

This is a serious challenge to the naïve self-interpretation theory, but the interpretive sensory-access theory has an obvious answer to it. Although there is no informative external behavioural cue in this case, the person can access her internal sensory cues, including inner speech and mental imagery, in order to identify her mental states. The interpretive sensory-access theory can handle Ken's case in a similar way; Ken's internal sensory cues inform him that he believes that his wife has been replaced by an impostor.

As a matter of fact, however, the interpretive sensory-access theory is not particularly promising when it comes to meeting my challenge. The main problem is that the internal cues are not informative for the purpose of identifying attitude-types. Even though Ken has access to his internal sensory cues such as the inner speech sentence "my wife has been abducted by Martians" or the mental image of Martians' abducting his wife, these sensory cues are not sufficient for him to conclude that he believes (rather than imagines, desires, wishes, etc.) that his wife was abducted by Martians.

Hume raises a similar issue concerning the difference between believing and imagining. He argues that sensory cues (or "ideas") are the same between somebody imagining that Caesar died in his bed and somebody believing the same thing. The believer "form[s] all the same ideas as [the imaginer] does", and the believer "can't conceive any idea that [the imaginer] can't conceive, or conjoin any ideas that [the imaginer] can't conjoin" (Hume 2007/1739: 66). But if Hume is correct, then one cannot tell whether one imagines that Caesar died in his bed or believes it by observing sensory cues.

Here is a possible solution to the problem. Inner speech sentences can be different between different attitude-types. In some cases, for example, we can easily distinguish beliefs from desires by observing inner speech sentences. For example, one might have "An apple is on the table" when believing that an apple is on the table, while one might have, "I want to eat an apple" when desiring to eat an apple.

But this response faces several problems. For example, the inner speech sentence "I want to eat an apple" might not express a desire. Rather it might express a desire-like imagination, or an i-desire (i.e., a conative imaginative attitude; Currie and Ravenscroft 2002; Doggett and Egan 2007). Another problem is that, even if this proposal works in distinguishing beliefs from desires, it cannot be generalized; in particular it does not work in distinguishing beliefs from imaginings. Perhaps the inner speech sentence is just the same (i.e., "an apple is on the table") both in believing that an apple is on the table and in imagining that an apple is on the table.

32   BELIEF, IMAGINATION, AND DELUSION

But, one might think, inner speech sentences can be different between believing and imagining. For example, believing brings some extra inner speech words, such as "exist" or "real"; e.g., "an apple EXISTS on the table" in believing that an apple is on the table. However, "an apple EXISTS on the table" can be taken as expressing an imagining rather than a belief, namely, the imagining that an apple exists on the table.

Another solution would be to follow Hume's suggestion that sensory cues are more vivid (more "forceful" and "vivacious" in Hume's terminology) in believing than in imagining. For example, I experience a highly vivid mental image of an apple on the table when I believe that an apple is on the table, while I experience a less vivid mental image of it when I imagine that an apple is on the table. Or, I experience a highly vivid inner speech sentence "an apple is on the table" when I believe that an apple is on the table, while I experience a less vivid inner speech sentence "an apple is on the table" when I imagine that an apple is on the table. This proposal might be called the "Humean interpretive sensory-access theory".

Even if this proposal works in the context of distinguishing beliefs from imaginings, it cannot be generalized; it does not work in the context of distinguishing beliefs from desires, hopes, wishes, acceptances, suppositions, etc. Is the mental image of an apple on the table, or the inner speech sentence "an apple is on the table", more vivid when believing that an apple is on the table than when desiring that an apple is on the table? The Humean interpretive sensory-access theory works only with the assumption that each attitude-type is associated with a distinctive level of vividness of sensory cues. But this assumption is not plausible.[12]

Summing up, the interpretive sensory-access theory is not immune to the challenge from delusion. Even if Ken has access to his internal sensory cues, the sensory cues are not informative enough for him to identify attitude-types. As a matter of fact, however, Ken does identify attitude-types; i.e., he regards his delusion as a belief (*Doxastic Recognition*). This means that it is not the case that Ken identifies his attitude-types by tracking internal sensory cues.

6. Tracking Phenomenology

6.1 Basic Ideas

Thus we have reached the (interim) conclusion that *Tracking Function* should be rejected. The rest of this chapter is for discussing the alternatives to *Tracking Function*.

---

[12] Another solution might be that inner speech sentences have some assertive force when they express beliefs but not when they express imaginings. For example, the inner speech sentence "an apple is on the table" has some assertive force when I believe that an apple is on the table, while the inner speech sentence does not have the assertive force when I imagine that an apple is on the table. Although this is an interesting proposal, just like the Humean interpretive sensory-access theory, it will face the problem of generalizability. This proposal works only with the assumption that each attitude-type is associated with a distinctive type of force. But it is difficult to find an independent reason to accept such an assumption.

The other options in the list are *Tracking Phenomenology, Tracking Content,* and *Tracking Brain.* Among them, *Tracking Content* does not seem to be a promising option. The problem for *Tracking Content* is analogous to the problem for the interpretive sensory-access theory; the representational content is not informative for distinguishing different attitude-types.[13] For example, the belief that an apple is on the table seems to be representationally equivalent to the imagining that an apple is on the table.

In response, one might argue that believing involves some distinctive representational content, such as EXIST or REAL; e.g., believing that a REAL apple is on the table/imagining that an apple is on the table. However, as Hume (2007/1739) points out, it is far from obvious that believing that a REAL apple is on the table is different from believing that an apple is on the table. Perhaps "REAL" does not add any representational content to the proposition that an apple is on the table.[14] Another problem is that, even if "REAL" does add some representational content (e.g., a "REAL apple" in the sense that it is not fake), it is far from obvious that "REAL" is peculiar to beliefs. Perhaps one can imagine, desire, hope, etc. that a REAL apple is on the table. A hungry person would desire that a REAL apple (as opposed to a fake one) is on the table, for example.

Then, we are left with two options: *Tracking Phenomenology* and *Tracking Brain.* Unlike *Tracking Function,* both *Tracking Phenomenology* and *Tracking Brain* can account for Ken's case, at least in principle. For example, Ken's delusion about his wife does not play the doxastic functional role of beliefs, but perhaps it has the distinctively doxastic phenomenology. Ken recognizes the doxastic phenomenology and identifies his delusion as a belief. Alternatively, the delusion's underlying neural properties are distinctively doxastic. Ken (or his sub-personal monitoring systems) recognizes the neural properties and identifies his delusion as a belief.

Although both *Tracking Phenomenology* and *Tracking Brain* are live options, I will focus on the former in the rest of this chapter; there is more to be said

---

[13] Hanks (2011, 2015) proposes an account of propositions according to which a proposition is individuated by an act of predicating a property of an object, where the act of predicating involves a judgement (i.e., judgement that the object has the property). This view denies the idea of propositions that are independent from acts, such as the act of judging or believing. But it is far from obvious that this proposal actually saves *Tracking Content.* For example, when I believe that an apple is on the table, I predicate the property of being on the table of an apple. But perhaps I perform the same act of predication when I imagine, rather than believe, that an apple is on the table. But then, even in this proposal, believing and imagining share the same propositional content. See Hanks (2015: Chapter 4) for a related discussion.

[14] Hume has another argument against this proposal; it implies an implausible version of doxastic voluntarism. Roughly, Hume's (2007/1739) reasoning goes as follows. If believing involves a peculiar idea, such as the idea of being REAL, then we should be able to believe anything voluntarily, which is obviously false. In general, we have the capacity of combining any ideas together voluntarily. Hence we should be able to combine, voluntarily, the idea of an apple and the idea of being REAL, if there is such an idea, to form the idea of a REAL apple. But this is nothing but (an implausible version of) doxastic voluntarism; forming the idea of a REAL apple is, according to the present proposal, to believe in the apple.

34   BELIEF, IMAGINATION, AND DELUSION

about the former than about the latter. According to *Tracking Phenomenology*, self-knowledge of attitude-types is achieved by tracking the phenomenology of the target states (Goldman 1993; see also Pitt 2004, 2011). This account presupposes that, for example, the belief that P has some distinctively doxastic phenomenology. As Russell writes; "believing P feels different from disbelieving it, supposing it, desiring it, or from any other propositional attitude towards it" (Russell 2009/1948: 108).

Interestingly, Goldman (1993) once favoured *Tracking Phenomenology* over *Tracking Brain*, but later (2006) he changed his mind and defended *Tracking Brain* instead. Goldman's main worry for *Tracking Phenomenology* is that it rests on the dubious assumption that each attitude-type is associated with a distinctive phenomenology. I agree with Goldman that this assumption can be questioned. But I do not think that this assumption is more questionable than what *Tracking Brain* assumes; i.e., each attitude-type is associated with a distinctive neural activity.

Moreover, the assumption that each attitude-type is associated with a distinctive phenomenology is not as problematic as it might seem initially. An interpretation (and perhaps Goldman's interpretation) of this assumption is that each attitude-type is associated with a distinctive *sensory* phenomenology. This assumption is not very plausible. What is, for example, the sensory phenomenal difference between the belief that an apple is on the table and the desire that an apple is on the table? Is the belief more vivid than the desire? But this idea sounds very similar to the Humean interpretive sensory-access theory. Another, and more plausible interpretation of the assumption would be that each attitude-type is associated with a non-sensory, *cognitive* phenomenology (Chudnoff 2015; Smithies 2013a, 2013b). I will say more about this below.

6.2 Clarifications

Here are some clarificatory remarks on *Tracking Phenomenology*.

(1) **Cognitive Phenomenology**: In principle, *Tracking Phenomenology* is neutral on the nature of the attitudinal phenomenology. *Tracking Phenomenology* presupposes only that, for example, the belief that P has some distinctively doxastic phenomenology, but it does not presuppose any particular view about the nature of the phenomenology. It can be sensory or non-sensory.

However, *Tracking Phenomenology* faces a problem if the doxastic phenomenology is sensory. This problem is analogous to the problem for the Humean interpretive sensory-access theory. As we saw above, we cannot distinguish beliefs from desires, hopes, wishes, acceptances, suppositions, etc. by the vividness of sensory cues. It is unlikely that each attitude-type is associated with a distinctive degree of vividness of sensory cues. Similarly, we cannot distinguish beliefs from desires, hopes, wishes, acceptances, suppositions, etc. by the sensory phenomenology. It is unlikely that each attitude-type is associated with a distinctive sensory phenomenology. This means that *Tracking Phenomenology* needs to be committed to the view that the doxastic phenomenology is non-sensory (or proprietary), cognitive phenomenology.[15]

(2) **Agential Phenomenology**: But it is too quick to conclude that we track cognitive phenomenology when we identify attitude-types. Another possibility would be that we track agential phenomenology;[16] e.g. the imagining that P involves agential phenomenology, while the belief that P does not. Ken regards his delusion as a belief rather than an imagining because the delusion does not involve agential phenomenology.

Currie (2000; Currie and Ravenscroft 2002) defends this idea. He thinks that beliefs and imaginings are normally distinguished by (the presence or the absence of) agential phenomenology. Ken's delusion is an imagining rather than a belief; Ken imagines that his wife has been replaced by an impostor, but he does not believe it, according to Currie. But Ken mistakenly regards the delusional imagining as a belief, and forms the false metacognitive belief that he believes that his wife has been replaced by an impostor. This metacognitive failure occurs because the delusional imagining about his wife is not accompanied by agential phenomenology, which is due to the abnormal lack of agential phenomenology in schizophrenia (Frith 1992).

I will not examine Currie's proposal as a whole; for example I will not discuss his idea that delusions are imaginings, or that schizophrenia involves the lack of agential phenomenology.[17] I only focus on his particular commitment that Ken regards his delusion as a belief because it does not involve agential phenomenology (which can be examined independently from other commitments in Currie's theory).

Currie's commitment is problematic. Beliefs do not have agential phenomenology, but there are many other mental states without agential phenomenology. For example, desires do not have agential phenomenology either. Even if it is true that Ken's delusion does not have agential phenomenology, the lack of agential phenomenology is not informative enough for Ken to reach the conclusion that his delusion is a belief rather than any other mental states without agential phenomenology. Why doesn't he reach the conclusion that he desires, not believes, that his wife has been replaced by an impostor, for example?

---

[15] Thus, I endorse Pitt's (2004, 2011) claim that cognitive phenomenology explains our capacity for self-knowledge. But Pitt's claim is not about attitudinal phenomenology.

[16] I am using the term "agential phenomenology" in a broad sense, referring to the subjective experience of a bodily movement or a mental event as an action; cf. "the experience of a movement (or a mental event) as: an action (of one's own); an action that one is in control of; an action that one is performing with a certain degree of effort; and as action that one is performing freely" (Bayne 2008: 183–4).

[17] For a detailed examination of Currie's proposal, see Bayne and Pacherie (2005).

36 BELIEF, IMAGINATION, AND DELUSION

Currie's proposal works once Ken somehow successfully narrows down the hypotheses to two; the hypothesis that he believes that his wife has been replaced by an impostor and the hypothesis that he imagines it. Then Ken chooses the former if the delusion does not have agential phenomenology, and the latter if it does have agential phenomenology. But this proposal is incomplete as a theory of self-knowledge unless the process of narrowing down is explained. And it is obvious that agential phenomenology cannot explain the process of narrowing down.

(3) **Individuation of Attitude-Types:** *Tracking Phenomenology* assumes that each attitude-type is associated with a distinctive phenomenology, but this does not necessarily mean that each attitude-type is individuated or defined by the phenomenology. For example, it is possible that the attitude of believing is associated with a distinctively doxastic phenomenology, but the attitude of believing is not individuated or defined by the phenomenology; it is individuated by its functional role.[18]

One might find it problematic to endorse *Tracking Phenomenology* without endorsing the idea that propositional attitudes are individuated by their phenomenology. Failing to endorse the latter invites a worry about reliability of self-knowledge. Suppose, for example, that the attitude of believing is individuated by the doxastic functional role rather than the doxastic phenomenology. The problem, then, is that the doxastic phenomenology and the doxastic functional role can come apart, at least in principle. It is at least conceivable that a mental state exhibits the doxastic functional role (and, hence, it is a belief), but does not have the doxastic phenomenology. In that case, *Tracking Phenomenology* predicts that the person fails to identify the belief as a belief. Again, it is at least conceivable that a mental state has the doxastic phenomenology, but does not exhibit the doxastic functional role (and, hence, it is not a belief). In that case, *Tracking Phenomenology* predicts that the person mistakenly regards the mental state as a belief.

However, I do not find these consequences especially problematic. I do not think that our self-knowledge of attitude-types is perfectly accurate or reliable. *Tracking Phenomenology* allows for the possibility that our self-knowledge fails in some cases (e.g., the cases in which the doxastic phenomenology and the doxastic functional role comes apart), but this implication does not seem to be a problem. In fact, if it turns out that delusions are not beliefs (which I do not rule out, at least in this chapter), then Ken's case turns out to be where a mental state that is not a belief (i.e., his delusion about his wife) is mistakenly regarded as a belief.

---

[18] Pitt (2004, 2011), in contrast, thinks that cognitive phenomenology is constitutive (of content, not of attitude), and he takes this to follow from *Tracking Phenomenology*. But I am inclined to think that this is too strong. One can know about a mental state by tracking its phenomenal properties even when the phenomenal properties are regularly correlated with, but not constitutive of, the state.

6.3 Objections

I will now discuss two objections to *Tracking Phenomenology*. The first objection is about whether *Tracking Phenomenology* is really plausible as a theory of self-knowledge, and the second objection is about whether *Tracking Phenomenology* can really account for the cases of delusion.

(1) **Dispositional Beliefs**: The first objection is that *Tracking Phenomenology* has an obvious difficulty in explaining our self-knowledge of dispositional beliefs (and any other dispositional states). Dispositional beliefs do not have doxastic phenomenology (or any phenomenology whatsoever). For instance, when I dispositionally believe that Caesar was assassinated by a group of senators, this belief does not have any phenomenology. Thus, I cannot identify them by tracking their doxastic phenomenology.

This objection can be formulated as follows. First, *Tracking Phenomenology* is not applicable to the self-knowledge of dispositional beliefs because they do not have any phenomenology. Second, a successful theory of self-knowledge needs to be applicable to occurrent as well as dispositional beliefs. Hence, *Tracking Phenomenology* is not a successful theory.

In response to this argument, I challenge the second premise that a successful theory of self-knowledge needs to be applicable to occurrent as well as dispositional beliefs. Empirical findings suggest that we do not have very good self-knowledge of dispositional states that are not consciously entertained. Psychological studies (such as confabulation studies; e.g., Nisbett and Wilson 1977; Gazzaniga 2000; Johansson et al. 2006) reveal systematic and predictable metacognitive errors. Some authors (e.g., Carruthers 2009, 2011) take these findings to be the evidence for the lack of direct metacognitive access to propositional attitudes in general, but in fact these findings do not support such a sweeping conclusion. Instead, a reasonable conclusion to draw from these findings would be that we do not have direct access to thoughts and decisions that are not consciously entertained at that moment or not consciously available in the first place. Wilson expresses this view in terms his adaptive unconsciousness hypothesis; "to the extent that people's responses are caused by the adaptive unconscious, they do not have privileged access to the causes and must infer them [...]. But to the extent that people's responses are caused by the conscious self, they have privileged access to the actual causes of these responses" (Wilson 2002: 106). This conclusion is perfectly consistent with *Tracking Phenomenology*, according to which we can track the phenomenal properties of propositional attitudes when they are consciously available.

Of course, it is not the case that we are completely clueless with regard to our dispositional beliefs. Perhaps we identify our dispositional beliefs by interpreting our behaviour.

(2) **Phenomenal Peculiarity of Delusion**: On the face of it, *Tracking Phenomenology* can account for cases of delusion. It is perfectly possible that Ken's delusion, although it does not play the doxastic functional role (*Non-Doxastic Function*), has the doxastic phenomenology. And Ken regards his delusion as a belief (*Doxastic Recognition*) on the basis of his awareness of the doxastic phenomenology. This account rests on the assumption that delusions have doxastic phenomenology, or that delusions and non-delusional beliefs share the same attitudinal phenomenology. For example, Ken's delusion about his wife and his non-delusional belief about the weather in London share the same attitudinal phenomenology.

However, some might challenge this assumption. In fact, several authors stress some qualitative peculiarities of delusions as well as some qualitative differences between delusions and non-delusional beliefs. For example, Louis Sass's points out that, unlike non-delusional beliefs, delusions are treated "with what seems a certain distance or irony" (Sass's 1994: 21). Similarly, Jennifer Radden observes that "[s]ubjective descriptions of both delusions and hallucinations are regularly accompanied by elaborate qualifications that echo these uncertainties over how to capture and represent such experiences" (Radden 2010: 48).

My response to this objection is that the qualitative peculiarities of delusions are perfectly compatible with the idea that delusions have the doxastic phenomenology.

First, there are different phases in the development of (schizophrenic) delusions, and different phases are associated with different experiences. Perhaps the peculiar, non-doxastic phenomenology can be seen in the prodromal phase of schizophrenia, before the onset of positive symptoms such as delusions. But it is not very surprising that the doxastic phenomenology is absent at the prodromal stage; after all, full-fledged delusions are not formed yet at that stage.

Second, as I pointed out above, delusions tend to wax and wane, vacillating between firm commitment and doubt. Perhaps Sass's remark on "distance" and "irony" as well as Radden's remark on "qualifications" and "uncertainties" are referring to the moment of doubt. But it is not very surprising that doxastic phenomenology is absent in the moment of doubt; perhaps delusional subjects do not (strongly) believe the delusional content in the moment of doubt.

Third, phenomenal differences between delusions and non-delusional beliefs are perfectly compatible with the idea that delusions have the doxastic phenomenology nonetheless. The idea that Ken's delusion about his wife and his non-delusional belief about the weather in London share doxastic phenomenology does not necessarily imply that the overall phenomenology at the time when Ken has the delusion about his wife and the overall phenomenology at the time when he has the non-delusional belief about the weather in London are completely the same. It is possible that Ken's delusion about his wife and his non-delusional belief about the weather in London share the doxastic phenomenology, but nonetheless the overall phenomenology at the time when Ken has the delusion about his wife is rather peculiar because of some peculiar experiences (e.g., perceptual experiences, affective experiences) in the stream of consciousness.[19]

7. Conclusion

The main claim of this chapter is that delusions provide a useful test case for investigating the nature of self-knowledge. A successful account of the self-knowledge of attitude-types needs to be coherent with the conjunction of two facts about delusions; the fact that people with delusions identify their delusions as beliefs (*Doxastic Recognition*), and the fact that delusions do not play the doxastic functional role (*Non-Doxastic Function*). This test in itself does not enable us to single out the true theory of self-knowledge, but it does enable us to narrow down the options. In particular, *Tracking Function* does not pass this test. And it implies the failure of the theories of self-knowledge that are associated with *Tracking Function*, such as the boxological monitoring theory and the self-interpretation theory. As an alternative to *Tracking Function*, I defended *Tracking Phenomenology*. Unlike *Tracking Function*, *Tracking Phenomenology* passes the test; it is coherent with the conjunction of *Doxastic Recognition* and *Non-Doxastic Function*.

Acknowledgments

An early version of this chapter was presented at the International Conference on Phenomenology and Philosophy of Mind (26 May 2019, at Huaqiao University). I thank Katsunori Miyahara, Uku Tooming, and Rui Kubota for their insightful comments. I also thank Ema Sullivan-Bissett for her helpful suggestions. I acknowledge the support of JSPS KAKENHI (grant number 18H00605, 20H00001, 21H00464).

References

American Psychiatric Association (2013). *Diagnostic and Statistical Manual of Mental Disorders*, 5th edition (Washington, DC: American Psychiatric Association).

Bayne, T. (2008). 'The Phenomenology of Agency', *Philosophy Compass* 3/1: 182–202.

Bayne, T. (2010). 'Delusions as Doxastic States: Contexts, Compartments, and Commitments', *Philosophy, Psychiatry, & Psychology* 17/4: 329–36.

---

[19] For a related discussion, see Clutton (2018).

40 BELIEF, IMAGINATION, AND DELUSION

Bayne, T. and Pacherie, E. (2005). 'In Defence of the Doxastic Conception of Delusions', *Mind & Language* 20/2: 163–88.

Bem, D. J. (1972). 'Self-Perception Theory', *Advances in Experimental Social Psychology* 6/1: 1–62.

Bortolotti, L. (2010). *Delusions and Other Irrational Beliefs* (New York: Oxford University Press).

Byrne, A. (2018). *Transparency and Self-Knowledge* (New York: Oxford University Press).

Carruthers, P. (2009). 'How We Know Our Own Minds: The Relationship between Mindreading and Metacognition', *Behavioral and Brain Sciences* 32/2: 121–38.

Carruthers, P. (2011). *The Opacity of Mind: An Integrative Theory of Self-Knowledge* (Oxford: Oxford University Press).

Chudnoff, E. (2015). *Cognitive Phenomenology* (London: Routledge).

Clutton, P. (2018). 'A New Defence of Doxasticism about Delusions: The Cognitive Phenomenological Defence', *Mind & Language* 33/2: 198–217.

Coltheart, M., Langdon, R., and McKay, R. (2011). 'Delusional Belief', *Annual Review of Psychology* 62: 271–98.

Currie, G. (1998). 'Pretence, Pretending and Metarepresenting', *Mind & Language* 13/1: 35–55.

Currie, G. (2000). 'Imagination, Delusion and Hallucinations', *Mind & Language* 15/1: 168–83.

Currie, G. and Jureidini, J. (2001). 'Delusion, Rationality, Empathy: Commentary on Martin Davies et al.', *Philosophy, Psychiatry, & Psychology* 8/2: 159–62.

Currie, G. and Ravenscroft, I. (2002). *Recreative Minds: Imagination in Philosophy and Psychology* (New York: Oxford University Press).

Doggett, T. and Egan, A. (2007). 'Wanting Things You Don't Want', *Philosophers' Imprint* 7/9: 1–17.

Egan, A. (2008). 'Imagination, Delusion, and Self-Deception', in T. Bayne and J. Fernández (eds.), *Delusion and Self-Deception: Motivational and Affective Influences on Belief Formation* (New York: Psychology Press), 263–80.

Fernández, J. (2013). *Transparent Minds: A Study of Self-Knowledge* (Oxford: Oxford University Press).

Fowler, D., Garety, P., and Kuipers, E. (1995). *Cognitive Behaviour Therapy for Psychosis: Theory and Practice* (Chichester: John Wiley & Sons).

Frith, C. D. (1992). *The Cognitive Neuropsychology of Schizophrenia* (New York: Psychology Press).

Gazzaniga, M. S. (2000). 'Cerebral Specialization and Interhemispheric Communication: Does the Corpus Callosum Enable the Human Condition?', *Brain* 123/7: 1293–326.

Goldman, A. I. (1993). 'The Psychology of Folk Psychology', *Behavioral and Brain Sciences* 16/1: 15–28.

Goldman, A. I. (2006). *Simulating Minds: The Philosophy, Psychology, and Neuroscience of Mindreading* (New York: Oxford University Press).

Gopnik, A. (1993). 'How We Know Our Minds: The Illusion of First-Person Knowledge of Intentionality', *Behavioral and Brain Sciences* 16/1: 1–14.

Hanks, P. W. (2011). 'Structured Propositions as Types', *Mind* 120/477: 11–52.

Hanks, P. (2015). *Propositional Content* (Oxford: Oxford University Press).

Hume, D. (2007/1739). *A Treatise of Human Nature* (Oxford: Oxford University Press).

Johansson, P., Hall, L., Sikström, S., Tärning, B., and Lind, A. (2006). 'How Something Can Be Said about Telling More than We Can Know: On Choice Blindness and Introspection', *Consciousness and Cognition*, 15/4: 673–92.

Lucchelli, F. and Spinnler, H. (2007). 'The Case of Lost Wilma: A Clinical Report of Capgras Delusion', *Neurological Sciences* 28/4: 188–95.

Miyazono, K. (2018). *Delusions and Beliefs: A Philosophical Inquiry* (New York: Routledge).

Nichols, S. and Stich, S. P. (2003). *Mindreading: An Integrated Account of Pretence, Self-Awareness, and Understanding Other Minds* (Oxford: Clarendon Press).

Nisbett, R. E. and Wilson, T. D. (1977). 'Telling More than We Can Know: Verbal Reports on Mental Processes', *Psychological Review*, 84/3: 231–59.

Pitt, D. (2004). 'The Phenomenology of Cognition or What Is It Like to Think That P?', *Philosophy and Phenomenological Research* 69/1: 1–36.

Pitt, D. (2011). 'Introspection, Phenomenality, and the Availability of Intentional Content', in T. Bayne and M. Montague (eds.), *Cognitive Phenomenology* (Oxford: Oxford University Press), 141–73.

Radden, J. (2010). *On Delusion* (New York: Routledge).

Reimer, M. (2010). 'Only a Philosopher or a Madman: Impractical Delusions in Philosophy and Psychiatry', *Philosophy, Psychiatry, & Psychology* 17/4: 315–28.

Russell, B. (2009/1948). *Human Knowledge: Its Scope and Limits* (New York: Routledge).

Sass, L. A. (1994). *The Paradoxes of Delusion: Wittgenstein, Schreber, and the Schizophrenic Mind* (Ithaca, NY: Cornell University Press).

Smithies, D. (2013a). 'The Nature of Cognitive Phenomenology', *Philosophy Compass* 8/8: 744–54.

Smithies, D. (2013b). 'The Significance of Cognitive Phenomenology', *Philosophy Compass* 8/8: 731–43.

Stone, T. and Young, A. W. (1997). 'Delusions and Brain Injury: The Philosophy and Psychology of Belief', *Mind & Language* 12/3–4: 327–64.

Wilson, T. D. (2002). *Strangers to Ourselves: Discovering the Adaptive Unconscious* (Cambridge, MA: Harvard University Press).

3

Contrast or Continuum?

The Case of Belief and Imagination

Amy Kind

Though philosophers have traditionally treated imagination and belief as distinct kinds of mental states, this orthodoxy has recently been challenged. According to what we might call the *continuum hypothesis*, imagination and belief should be seen as lying on a continuum, with at least some of the intermediary states along this continuum best thought of as imagination-belief hybrids. In support of this hypothesis, its defenders often argue that certain phenomena cannot be adequately explained unless we reject the view that there is a sharp division between imagination and belief. The two phenomena that have been most often invoked in this context are delusion and imaginative immersion.

In this chapter, I review the case for the continuum hypothesis. After setting out the philosophical consensus that is challenged by the continuum hypothesis, I turn to a consideration of the hypothesis itself and I attempt to clarify more precisely what exactly it amounts to. As we will see, though this hypothesis has been associated with work by Gregory Currie and Jon Jureidini (2004), Susanna Schellenberg (2013), and Andy Egan (2008), there are really two different views on offer: what I will call *the cluster view* and *the continuum view*. Focusing in on the continuum view, I look more specifically at two arguments that have been offered in defence of it. As I will suggest, the case that has been offered is not nearly as strong as its defenders would have us believe. Finally, in the last section I attempt to draw out some morals from our discussion and briefly point the way forward.

1. Understanding the Orthodoxy

Consider Betty, who has had a hankering for brownies all day. Sitting in her office, she imagines herself walking down the hall to the department lounge and discovering a platter of freshly baked brownies on the counter. This imaginative exercise might take place in a variety of ways, either alone or in conjunction with one another. In particular, she might imagine that there are brownies on the counter. She might imagine herself tasting the brownies. Or she might just imagine the brownies themselves.

Amy Kind, *Contrast or Continuum? The Case of Belief and Imagination* In: *Belief, Imagination, and Delusion.* Edited by: Ema Sullivan-Bissett, Oxford University Press. © Oxford University Press 2024. DOI: 10.1093/oso/9780198872221.003.0003

CONTRAST OR CONTINUUM? BELIEF AND IMAGINATION   43

These different ways of imagining are often categorized, respectively, as propositional imagining, experiential imagining, and objectual imagining. When philosophers compare belief and imagination, they tend to have propositional imagining in mind. Both propositional imagining and belief are treated as propositional attitudes, i.e., attitudes that one can take toward a certain content. On another occasion, instead of imagining that there are brownies on the counter, Betty might believe that there are brownies on the counter. And of course, she might take other attitudes toward this same content as well: she might desire that there are brownies on the counter, fear that there are brownies on the counter, and so on.

According to the philosophical orthodoxy, just as believing is a different propositional attitude from desiring, so too is it a different propositional attitude from imagining.[1] When it comes to belief and desire, the distinction can be in large part explained in terms of direction of fit. While belief has a mind-to-world direction of fit, in that we aim for the contents of our beliefs to match the world, desire has a world-to-mind direction of fit, in that we aim for the world to match the contents of our desire. But the notion of direction of fit does not seem to help us to distinguish between belief and imagining. Insofar as imagination has a direction of fit (and not everyone agrees that it does[2]), it appears to be mind-to-world—though in this case the world in question is perhaps best understood not as the actual world but rather as an imagined world. Another way to make the point: While desire is a *conative* attitude, imagination and belief are both *cognitive* attitudes.[3]

This last way of putting the point also yields the common framing of the philosophical orthodoxy as the *distinct cognitive attitude view*, i.e., that imagination is best treated as a cognitive attitude distinct from belief. When modeling the cognitive architecture for the mind—which is often done by way of boxological diagrams where different boxes pick out functionally distinct components of the mind—we need to have a separate box for imagination in addition to the box for belief.[4] For our purposes here, however, I prefer to call the view in question the

---

[1] Philosophers who embrace this philosophical orthodoxy include Nichols and Stich (2000), Weinberg and Meskin (2006), Schroeder and Matheson (2006), Neil Van Leeuwen (2016), and many others—this list should just be seen as providing a few illustrative examples.

[2] See, e.g., Humberstone (1992).

[3] Some philosophers have argued that attitude imagining comes in both cognitive and cognitive varieties (see Currie and Ravenscroft 2002; Doggett and Egan 2007). These two varieties are sometimes referred to respectively as belief-like imagination and desire-like imagination. But even if we were to accept the existence of desire-like imagination (and not everyone does; see, e.g., Kind 2011 and Spaulding 2015), the question discussed in the text about the relationship between belief and (belief-like) imagination would still arise.

[4] This way of framing the view is often traced back to Stich and Nichols (2000), although they don't use this exact phrasing. Rather, they postulate the existence of the *Possible World Box*. For related discussion of imagination's role in the cognitive architecture of mind, see Omoge, this volume.

44 BELIEF, IMAGINATION, AND DELUSION

contrast view. As we will see, casting the view in these terms will provide us with a nice way to highlight the disagreement with the continuum view.[5]

How, then, does the contrast view explicate the contrast that it sees between the two cognitive attitudes of belief and imagination? Perhaps the most fundamental distinction between these two attitudes concerns their relationship to truth. When a subject believes a given content, they take that content to be true. But this need not be the case for an imagining. Consider again Betty's imagining that there are brownies on the counter in the department lounge. Betty can engage in this imagining even if she does not take it to be true that there are brownies on the counter in the department lounge. So, imagination does not have the same kind of connection to truth that belief does. Importantly, however, this should not be taken to imply that a subject's imagining a given content entails that she takes that content to be untrue or even just that she fails to take that content to be true. Even if Betty takes it to be true that there are brownies on the counter, she can still engage in the same imagining. Suppose, for example, that Betty walked through the department lounge earlier in the day and came to believe that there are brownies on the counter. That afternoon, one of her colleagues does something that really annoys her. Sitting at her desk, she then engages in a revenge fantasy in which she imagines herself walking into the department lounge, imagines that there are brownies on the counter, and then imagines herself knocking the whole platter onto the floor just as her colleague is starting to reach for one. Granted, this is not that interesting as revenge fantasies go. But it nonetheless provides a case where someone imagines something—namely, that there are brownies on the counter—despite taking it be true.

Sometimes the difference between belief and imagination with respect to truth is put in normative terms. Beliefs, but not imaginings, *ought* to be true. This is sometimes put by saying that belief *aims* at the truth or that we aim at the truth in forming beliefs. In saying that we should aim our beliefs at truth, however, it is not thereby implied that one should aim to believe *as many truths as possible* or even, if we set aside trivial truths, *as many useful truths as possible*. Rather, as David Velleman notes, the relevant aim that distinguishes belief from imagining needs to be specified more carefully: "What distinguishes believing a proposition from imagining or supposing it is . . . the aim of getting the truth-value of that particular proposition right, by regarding the proposition as true only if it really is" (Velleman 2015: 252).[6]

---

[5] Another reason to dislike the name the *distinct cognitive attitude view* is that this may seem to privilege belief. Though the view could be explicated in neutral terms by saying that belief and imagining are distinct cognitive attitudes (thereby setting the two attitudes on equal terms), it is more commonly explicated by saying that imagining should be seen as a cognitive attitude distinct from belief (which does not set the attitudes on equal terms but instead presupposes a certain treatment of belief). Better, then, just to adopt a different name.

[6] For a discussion of different ways of understanding the aim of belief, see Noordhof, this volume. In his chapter, Noordhof explores how these different accounts might explain doxastic transparency and our inability to believe at will.

Alternatively, we might also explicate the difference between belief and imagination with respect to truth in functional terms. With respect both to formation and revision, belief seems to be both dependent on and responsive to evidence in a way that imagination is not. If Betty is provided with evidence that one of her colleagues has eaten the last of the brownies, she revises her belief about whether there are brownies on the counter. But even with this evidence, she may still engage in the very same revenge fantasy, i.e., one that involves imagining that there are brownies on the counter.[7]

The functional profiles of belief and imagination are not only specified in terms of their relationship to evidence, but also in terms of their relationship to action, emotion, and so on. Generally speaking, belief is thought to have a more expansive role with respect to guiding behaviour and generating affective responses, while imagining is thought to have a much more circumscribed role in these regards. Suppose that Betty wants a brownie. In that case, her belief that there are brownies in the kitchen will likely make her happy and cause her to get up from her desk and go to the kitchen. But her imagining that there are brownies in the kitchen is unlikely to have either of these effects. Likewise, the inferential role played by belief is thought to be considerably more expansive than the inferential role played by imagination. When Betty comes to believe that a plate of brownies has been placed on the kitchen counter, she will also come to believe that the counter is not empty. But when Betty imagines that a plate of brownies has been placed on the kitchen counter, this will not have any effects on her beliefs about whether the kitchen counter is or is not empty. This point is often put in terms of quarantining: though an imagining is typically quarantined off from one's set of beliefs, a belief is not.

The use of words like "expansive" and "circumscribed" in setting out these functional roles may seem to leave a lot of wiggle room, and in fact, that will turn out to be important later on. As we will see, how exactly we are to understand these functional profiles will play a central part in evaluating the arguments offered for the continuum hypothesis. I will thus forestall further discussion of this issue until we turn to the relevant arguments. For now, we should have enough of a sense of the normative and functional considerations usually invoked to have a sense of how the contrast view has typically been motivated and to understand the kinds of challenge that proponents of the continuum view raise for it.

2. Clarifying the Challenge

Challenges to the contrast view can be pursued in a variety of ways. In questioning whether belief and imagination should really be classified as distinct cognitive

---

[7] For related discussion of how belief and imagination differ with respect to responsiveness to evidence, see Ichino, this volume.

46 BELIEF, IMAGINATION, AND DELUSION

attitudes, one might try to reduce one of these states to the other. This kind of reductive project has recently been pursued by Peter Langland-Hassan; on his view, "propositional imagination just is a form of believing" (Langland-Hassan 2012: 155). The kind of challenge I am considering in this chapter takes a different form. Rather than trying to reduce one state to another, this challenge attempts to undermine the contrast view by blurring the lines between the two allegedly distinct states. In exploring this challenge, I will start by looking at three different papers in which it has been developed, one by Gregory Currie and Jon Jureidini (2004), one by Andy Egan (2008), and one by Susanna Schellenberg (2013). Though these authors have different aims, they all share a commitment to the idea that we should consider (or even accept) the existence of states that are in some way intermediate between belief and imagination.

Currie and Jureidini come to the issue by way of a discussion of narrative and coherence, and more specifically, the phenomenon of over-coherence. Over-coherence can be characterized in terms of a tendency to seek some kind of grand, unifying story that mistakenly ties together actions or events. Generally speaking, this tendency can be seen to lie in an individual's mistaken conception of how agency operates in the world—either because they see their own agency as powerless in the face of the machinations of mysterious beings or because they see their own agency as having power to affect things that are actually outside of their control. Consider someone who thinks that they're under the control of someone else and thus that all of their actions derive from the manipulations of this puppet-master. Or consider someone who sees themself as the puppet-master and thus sees other people's actions as owing to their own manipulations. Or finally, consider someone who—while not seeing themself as a puppet-master—nonetheless thinks that in some way the world revolves around them, that everything depends on what they themself do. All three of these examples offer different ways of exemplifying the tendency of over-coherence. It's as part of their effort to account for this phenomenon that Currie and Jureidini explore the idea that belief and imagination are not exclusive categories, since in their view the mental states most naturally attributed to the person who seeks over-coherence do not neatly fit the functional profile of either belief or imagination. Ultimately, they propose a framework that allows for the possibility of states that "while neither fitting well into the category of beliefs or imaginings, exhibit some features of both" (Currie and Jureidini 2004: 424).

Egan's development of the challenge occurs in the course of a discussion of delusion. The phenomenon of delusion has some commonalities with the phenomenon of over-coherence, since someone who has the tendency to impose coherence where there in fact is none might naturally be characterized as operating with a delusional conception of the world. But Egan focuses on two different varieties of delusion: Capgras delusion, a phenomenon in which a person sincerely reports that their spouses or other family members have been replaced by identical impostors; and Cotard delusion, a phenomenon in which a person sincerely reports that they themselves are dead. On Egan's view, the mental states involved in these delusions, mental states that have some of the distinctive features of belief and some of the distinctive features of imagining, might naturally be thought as intermediate between belief and imagination. We will discuss his arguments for this in more detail below, but for now let's simply note that his discussion leads him to suggest the following: "[T]here seems to be no principled reason to think that we can't get a spectrum of cases, from clear totally non-belief-like imaginings to clear, full-blooded paradigmatic beliefs, with intermediate, hard-to-classify states in the middle" (Egan 2008: 274). He proposes that we refer to these intermediate states as *bimagination*.

Schellenberg's development of the challenge proceeds in an effort to account for imaginative immersion. Imaginative immersion is a phenomenon that sometimes occurs when someone is engaged in an activity like make-believe or acting. As Schellenberg puts it, "The most relevant characteristic of imaginative immersion is that the subject does not consciously think about the fact that she is imagining. She is immersed in fiction" (2013: 507). Like the other authors we've just considered, Schellenberg too posits the existence of states intermediate between imagination and belief in her attempt to explain the phenomenon in which she is interested. Unlike the other authors, however, she is especially explicit in putting this in terms of a *continuum*. She also attempts to clarify what the notion of a continuum means in this context, in particular, that the "sense in which there is a continuum of mental states between imaginings and beliefs is at least in some respects analogous to the sense in which there is a continuum of colors between yellow and red" (Schellenberg 2013: 509). This analogy yields two important insights. First, when someone is in one of the intermediate states between belief and imagination, their mental state may not be easily categorized in terms of either of these attitudes, "analogous to the way shades between yellow and red may not be easily categorized as either yellow or red" (Schellenberg 2013: 510). But second, accepting the existence of a continuum does not mean that we have to deny that there is a conceptual distinction between belief and imagination. We accept that there is a conceptual distinction between yellow and red even though we also accept that the existence of intermediate states that are hard to classify either way. On Schellenberg's view, we should do likewise for belief and imagination.

This last point, however, shows that Schellenberg's proposal differs in an important respect from the proposal offered by Currie and Jureidini. Unlike Schellenberg, when Currie and Jureidini advocate for the possibility of intermediate states between belief and imagination, they do so as part of an explicit effort to call into question the coherence of a distinction between these two states. The possibility they propose involves "the abandonment of a categorical belief/imagination distinction in favour of vaguely specified clusterings in a many-dimensional cognitive space" (Currie and Jureidini 2004: 409).

48 BELIEF, IMAGINATION, AND DELUSION

As we saw in Section 1, there are a variety of different dimensions on which the functional roles of belief and imagination differ, and this gives us a variety of different features associated with one or the other state: expansive behaviour guidance, circumscribed behaviour guidance, evidence-dependence, evidence-independence, and so on. To make things simple, suppose that we can identify three such dimensions and thus six such features, and let's just refer to these features as A through F. The story that Currie and Jureidini tell can thus be put as follows: In our efforts to categorize mental states, we've noticed that A, B, and C often seem to be found together, and we've used the term "belief" to refer to states that exhibit this cluster of features. Likewise, we've noticed that D, E, and F often seem to be found together, and we've used the term "imagining" to refer to states that exhibit this cluster of features. But in focusing on these common groupings, we have lost sight of the fact that the six features do not always cluster in these patterns. As a result, our mental state taxonomies are inaccurate, as we've been forced to slot various instances of mental states into categories in which they don't naturally fit. Once we recognize that there are other ways for these features to cluster, we can develop a richer taxonomy that includes a greater variety of clusterings. Moreover, we may find that for some explanatory purposes we are better served by focusing on one subset of these clusterings whereas in other explanatory contexts we're better served by focusing on a different subset.

With this picture of Currie and Jureidini's view before us, it becomes clear that what we have thus far been treating as a single kind of challenge to the contrast view should really be seen as two distinct kinds of challenges—one that might be described as the *continuum view* and one that might be described as the *cluster view*. Granted, these two views have much in common with one another. In particular, they share the assumption that there exist states best described as in between belief and imagination, at least as belief and imagination are typically understood. But despite this shared assumption, the two views turn out to be importantly different, most importantly in terms of what they say about the robustness of the categories of belief and imagination. Though some of the considerations that motivate one of these views would also motivate the other, there are some considerations that do not support them both equally. Thus, going forward I am going to focus on the specific challenge posed by the continuum view.

3. Two Arguments

Focusing in on the continuum view means that we will set aside considerations relating to over-coherence and instead concentrate on delusion and imaginative immersion. As we have seen, the motivating thought can be put as follows: In both of these phenomena, mental states occur that are not neatly categorized as either belief or imagination; rather, they have a functional profile that is somewhere in-between the two. In imaginative immersion, there is a further issue, namely, that someone who is immersed might sometimes move "seamlessly from mental states that could be called pure imaginings to mental states that are at least to some degree belief-like" (Schellenberg 2013: 509). To my mind, these issues are best kept separate, and that's how I'll proceed in what follows. In that spirit, I would like to tease out two different arguments that seem operative in the case for the continuum view and against the contrast view. Let's call these *the argument from functional profiles* and *the argument from seamless transition*. Here's a rough schematization of each:

The argument from functional profiles
1. Delusion does not perfectly match the functional profile of either imagination or belief but instead partly matches one and partly matches another.
2. This would only be possible if imagination and belief were on a continuum.
3. Imagination and belief are on a continuum.

The argument from seamless transition
1. In imaginative immersion, we start off in a state that is a pure imagining and then seamlessly move to a state that is belief-like.
2. This would only be possible if imagination and belief were on a continuum.
3. Imagination and belief are on a continuum.

In what follows, I'll discuss both of these arguments in detail. As I'll suggest, they should both be rejected. I'll start with the argument from seamless transition. I do this in part because I think it's the argument that can be dismissed most easily. But perhaps more importantly, starting with this argument teaches us certain lessons that will prove instructive to our subsequent consideration of the argument from functional profiles.

Before I take up either of these arguments, however, I want to pause for a moment to note what their proponents take themselves to be showing in offering them. Importantly, Egan is considerably less decisive in his support of the continuum thesis than Schellenberg is, and he thus takes the case on offer to establish less than Schellenberg does. Schellenberg explicitly commits herself to the truth of the continuum thesis.[8] Moreover, in the context of her larger project, a project that aims to explain how imaginings, beliefs, and desires relate to produce actions/affective responses, Schellenberg takes the continuum thesis to impose a constraint on which candidate explanations are viable. In contrast to Schellenberg, however, Egan does not take his discussion to establish the truth of the continuum

---

[8] See, e.g., her claim that "There is a continuum between imaginings and beliefs" (Schellenberg 2013: 497).

50 BELIEF, IMAGINATION, AND DELUSION

thesis. Rather, he simply takes himself to have cleared conceptual space for it: "Although I don't take myself to have established that some intermediate-state account of delusion or self-deception is *true*, I do take myself to have established that it's not *crazy*" (Egan 2008: 277). As he goes on to note, "[P]ostulating such intermediate states is not conceptually incoherent and not incompatible with any obvious facts about our actual psychologies" (Egan 2008: 277). As we consider these two arguments, then, it is worth keeping in mind that even one of their proponents is hesitant about how much should be concluded from them.

3.1 The Argument from Seamless Transition

Evaluating the argument from seamless transition requires us to take a closer look at cases of imaginative immersion. Let's consider a case of pretence. Suppose that a parent is playing a game of make-believe with her child. Perhaps they are pretending to be wizards. At the start of the game, the parent is fully cognizant of the fact that she is only playing a game, that she is not really a wizard, and so on. Even while engaged in this activity, thoughts about other things—the work she needs to get done, the errands she needs to run—may be front and centre before her mind. But, sometimes, as the game goes on the parent may become more engrossed by it. Those other thoughts recede and the pretend world of wizardry starts to come alive to her. She no longer needs to think, "What would a wizard do now?" but can instead simply and effortlessly engage in wizard-like actions.

With this kind of case in mind, Schellenberg notes that as the parent becomes immersed in the game of make-believe, "the cognitive role of her mental state may start taking on characteristics of the cognitive role of a belief" (Schellenberg 2013: 510). She may "start to take it to be true" that she is a talented wizard (Schellenberg 2013: 508). More generally, "In cases of imaginative immersion, the imagining subject has mental states that are belief-like in that the imagining subject comes close to taking the subject matter of her imagination to be true" (Schellenberg 2013: 509). And, importantly, the move from the initial state of "pure imagining" to the later state that is more belief-like is a seamless one. As Schellenberg notes, the ability to make this transition seamlessly is part what makes someone a good pretender or actor.

This gives us the first premise of the argument from seamless transition:

> In imaginative immersion, we start off in a state that is a pure imagining and then seamlessly move to a state that is belief-like.

According to the second premise, this would only be possible if imagination and belief were on a continuum. We can spell out the motivation for this premise by recalling a point briefly mentioned earlier, namely, that philosophers often model the cognitive architecture of the mind by way of boxological diagrams, with a different box for each functionally distinct element of mind. In line with this approach, if we adopt the contrast view, imagination and belief would constitute different boxes. A particular token state can't be partly in one box and partly in another; it's either in a box or it's not, and it can only be in one box. Nor is there any transition process between one box and another. So in order to account for Premise 1, we need to discard the distinct boxes and instead adopt a different approach which sees imagination and belief as continuous with one another, perhaps occupying only a single box.

In response to this argument, I want to make three points. First, it's worth noting that Schellenberg seems hesitant to claim that the immersed actor or pretender ever actually ends up with a belief. Her claims are usually somewhat hedged. For example, as we've seen, she notes that someone who is pretending to be a talented wizard might come "close" to taking it to be true that she's a talented wizard, and thus her state is "belief-like". But is it actually a belief? If not, then it's not clear that we can't account for it completely within the imagination box. Perhaps within the class of imaginings, some are more belief-like and some less so. There might be independent reason to accept this claim when we think about imaginings in other contexts, particularly those contexts that are epistemically useful.[9] When I am trying to figure out whether the couch I just bought will fit through the doorway, I might engage in two different imaginings: the first where I imagine myself holding the couch and manipulating it at various angles, and the second where I imagine myself sprinkling the couch with fairy dust and its magically shrinking down to a miniature size (the fairy dust lasts just long enough for me to get it through the doorway, and then the couch restores itself to its original size). It seems plausible that there are various respects in which the first of these imaginings, while still an imagining, is more belief-like than the second. This is not just to say that it is more realistic, but rather, that the way that it connects to my actions and motivations is more belief-like than the way the second imagining does. (I'll have more to say on this when we turn to the argument from functional profiles below.)

Second, and more significantly, I think there is good reason to question the truth of Premise 1—or at least, to question whether it picks out the kind of robust phenomenon that would be needed to motivate the truth of Premise 2. Part of what makes Premise 2 seem so plausible is that it seems like immersion is a pretty widespread occurrence. Children seem to get really immersed in their games all the time, and actors often seem to get really immersed in their roles. This makes it looks like something pervasive for which we really need to account, and insofar as the contrast view can't handle it, the continuum view gains plausibility. But, as

---

[9] For discussion of imaginings that have epistemic usefulness, see the contributions in Badura and Kind (2021) and Kind and Kung (2016).

52 BELIEF, IMAGINATION, AND DELUSION

I want now to suggest, we can recognize the fact that children sometimes (maybe even frequently) get immersed in their games, and that actors sometimes (maybe even frequently) get immersed in their roles, without committing ourselves to Premise 1. In short, in the usual cases of children getting immersed in their games, or actors getting immersed in their roles, I don't see any reason to think that we see transitions from imaginings to belief, or even to significantly belief-like states.

Consider a child who is pretending to be a dog and who might naturally be described as having become immersed in the pretence. What does this amount to? I take it that it usually involves things like the following: The child persistently won't answer (in English) when you talk to them but instead simply barks; they persistently refuse to respond to their human name; they persistently "paw" at the door rather than opening it; and so on. But even though there are all sorts of ways in which they don't break character, what happens when you put a bowl of dog food down in front of them? I doubt that they start to lap it up. Or what happens when you turn on the television or computer and start to stream their favorite video? Here too, I doubt they keep "pawing" at the door. Rather, I suspect they're more likely to stand up from all fours and settle in on the couch to watch. It doesn't take much examination of their behaviour to see how unlikely it would be to suggest that they've really stopped believing that they're a little human and started to believe that they're a dog. Yes, they are immersed in their make-believe games, but this immersion is perhaps best described as a kind of investment or commitment than as a case where they've lost sight of the truth.

Parallel arguments have been raised in a slightly different context relating to belief and imagination, i.e., in connection with Velleman's argument (2000) that belief and imagination share the same motivational role. In the course of this argument, Velleman suggests that in cases of child's play, pretenders that p behave "as would be desirable if p were true" (Velleman 2000: 256). For example, when a child "imagines that he is an elephant, he is disposed to behave as if he were an elephant." But in response to this case, philosophers such as Paul Noordhof and Lucy O'Brien have noted the limitations of these dispositions. Noordhof questions whether the child would "seek to live outdoors, consume elephant edibles, and so on? Would he or she be worried at the transformation?" (Noordhof 2001: 253; see also Noordhof, this volume, esp. section 2). Likewise, O'Brien notes that if one were actually come to believe that one were an elephant, one would likely try to find ways to break it to one's family, arrange for a larger bed, resign from one's job (or, in the child's case, get out of going to school), and so on. But one does not feel motivated to do any of these things when pretending to be an elephant (O'Brien 2005: 59). For our purposes, what's important is that this lack of motivation is apparent even in immersed cases of pretending.

The problem, in short, is that there seem to be two different senses of immersion in play. Let's call these *ordinary immersion* (or *o-immersion*) and *Schellenberg immersion* (or *s-immersion*). The case I just described—where the immersion manifests primarily as a deep (and temporarily sustained) commitment—is what I mean as an example of o-immersion, and to my mind, most of the cases of immersion that we come across in day-to-day life, cases involving pretenders and actors, are of this sort. S-immersion requires something more than just a deep commitment; it involves the kind of switch from imagining to belief that she describes. Perhaps s-immersion is conceptually possible. But I don't think it's what we typically have in mind when we talk about immersed pretenders, and I think that it's a rare occurrence at best.

Of course, my concession that s-immersion is a conceptual possibility might seem to be enough for the argument from seamless transition to go through. For if it were conceptually possible for there to be cases of seamless transition from imagining to belief, then perhaps that's enough for Schellenberg to show that we should treat these states as on a continuum. But this brings me to the third point I'd like to make about the argument from seamless transition. The fact that there may be cases in which someone starts off imagining P and ends up believing P, and even cases where we'd want to describe this transition as seamless, doesn't mean that the transition is best described as a gradual movement along a continuum.[10] Rather, there might have simply been a change from being in one mental state to being in another. Compare the change from believing P to not believing P (or from not believing P to believing P). Some belief changes happen instantaneously, but many do not. But even when a belief change is best described as taking place over time, we don't typically think that this demands that we recognize a continuum between belief and not-belief. We can see the same thing in all sorts of other mental state transitions. One can move from love to hate without being in a state that's sort of love-like and sort of hate-like. One can move from enjoyment to disgust without being in a state that's sort of enjoyment-like and sort of disgust-like. So why can't the same thing be said for the change from imagining P to believing P? And if it can, then we have no reason to think that imagination and belief can't be different "boxes," that is, we have no reason to reject the contrast view.

Ultimately, then, the argument from seamless transition should be rejected. Either the first premise is false (since cases of immersion are best understood as o-immersion), or if it's not false, the way that it is true does not demand 2. As we'll see as in the next subsection as we turn to the argument from functional profiles, a similar kind of problem emerges there as well.

---

[10] This connects to another worry about the continuum view that I don't have the space to develop here. If we think that we can seamlessly (and gradually) move from imagining to belief, then one would expect that we can seamlessly (and gradually) move from belief to imagining. But what would an example of this look like? I find it surprising, and perhaps telling, that Schellenberg doesn't consider transitions in this reverse direction.

54 BELIEF, IMAGINATION, AND DELUSION

3.2 The Argument from Functional Profiles

To start our discussion of this argument, let's recall how it works:

1. Delusion does not perfectly match the functional profile of either imagination or belief but instead partly matches one and partly matches another.
2. This would only be possible if imagination and belief were on a continuum.
3. Imagination and belief are on a continuum.

As mentioned earlier, Egan's defence of this argument revolves around consideration of two specific forms of delusion: Cotard delusion and Capgras delusion. In support of the argument, Egan points to various ways in which delusions do not exhibit the normal functional profile of belief.

Perhaps the most obvious discrepancy concerns evidence dependence and responsiveness, since the delusions are formed without connection to any evidence (and persist in the face of contrary evidence). But we also see important differences with respect to delusions' inferential role and their connection to both behaviour and affect. For example, as Egan notes, someone who has Capgras delusion and believes that their spouse has been replaced by an impostor is "likely *not* to adopt an overall worldview" according to which this makes sense—their delusion isn't well incorporated into their overall belief system (Egan 2008: 266).

As was just alluded to at the end of the previous subsection, my criticism of this argument will take roughly the same form as my criticism of the argument from seamless transition. In brief, what I want to suggest is that either the first premise is false, or if it's not false, the way that it is true does not demand Premise 2. My discussion depends on a point I'm going to call *smudginess*. As I will suggest, the functional roles of ordinary belief and ordinary imagining are a lot smudgier than this argument would have us believe. And, importantly, we are perfectly comfortable tolerating this smudginess.[11]

Let's start with an example. Consider a woman whose spouse has just died. She believes that her spouse is dead. But she keeps acting in ways that don't fit well with this belief, and she manifests other beliefs that don't fit well with this belief. She shuts her alarm off quickly in the morning so as not to wake her spouse. She pours two glasses of wine when she is making dinner. When her phone buzzes, she expects that it's a text from her spouse. And so on. Her belief that her spouse is dead thus doesn't have the usual behaviour-guiding role that beliefs normally have. How can we best describe what's going on? Is she imagining her spouse is alive? (Or bimagining that her spouse is alive?) This doesn't seem to me how we would

---

[11] Although she does not put things in terms of "smudginess", Tamar Gendler's discussion of imaginative contagion (2006) offers some additional considerations in support of the argument of this section.

CONTRAST OR CONTINUUM? BELIEF AND IMAGINATION   55

most naturally categorize it. Rather, I think we would be more likely to treat her as having inconsistent beliefs. In accounting for the inconsistency, we might note that her belief that her spouse is dead hasn't yet been fully integrated into her overall belief network or fully incorporated into her cognitive network.[12] But even though her belief that her spouse is dead doesn't match well with the functional profile of belief, I don't think we're inclined to deny that this is genuinely a belief.

This kind of case falls into a generally category that I'll call *disruptive belief*. Certain beliefs, especially when they are first acquired, are so disruptive to one's cognitive network that they don't always function as beliefs normally do. In particular, they don't seem to play the typically expansive inferential role of beliefs, and they also don't seem to play the typically expansive behaviour-guidance role of beliefs. Insofar as we are nonetheless inclined to count them as belief, support is provided for my claim about smudginess.

This claim is further supported by consideration of different categories of beliefs. Consider superstitious beliefs, like someone's belief that she'll suffer seven years of bad luck if she breaks a mirror. While this superstition might play the typically expansive behaviour-guidance role associated with beliefs, it doesn't seem to match the functional profile of belief with respect to evidence-dependence or evidence-responsiveness. Yet again, we nonetheless tend to treat these superstitions as beliefs.[13]

Consideration of various kinds of imaginings provides yet further support. Certain imaginings—what I'll call *unwelcome imaginings*—suggest that we tolerate smudginess not only with respect to the functional role of beliefs but also with respect to the functional role of imaginings. Consider a child who, alone in their bedroom right after the lights have been turned off, starts imagining that there is a monster under the bed—even though they know full well there's not, as their parents did a full under-bed check before saying goodnight. Or consider an adult who, unable to reach their partner by phone or by text, starts imagining that their partner is having an affair—even though they know full well that it's an especially busy time for their partner at work. While these states manifest the usual circumscribed inferential role of imaginings, they will likely not have the usual circumscribed role with respect to affective response, and similarly with respect to behaviour guidance.

Once we recognize the smudginess in the specification of the functional roles for belief and imagination, it no longer seems nearly as plausible that the first premise of the argument from functional roles is plausible—or at the very least,

---

[12] Alternatively, we might simply make this point about lack-of-integration without also claiming that the woman has inconsistent beliefs. Thanks to an anonymous referee for suggesting this point.

[13] Interestingly, Anna Ichino (2020) has recently argued that superstitions might best be classified as imaginings and not beliefs. Perhaps this is right, but to my mind, that classification will still require acceptance of smudgy functional roles, only in this case the smudginess will concern the functional role of imagining rather than that of belief. For additional discussion of superstition, see Levy, this volume.

56 BELIEF, IMAGINATION, AND DELUSION

insofar as it's true, it does not demand the truth of Premise 2. Moreover, if there are oddities in the functional profile of delusions that go beyond the usual kind of smudginess that I've pointed to, there are other explanations available to us. First, we might be able to explain some of these oddities in virtue of other facts about the delusional subject—for example, the fact that their delusion might be the result of brain damage. Second, it seems plausible that certain aspects of a belief's functional profile become more salient when the belief is occurrent. Given that a particular delusion is often not occurrent, this too can explain the apparent anomalies in its functional profile.

Ultimately, then, the argument from functional profiles fares no better than the argument from seamless transition. Both arguments fail for the same reason: either the first premise is false, or if it's not false, the way that it is true does not demand Premise 2. In the final section of this chapter, I will attempt to draw out some morals from the discussion thus far—morals that will extend beyond the case of belief and imagination to mental state taxonomy more generally.

4. The Way Forward

As the discussion of the previous section has shown, there is good reason to reject both the argument from seamless transition and the argument from functional profiles. These arguments do not force the adoption of the continuum hypothesis, and the case for this hypothesis is far weaker than its proponents would have us believe.

At this point, however, one might wonder where things stand. In particular, one might wonder whether the discussion thus far puts us at something of a stalemate. Though the contrast view has long been treated as the philosophical orthodoxy, we haven't reviewed the case for it. And so perhaps one might naturally wonder whether the case for the contrast view, too, is considerably weaker than its proponents would have us believe. Why, in other words, does the contrast view win by default once we've undermined the case for the continuum view?

In some sense, a full answer to this question would require another whole paper—one that develops and defends the case for the contrast view. As is perhaps obvious, that's not something that I can do here.[14] But I do think we can make some progress toward addressing the question in the absence of that defence.

Perhaps the most important consideration concerns explanatory usefulness. In a discussion of similar issues, Shen-yi Liao and Tyler Doggett have argued that methodological considerations might point in favour of the contrast view. As they

---

[14] See Kind (2016) for some discussion in this regard.

suggest, a cognitive architecture that relies on borderline cases in justifying the collapse of distinctive attitudes—as is done by the continuum view—is unlikely to be explanatorily fruitful (Liao and Doggett 2014).

This point, which I find compelling, also points us toward some more general questions about what exactly we're doing when we're developing a cognitive architecture, i.e., when we're developing a mental state taxonomy. Lying behind the arguments for the continuum view are several big background assumptions—assumptions such as functionalism and the representational theory of mind. Both of these are intimately connected to a further background assumption, namely, that we should approach our mental state taxonomy by way of a boxological approach and, moreover, that the different boxes should be defined in terms of functional/causal roles. I don't mean to suggest that these assumptions are hidden—indeed they're often made quite explicit. Certainly they're explicit in both Egan and Schellenberg. And to a large extent these same assumptions are accepted by proponents of the contrast view as well. But they seem particularly important to the continuum view, since it's only in virtue of this boxological approach that phenomena such as the smudginess I've discussed look problematic.

The defence of the continuum view fits a general pattern that's become increasingly common in recent years, a pattern that urges the need for revisiting our traditional mental state taxonomies. We see this, for example, in discussion of i-desires (Doggett and Egan 2007) and alief (Gendler 2008). But one moral that might be drawn from the discussion in this chapter is that there's perhaps a different, and better way forward. Instead of seeing the pressure on our existing mental state categories as decisive reason to reject them, we might instead revisit the way we divide mental states into different categories, i.e., we might question the assumptions lying behind our taxonomical enterprise.

Going forward, I expect we're going to see continued—perhaps even increasing—pressure on our standard taxonomical categories. But we have to be careful about giving in to this pressure. Of course, we may find that some of the ways we've traditionally carved things up turn out to be mistaken. And we shouldn't hold on to traditional categories just for the sake of tradition. But we also shouldn't be too quick to jettison our traditional categories at the first sign of trouble.

Indeed, in an attempt to ease the pressure—in an attempt to accommodate the puzzling "intermediary" phenomena with which we're presented—we'd perhaps do best first to make sure that we adequately understand the categories with which we're dealing. Do we really understand the functional profile of belief? Of imagining? Much of what I said earlier with respect to "smudginess" is relevant here. Before we discard the taxonomies with which we're working, my own sense is that we'd do better to see if they can be amended to accommodate the relevant pressure.

Acknowledgments

Some of these ideas were originally floated during a talk entitled "Rethinking Mental State Taxonomy: The Case of Belief & Imagination" at the Eastern APA in 2016. Thanks to the participants there for discussion. In 2019, I presented this chapter at "The Mind's Eye" conference at Bilkent University. I am grateful to the participants at that conference, and especially my commentator Bill Wringe, for useful feedback and discussion. Thanks also to Ema Sullivan-Bissett and a reader at OUP for comments on a previous draft of this chapter.

References

Badura, C. and Kind, A. (eds.) (2021). *Epistemic Uses of Imagination* (London: Routledge).

Currie, G. and Jureidini, J. (2004). 'Narrative and Coherence', *Mind & Language* 19/4: 409–27.

Currie, G. and Ravenscroft, I. (2002). *Recreative Minds* (Oxford: Oxford University Press).

Doggett, T. and Egan, A. (2007). 'Wanting Things You Don't Want: The Case for an Imaginative Analogue of Desire', *Philosophers' Imprint* 7/9: 1–17.

Egan, A. (2008). 'Imagination, Delusion, and Self-Deception', in T. Bayne and J. Fernández (eds.), *Delusion and Self-Deception: Affective and Motivational Influences on Belief Formation* (New York: Psychology Press).

Gendler, T. (2006). 'Imaginative Contagion', *Metaphilosophy* 37/2: 183–203.

Gendler, T. (2008). 'Alief and Belief', *The Journal of Philosophy* 105/10: 634–63.

Humberstone, I. L. (1992). 'Direction of Fit', *Mind* 101/401: 59–83.

Ichino, A. (2020). 'Superstitious Confabulations', *Topoi* 39: 203–17.

Kind, A. (2011). 'The Puzzle of Imaginative Desire', *Australasian Journal of Philosophy* 89/3: 421–39.

Kind, A. (2016). 'Introduction: Exploring Imagination', in A. Kind (ed.), *The Routledge Handbook of Philosophy of Imagination* (Abingdon: Routledge), 1–11.

Kind, A. and Kung, P. (eds.) (2016). *Knowledge Through Imagination* (Oxford: Oxford University Press).

Langland-Hassan, P. (2012). 'Pretense, Imagination, and Belief: The Single Attitude Theory', *Philosophical Studies* 159: 155–79.

Liao, S. and Doggett, T. (2014). 'The Imagination Box', *The Journal of Philosophy* 111/5: 259–75.

Nichols, S. and Stich, S. (2000). 'A Cognitive Theory of Pretense', *Cognition* 74/2: 115–47.

Noordhof, P. (2001). 'Believe What You Want', *Proceedings of the Aristotelian Society* 101/1: 247–65.

O'Brien, L. (2005). 'Imagination and the Motivational View of Belief', *Analysis* 65/1: 55–62.

Schellenberg, S. (2013). 'Belief and Desire in Imagination and Immersion', *Journal of Philosophy* 110/9: 497–517.

Schroeder, T. and Matheson, C. (2006). 'Imagination and Emotion', in S. Nichols (ed.), *The Architecture of the Imagination: New Essays on Pretence, Possibility, and Fiction*, 19–39.

Spaulding, S. (2015). 'Imagination, Desire, and Rationality', *Journal of Philosophy* 112/9: 457–76.

Van Leeuwen, N. (2016). 'The Imaginative Agent', in A. Kind and P. Kung (eds.), *Knowledge Through Imagination* (Oxford University Press), 85–109.

Velleman, D. (2015). *The Possibility of Practical Reason*, 2nd edition (Oxford: Oxford University Press).

Weinberg, J. M. and Meskin, A. (2006). "Puzzling Over the Imagination: Philosophical Problems, Architectural Solutions', in S. Nichols (ed.), *The Architecture of the Imagination: New Essays on Pretence, Possibility, and Fiction* (Oxford University Press), 175–202.

4

Imagination, Agency, and Predictive Processing

Philip R. Corlett

1. Introduction

This chapter is about delusions, hallucinations, and imagination. Delusions and hallucinations are symptoms of psychotic illnesses like schizophrenia, wherein beliefs and percepts depart from consensual reality. However, such departures also occur in neurological illnesses, closed head injuries, and autoimmune illnesses, as well as in attenuated forms along continua in the general (non-clinical) population. My work aims to understand this departure in terms of the mechanisms of belief formation and updating, with a particular focus on how they are implemented in the brains of people with psychosis and people who have hallucination-like experiences and delusion-like beliefs.

Thus far, I have taken a reductionist approach, grounded in formal associative learning and reinforcement learning theories and, by extension, predictive coding, which aims to subvert human chauvinism and explain apparently 'special' capabilities and phenomena, considered as higher-level cognitive operations, in terms that are amenable to inquiry in simpler model systems (like primates, rodents, and even *in silico*).

I like things to be as simple as possible (but no simpler) and I believe that understanding the implementation of these cognitive operations in cells, circuits, and systems will illuminate the shape of minds and the allowable interactions between components of minds.

This attitude means that I am skeptical of explanations that evoke bespoke modular gadgets that solve theoretical problems (coalitional threat detection system, cheater detection gadget, etc.). Instead, I am interested in how simple precision weighted learning and belief updating can subsume the functioning of many of those gadgets (Heyes and Pearce 2015; Heyes 2018), and how much of delusionality can be accounted for with that domain-general learning process.

This has furnished heated debate and disagreement between me and people who appeal to domain-specific processes (to confer delusion contents for example). This has been immensely generative and allowed my collaborators and I to hone our account closer and closer to a more complete explanation of

Philip R. Corlett, *Imagination, Agency, and Predictive Processing* In: *Belief, Imagination, and Delusion*. Edited by: Ema Sullivan-Bissett, Oxford University Press. © Oxford University Press 2024. DOI: 10.1093/oso/9780198872221.003.0004

delusions. Some things are still lacking though (like how delusions have their characteristic contents; but see Corlett et al. 2010).

In this chapter I try to reconcile a different class of explanation with the reductionist approach. Some philosophers have pointed out that delusions and hallucinations might be understood as confusions between having imagined some stimulus (or circumstance) and having perceived (or believed) it (Currie 2000). In what follows, I am going to try to adumbrate a path through which the predictive coding theory of psychosis might be aligned with these important ideas.

This will involve clarifying how imagination might work in the context of reinforcement learning and predictive coding, and what the relationships between associative and reinforcement learning and imagination might be. It will entail some consideration of the history of the basic neuroscience of associative learning (with particular emphasis on dopamine and glutamate) and how it has recently been extended to imagination. I will then discuss the intersection of that work with predictive coding theories and data on hallucinations and delusions. I will conclude by speculating about a key role for imagination in a novel neural network architecture, the Generative Adversarial Network (GAN). I will suggest that failures in this network portend different dysfunctions of conscious experience, including delusions and hallucinations.

2. Algorithms for Learning and Belief

The psychology and neurobiology of decision-making, belief formation, and updating have been enriched by the application of reinforcement learning principles. Put simply, we learn to believe things that facilitate choices which increase our adaptive fitness, by, for example, increasing contact with rewards and decreasing contact with punishments.

There are many algorithms that might explain or even underwrite how organisms solve these problems. Analyzing their tractability as well as the ways in which they parameterize decisions can yield insights into how beliefs are formed and updated, with relevance not only to the adaptive case, but also to instances wherein we err in our beliefs.

Presently, I shall argue that whilst imaginative reconstruction of possible outcomes is useful for goal-directed action choice, such powerful mechanisms are extremely sensitive to noise and uncertainty, and can perhaps lead to gross mischaracterizations of states, and ultimately, to perception, actions, and beliefs that do not reflect reality.

The dopamine rich basal ganglia and their reciprocal connections with the frontal cortices and the hippocampus are implicated in reinforcement learning, credit assignment (apportioning blame for outcomes to the appropriate actions and agents), imagination, and psychosis. The late Jeffrey Gray, in collaboration

62   BELIEF, IMAGINATION, AND DELUSION

with David Hemsley and others at the Institute of Psychiatry in London developed a model integrating the neurobiology and neurochemistry of the basal ganglia as well as their input and output structures with the cognitive and phenomenological experiences of psychotic patients (Gray et al. 1991; Hemsley 1992, 1993, 1994a, 1994b, 2005a, 2005b; Gray 1993, 1995, 1998a, 1998b). It focused on the hippocampus and its dopaminergic inputs to the nucleus accumbens, suggesting that the hippocampus served as a comparator, comparing the perceptual inputs to which the organism was exposed with the organism's internal model of the world (the regularities and contingencies which it learned by prior experience; Gray et al. 1991).

If there was a mismatch between what was expected and experienced, a novelty or salience signal would be sent to the striatum, inhibiting ongoing actions and eliciting an orienting response.

Gray, Hemsley, and colleagues argued that in experimental animals treated with amphetamine and individuals with psychosis, such mismatch signals occur inappropriately, driving attention towards irrelevant environmental stimuli and internal thought processes, culminating in the attribution of delusional significance to external stimuli and events and in the experience of hallucinations (Gray et al. 1991).

Mismatches between expectancy and experience, or prediction errors, dominate theories of learning (Rescorla and Wagner 1972; Mackintosh 1975b; Pearce and Hall 1980; Grossberg 1982) and dopamine function (Schultz and Dickinson 2000; Waelti et al. 2001; Schultz 2004). In the classic studies, dopamine neurons deep in the monkey's midbrain report the surprising presence or absence of rewards, with learning, they respond to cues (e.g., visual stimuli) that predict the presence or absence of rewards.

3. Prediction Errors

Psychological models of prediction error driven learning posit that prediction errors contribute to learning directly, updating organisms' expectancies of particular stimuli (Rescorla and Wagner 1972) and indirectly, driving the subsequent allocation of attention to stimuli that predict important events (Mackintosh 1975b; Grossberg 1982) and to stimuli that have an unpredictable or uncertain relationship with important events (Pearce and Hall 1980; Grossberg 1982), both of which are salient. Gray and colleagues (1991) thesis provided a mechanistic link between brain function and psychotic symptoms via dopamine dysregulation and inappropriate attentional learning. However, to borrow Gray's phraseology, some of that particular wall had also been laid down previously (Gray 2004).

Robert Miller first made the connection between dopamine dysfunction, aberrant associative learning, and delusion formation, suggesting that increased

IMAGINATION, AGENCY, AND PREDICTIVE PROCESSING   63

dopamine signaling in the basal ganglia in schizophrenia lowered the significance threshold on conclusions that stimuli and events were related and that those relationships were important (Miller 1976). Roy King provided mathematical models of chaotic dopamine function in schizophrenia that could explain the dopamine responsivity independent of cue and context that Shitij Kapur proposed to be the mediator of aberrant salience (King et al. 1981, 1984).

The elegant tonic/phasic dopamine hypothesis of Anthony Grace offered further conciliation between brain dopamine dysfunction in frontal, temporal, midbrain, and striatal systems, the psychological processes of learning and attentional allocation, and psychotic symptoms (Grace 1991). It also highlighted the importance of glutamatergic regulation of the balance between tonic and phasic dopamine (Grace 1991). With reference to the phasic/tonic dopamine balance and signal-to-noise ratio in the dopamine system, Manfred Spitzer outlined an account of delusion formation and maintenance, suggesting that under conditions of high signal-to-noise ratio, an individual would experience "significant events" when merely ordinary events were in fact happening and those experiences, once generated, would be less likely to passively decay or be actively erased—manifest clinically as a delusional belief (Spitzer 1995).

Phasic dopamine release is held to carry the prediction error signals recorded from midbrain and striatal dopamine neurons by Wolfram Schultz. Tonic dopamine levels in the synapse are impacted by that release and spill-over, as well as feedback from the prefrontal cortex (Grace 1991). They set the gain on the system, modulating the impact of a particular phasic, prediction error related release.

In the absence of prefrontal feedback regulation, the signal-to-noise ratio of the system is altered, such that the phasic dopamine component becomes over-responsive, precipitating positive symptoms (Grace 1991). Recently, the tonic/phasic scheme has been integrated with Gray and colleagues model, such that the ventral hippocampus impacts upon the responsivity of midbrain dopamine, prediction error coding neurons, increasing the number of neurons that are recruited to readily excitable neuron pools in the ventral tegmental area (VTA) which respond to a particular stimulus (Lodge and Grace 2006). Disruption of this hippocampal modulation of VTA neurons, under conditions of dopamine hyperactivity or glutamate hypofunction could result in the excessive and chaotic stimulation of the striatum and prefrontal cortex, producing positive psychotic symptoms according to the Gray and colleagues model (Gray et al. 1991; Lisman and Grace 2005).

This aberrant learning model has been tested preclinically, in pharmacological and lesion models (Kaye and Pearce 1987; O'Tuathaigh et al. 2003), as well as clinically in human subjects with schizophrenia (Jones et al. 1992; Oades et al. 1992, 1996; Moran et al. 2008), and in healthy individuals with high scores on schizotypal personality scales (Jones et al. 1990; Moran et al. 2003).

4. Associative Learning

Two learning phenomena are frequently employed in examinations of the hypothesis; both of which measure the allocation of attention to and learning about irrelevant stimuli, namely blocking (Kamin 1969) and latent inhibition (Lubow and Moore 1959).

Both of these paradigms involve the adaptive down regulation of the salience of a stimulus, either due to pre-exposure to that stimulus in the absence of important consequences (latent inhibition) or due to pairing of those important consequences with a salient and predictive stimulus which then "blocks" subsequent learning about any novel stimulus paired with that pre-trained stimulus. Both blocking and latent inhibition are held to reflect the adaptive use of environmental regularities to guide behaviour and filter out irrelevant and potentially distracting stimulation. However, in psychosis, this filtering process is impaired, leading to sensory overload, inappropriate attribution of significance to inconsequential or irrelevant stimuli, and positive symptoms.

5. Imagination

The learning accounts and behavioural phenomena considered so far have been rather passive, and anchored in learning about the external world. As noted in the introduction, imagining possible future states and the fictive consequences of action choices might enhance the learning and adaptation of an agent to its environment.

Edward Tolman was a neo-behaviourist. He believed even rodents were capable of generating elaborate internal models of their environment (Tolman 1932). Guthrie, a more traditional behaviourist, quipped that Tolman's rats would be "*buried in thought*", incapable of responding because of the elaborate thought processes in which they were engaged (Guthrie 1952). In new data, Yuji K. Takahashi and colleagues exhume Tolman's ideas—showing with careful neural and behavioural studies that rats can imagine outcomes they have never experienced (Takahashi et al. 2013).

Pavlov's dogs learned to salivate in response to a bell that predicted food (Pavlov 1927). Follow-up studies have demonstrated summation; if animals learn that another cue, say a light, predicts the same food, and they experience light and bell together, then they expect double helpings of reward. This over-expectation, based on summed expectancies is manifest as vigorous behavioural responses following the compound of the two predictive cues (Thein et al. 2008).

Takahashi and colleagues demonstrate that this over-expectation is mediated by the orbitofrontal cortex (OFC) in rodents. The neurons in this region increase in responding as the animals learn about the cues. They respond most strongly to the compound cues in a manner that predicts subsequent over-expectation behaviour. Finally, using optogenetics, a technique that allows light to inhibit the over-expecting cells, they show that animals summate less when their OFC neurons are inhibited.

People often seem uncomfortable with the idea of rats having rich representations and even being able to imagine. Yet many allow for working memory in rats—the maintenance of information over a delay in the absence of sustaining environmental stimuli. Imagination is really nothing more than an internally generated representation with much in common with that which mediates working memory. Problems with animal imagination are further puzzling when we consider the field of translational neuroscience studying mental illnesses like schizophrenia and addiction with animal models.

Takahashi and colleagues lend a neural reality to a relatively high-level cognitive capacity—that of creative expectation or imagination in rodents.

6. Imagination and Psychosis

Stephen Grossberg's (2000) computational theory of hallucinations bridged the gap between conditioning and incentive models of hallucination (Grossberg 2000). He equated hallucinations with the subjective experience of imagination. Grossberg conceptualized imagination as the willed deployment of top-down influences on perception. Like Christopher Frith (Frith 1987), he suggested that in schizophrenia, actions can occur in the apparent absence of conscious intentions, due to dysregulated dopaminergic volitional signals, and in such situations the sensations generated are perceived as externally generated hallucinations (Grossberg 2000). The conditioned hallucinations of C. E. Seashore, D. G. Ellson, and others are an example of how top-down expectancies can modulate experience (Seashore 1895; Ellson 1941; Kot and Serper 2002). In the psychotic individual this process is thought to occur endogenously and inappropriately under the influence of an aberrant dopamine system (Gray et al. 1991; Miller 1993; Kapur 2003). There is some evidence that sensory "hallucinations" can be conditioned in healthy and psychotic volunteers using a sensory discrimination procedure (Seashore 1895; Ellson 1941; Kot and Serper 2002). In brief, subjects are instructed that their sensory thresholds are being measured, each trial begins with the illumination of a light (the conditioned stimulus, CS), and subsequently a tone of increasing intensity is played (the unconditioned stimulus, US). Subjects are instructed to make a button-push response when they hear the tone. On certain trials, the tone is omitted. A hallucination is said to have occurred if subjects report hearing a tone when no tone was played. Seashore has demonstrated this phenomenon with olfactory, tactile, and electrodermal conditioning (Seashore 1895) and, while an explanation could be conceived in terms of response biases, these and other data suggest some role of prior knowledge and expectancies in generating perceptual experiences, both normal (Frith and Dolan 1997) and abnormal (Frith and Dolan 2000).

More recently, visual-auditory conditioning has been employed to demonstrate that voice-hearing schizophrenia patients are significantly more susceptible to this effect than patients without hallucinations and controls (Kot and Serper 2002). These conditioned hallucinations are mediated by strong prior beliefs, and those priors are stronger in people who hallucinate (in a manner that correlates with hallucinations) (Powers et al. 2017b). Furthermore, people with a diagnosed psychotic illness are less likely to update those prior beliefs in light of new evidence (Powers et al. 2017b). Critically, the neural circuit underlying these conditioned phenomena—including superior temporal gyrus and insula—largely overlapped with the circuit engaged when patients report hearing voices in the scanner (Jardri et al. 2011; Powers et al. 2017b). These studies underline the role of learning and, more specifically, a bias towards learned top-down information in the genesis of auditory verbal hallucinations (AVHs).

Further support for this strong prior account of hallucinations comes from findings that prior knowledge of a visual scene confers an advantage in recognizing a degraded version of that image and that patients at risk for psychosis—and, by extension, voice-hearing—were particularly susceptible to this advantage, and its magnitude correlated with hallucination-like percepts outside of the laboratory (Teufel et al. 2015). Similarly, there is a version of this effect in audition; voice-hearing participants appear to have an enhanced prior for speech in degraded auditory stimuli even when not explicitly instructed (Alderson-Day et al. 2017). That is, speech is perhaps the most salient biological signal for our species, and the auditory system of AVH-prone individuals may be predisposed to inferring speech.

This raises an important possible distinction between clinical and non-clinical voice hearers. Since non-clinical voice hearers have a ready explanatory framework and have spent time cultivating their volitional control over perception (likely over the weighting of their prior expectations (regarding some imagined event) relative to the sensory evidence (that the event is not occurring)), then they can better anticipate hallucination episodes and can understand them through their preferred explanatory lens (Powers et al. 2016). This would be consistent with the sensitivity of the non-clinical voice hearers to environmental volatility—the rate of change of environmental contingencies: they are able to update their beliefs rapidly and appropriately through learning, unlike the clinical groups (Powers et al. 2017b). If one can move between possible priors with alacrity, reconfiguring one's expectations smoothly and accurately, one would likely have strong attentional control over learning and belief updating, and by extension, imagination.

7. Reinforcement Learning and Imagination

Contemporary models of reinforcement learning and artificial intelligence have an imaginative, simulation component, that has been evidenced in humans (Gershman et al. 2017). In some cases, imagined reinforcers can maladaptively bias real-world decisions—imagining that you have been rewarded can change your subsequent reward seeking (Gershman et al. 2017). The adaptive use of imagination depends on its obedience to real-world constraints (perhaps as observed in non-clinical voice hearers). If untethered, then we may find ourselves transcending reality too much (Gershman et al. 2017), and ultimately failing to learn from the real world (Gershman et al. 2017) (as observed in patients with psychosis).

8. Source Monitoring

It is important to distinguish reality testing (discriminating between real and imagined stimuli in perception) and reality monitoring (discriminating between real and imagined stimuli in memory). The bulk of the work in psychosis has—ironically perhaps—focused on monitoring (i.e., a mnemonic process) rather than the more perceptual—testing or filtering of reality.

Imagining leaves a trace in memory, and we must then be able to discriminate between these memories and memories of observed stimuli (Johnson and Raye 1981). Deficits in such discrimination have been related to delusions (Simons et al. 2008) and hallucinations, though not consistently (Alderson-Day et al. 2019), and perhaps not in non-clinical voice hearers (Garrison et al. 2017).

One animal learning phenomenon that may unite prior weighting and source monitoring views of psychosis is representation mediated learning, wherein the value of an expected cue is updated even though that cue is never presented with a salient outcome (like a food reward). Through associations, an expectation of a stimulus (S2) is engendered, contingent on the presentation of a stimulus that predicts it (S1). The expected stimulus (S2) is not presented; however, it is, through those learned associations retrieved from memory when its predictor S1 is presented. Representation mediated learning occurs when that retrieved representation is updated in light of some change in the value of S1 (pairing it with reward or punishment for example). Mediated learning probes the extent to which animals can distinguish between real percepts and internally retrieved representations of cues (McDannald and Schoenbaum 2009; McDannald et al. 2011; Kim and Koh 2016; Koh et al. 2018; Fry et al. 2020; Koh and Gallagher 2020).

It typically proceeds through three phases: (1) associative phase: odour (stimulus 1; S1) + flavour (stimulus 2; S2) pairings; (2) devaluation phase (e.g., aversion training): the flavour (S2) is devalued by an injection of lithium chloride (LiCl) to induce gastric malaise to alter its "value"; and (3) a test phase to determine if both the associated odour (S1), in addition to the experienced flavour (S2), are devalued (i.e., mediated and direct learning, respectively). Patterns of neural activity that correspond to the representation of the S1 cue, recorded during the devaluation phase when this cue is absent, but expected, can predict stronger expression of mediated learning at test (Kerfoot et al. 2007; Saddoris et al. 2009). Mediated learning bridges perceptual decision-making and conditioned hallucination tasks because it assesses retrieved cue representations, with translational relevance (Wimmer and Shohamy 2012; Zeithamova et al. 2012; Barron et al. 2020; Wang et al. 2020).

Various manipulations that produce psychosis-like phenotypes in rodents, including chronic ketamine (Koh et al. 2018), increase mediated learning (McDannald and Schoenbaum 2009; McDannald et al. 2011; Busquets-Garcia et al. 2017; Koh et al. 2018; Fry et al. 2020; Wu et al. 2020). Furthermore, antipsychotic medications can rescue the phenotype in some models (Busquets-Garcia et al. 2017; Koh et al. 2018; Fry et al. 2020). The potential of mediated learning has yet to be explored in humans with psychosis; however, the preclinical data and theory suggest that representation mediated learning ought to be enhanced in people who hallucinate, and perhaps in those who harbour delusional beliefs too. Critical to the phenomenon is a confusion of having remembered a stimulus (perhaps very richly) with having perceived it. In the final section of this chapter, I will speculate on how the brain might distinguish imagination from perception, and how those mechanisms might break down, portending various changes in the sense of reality of conscious perception. I believe these examples may be relevant to psychosis, and taken together, this approach proffers the exciting possibility of unifying source monitoring and learning based explanations of psychotic symptoms (Griffin and Fletcher 2017).

9. Simple Mechanisms, Complex Phenomena

Throughout this chapter I have suggested that basic reinforcement learning mechanisms, co-opted towards perception and belief, give rise to delusions and hallucinations. I have suggested that something like simple cued-associative retrieval can evoke representations into a space akin to a simple form of imagination, and that those evoked representations can be confused for real percepts, especially in neurochemical and neurobiological contexts that resemble psychosis. I would like to try to relate my argument back to delusions and I will use paranoia and persecutory delusions as an example.

Recent work in the cognitive science of paranoia has suggested that paranoia—the belief that others intend to harm one—is the purview of an evolved mechanism for detecting coalitional threats (Raihani and Bell 2019). This mechanism is held to be defective in people who are paranoid. The hypothesis has largely been examined in the context of game theory based iterative interactions, and indeed, people who are paranoid seem to have trouble generating and using representations of the agents they are interacting with (Barnby et al. 2022). Theorists of this bent often appeal to mechanisms like recursive mentalizing, thinking a number of moves ahead about the counterfactuals: "what should I do if they do this, and how will they respond?" (Barnby et al. 2022). This type of mentalizing has much in common with theory of mind tasks, performance of which, perhaps surprisingly, is not consistently or strongly related to paranoia (Pinkham et al. 2016) (though of course it is possible that these older tasks were not recursive enough).

In work from my lab on this topic, we find that people who are paranoid have appropriate prior expectations about the advice of minimal-group partners; they expect that someone on their team will help them, and that someone competing might mislead them. Neither effect is exaggerated in paranoia (Rossi-Goldthorpe et al. 2021). Rather, paranoid people will rely on advice from collaborators or competitors, particularly when decisions are difficult, and they do so especially when they find their own perceptual decisions to be unreliable (Rossi-Goldthorpe et al. 2021). This centres paranoia not in group cognition, but rather in noisy personal level perceptual decision-making. Further work from my group suggests that this may be a fundamental expectation in people who are paranoid (including patients with schizophrenia who have persecutory delusions; Sheffield et al. 2022); they expect that the world will be volatile and changeable (Reed et al. 2020, Suthaharan et al. 2021). We even find evidence in basic preclinical animal models: rats treated with methamphetamine have stronger prior beliefs about volatility (Reed et al. 2020). We contend that what looks like mentalizing may actually—like representation mediated learning—be a much simpler version of cue driven learning, and that delusions involve aberrations of this basic learning mechanism, rather than mentalizing proper. Of course it remains an empirical question whether these simple mechanisms undergird more baroque social cognition, but, following Occam's razor, I prefer not to evoke something specifically or separately social before we have exhausted the reach of simpler mechanisms.

There are many other complexities, beyond symptom contents, that demand our attention. In what remains, I will try to sketch a version of how the predictive coding theory of mind and psychosis might address the sense of reality of percepts relative to imagination, and, by extension, hallucinations.

10. The Reality of Perception

Where might the sense of reality (or imagination) arise in a purely inferential model? Anil Seth has argued that sensorimotor counterfactuals are critical (Seth 2014). People perceive something as real to the extent that their perceptual

70 BELIEF, IMAGINATION, AND DELUSION

hypothesis testing is satisfied (Seth 2014). For example, real things rarely move in perfect synchrony with our eye movements. If an object in the visual field moves when our eyes move, we will likely infer that it is not real. Furthermore, real things are unlikely to retreat in synchrony with our investigative reaching movements. This is a perspicuous idea; however, people who are unable to move their eyes may experience low sensorimotor contingency, but can still discriminate real from imagined stimuli.

Perhaps a more in-depth consideration of our sense of visual reality might help clarify? In the neuropsychology of vision there are patients whose brain damage and subsequent dysfunction help us think about the perception of reality. Blindsight describes the covert visual abilities of brain damaged individuals who deny conscious visual perception. It is contrasted with Anton's syndrome, wherein blind individuals claim to be sighted and behave as though they are (walking through the world, but colliding with objects in it). Both of these syndromes are characterized by acquired damage to the visual cortex in individuals whose development (and interaction with the visual world) was otherwise typical. The syndromes are consistent with a Bayesian Prediction Error Minimization Model of conscious perception, wherein candidate percepts are predicted and visual experiences are consistent with those model predictions. The syndromes differ in the richness with which those predictions are experienced. Blindsight has low richness which conflicts with behavioural detection of stimuli. Anton's has high richness that conflicts with reality. How is this possible in the model? And how are these cases instructive with regards to blindness and psychosis?

The computational motif of generative adversarial networks may be instructive. These involve:

1. A training set of images (containing e.g., dogs)
2. A Generator Network
3. A Critic Network

First, the Generator is trained with the training set (so that it learns a given exemplar is a picture of a dog). Then it is inverted to produce novel content (images of dogs). The Critic decides whether a generated image belongs amongst the training set (is this a dog?). It is reinforced for correctly rejecting what the Generator produces. The Generator is reinforced for fooling the Critic. Thus, the two networks train one another. This arrangement is one mechanism through which predictive coding could implement reality monitoring, and give rise to conscious perception (Lau 2008).

In blindsight, it is possible that the Generator is impaired. And in Anton's syndrome, the Critic may be impaired. In Charles-Bonnet syndrome, character-ized by visual hallucinations, wherein the retina is degenerating, the Generator may be hyper-engaged (Reichert et al. 2013); however, the Critic is somewhat intact, since Charles-Bonnet syndrome cases often appreciate that they are hallucinating. The congenitally blind never achieve a fully formed generative network, and as such they do not suffer the deleterious impact of perturbations within that network. And endogenous psychosis involves *both* noise and compensation within the generative network *and* a failure of reality monitoring by the Critic.

This sounds rather like a two-factor theory of delusions and psychosis—which demands two independent deficits, one in perception (a broken Generator), and one in belief evaluation (a broken Critic) (Gershman 2019). However, let us consider the information flow within a GAN. The premier two-factor theory of delusions—based on monothematic delusions secondary to neurological damage—holds that people with these delusions have a deficit in perception (Factor 1) and belief evaluation (Factor 2) (Coltheart 2010). Under the encapsulated modularity of two-factor theory, the flow of information is unidirectional, from perception to belief (Ross et al. 2016). For two-factor theory, beliefs cannot influence perception (otherwise only damage to the mechanisms of belief would be necessary for delusions to arise; Corlett 2019).

As an aside, such an architecture would demand quite a specific and unlikely set of insults, in which odd experiences led to a final instance of belief updating, and thence beliefs were concretized (McKay 2012; Corlett 2019).

Now, careful consideration of GANs reveals that they have no such unidirectional flow of information. The Generator also learns from the Critic—particularly its inaccuracies (or prediction errors perhaps), which tell the Generator how convincingly it has emulated the data distribution pertaining to reality (Gershman 2019). It is possible then, that although GANs appear aligned with modularity and two-factor theory, they are actually underwritten by mechanisms that share more with predictive processing. Indeed, computer scientists argue that the 'clamping' of layers within a hierarchy that permits inception—as in Google Deep Dream—could instantiate the type of generative activity required for adversarial functionality (Sun and Orchard 2020).

The question remains, how would such a network 'know' that it was in generative mode? Does the precision of prediction errors in the Critic change when we imagine? This would allow prior beliefs to dominate our inferences.

These are exactly the circumstances that Jean-Rémy Martin and Elisabeth Pacherie argue obtains during hypnosis (Martin and Pacherie 2019). Perhaps then, there is the potential for rapprochement—the Grossberg account has its prior beliefs that predominate, Frith has intention being brought to the fore (through the down regulation of prediction error—the suspension of disbelief). This is the state that clairaudient psychics might achieve, as do those who practice tulpamancy (Powers et al. 2016). The difference between them and individuals with psychotic illness, is that those with an illness wield less control over the precision of their prediction errors and as such, they do not control the phenomenology they experience to the same degree (Powers et al. 2017a).

72 BELIEF, IMAGINATION, AND DELUSION

In summary then, there is much to be gleaned from considering hallucinations and delusions through the lens of imagination and belief. In so doing, we learn more about the potential functions imagination might serve (simulation, planning, tuning our generative model of the world) and the sorts of algorithms that might underwrite it. While it remains to be shown definitively, evidence mounts that beliefs might well influence perception and that perhaps strict distinctions between these two are challenged by the data on imagination, as well as on hallucination and delusion.

References

Alderson-Day, B., C. F. Lima, S. Evans, S. Krishnan, P. Shanmugalingam, C. Fernyhough, and S. K. Scott (2017). "Distinct processing of ambiguous speech in people with non-clinical auditory verbal hallucinations". *Brain* 140(9): 2475–89.

Alderson-Day, B., D. Smailes, J. Moffatt, K. Mitrenga, P. Moseley, and C. Fernyhough (2019). "Intentional inhibition but not source memory is related to hallucination-proneness and intrusive thoughts in a university sample". *Cortex* 113: 267–78.

Barnby, J. M., N. Raihani, and P. Dayan (2022). "Knowing me, knowing you: Interpersonal similarity improves predictive accuracy and reduces attributions of harmful intent". *Cognition* 225: 105098.

Barron, H. C., H. M. Reeve, R. S. Koolschijn, P. V. Perestenko, A. Shpektor, H. Nili, R. Rothaermel, N. Campo-Urriza, J. X. O'Reilly, D. M. Bannerman, T. E. J. Behrens, and D. Dupret (2020). "Neuronal computation underlying inferential reasoning in humans and mice". *Cell* 183(1): 228–243.e221.

Busquets-Garcia, A., E. Soria-Gómez, B. Redon, Y. Mackenbach, M. Vallée, F. Chaouloff, M. Varilh, G. Ferreira, P. V. Piazza, and G. Marsicano (2017). "Pregnenolone blocks cannabinoid-induced acute psychotic-like states in mice". *Molecular Psychiatry* 22(11): 1594–603.

Coltheart, M. (2010). "The neuropsychology of delusions". *Annals of the New York Academy of Sciences* 1191: 16–26.

Corlett, P. R. (2019). "Factor one, familiarity and frontal cortex: A challenge to the two-factor theory of delusions". *Cognitive Neuropsychiatry* 24(3): 165–77.

Corlett, P. R., J. R. Taylor, X. J. Wang, P. C. Fletcher, and J. H. Krystal (2010). "Toward a neurobiology of delusions". *Progress in Neurobiology* 92(3): 345–69.

Currie, G. (2000). "Imagination, delusion and hallucination". In M. Coltheart and M. Davies (eds.), *Pathologies of Belief*. Malden, MA: Blackwell Publishing, 167–82.

Ellson, D. G. (1941). "Hallucinations produced through sensory conditioning". *Journal of Experimental Psychology* 28: 1–20.

Frith, C. (1987). "The positive and negative symptoms of schizophrenia reflect impairments in the perception and initiation of action". *Psychological Medicine* 17(3): 631–48.

Frith, C. and R. J. Dolan (1997). "Brain mechanisms associated with top-down processes in perception". *Philosophical Transactions of the Royal Society B: Biological Sciences* 352(1358): 1221–30.

Frith, C. and R. J. Dolan (2000). *The Role of Memory in the Delusions Associated with Schizophrenia.* Cambridge, MA: Harvard University Press.

Fry, B. R., N. Russell, R. Gifford, C. F. Robles, C. E. Manning, A. Sawa, M. Niwa, and A. W. Johnson (2020). "Assessing reality testing in mice through dopamine-dependent associatively evoked processing of absent gustatory stimuli". *Schizophrenia Bulletin* 46(1): 54–67.

Garrison, J. R., P. Moseley, B. Alderson-Day, D. Smailes, C. Fernyhough, and J. S. Simons (2017). "Testing continuum models of psychosis: No reduction in source monitoring ability in healthy individuals prone to auditory hallucinations". *Cortex* 91: 197–207.

Gershman, S. J. (2019). "The generative adversarial brain". *Frontiers in Artificial Intelligence* 2: 18.

Gershman, S. J., J. Zhou, and C. Kommers (2017). "Imaginative reinforcement learning: Computational principles and neural mechanisms". *Journal of Cognitive Neuroscience* 29(12): 2103–13.

Grace, A. A. (1991). "Phasic versus tonic dopamine release and the modulation of dopamine system responsivity: A hypothesis for the etiology of schizophrenia". *Neuroscience* 41(1): 1–24.

Gray, J. A. (1993). "Consciousness, schizophrenia and scientific theory". *Ciba Foundation Symposium* 174: 263–73; discussion 273–81.

Gray, J. A. (1995). "Dopamine release in the nucleus accumbens: The perspective from aberrations of consciousness in schizophrenia". *Neuropsychologia* 33(9): 1143–53.

Gray, J. A. (1998a). "Abnormal contents of consciousness: The transition from automatic to controlled processing". *Advances in Neurology* 77: 195–208; discussion 208–11.

Gray, J. A. (1998b). "Integrating schizophrenia". *Schizophrenia Bulletin* 24(2): 249–66.

Gray, J. A. (2004). "On biology, phenomenology, and pharmacology in schizophrenia". *American Journal of Psychiatry* 161(2): 377; author reply 377–8.

Gray, J. A., J. Feldon, J. N. P. Rawlins, D. Hemsley, and A. D. Smith (1991). "The neuropsychology of schizophrenia". *Behavioral and Brain Sciences* 14: 1–84.

Griffin, J. D. and P. C. Fletcher (2017). "Predictive processing, source monitoring, and psychosis". *Annual Review of Clinical Psychology* 13: 265–89.

Grossberg, S. (1982). "Processing of expected and unexpected events during conditioning and attention: A psychophysiological theory". *Psychological Review* 89(5): 529–72.

Grossberg, S. (2000). "How hallucinations may arise from brain mechanisms of learning, attention, and volition". *Journal of the International Neuropsychological Society* 6(5): 583–92.

74 BELIEF, IMAGINATION, AND DELUSION

Guthrie, E. R. (1952). *The Psychology of Learning*. New York: Harper and Brothers.

Hemsley, D. R. (1992). "Cognitive abnormalities and schizophrenic symptoms". *Psychological Medicine* 22(4): 839–42.

Hemsley, D. R. (1993). "A simple (or simplistic?) cognitive model for schizophrenia". *Behaviour Research and Therapy* 31(7): 633–45.

Hemsley, D. R. (1994a). "A cognitive model for schizophrenia and its possible neural basis". *Acta Psychiatrica Scandinavica, Supplement* 384: 80–6.

Hemsley, D. R. (1994b). "Perceptual and cognitive abnormalities as the bases for schizophrenic symptoms". In A. S. David and J. C. Cutting (eds.), *The Neuropsychology of Schizophrenia*. Mahwah, NJ: Lawrence Erlbaum Associates, 97–118.

Hemsley, D. R. (2005a). "The development of a cognitive model of schizophrenia: Placing it in context". *Neuroscience & Biobehavioral Reviews* 29(6): 977–88.

Hemsley, D. R. (2005b). "The schizophrenic experience: Taken out of context?" *Schizophrenia Bulletin* 31(1): 43–53.

Heyes, C. (2018). "Précis of *Cognitive Gadgets: The Cultural Evolution of Thinking*". *Behavioral and Brain Sciences* 42: e169.

Heyes, C. and J. M. Pearce (2015). "Not-so-social learning strategies". *Proceedings of the Royal Society B: Biological Sciences* 282(1802): 20141709.

Jardri, R., A. Pouchet, D. Pins, and P. Thomas (2011). "Cortical activations during auditory verbal hallucinations in schizophrenia: A coordinate-based meta-analysis". *American Journal of Psychiatry* 168(1): 73–81.

Johnson, M. K. and C. L. Raye (1981). "Reality monitoring". *Psychological Review* 88 (1): 67–85.

Jones, S. H., J. A. Gray, and D. R. Hemsley (1990). "The Kamin blocking effect, incidental learning and psychoticism". *British Journal of Psychology* 81(Pt 1): 95–109.

Jones, S. H., J. A. Gray, and D. R. Hemsley (1992). "Loss of the Kamin blocking effect in acute but not chronic schizophrenics". *Biological Psychiatry* 32(9): 739–55.

Kamin, L. J. (1969). "Predictability, surprise, attention and conditioning". In R. Church and B. Campbell (eds.), *Punishment and Aversive Behavior*. New York: Appleton-Century-Crofts, 279–96.

Kapur, S. (2003). "Psychosis as a state of aberrant salience: A framework linking biology, phenomenology, and pharmacology in schizophrenia". *American Journal of Psychiatry* 160(1): 13–23.

Kaye, H. and J. M. Pearce (1987). "Hippocampal lesions attenuate latent inhibition and the decline of the orienting response in rats". *Quarterly Journal of Experimental Psychology B: Comparative and Physiological Psychology* 39(2): 107–25.

Kerfoot, E. C., I. Agarwal, H. J. Lee, and P. C. Holland (2007). "Control of appetitive and aversive taste-reactivity responses by an auditory conditioned stimulus in a devaluation task: A FOS and behavioral analysis". *Learning & Memory* 14(9): 581–9.

Kim, H. J. and H. Y. Koh (2016). "Impaired reality testing in mice lacking phospholipase Cβ1: Observed by persistent representation-mediated taste aversion". *PLoS One* 11(1): e0146376.

King, R., J. D. Barchas, and B. A. Huberman (1984). "Chaotic behavior in dopamine neurodynamics". *Proceedings of the National Academy of Sciences of the United States of America* 81(4): 1244–7.

King, R., J. D. Raese, and J. D. Barchas (1981). "Catastrophe theory of dopaminergic transmission: A revised dopamine hypothesis of schizophrenia". *Journal of Theoretical Biology* 92(4): 373–400.

Koh, M. T., P. S. Ahrens, and M. Gallagher (2018). "A greater tendency for representation mediated learning in a ketamine mouse model of schizophrenia". *Behavioral Neuroscience* 132(2): 106–13.

Koh, M. T. and M. Gallagher (2020). "Using internal memory representations in associative learning to study hallucination-like phenomenon". *Neurobiology of Learning and Memory* 175: 107319.

Kot, T. and M. Serper (2002). "Increased susceptibility to auditory conditioning in hallucinating schizophrenic patients: A preliminary investigation". *Journal of Nervous and Mental Disease* 190(5): 282–8.

Lau, H. C. (2008). "A higher order Bayesian decision theory of consciousness". *Progress in Brain Research* 168: 35–48.

Lisman, J. E. and A. A. Grace (2005). "The hippocampal-VTA loop: Controlling the entry of information into long-term memory". *Neuron* 46(5): 703–13.

Lodge, D. J. and A. A. Grace (2006). "The hippocampus modulates dopamine neuron responsivity by regulating the intensity of phasic neuron activation". *Neuropsychopharmacology* 31(7): 1356–61.

Lubow, R. E. and A. U. Moore (1959). "Latent inhibition: The effect of nonreinforced pre-exposure to the conditional stimulus". *Journal of Comparative and Physiological Psychology* 52: 415–19.

McDannald, M. and G. Schoenbaum (2009). "Toward a model of impaired reality testing in rats". *Schizophrenia Bulletin* 35(4): 664–7.

McDannald, M. A., J. P. Whitt, G. G. Calhoon, P. T. Piantadosi, R.-M. Karlsson, P. O'Donnell, and G. Schoenbaum (2011). "Impaired reality testing in an animal model of schizophrenia". *Biological Psychiatry* 70(12): 1122–6.

McKay, R. (2012). "Delusional inference". *Mind & Language* 27(3): 330–55.

Mackintosh, N. J. (1975a). "Blocking of conditioned suppression: Role of the first compound trial". *Journal of Experimental Psychology: Animal Behavior Processes* 1(4): 335–45.

Mackintosh, N. J. (1975b). "A theory of attention: Variations in associability of stimuli with reinforcement". *Psychological Review* 82(4): 276–98.

Martin, J. R. and E. Pacherie (2019). "Alterations of agency in hypnosis: A new predictive coding model". *Psychological Review* 126(1): 133–52.

Miller, R. (1976). "Schizophrenic psychology, associative learning and the role of forebrain dopamine". *Medical Hypotheses* 2(5): 203–11.

Miller, R. (1993). "Striatal dopamine in reward and attention: A system for understanding the symptomatology of acute schizophrenia and mania". *International Review of Neurobiology* 35: 161–278.

Moran, P. M., M. M. Al-Uzri, J. Watson, and M. A. Reveley (2003). "Reduced Kamin blocking in non paranoid schizophrenia: Associations with schizotypy". *Journal of Psychiatric Research* 37(2): 155–63.

Moran, P. M., L. Owen, A. E. Crookes, M. M. Al-Uzri, and M. A. Reveley (2008). "Abnormal prediction error is associated with negative and depressive symptoms in schizophrenia". *Progress in Neuro-Psychopharmacology & Biological Psychiatry* 32(1): 116–23.

O'Tuathaigh, C. M., C. Salum, A. M. Young, A. D. Pickering, M. H. Joseph, and P. M. Moran (2003). "The effect of amphetamine on Kamin blocking and overshadowing". *Behavioural Pharmacology* 14(4): 315–22.

Oades, R. D., D. Bunk, and C. Eggers (1992). "Paranoid schizophrenics may not use irrelevant signals: The use of measures of blocking and of urinary dopamine". *Acta Paedopsychiatrica* 55(3): 183–4.

Oades, R. D., B. Zimmermann, and C. Eggers (1996). "Conditioned blocking in patients with paranoid, non-paranoid psychosis or obsessive compulsive disorder: Associations with symptoms, personality and monoamine metabolism". *Journal of Psychiatric Research* 30(5): 369–90.

Pavlov, I. P. (1927). *Conditioned Reflexes: An Investigation of the Physiological Activity of the Cerebral Cortex*. Oxford: Oxford University Press.

Pearce, J. M. and G. Hall (1980). "A model for Pavlovian learning: Variations in the effectiveness of conditioned but not of unconditioned stimuli". *Psychological Review* 87(6): 532–52.

Pinkham, A. E., P. D. Harvey, and D. L. Penn (2016). "Paranoid individuals with schizophrenia show greater social cognitive bias and worse social functioning than non-paranoid individuals with schizophrenia". *Schizophrenia Research: Cognition* 3: 33–8.

Powers, A. R., III, M. Kelley, and P. R. Corlett (2016). "Hallucinations as top-down effects on perception". *Biological Psychiatry: Cognitive Neuroscience and Neuroimaging* 1(5): 393–400.

Powers, A. R., III, M. Kelley, and P. R. Corlett (2017a). "Varieties of voice-hearing: Psychics and the psychosis continuum". *Schizophrenia Bulletin* 43(1): 84–98.

Powers, A. R., III, C. Mathys, and P. R. Corlett (2017b). "Pavlovian conditioning-induced hallucinations result from overweighting of perceptual priors". *Science* 357(6351): 596–600.

Raihani, N. J. and V. Bell (2019). "An evolutionary perspective on paranoia". *Nature Human Behaviour* 3(2): 114–21.

Reed, E. J., S. Uddenberg, P. Suthaharan, C. D. Mathys, J. R. Taylor, S. M. Groman, and P. R. Corlett (2020). "Paranoia as a deficit in non-social belief updating". *Elife* 9: e56345.

Reichert, D. P., P. Series, and A. J. Storkey (2013). "Charles Bonnet syndrome: Evidence for a generative model in the cortex?" *PLoS Computational Biology* 9(7): e1003134.

Rescorla, R. A. and A. R. Wagner (1972). "A theory of Pavlovian conditioning: Variations in the effectiveness of reinforcement and non-reinforcement". In A. H. Black and W. F. Prokasy (eds.), *Classical Conditioning II: Current Research and Theory*. New York: Appleton-Century-Crofts, 64–99.

Ross, R. M., R. McKay, M. Coltheart, and R. Langdon (2016). "Perception, cognition, and delusion". *Behavioral and Brain Sciences* 39: 47–8.

Rossi-Goldthorpe, R. A., Y. C. Leong, P. Leptourgos, and P. R. Corlett (2021). "Paranoia, self-deception and overconfidence". *PLoS Computational Biology* 17(10): e1009453.

Saddoris, M. P., P. C. Holland, and M. Gallagher (2009). "Associatively learned representations of taste outcomes activate taste-encoding neural ensembles in gustatory cortex". *The Journal of Neuroscience* 29(49): 15386–96.

Schultz, W. (2004). "Neural coding of basic reward terms of animal learning theory, game theory, microeconomics and behavioural ecology". *Current Opinion in Neurobiology* 14(2): 139–47.

Schultz, W. and A. Dickinson (2000). "Neural coding of prediction errors". *Annual Review of Neuroscience* 23: 473–500.

Seashore, C. E. (1895). "Measurements of illusions and hallucinations in normal life". *Studies from the Yale Psychological Laboratory* 3: 1–67.

Seth, A. K. (2014). "A predictive processing theory of sensorimotor contingencies: Explaining the puzzle of perceptual presence and its absence in synesthesia". *Cognitive Neuroscience* 5(2): 97–118.

Sheffield, J., P. Suthaharan, and P. Leptourgos (2022). "Belief updating and paranoia in individuals with schizophrenia". *Biological Psychiatry: Cognitive Neuroscience and Neuroimaging* 7(11): 1149–57.

Simons, J. S., R. N. Henson, S. J. Gilbert, and P. C. Fletcher (2008). "Separable forms of reality monitoring supported by anterior prefrontal cortex". *Journal of Cognitive Neuroscience* 20(3): 447–57.

Spitzer, M. (1995). "A neurocomputational approach to delusions". *Comprehensive Psychiatry* 36(2): 83–105.

Sun, W. and J. Orchard (2020). "A predictive-coding network that is both discriminative and generative". *Neural Computation* 32(10): 1836–62.

Suthaharan, P., E. Reed, P. Leptourgos, J. Kenney, S. Uddenberg, C. Mathys, L. Litman, J. Robinson, A. Moss, J. Taylor, S. Groman, and P. Corlett (2021). "Paranoia and belief updating during the COVID-19 crisis". *Nature Human Behaviour* 5: 1190–202.

Takahashi, Y. K., C. Y. Chang, F. Lucantonio, R. Z. Haney, B. A. Berg, H. J. Yau, A. Bonci, and G. Schoenbaum (2013). "Neural estimates of imagined outcomes in the orbitofrontal cortex drive behavior and learning". *Neuron* 80(2): 507–18.

Teufel, C., N. Subramaniam, V. Dobler, J. Perez, J. Finnemann, P. R. Mehta, I. M. Goodyer, and P. C. Fletcher (2015). "Shift toward prior knowledge confers a perceptual advantage in early psychosis and psychosis-prone healthy individuals". *Proceedings of the National Academy of Sciences of the United States of America* 112(43): 13401–6.

Thein, T., R. F. Westbrook, and J. A. Harris (2008). "How the associative strengths of stimuli combine in compound: Summation and overshadowing". *Journal of Experimental Psychology: Animal Behavior Processes* 34(1): 155–66.

Tolman, E. C. (1932). *Purposive Behavior in Animals and Men.* New York: Appleton-Century-Crofts.

Waelti, P., A. Dickinson, and W. Schultz (2001). "Dopamine responses comply with basic assumptions of formal learning theory". *Nature* 412(6842): 43–8.

Wang, F., J. D. Howard, J. L. Voss, G. Schoenbaum, and T. Kahnt (2020). "Targeted stimulation of an orbitofrontal network disrupts decisions based on inferred, not experienced outcomes". *Journal of Neuroscience* 40(45): 8726–33.

Wimmer, G. E. and D. Shohamy (2012). "Preference by association: How memory mechanisms in the hippocampus bias decisions". *Science* 338(6104): 270–3.

Wu, J. L., R. P. Haberman, M. Gallagher, and M. T. Koh (2020). "Probing for conditioned hallucinations through neural activation in a ketamine mouse model of schizophrenia". *Neuroscience Bulletin* 36(8): 937–41.

Zeithamova, D., A. L. Dominick, and A. R. Preston (2012). "Hippocampal and ventral medial prefrontal activation during retrieval-mediated learning supports novel inference". *Neuron* 75(1): 168–79.

PART II
BELIEF AND IMAGINATION
IN THE WILD

5

Religious Imaginings

Anna Ichino

A recurrent theme in the contemporary philosophy of imagination has to do with the idea that imaginings might play a larger role in our cognitive lives than we used to think. While imaginings traditionally have been invoked to explain phenomena like engagement with fiction, pretence, or daydreaming, in the last few decades many philosophers have argued that they play key explanatory roles also in a variety of other domains—from self-deception (Lazar 1999; Gendler 2010: Ch.8), to psychopathology (Currie and Ravenscroft 2002; Egan 2008), to implicit bias (Sullivan-Bissett 2019, 2023), and beyond. In this chapter I argue that religion, too, is a domain of this sort, in which imagination turns out to be the key cognitive attitude: many of the attitudes that we commonly call "religious beliefs" are actually not beliefs, but imaginings.

The negative part of this claim is not new. The idea that religious attitudes are not (always) beliefs is familiar in debates about the nature of faith, where non-doxastic approaches are increasingly common (Schellenberg 2005; Alston 1991; Howard-Snyder 2013). And recently this idea has been forcefully defended by Neil Van Leeuwen (2014, 2017a, 2017b), who argued that many instances of religious attitudes are best described in terms of the *sui generis* non-doxastic category of 'religious credence'. Whilst recognizing that religious attitudes are not beliefs, however, none of these authors has gone further to argue that they are imaginings instead—as I will do here.

I will provide some key reasons in favour of non-doxasticism, and I will argue that those same reasons should lead us to recognize religious attitudes' imaginative nature (§§1–4). I will then explain the advantages of my view over Van Leeuwen's view (§5). I will conclude by examining two forms in which religious imaginings typically come and by clarifying their relation to the notion of religious faith (§6).[1]

---

[1] The main cases that I've got in mind concern the religious attitudes of contemporary Western Christian people: attitudes having to do with the idea that there is one God, conceived as an immaterial being with psychological properties such as omniscience, omnipotence, and infinite goodness, who created the universe and everything in it, and whose son, Jesus of Nazareth, died and was resurrected for us. I actually hold that most of what I say could be extended to other religions, epochs, and cultures—as the psychology of religious people is likely to display some universal features. But I don't commit myself to this broader view here, since the empirical evidence on which I rely is mostly about this class of 'believers'. Vice versa, I acknowledge exceptions to my claims even among contemporary Western Christians, who are in important respects a motley crew. My claims from now on should then

---

Anna Ichino, *Religious Imaginings* In: *Belief, Imagination, and Delusion*. Edited by: Ema Sullivan-Bissett,
Oxford University Press. © Oxford University Press 2024. DOI: 10.1093/oso/9780198872221.003.0005

82   BELIEF, IMAGINATION, AND DELUSION

My arguments will show that re-categorizing religious attitudes as imaginings is important not only for a better understanding of the nature of those attitudes, but also for a better understanding of the imagination itself.

1. Religious Attitudes, Beliefs, and Imaginings

Here are three reasons for thinking that religious attitudes are genuine beliefs. The first two reasons concern features that are generally taken to be constitutive of belief.

(i) **Sensitivity to Evidence.** Religious people justify their attitudes by appeal to at least two sorts of evidence. First, a (kind of) testimonial evidence from the sacred tradition: most notably, the sacred texts of the biblical canon, but possibly also other sources—like official catechisms, traditional narratives about the lives of saints, and so on. Second, (quasi-)perceptual evidence from peculiar spiritual experiences—such as the purported awareness of God's disembodied presence, an overwhelming feeling of his warming love, and other such things (cf. James 1902/2008; Alston 1991).

(ii) **Coherent Integration.** Religious attitudes seem to form an internally coherent system and seem to be reasonably well-integrated with subjects' other mundane beliefs. The religious idea that our world is God's creation, for instance, might be taken to explain many beliefs that we have about such a world, including those about the scientific laws that govern it.

(iii) **Sincere Avowals.** A third reason to classify religious attitudes as beliefs has to do with a feature which—if not constitutive of belief—plays a crucial role in our practices of belief ascription: typically, a subject who believes that p does also believe that she believes that p, and is disposed to verbally manifest such belief.[2] This is arguably the most straightforward reason to credit religious people with authentic beliefs: they earnestly avow such beliefs. Avowals of religious 'beliefs' are indeed very common—possibly even more common and emphatic than avowals of other mundane beliefs. While in ordinary talk we often omit explicit expressions of belief towards our own assertions, in

---

be intended as concerning a *distinctive and large enough to be interesting* number of contemporary Western Christians—even if, for ease of exposition, I will often talk unqualifiedly about religious 'people' and religious 'attitudes'.

[2] Levy (this volume) discusses various cases of alleged beliefs that do not display this feature—i.e., cases in which people's beliefs are not aligned with their sincere avowals. His examples include delusional and superstitious beliefs; as I shall argue in §5.1, though, I doubt that such cases are indeed genuine cases of belief.

RELIGIOUS IMAGININGS   83

religious contexts the opposite seems true. The public profession of the
"Credo" ("I believe"), for instance, is a central part of the Catholic
Mass—and it is explicitly encouraged in many other contexts as well.[3]

Since we generally have no reason to take such public avowals to be insincere—
and given reasons (i) and (ii) above—it seems reasonable to treat religious
attitudes as authentic beliefs.

However, I shall argue that we shouldn't do that: in spite of appearances,
religious attitudes are better classified as imaginings. I will show that reasons
(i)–(iii) can be overturned into opposite non-doxastic reasons that speak in favour
of their imaginative nature.

Before doing that, however, some preliminary clarifications about imagination
and belief themselves are in order.

1.1 Imagination and Belief

The sort of imagination that is at stake in the present discussion is *propositional,
belief-like imagination* (aka 'make-believe'): a distinctive propositional attitude
that is functionally similar to belief, and yet not identical to it.[4] The similarity
between the two can be observed at the cognitive, affective, as well as motivational
level. For instance, imagining something scary can produce thoughts, emotions,
and behavioural responses similar to those that would be produced by believing
something scary—even though the precise extent of those similarities is debated
(more on this in §5).

Among the respects in which imagination and belief are widely agreed to differ,
on the other hand, there are the evidence-sensitivity and inferential integration
that we just discussed.[5] Imaginings are not constrained by evidence in the
same ways in which beliefs are, and in particular they are not constrained by
that sort of 'inferential evidence' that makes our beliefs integrated into a more
or less holistically coherent system.[6] Vice versa, imaginings can respond to a
variety of evidence-insensitive factors—including, notably, our will and intentional deliberations.

---

[3] See e.g., the Apostolic Letter *Porta Fidei*, which exhorts Catholics to engage in acts of "public
testimony and commitment" (Ratzinger 2011: §10), quoting Paul of Tarsus' passage about the
importance of "confessing with the lips" (Epistle to the Romans, 10:10); or the *Catechism of the
Catholic Church* (Part I, Ch. 3, Art. 2) on the "duty of public profession".

[4] The specification 'belief-like' is necessary since according to some authors, propositional imagination can also come in different, *desire-like* forms (see e.g., Currie and Ravenscroft 2002).

[5] Relatedly, see Kind (this volume) on the different relationships that imagination and belief bear to
truth.

[6] I call 'inferential evidence' the evidence constituted by a subject's pre-existing beliefs.

84 BELIEF, IMAGINATION, AND DELUSION

Importantly, this does not mean that imaginings cannot hold if there is evidence that supports their contents. To say that they are not constrained by evidence simply means that their holding is not *contingent* upon evidence. The evidence at our disposal can prompt us to imagine a number of things, but what we imagine is not tied to such evidence in the way in which what we believe is. This is revealed most clearly when it comes to revision procedures: the fading of the relevant evidence about *p* would only lead us to revise/abandon a belief that *p*, but not (necessarily) to revise/abandon an imagining that *p*.

The fact that evidence *can*—although does *not need* to—play a role in the formation and maintenance of our imaginings is what explains why it is often easy to mistake imaginings for beliefs: the mere presence of evidence (or alleged such) might mislead us into taking as doxastic an attitude that is in fact imaginative. This is indeed, I shall argue, what happens in many cases of religious attitudes—where the evidence to which religious people appeal does not play the critical role that it would play in a genuinely doxastic context. Moreover, I shall argue that also the alleged 'coherent integration' of religious attitudes is in fact dubious. So, in both these key respects having to do with the features mentioned in (i) and (ii) above, religious attitudes turn out to match the functional profile of imagination better than the functional profile of belief—and something similar happens with respect to (iii).

2. 'Appeals to Evidence' vs. 'Sensitivity to Evidence'

In order for a propositional attitude to be sensitive to evidence, the subject to whom we ascribe that attitude must display some openness to revise it in the face of counterevidence—even if her criteria for revision are far from perfectly rational. Religious attitudes do not typically display relevant degrees of such sensitivity. They are related to evidence in the sense that religious people appeal to some evidence to justify them; but the evidence which is appealed to seems to be available only to corroborate, rather than to revise and falsify. Appealing to evidence is not the same as being sensitive to it.

A striking illustration of this imperviousness to contrary evidence is provided by attitudes concerning biblical prophecies and doomsday scenarios—which have drawn scholars' attention because apparently not only do they persist in the face of counterevidence, but they might even get reinforced by it. As a now famous study by Leon Festinger and colleagues pointed out, when a prophecy fails, its followers may deepen, rather than weaken, their commitment to it—a phenomenon that has been repeatedly observed in the history of Christian movements such as Anabaptists, Mormons, and Jehovah's Witnesses (Festinger et al. 1956; Zygmunt 1970; Boyer 2001: 346–7).

But something similar, even though in less glaring forms, holds more generally for all sorts of religious attitudes—whose resilience is a prominent feature: these attitudes seem crucially characterized by the capacity to persist when the relevant evidence is weak or lacking, or even in the face of blatant counterevidence.

Indeed, the very idea of an omnipotent, loving, and just God is challenged by much of what goes on in this world, and this is not lost on religious people. On the contrary, as the anthropologist Tania Luhrmann observes—based on her fieldwork among American Evangelicals:

> This is the problem for ordinary Christians: it is the problem of how to commit to what the Bible says is true, *in the face of contradictions they experience in their world*. They believe—or want to believe—that the world is fundamentally good or was at least created by a fundamentally good power that is still present and responsive. *Yet, they see around themselves a world of great injustice*. They believe, or they think they should believe, that God loves them—*and yet they don't really experience themselves, in their heart of hearts, as loved and lovable*. They sit down to pray, *but they cannot persuade themselves that anyone is listening*. Or they believe in God, *but what they interpret as God's will has just been flatly contradicted by someone they know and trust*...
>
> (Luhrmann 2012: 7; emphasis mine)

This is not meant to deny that religious people may have—or at least think they have—evidence that supports their attitudes. As I said, I grant that they do. But the point is that they do also see much conflicting evidence that pulls in the opposite direction. And what is most interesting for us here is that their 'solution' to this conflict seems to be in important respects a matter of deliberate decision— "a decision based not on evidence but on the way in which they choose to live in the face of inadequate evidence", as Luhrmann puts it (2012: 9).

Indeed, a prominent feature of religious attitudes is the fact of involving a significant voluntaristic component, which is recognized as such by religious people. The commitment to the idea of an omnipotent, loving God has been variously described as "a personal choice" (Kung 1976), "a decision" (Kierkegaard; Barth 1964/2003: 23), "a bet" (Pascal 1670), "a human act, conscious and free" (*Catechism of the Catholic Church*, Part I, Ch. 3, Art. 1)—in any case, as something that springs in important respects from inner motivation and deliberation.

These voluntaristic characterizations are in tension with doxastic status. As Bernard Williams (1970) famously argued, "deciding to believe" is a contradiction in terms.[7] Vice versa, as we have seen, imagination is precisely the sort of attitude that one can *choose* to entertain irrespective of evidence and reasons.

---

[7] The idea that beliefs are not a matter of decision (at least of conscious and deliberate decision) is widely accepted. Although it must be acknowledged that there is a growing literature defending varieties of doxastic voluntarism (see e.g., McCormick 2015 and Rinard 2018 for interesting discussions).

This is then a first important respect in which religious attitudes seem better classified as imaginings.

As it turns out, the distinction that I introduced above between *appeals* and *sensitivity* to evidence is not just a matter of degree. Of course, evidence-sensitivity in itself does come in degrees; and we know that the sensitivity of most ordinary beliefs is much lower than one would expect from a perfectly rational subject. But the point here is not that religious attitudes' sensitivity to evidence is too low—even lower than the already low average—in order for them to count as beliefs. What I have argued suggests that their relation to evidence is of a rather different kind, which parallels closely that of paradigmatic instances of imagination. Religious attitudes are not 'very resistant to counterevidence', but seem to depend on factors other than evidence—factors among which our will plays a crucial role, as it does with imaginative states.

This does not mean that religious attitudes are *entirely* the outcome of an intentional deliberation. On the contrary, research in the cognitive psychology of religion emphasizes the intuitive—hence non-reflective and non-deliberative—origin of such attitudes, suggesting that they arise naturally out of our evolved tendency to overestimate the presence of agents and intelligent design in the world (as per the operations of our "hypersensitive *agency detection device*"; Boyer 2001; Barrett 2004). But this account of the origins of religious attitudes is compatible with what we said about their voluntaristic component, since such a component is not supposed to explain how religious attitudes are originally formed, but rather how, once they are formed, they are maintained in the face of counterevidence. It is at this maintenance stage that the voluntaristic component comes into the picture—as it does in the case of imaginative attitudes.

Indeed, imaginings, too, often 'come to our mind' without a previous decision, and even against our will—as a result of intuitive automatic associations triggered by either external or internal stimuli. What matters to us here is that, like religious attitudes, once they are in our mind they can be kept there out of a deliberate choice.

The point I am making, then, is simply this: whilst neither imaginings nor religious attitudes are entirely subject to the will and impervious to evidential inputs, both of them can—and in many cases do—respond to our will in a way in which genuine beliefs cannot.

And, it is also worth noting, this does not make them epistemically irrational: like imaginings, religious attitudes do not seem to undergo the same normative constraints that beliefs undergo. Whilst the tendency to confirmation bias is clearly a fault of ordinary beliefs, the firmness and steadiness of religious attitudes (in the absence of evidence, or even in the face of overwhelming counterevidence) is rather celebrated as a virtue—as even just a cursory look at religious normative practices makes clear.

2.1 Normative Excursus—Job vs. Thomas

Consider for instance the two key biblical figures—from the Old and the New Testament, respectively—of Job, on the one hand, and the disciple Thomas, on the other. Whilst Job, who keeps 'believing' in the existence and goodness of God when every possible piece of evidence at his disposal would suggest otherwise, has been celebrated ever since as an upstanding religious 'believer', a diametrically opposite treatment is reserved for Thomas, whose refusal to believe in Jesus' resurrection unless he "sees in his hands the prints of the nails" (John 20:25) is reprimanded by Jesus himself with these famous words: "Have you believed because you have seen me? Blessed are those who have not seen and yet have believed" (John 20:29). With this renowned blessing that closes John's gospel (and with it the entire evangelical section of the New Testament), the capacity to 'believe' in the absence of evidence is set as a normative ideal for the Christians to come.[8]

But these roles of hero and antihero that Job and Thomas are assigned in the religious paradigm, would be clearly reversed in the doxastic paradigm—where believing against/without the available evidence is all but a virtue. And this is then a further respect in which religious attitudes seem to fit the imaginative domain better than the belief domain. Indeed, although imaginings can be subject to different constraints depending on the different contexts in which they arise and on the different functions they serve in each context, they are not tied to epistemic evidential constraints in the ways in which beliefs are. This flexibility in imagination's normative profile makes it more suited to accommodate religious attitudes' peculiar normativity.

But let's now go back from the normative to the functional level which is the focus of the present inquiry, considering a second functional respect in which, in spite of appearances, religious attitudes resemble imaginings much more than beliefs.

3. Religious Contradictions

The supposed *coherent integration* of religious attitudes pointed out in reason (ii) above is also far from clear.

For one thing, there are often internal incoherencies within the set of a subject's own religious attitudes. For instance, in a series of famous studies Justin Barrett and colleagues found that when religious subjects are asked in the abstract to describe what God is like, they give 'theologically correct' descriptions which

---

[8] For a paradigmatic celebration of Job's "unshakable belief", see e.g., Kung (1976: 298–9).

88 BELIEF, IMAGINATION, AND DELUSION

depict him as a supernatural, ontologically *sui generis* agent (eternal, ubiquitous, and endowed with unlimited power and knowledge); but when asked to describe how God would deal with particular problems, they fall back on rather anthropomorphic representations of him as a human-like agent with spatial, temporal, and cognitive limitations. These mutually inconsistent representations of God coexist in the religious mind (Barrett and Keil 1996; Barrett 1998; for discussion, see also Boyer 2001: Chs. 2 and 9).

To be sure, in many of these cases the inconsistency may not have been immediately salient to the subjects, since only the 'theologically correct' representation was explicitly endorsed by them, whilst the other 'incorrect' one was only implicitly relied upon. And the studies in question did not test how subjects would react if the inconsistency were made salient. But there is reason to think that subjects might have let the said inconsistency stay even in such a case, as indeed they do with other contradictions internal, and even central, to their religious system. The Christian doctrine of the Trinity, and the related one of a God who 'made himself man', for instance, involve blatant contradictions—or, at least, what many religious people are likely to take as such. Yet, such doctrines are openly accepted and endorsed in the "Credo", and they lay the basis for further paradoxical views—like that of a God who is omnipotent *and yet* unable to prevent our suffering, which he does rather 'share with us'.[9] The acceptance of these internal contradictions—which following Tim Crane we can trace back to that "sense of mystery [...] that is central to Western monotheism" (2017: 56)—resembles closely the way in which we accept the contradictions that often characterize our imaginative contents (see Gendler 2010: 153–4).

Moreover, and most importantly, there are also *external* incoherencies between subjects' religious attitudes and their ordinary beliefs. Many common religious views appear to be in tension with widely accepted scientific beliefs, as well as with other natural beliefs that follow more or less directly from the scientific ones.[10] The point here, again, is not that religious people hold views that a careful analysis reveals to be inconsistent with each other— which is something that happens frequently in our imperfect doxastic systems. In fact, it is not even obvious that a careful analysis would, ultimately, reveal an inconsistency—the question of whether there may be ways to reconcile religious and natural perspectives is a highly controversial one, which I should not try to settle here.[11] What matters here is that religious people often entertain views that are *prima facie* inconsistent—and that, most

---

[9] For a position of this sort defended after a recent earthquake in Italy see: https://www.lavoce.it/dio-non-crea-il-dolore-lo-combatte-con-noi/.
[10] See Lipton (2007: 33) for many examples.
[11] Cf. the controversy in Dennett and Plantinga (2011).

RELIGIOUS IMAGININGS   89

importantly, *they do take to be* inconsistent; without, however, attempting to overcome such inconsistency.[12]

Take for instance common views about death and afterlife—where religious and natural approaches *seem* to pull in opposite directions, inviting us to see death, respectively, as a *transition* after which our disembodied minds/souls continue to enjoy conscious existence, and as the total *cessation* of any physical and mental process.

Research by Paul Harris and colleagues suggests that religious people do indeed hold both these *prima facie* inconsistent views, recognizing them as such; and yet they do not make any serious attempt to reconcile them. They do not modify, let alone abandon, either of the two views; instead, they keep both views 'in parallel', one alongside the other, preventing them from mutual interactions.

This emerged clearly in a study by Harris and Marta Giménez (2005), who presented Spanish Catholic children from seven to eleven years old with two stories where one of the characters dies, framing each story into a different narrative context: a medical context highlighting biological aspects of death, in one case, and a religious context highlighting spiritual aspects of death, in the other case. After hearing each story, children were asked to judge whether (and why) either the mind or the body of the deceased could still work after death; plus, some other questions about what happens after death to people in general.

In reviewing children's responses, three main patterns emerged: (i) a 'consistently biological' pattern (when a child's responses across the interview consistently deployed a biological conception of death[13]); (ii) a 'consistently religious' pattern (when a child's responses across the interview consistently deployed a religious conception of death[14]); and (iii) a 'mixed pattern' (when a child's responses deployed different conceptions of death at different points in the interview). The 'consistently biological' pattern was dominant among younger children: 61 per cent of the seven-year-olds replied to *all* questions—including those concerning the religiously framed story—based on an idea of death as a total annihilation, without any reference to the notion of afterlife (which, apparently, they hadn't quite mastered yet). This percentage of 'consistently biological' thinkers sharply declined with age. But this was not due to an increase in the percentage of children adopting a 'consistently religious' stance, which remained

---

[12] Or, better, without attempting to overcome it by abandoning either of the contents from which it arises. As Lipton (2007: 32) pointed out, indeed, there are two possible strategies to overcome the inconsistencies that arise within our religious and natural views—one strategy that amounts to *adjusting content* and one that amounts to *adjusting attitude*: "adjusting content means giving up some claims. Adjusting attitude means keeping the claims but changing one's epistemic attitude toward at least some of them." Lipton himself advocates a version of the adjusting attitude strategy which amounts to adopting an imaginative attitude towards his religious views, whilst keeping a doxastic attitude towards the natural/scientific ones. What I argue is that this same strategy is adopted—although possibly in less self-aware ways—by most religious people.

[13] For example, responses like: "If he is dead, nothing can work".

[14] For example, responses like: "When she dies and goes to heaven, God will give her a brain again".

90 BELIEF, IMAGINATION, AND DELUSION

pretty low at all ages (only 10 per cent of the seven-year-olds and 16 per cent of the eleven-year-olds). What the majority of children did as they grew up was rather to adopt the 'mixed' stance: 67 per cent of the eleven-year-olds appeared to *swing* between a religious notion of death as spiritual transformation, and a biological notion of death as total terminus.

Quite predictably, the direction of this swing was influenced by the story-framing at play on each occasion. But whatever the primer for the reliance upon one view or the other was, what matters most to us here is the picture of the relation between the two views that emerges from the findings just reported. As Harris (2012) observes:

> The fact that the proportion of children displaying both conceptions increases with age [...] suggests that what happens is *not* that children first construct a conception of death as a biological terminus and then proceed to dismantle it as they get older. Instead, they leave that early emerging biological conception intact, but on top of it they build a different, religious conception – one that is especially likely to be activated when they are asked to think about death in a religious rather than a medical context [...]. Stated differently, there is no evidence in these data that older children end up rejecting the biological facts. Rather, they construct an *alternative or parallel* conception of death – one that includes an afterlife – in the face of those facts. Especially in the minds of older children, the biological and the religious conception of death appear to *co-exist alongside* one another.   (Harris 2012: 206–7; emphasis mine)

Harris's talk about two 'alternative views', coexisting 'in parallel', 'alongside one another' here denotes the lack of proper interactions between such views: i.e., the fact that children swing between such views did *not* typically take the form of an attempt to bridge the gap between them, by integrating them into a globally consistent perspective. Indeed, only a tiny minority of the children who adopted the mixed stance ever did appeal to the two different conceptions of death within the same piece of reasoning (i.e., within the breath of a single response to one question). What happened in over 80 per cent of the cases, instead, was that children invoked only one of the two conceptions at a time—framing each of their responses either in entirely biological terms, or in entirely religious terms, and reverting to the other conception only when they were asked a new, different question.

This was arguably because—as Harris goes on to notice—"at some level, however tacit, children do conceive of the afterlife as a negation or denial of the biological facts" (2012: 219). And yet, not being ready to question neither the afterlife, nor the biological facts that contradict it, they simply keep their views about these two things apart from each other, recruiting them in different contexts.

RELIGIOUS IMAGININGS 91

These findings were replicated and extended in a follow-up study which Harris conducted with Rita Astuti among the Vezo—a religious community of rural Madagascar, who profess "beliefs" about an afterlife where the ancestors survive with their own cognitive functions intact. A striking fact about those professed beliefs, again, is their pacific coexistence with the Vezo's natural beliefs about death, which seem patently inconsistent with them:

> Although such different conceptions of death might be regarded as objectively incompatible with one another, it is unlikely that Vezo experience tension. [...] Each conception is likely to be activated in different, non-overlapping circumstances. For example, when people are confronted with a dead person, they will consider it at one moment as a corpse and at another moment as an ancestor, behaving accordingly toward it. When they wash and prepare the corpse, Vezo treat it as a non-sentient entity. The body is washed with cold water because "it can't feel anything," and the entangled hair is pulled and yanked because "she no longer feels any pain." But when the children are shown the face of their dead parent for the last time and told never to call his or her name again, the dead person is treated as a sentient being capable of returning to, and interfering with, the everyday life of the community.   (Astuti and Harris 2008: 733–4)

By involving a much wider age range of participants (from eight to seventy-one years old), this follow-up study suggests that the same sort of coexistence of religious and natural conceptions that Harris and Giménez had observed in children, persists also in adulthood, becoming a characteristic feature of the religious mind.

And what I argue is that this feature is best explained if we understand the relationship between religious and natural views on the model of the relationship between imaginings and beliefs. The way in which religious and natural views about death are 'let stand alongside each other' is strikingly reminiscent of the way in which imaginings and beliefs with conflicting contents are let stand alongside each other—as in our engagement with a game of pretence where, for instance, we can look at one and the same doll *both* as a real baby *and* as an inanimate object, without thereby feeling compelled to abandon either of those conflicting representations.

Importantly, what I said about religious ideas on death and afterlife seems to happen also with other religious ideas, since the first moments when they are acquired. Jaqueline Woolley (2000) observes that children's developing beliefs about various kinds of natural causal relations are not influenced by their simultaneous acquirement of religious ideas about supernatural relations. For example, when children around three/four years old become aware of the fact that other minds and the physical world cannot be modified by thought alone, those educated in religious families are also introduced to the idea of silent inner prayer;

92 BELIEF, IMAGINATION, AND DELUSION

but even though the efficacy of such prayer presupposes mechanisms that run against the natural mechanisms of mental-mental or mental-physical causation that children are mastering, their developing understanding of such mechanisms apparently is not affected.

To explain these findings, Woolley appeals to the same notion of *quarantining* that has been introduced by Alan Leslie (1987) to characterize our imaginative attitudes—and in particular our capacity to prevent our imaginings from 'infecting' the belief-system, confusing us about what is real and what is merely pretended: "I see it [i.e., religious quarantining] as potentially similar in this sense to the decoupling mechanism that Leslie has proposed to account for the fact that young children do not become confused by their pretend stipulations" (Woolley 2000: 126).

In line with what I suggested, we can then say that, similarly to how they do with their imaginative attitudes towards fiction and pretence, children do somehow quarantine their religious attitudes, preventing them from influencing their understanding of natural mechanisms.[15]

A remaining question is how children come to realize that they should keep this 'quarantined attitude' towards religion, notwithstanding that, differently from fictional stories, religious matters are presented seriously, just as real beliefs. This leads us to the question of religious people's belief avowals.

4. Religious Avowals Unmasked

The third reason for doxasticism that I presented above appealed to a principle of first-person authority, which considers self-reports as 'true by default': i.e., true until proof to the contrary. If acceptance should be our default attitude towards people's self-reports—that was the point of reason (iii)—surely it should be our attitude towards religious self-reports, which are expressed with special emphasis and conviction. So, why not credit religious people with genuine religious beliefs? My answer to this question, of course, is that the anti-doxastic reasons just presented in §§2–3 do constitute the relevant proof to the contrary in the case of religious beliefs: religious people's avowals are controverted by the insensitivity to evidence and inferential isolation of their supposed 'beliefs'.

In fact, I would push this even further: the characteristic emphasis with which religious 'beliefs' are avowed—and indeed the very fact that they are avowed more often and eagerly than beliefs on other mundane matters—may even provide further proof *against* their doxastic status.

---

[15] For a philosophical discussion of imagination's quarantining, see Gendler (2010: Ch. 7).

This is indeed one of the hypotheses that have been suggested to explain how children come to quarantine the religious attitudes that they acquire from adults' testimony. Considering testimonies about entities that they cannot experience by first-hand observation, children use what psychologists call a 'presupposition metric': depending on whether the existence of such entities is unreflectively presupposed or vice versa ostentatiously affirmed, they draw different conclusions about the sort of attitude that their informants bear towards the entities in question (Harris 2012; Harris and Corriveau 2014). Compare for instance what children hear about invisible scientific entities like germs and oxygen, with what they hear about invisible religious entities like God. Children will typically hear remarks that take the existence of germs and oxygen for granted, without making it explicit—e.g., remarks like "Wash your hands, which are full of germs!", or "Anyone needs oxygen to breathe"; while they will hardly hear explicit remarks like: "There really exist germs, and they can hurt us", or "I believe in oxygen". On the other hand, they will often hear such explicit assertions about God, as well as about fictional characters like Santa Claus: "I believe in God!"; or "Trust me, Santa really exists!" This is how children will come to the conclusion that God's existence is not considered by adults in the same way in which oxygen's existence is considered. And they will do the same, keeping God and Santa Claus apart from the entities that populate their real-world beliefs.[16]

There are also other linguistic differences that children's sensitive antennae might capture—differences between our uses of "belief" in religious and ordinary contexts, which reveal substantial differences in the underlying mental attitudes. While in ordinary contexts "I believe" weakens our assertions, in religious contexts it typically has an opposite, intensifying role. Compare: "I believe they never met before" vs. "I believe that God will listen to my prayers!" In the former case, "I believe" expresses an attitude which is open to corrections ("as far as I know, they never met...But I might be wrong"); in the latter, it expresses a strong conviction, based on self-sufficient inner trust, which doesn't seem to look for further confirmation ("I think so...And that's all!").

A related difference between religious and ordinary talk of "belief" has to do with the use of "believe in" vs. "believe that". Actually, we do happen to use "believe in" also in non-religious contexts—e.g., for encouragements such as: "you can do that, I believe in you!" But this is arguably because in similar cases—as in most cases of religious avowals—we do not use "believe" to express our opinion on how we deem things to be, but rather to express something different, which can be

---

[16] A related possibility that psychologists point out is that children use a "consensus metric", registering the degree of expressed consensus concerning the existence of the invisible entities they are told about (Harris and Koenig 2006; Harris and Corriveau 2014).

94 BELIEF, IMAGINATION, AND DELUSION

an exhortation, an assurance, a hope, a wishful hypothesis, but not really an evidence-grounded judgement.[17]

As it turns out, then, sincere religious avowals are not only insufficient to credit people with genuine religious beliefs; such avowals may even provide positive reasons not to do so, suggesting that we ascribe a different sort of attitude instead. What I argued in §§2–3, in turn, suggests that this attitude displays striking functional similarities with imagination.

Admittedly, this might still not be enough to warrant my conclusion that religious attitudes are imaginings. Van Leeuwen (2014, 2017a, 2017b) argued that to characterize them properly we need to postulate a distinctive cognitive attitude which is similar to imagination, but not identical to it: what he calls 'religious credence'. In the next section I shall discuss Van Leeuwen's view, arguing that he does not provide compelling reasons to postulate such a novel mental category: religious attitudes' functional profile matches neatly the functional profile of imagination, and recognizing this teaches us important lessons about the nature of imagination itself.

5. Religious Imaginings and Religious "Credences"

Van Leeuwen recognizes that religious attitudes have more in common with imagination than with belief. On his view, both religious attitudes and imaginings are "secondary cognitive attitudes", characterized by the lack of such key features of belief as "evidential vulnerability" (i.e., what here I called "sensitivity to evidence") and "cognitive governance" (i.e., that feature by virtue of which belief supplies to other cognitive attitudes the informational background for inferences).

However, on his view religious attitudes have peculiar features that differentiate them from other secondary attitudes—hence also from imaginings. First, and most importantly, they differ with respect to action-guidance. Unlike beliefs, which guide our actions in all situations in which their contents are relevant, secondary cognitive attitudes are "practical setting dependent": they guide our actions only in specific situations, and each cognitive attitude is distinguished from the others by the sorts of situations in which it does so. In particular, imaginings guide action only when we represent ourselves to be in the practical setting of pretence play; while religious attitudes guide action only when we represent ourselves to be in the practical setting of religion.[18] Moreover, Van Leeuwen mentions three other features that make religious attitudes "unique

---

[17] On the functional difference between belief-that and belief-in, see also Price (1969: Ch. 9).

[18] It is important to note that, if secondary attitudes guide actions in their proper settings, this is not by virtue of a magical connection, but because subjects do somehow take themselves to be in the relevant setting—which is why what is necessary for action-guidance is a relevant practical setting *representation*.

RELIGIOUS IMAGININGS   95

among secondary cognitive attitudes": susceptibility to free elaboration, vulnerability to special authority, and perceived normative orientation.

I shall argue that actually none of these features discussed by Van Leeuwen give us good reason to postulate the existence of a mental category of credence distinguished from imagination to characterize religious attitudes. As to practical setting dependence, it is not really a feature of religious attitudes and imaginings in the first place; so, *a fortiori* it is not a feature that distinguishes them from each other, requiring us to introduce a new mental category. As to susceptibility to free elaboration, vulnerability to special authority, and perceived normative orientation, they are indeed characteristic features of religious attitudes, but they are all features that we also find in paradigmatic instances of imaginings; so, again, no new state other than the imagination is required to do the relevant explanatory work here. Insofar as this is right, the case for a new category of credence distinct from imagination is unconvincing.

Let's begin with the alleged "practical setting dependence" of religious attitudes—which in Van Leeuwen's view is what explains some otherwise puzzling facts about the ways in which religious people behave. He brings examples like the stereotypical 'once-a-week Christians' who act upon their religious attitudes only on Sundays, ignoring them the rest of the week—as in a study which found that on Sundays people in predominantly Christian states look at pornography *less* than the rest of the population, while looking at it *more* than average during week-days (Van Leeuwen 2017a: 206[19]). These baffling action tendencies, Van Leeuwen argues, depend on the fact that religious attitudes motivate only when people take themselves to be in a religious practical setting, thereby differing not just from beliefs, which motivate across all practical settings, but also from imaginings, which motivate only when one takes herself to be in the practical setting of pretence.

As I have it, this motivational difference between religious attitudes and imaginings does not hold. Nor indeed—as Maarten Boudry and Jerry Coyne (2016) and Levy (2017) already argued—holds the difference between them and beliefs. It is indeed the whole picture that Van Leeuwen articulates about the motivating powers of different cognitive attitudes, based on the notion of practical settings in/dependence, that is problematic. On the one hand, it overestimates the action-guiding role of beliefs—which are less 'independent' than he suggests; on the other hand it underestimates the action-guiding role of religious attitudes and imaginings—which are less 'dependent' than he suggests. By showing that the attitudes in question are in fact motivationally equivalent, I will undercut Van Leeuwen's main argument to postulate a distinctive category of religious credence.

Van Leeuwen's claim that belief guides action in all situations in which its contents are relevant, as it is, can't be right. For any belief that *p* there are many

---

[19] Cf. Edelman (2009).

96 BELIEF, IMAGINATION, AND DELUSION

situations in which, even if p is relevant, it fails to motivate us due to the interference of other factors. The belief that *white wine gives me migraine* is surely relevant when I am ordering my drinks; yet, it may fail to guide my actions, due to a strong desire to try the fine Prosecco on offer. And so, the belief that *my keys are in the backpack* is surely relevant when I want to open the door, but it may fail to guide my actions due to my lagging habit of searching for the keys in my right pocket. Belief's connection to action is indeed a dispositional connection, which is only manifested if a number of relevant conditions hold—conditions that include, but are not exhausted by, the presence of the relevant desires. To show that this dispositional connection is different from the dispositional connection to action of religious and imaginative attitudes, Van Leeuwen should have carefully examined the conditions of manifestation of the dispositions in question, indicating precisely where they come apart. But he doesn't do that. And what I argue is that, once we do that, we find no clear difference between them.

To see this point, consider again the example of once-a-week Christians who lower their pornography consumption on Sundays, while increasing it in other days of the week. These behaviours are easily explained by the fact that during the week those people's sexual desire becomes phenomenologically predominant over the religious desire to please God; and that sexual desire, in turn, makes the cognitions that are relevant to its satisfaction become predominant over the cognitions that are relevant to the satisfaction of the religious desire. In other words, it is likely that, as the sexual desire increases (due to natural physiological causes), subjects will tend to think about how to fulfil it more than they think about how to fulfil the desire to please God; hence the motivating force of their religious cognitive attitudes will be overcome by the motivating force of their cognitive attitudes concerning pornography. None of this reveals the sort of practical setting dependence that Van Leeuwen suggests; but simply the fact that the behavioural manifestations of religious attitudes critically depend on the presence and strength of relevant desires—something that is true also of beliefs and, as we shall see, of imaginings.[20]

The practical setting dependence that Van Leeuwen ascribes to religious attitudes and imaginings is not only unnecessary to explain their behavioural manifestations. It does also yield incorrect predictions about them. If Van Leeuwen were right, we would never be moved to act by religious and imaginative attitudes unless we took ourselves to be, respectively, in the practical settings of religion or in that of pretence. But this is not what happens.

---

[20] This is in line with Levy's (2017) criticism which notes that, like religious attitudes, ordinary beliefs also fail to guide action in many contexts where their contents are relevant. Levy's explanation for these 'motivational failures' is based on the idea that in the said contexts religious attitudes and beliefs aren't fluently processed, so they are unintuitive. Whilst I don't want to commit myself to this specific explanation (due to the worries raised by Van Leeuwen 2017a), I showed that alternative explanations are available—and I hold Levy's basic point to be right.

RELIGIOUS IMAGININGS   97

In the case of religious attitudes, the implausibility of this claim emerges clearly as soon as we consider the complex and (deliberately) broad way in which Van Leeuwen defines the religious setting:

> What then is the practical setting of religious credence? We should not attempt to be too specific at this point, since that setting takes different forms in different cultures. But [...] "existential" problems and situations that evoke them are central to religions cross-culturally. These include confrontation with death, birth, illness that can't be explained otherwise, unexplainable coincidences that seem to change one's life, challenges to one's identity, and the like. In addition [...] many religions construct practices and physical spaces that evoke or are symbolic of these problems and situations and hence toggle on religious credences as well. This is the extended practical setting. And since religious credences are part of one's identity, many situations that challenge one's identity or group allegiance can activate credences as well.   (Van Leeuwen 2014: 706)

Especially insofar as the religious practical setting is so elusively characterized, positing representations about it as necessary conditions for an agent to be moved by her religious attitudes is problematic.[21] It is not even clear what precisely the relevant representations should be: should one hold representations like "My identity is being challenged", or "I'm in a church", in order to act upon one's religious attitudes? This is implausible. What might be plausible is that challenges to one's identity, existential problems, and the various other factors by which Van Leeuwen characterizes religious settings, exert a sort of priming effect upon religious attitudes, making them occurrently present in our minds. For example, entering a church prompts me to think about God—it makes me occurrently attend to the idea that God is watching me. But once such attitudes are occurrently present in my mind—*however they got there*—they seem able to guide action whether or not I take myself to be in the relevant practical setting.[22]

Parallel considerations hold for standard instances of imaginative attitudes, that do not require "pretence setting representations" in order to motivate us. So-called *expressive actions* (i.e., actions expressive of an emotion) are clear examples of

---

[21] Boudry and Coyne (2016: 610–611) criticize the broadness of Van Leeuwen's characterization of the religious setting also in a different way, observing that (notably because of the reference to "situations that challenge one's identity", which can include a very wide range of situations) it makes it hard to find settings that do *not* qualify as 'religious'—thereby suppressing the very motivational difference between credences and beliefs that Van Leeuwen is trying to establish.

[22] As a reader for OUP helpfully pointed out, Van Leeuwen's practical setting requirement looks even more problematic if we consider examples of pervasive religious behaviours which result from norms concerning eating, dressing, cross-sex relations, and other key aspects of our everyday lives. If a 'religious setting representation' were indeed necessary to motivate religious actions, religious people who routinely adopt those behaviours should be almost *constantly* representing themselves to be in a religious setting. For the reasons we have seen, this is an implausible requirement; and, again, it would make unclear in which sense religious credences are motivationally more circumscribed than beliefs.

cases where that requirement is implausible. As various philosophers (Van Leeuwen included) suggest, actions like kissing the picture of your loved one when you miss her/him are imagination-driven: you act out of the imagining that kissing the picture *is* actually kissing your loved one. In cases like this, you don't need to (nor, indeed, typically do you) take yourself to be in a pretence setting in order to be moved to act: all you need is a desire to kiss your loved one, which will pair up with your imagining that you can do that by kissing the picture.[23] Other examples of imagination-driven actions where the pretence setting representation condition would be implausible include actions performed out of self-deception (Gendler 2010: Ch.8), out of delusion (Currie and Ravenscroft 2002: Ch.8), and out of implicit bias (Sullivan-Bissett 2019).

Of course, there are also cases in which imaginings do not motivate any action—like some classic cases of daydreams. But we know already that this is true of all cognitive attitudes—whose motivational power is only manifested under certain conditions. Van Leeuwen does not show that these conditions are peculiar in cases of imaginings, differentiating them from religious attitudes and beliefs.

As we have seen, Van Leeuwen identifies also some other features that are supposed to set religious attitudes apart from other secondary cognitive attitudes: susceptibility to free elaboration, vulnerability to special authority, and perceived normative orientation. However, these are features that characterize also paradigmatic instances of imaginings. For instance, as Van Leeuwen himself explicitly recognizes (2014: 711), daydream imaginings are clearly susceptible to the sort of free elaboration that he describes. And imaginings in response to fiction are clearly vulnerable to special authority—most notably, the special authority of the author. As to perceived normative orientation—i.e., that property by virtue of which actions guided by religious attitudes are taken to be *ipso facto* virtuous—it not clear whether it should be understood as a functional property or a normative one. If the latter is the case, it would matter less to the present inquiry, which is primarily concerned with religious attitudes' functional status. But anyway, again, it seems to be a property that at least some kinds of imaginings are likely to display (for instance, the imaginings one might form in response to moralistic fictional tales); and Van Leeuwen does not provide any reason to think otherwise.

This is why the weight of his argument for distinguishing religious attitudes from imaginings rests upon their alleged motivational differences. Given that, as we have seen, such differences do not hold, there seem to be no grounds to draw the distinction at a functional level. Functionally speaking, religious attitudes are best classified as imaginings.

---

[23] For accounts along these lines, see e.g., Velleman (2000); Currie and Ravenscroft (2002: Ch. 6); Van Leeuwen (2016); Ichino (2019).

5.1 Imagination and Belief—Again

What I have just argued suggests that motivational factors are insufficient to distinguish religious attitudes not only from imaginings, but also from beliefs. Yet, in §§2–4 I showed that there are other important reasons to distinguish religious attitudes from beliefs: reasons based on their (non-evidential) inputs, their inferential properties, and their linguistic correlates. This is where I diverge from the other critics of Van Leeuwen I mentioned above—such as Boudry and Coyne (2016) and Levy (2017)—who not only reject Van Leeuwen's claim that religious attitudes and beliefs differ with respect to motivational outputs, but deny altogether that they differ in *any* substantial respects—contending that religious attitudes are, after all, genuine beliefs.

Importantly, these authors recognize that religious attitudes are by and large insensitive to evidence and incoherent with many other beliefs that religious people hold. But their point is that this is true also of various other states that we commonly qualify as beliefs—such as some 'beliefs' in pseudoscience or in conspiracy theories (Boudry and Coyne 2016: 607; Levy 2017: 113).

Whilst I agree with them that, alongside religious attitudes, there are various other cases where mental states that lack evidence-sensitivity and coherent integration motivate us to act in relevant ways, I think that—insofar as this is true—it may well be a good reason to recognize that (at least some of) the mental states in question are *not beliefs, either*.[24] In other words, rather than inducing us to broaden our category of belief so as to also include states that lack relevant degrees of evidence-sensitivity and coherent integration, attitudes towards pseudo-scientific or conspiracy theories provide further reason to recognize that mental states other than beliefs motivate actions more often than we commonly think.

Indeed, our category of belief is already broad and heterogeneous enough, allowing for many different sorts of evidence to which beliefs respond (e.g., perceptual, testimonial, introspective evidence)—corresponding to different sorts of beliefs (i.e., perceptual, testimonial, introspective beliefs). I don't think we should broaden it *even more*, including in it also states that are by and large insensitive to any sort of evidence whatsoever. We shouldn't, also because for states of this latter sort we do possess a better category: imagination.

Of course, imagination on this view turns out to be a broad and heterogenous category, too—no less than belief is. As there are different sorts of evidence to which beliefs respond, so there are different sorts of evidence-insensitive factors to which imaginings respond. To say that religious attitudes are better qualified as imaginings than as beliefs, then, does not mean that they are *just like* any other

---

[24] I defend this view in relation to 'beliefs' in pseudoscience, superstition, and conspiracy theories in Ichino (2018, 2022), Ichino and Raikka (2020), and Ichino (2022). For a discussion of these and other similar sorts of 'beliefs', see Levy (this volume).

imaginings we are familiar with. It simply means that they fit better in the broad functional category of imagination, than in that of belief.

This, however, shouldn't suggest that the difference between Van Leeuwen's and my own position is mostly terminological, with his 'credence' being simply a finer-grained category that picks up a sub-class of my 'imaginings'. His credences and my imaginings are functionally distinguished by their motivating powers. Credences can motivate only in religious settings. Imaginings motivate across different settings, as beliefs do; and I have argued that they are therefore better suited to characterize religious attitudes, which do indeed motivate in a heterogeneous variety of situations.

Van Leeuwen (2017b) advances a further reason—somewhat independent from functional considerations—to resist this conclusion. Classifying religious attitudes as imaginings, he observes, might suggest that religious people are *fakers*—which is obviously an undesirable consequence. Indeed, religious people do a number of things that manifest religious *beliefs*—including, most notably, publicly avowing them as such. And someone who avows to believe something that in fact she just imagines, is arguably a faker.

Whilst I agree that charging religious people with insincerity would be undesirable, however, I don't think this is an unavoidable consequence of the view that religious attitudes are imaginings. To conclude my defence of such view, I will show how this consequence can be avoided, suggesting two alternative interpretations of religious believers' avowals—which correspond to two different forms that religious imaginings commonly take.

6. Two Forms of Religious Imaginings—and Their Place in Religious Faith

Van Leeuwen's observation raises an important point. On the view I defended, religious people avow to believe something that in fact they do not believe, but just imagine. I owe an explanation of why religious people make such avowals.

As I said, I grant that insincerity cannot be the norm. But there at least two other plausible interpretations of religious avowals which do not involve any insincerity or hypocrisy.

On the one hand, we may take such avowals literally, as genuine expressions of belief, thereby holding religious people to have faulty self-knowledge. On the other hand, we may take religious beliefs' avowals to be made with the intention of communicating something different from their literal meaning: rather than revealing faulty self-knowledge, they could be lucid expressions of (a specific form of) imaginative attitude. These interpretations correspond to two different forms in which religious imaginings may come.

Sometimes, they will be 'misrecognized imaginings'. Roughly, what may happen in such cases is that some powerful mental state—such as fear of death, a desire for meaning, or for social homologation—blurs religious people's view of their minds, and in particular it shuts out their awareness that God's existence is purely imagined, leading them to believe that they believe it.[25] In cases like these, the relevant non-doxastic factors (such as emotions, desires, or social pressures) that are causally responsible for the metacognitive mistake are not recognized as such by religious people. This might well involve some epistemic irrationality on their part; but no insincerity.

More often, however, the imaginative nature of religious attitudes is likely to be correctly identified as such by religious people, who deliberately allow imagination to play an expanded role in their lives. To understand how this might happen, we should note that belief is 'negation incomplete': there are propositions that a subject neither believes nor disbelieves. The fact that religious people do not believe that God exists, thus, does not imply that they believe that God does *not* exist. They may simply lack a definite belief about whether God exists or not, while having an inclination (perhaps arising from their spiritual experiences), or a preference (perhaps arising from a need for meaning, or even from a rational calculus) for the view that he exists. Their penchant for such a view makes religious people willing to entertain the corresponding imaginings, i.e., to 'make-believe' that such a view is true—since this provides a good approximation to the experience that they would have if it were indeed true. And in order to make-believe at best that p is the case, one should behave, to some extent at least, as if she believed that p; hence she might also end up avowing to believe so. If, on the contrary, she avowed to merely imagine that, this would damage her participation in the quasi-experience of God's existence (cf. Walton 1990: Part IV).

This can explain why religious people avow beliefs in God, while being aware that their attitudes are not really beliefs. But note that, in so doing, they might not be merely *pretending to avow* a belief. By means of such a pretence they might well be *seriously avowing* a different attitude:[26] an attitude of *faith*, which, in turn, can be seen as involving a decision to give space in their lives to an imagining—an imagining that they do not take as mere fiction, but rather as a serious hypothesis through which to look at, and make sense of, the world.

As I said, I take this latter, more mindful, form in which religious imaginings may come, to be more common than the first, 'misrecognized' form I described.

---

[25] Similar mistakes are not implausible: empirical research tells us that our knowledge of our own minds is far from perfect (as phenomena like so-called 'choice blindness' and confabulation indicate—see Carruthers 2010 for review and discussion). This said, as I am about to argue, I do not take such mistakes to be the norm among religious people.

[26] What I have in mind here is something similar to what happens in irony, according to the 'pretence theory' of such phenomenon (see e.g., Currie 2006): by *pretending to say* something (e.g., "What a lovely sunny day!"), we may *seriously say* something else ("What a dreadful rainy day!").

102   BELIEF, IMAGINATION, AND DELUSION

But it is of course possible for the latter to harden into the first: when you give much space to an imagining in your life, you may end up believing that you believe it.

6.1 Religious Imaginings and Religious Faith

Importantly, to say that religious faith *involves* religious imaginings does not mean that it *amounts* to them. Faith is a complex stance which involves different psychological dimensions—among which here I've only examined the cognitive one.[27] Providing an exhaustive account of faith that also encompasses its other non-cognitive dimensions is not part of the present project. To conclude, however, I wish to highlight the good fit between my view and some accounts of faith that have recently been defended.

Howard-Snyder (2013, 2019), for instance, has argued that often the cognitive component of faith is not belief, but 'assumption': a propositional cognitive attitude that he characterizes as functionally similar, but not identical, to belief—in a way almost overlapping with the way in which I have characterized the imaginative attitude.[28] And although he does not exclude that the cognitive component of faith *might* also be a belief, his multidimensional model of faith's functional architecture suggests that imaginings are actually much better suited than beliefs to play the relevant role. According to his model:

Faith that p is a complex propositional attitude consisting of:

(i) a positive evaluation of p,
(ii) a positive conative orientation toward p,
(iii) a positive cognitive stance toward p, and
(iv) resilience to new counter-evidence to p. (Howard-Snyder 2013: 370)

It is not hard to see why imaginings are much better candidates than beliefs to fill the cognitive slot of this model—i.e., its component (iii). The reason why it is so, has to do with two other components of the model: (ii) and (iv).

As to (iv), insofar as faith involves resilience to counterevidence, surely cognitive states like imaginings, that are by their very nature unconstrained by evidence and responsive to the will, fit better with it than beliefs, which are—and ought to be—evidence-sensitive at least to some degree.

Something similar holds with respect to (ii), according to which faith that p involves "a positive conative orientation towards p"—which Howard-Snyder

---

[27] Other non-cognitive dimensions of faith that are standardly identified include affective, evaluative, and volitional ones (see Howard-Snyder's account considered below for discussion).

[28] Although Howard-Snyder does not make any reference to the philosophy of imagination literature, indeed, the idea that assuming (or 'supposing') is a sub-type of propositional imagination has been defended by various authors (for a review, see Currie and Ravenscroft 2002: Ch. 2).

characterizes as "a desire for p's truth" (2013: 367). Indeed, there seems to be some psychological tension—or at least some oddity—in desiring and believing one and the same proposition at the same time. Generally speaking, if I desire p to be true, acquiring the belief that p is indeed true is likely to extinguish my desire (possibly giving way to 'happiness' about p, or to some other positive appraisal of p—but those are different, no more conative, states). Vice versa, desiring something to be true is typically associated with imagining scenarios in which it is so: this is indeed the way in which much of our daydreams and fantasies come about (cf. Velleman 2000; Currie and Ravenscroft 2002). Hence, again, insofar as faith that p requires a positive conation towards p, imaginings will fit better with it than beliefs.

As it turns out, then, the account of religious (cognitive) attitudes that I defended in this chapter is not only compatible with the account of religious faith defended by Howard-Snyder, but it gains support from it: insofar as his account is true, it makes my account more likely to be true. Moreover, my account indicates a way in which Howard-Snyder's account might be sharpened, showing that some states are better suited than others to play the relevant cognitive role in his model.

This makes room to envisage similarly fruitful connections also between my account and other non-doxastic accounts of faith. An exhaustive discussion of these accounts will have to wait for a different occasion; but hopefully what I argued in this chapter lays the basis for that.

7. Conclusion

I have defended the view that many instances of religious attitudes are best characterized as imaginings. I have discounted some apparently obvious reasons to classify them as beliefs, as well as Van Leeuwen's reasons to classify them as "credences". I have argued that religious attitudes' functional profile matches neatly that of paradigmatic imaginative states, showing that this view does not have the undesirable consequences that it may *prima facie* seem to have. It does not force us to say that religious people are hypocrites, nor that they have faulty self-knowledge. On the contrary, it helps us to make more rational sense of their sincere religious avowals. This view fits nicely with some recent accounts of the multidimensional nature of faith, laying the basis for a more comprehensive picture of the religious mind.

Acknowledgements

This chapter has a long story. I wrote its original draft in 2011, as the first chapter of my PhD dissertation (it then ended up being its last chapter—as I realized that in order to argue for the imaginative nature of so-called 'religious belief' I first needed an extensive inquiry into the nature of imagination and belief themselves). Since then, I have presented it in many places and talked about it with many people, whose feedback has been really important to develop and refine my view. Among them, I wish to thank in particular Greg Currie, Paul L. Harris, Komarine Rohmden-Romluc, Shen-yi Liao, Lisa Bortolotti, Stefano Predelli, Kengo Miyazono, Dave Ingram, Tim Bayne, Hanna Pickard, Bence Nanay, Alon Chasid, and Paolo Spinicci. Last but not least, I'm very grateful to Ema Sullivan-Bissett, for her precious comments and also for encouraging me to get this published and giving me the chance to do that in this volume.

References

Alston, W. (1991). *Perceiving God: The Epistemology of Religious Experience*. Ithaca, NY: Cornell University Press.

Astuti, R. and Harris, P. L. (2008). "Understanding Mortality and the Life of the Ancestors in Rural Madagascar", *Cognitive Science*, 3, 4: 713–40.

Barrett, J. (1998). "Cognitive Constraints on Hindu Concepts of the Divine", *Journal for the Scientific Study of Religion*, 37, 4: 608–19.

Barrett, J. (2004). *Why Would Anyone Believe in God?* Lanham, MD: AltaMira Press.

Barrett, J. and Keil, F. (1996). "Conceptualizing a Non-Natural Entity: Anthropomorphism in God Concepts", *Cognitive Psychology*, 31: 220–47.

Barth, K. (1964/2003). *God Here and Now*. New York: Routledge.

Boudry, M. and Coyne, J. (2016). "Disbelief in Belief: On the Cognitive Status of Supernatural Beliefs", *Philosophical Psychology*, 29: 601–15.

Boyer, P. (2001). *Religion Explained*. New York: Vintage Books.

Carruthers, P. (2010). "Introspection: Divided and Partly Eliminated", *Philosophy and Phenomenological Research*, 80: 76–111.

Crane, T. (2017). *The Meaning of Belief: Religion from an Atheist's Point of View*. Cambridge, MA: Harvard University Press.

Currie, G. (2006). "Why Irony is Pretence", in S. Nichols (ed.), *The Architecture of the Imagination: New Essays on Pretence, Possibility, and Fiction*. Oxford: Clarendon Press, 111–34.

Currie, G. and Ravenscroft, I. (2002). *Recreative Minds: Imagination in Philosophy and Psychology*. Oxford: Oxford University Press.

Dennett, D. and Plantinga, A. (2011). *Science and Religion: Are They Compatible?* Oxford: Oxford University Press.

Edelman, B. (2009). "Markets: Red Light States: Who Buys Online Adult Entertainment?", *Journal of Economic Perspectives*, 23: 209–20.

Egan, A. (2008). "Imagination, Delusion, and Self-Deception", in T. Bayne and J. Fernández (eds.), *Delusion and Self-Deception: Affective Influences on Belief Formation*. New York: Psychology Press, 263–80.

Festinger, L., Riecken, H., and Schachter, S. (1956). *When Prophecy Fails: A Social and Psychological Study of a Modern Group That Predicted the Destruction of the World.* New York: Harper Torchbooks.

Gendler, T. (2010). *Intuitions, Imagination, and Philosophical Methodology.* Oxford: Oxford University Press.

Harris, P. L. (2012). *Trusting What You Are Told: How Children Learn from Others.* Cambridge, MA: Harvard University Press.

Harris, P. L. and Corriveau, K. (2014). "Learning from Testimony about Religion and Science", in E. Robinson and S. Einav (eds.), *Trust and Skepticism: Children's Selective Learning from Testimony.* New York: Psychology Press, 28–41.

Harris, P. L. and Giménez, M. (2005). "Children's Acceptance of Conflicting Testimony: The Case of Death", *Journal of Cognition and Culture*, 5: 143–64.

Harris, P. L. and Koenig, M. (2006). "Trust in Testimony: How Children Learn about Science and Religion", *Child Development*, 77: 505–24.

Howard-Snyder, D. (2013). "Propositional Faith: What It Is and What It Is Not", *American Philosophical Quarterly*, 50: 357–72.

Howard-Snyder, D. (2019). "Three Arguments to Think That Faith Does Not Entail Belief", *Pacific Philosophical Quarterly*, 100: 114–28.

Ichino, A. (2018). "Superstitious Confabulations", *Topoi: An International Review of Philosophy*, 39: 203–17.

Ichino, A. (2019). "Imagination and Belief in Action", *Philosophia*, 47: 1517–38.

Ichino, A. and Raikka, J. (2020). "Non-Doxastic Conspiracy Theories", *Argumenta*, 11: 1–18.

Ichino, A. (2022). "Conspiracy Theories as Walt-Fiction", in P. Engisch and J. Langkau (eds.), *The Philosophy of Fiction: Imagination and Cognition.* New York: Routledge, 240–61.

James, W. (1902/2008). *The Varieties of Religious Experience.* New York: Routledge.

Kung, H. (1976). *On Being a Christian.* New York: Doubleday & Company.

Lazar, A. (1999). "Deceiving Oneself or Self-Deceived?", *Mind*, 108: 265–90.

Leslie, A. (1987). "Pretense and Representation: The Origins of 'Theory of Mind'", *Psychological Review*, 94: 412–26.

Levy, N. (2017). "Religious Beliefs Are Factual Beliefs", *Cognition*, 161: 109–16.

Lipton, P. (2007). "Science and Religion: The Immersion Solution", in A. Moore and M. Scott (eds.), *Realism and Religion.* Aldershot: Ashgate, 31–46.

Luhrmann, T. (2012). *When God Talks Back: Understanding the American Evangelical Relationship with God.* New York: Vintage Books.

McCormick, M. (2015). *Believing Against the Evidence: Agency and the Ethics of Belief.* New York: Routledge.

Pascal, B. (1670). *Pensées.* Paris: Port Royal.

Price, H. H. (1969). *Belief: The Gifford Lectures.* Muirhead Library of Philosophy. London: George Allen & Unwin.

106 BELIEF, IMAGINATION, AND DELUSION

Ratzinger, J. (2011). *Porta Fidei*. http://w2.vatican.va/content/benedict-xvi/en/motu_proprio/documents/hf_ben-xvi_motu-proprio_20111011_porta-fidei.html.

Rinard, S. (2018). "Believing for Practical Reasons", *Noûs*, 4: 763–84.

Schellenberg, J. L. (2005). *Prolegomena to a Philosophy of Religion*. Cornell University Press.

Sullivan-Bissett, E. (2019). "Biased by Our Imaginings", *Mind & Language*, 34: 627–47.

Sullivan-Bissett, E. (2023). "Implicit Bias and Processing", in R. Thompson (ed.), *The Routledge Handbook of Philosophy and Implicit Cognition*. New York: Routledge, 115–26.

Van Leeuwen, N. (2014). "Religious Credence Is Not Factual Belief", *Cognition*, 133: 698–715.

Van Leeuwen, N. (2016). "Imagination and Action", in A. Kind (eds.), *The Routledge Handbook of Philosophy of Imagination*. Routledge, 111–23.

Van Leeuwen, N. (2017a). "Two Paradigms for Religious Representation: The Physicist and the Playground (a Reply to Levy)", *Cognition*, 164: 206–11.

Van Leeuwen, N. (2017b). "Beyond Fakers and Fanatics: A Reply to Boudry and Coyne", *Philosophical Psychology*, 29: 1–6.

Velleman, J. D. (2000). *The Possibility of Practical Reason*. Oxford: Clarendon Press.

Walton, K. L. (1990). *Mimesis as Make-Believe: On the Foundations of the Representational Arts*. Cambridge, MA: Harvard University Press.

Williams, B. (1973). "Deciding to Believe", in *Problems of the Self*. Cambridge: Cambridge University Press, 136–51.

Woolley, J. (2000). "The Development of Beliefs about Direct Mental-Physical Causality in Imagination, Magic and Religion", in K. Rosengren, P. L. Harris, and C. Johnson (eds.), *Imagining the Impossible*. Cambridge: Cambridge University Press, 99–129.

Zygmunt, J. F. (1970). "Prophetic Failure and Chiliastic Identity: The Case of Jehovah's Witnesses", *American Journal of Sociology*, 75: 926–48.

6

On the Place of Imagination in the Architecture of the Mind

Michael Omoge

1. Introduction

Standardly, when mapping out the functional connections between various components of the mind, the approach is to treat imagination as a functionally distinct propositional attitude on par with belief. That is, in the cognitive architecture of the mind, belief-like imagination is treated as an attitude that can take propositional contents and interact with various psychological mechanisms. This architectural framework has been useful in clarifying the epistemic roles of propositional imagination in pretence (e.g., Carruthers 2006b), thought experiments (e.g., Nichols 2008), modal epistemology (e.g., Omoge 2021), creativity (e.g., Carruthers 2006a), mindreading (e.g., Nichols and Stich 2003), fiction (e.g., Nichols 2004), delusion (e.g., Miyazono, this volume), and so on. Call all these views *cognitive support*.

Philosophers often take cognitive support to encompass two claims: (i) imagination has a space in the architecture of the mind, and (ii) perception-like (or experiential) imagination is excluded in architecture talk.[1] However, (ii) has been used to challenge (i). According to a view that we might call *cognitive dissent*, imagination has no space in the architecture of the mind ('cognitive architecture', hereafter) not least because imagination is not limited to propositional imagination which is the prerogative in architecture talk—there is also experiential imagination—but also because both experiential and propositional imagination share identical neural substrates with perception and language, respectively (Carruthers 2002, 2006a). Consequently, cognitive dissent holds that experiential and propositional imagination are by-products of perception and language, respectively, and, so, what we need to make space for in cognitive architecture are the latter, not the former.

---

[1] There are other kinds of imagination besides the propositional and experiential kinds, however, e.g., objectual, conceptual, spontaneous, and so on. In short, imagination is notoriously heterogeneous (see, e.g., Kind 2013).

Michael Omoge, *On the Place of Imagination in the Architecture of the Mind* In: *Belief, Imagination, and Delusion.* Edited by: Ema Sullivan-Bissett, Oxford University Press. © Oxford University Press 2024. DOI: 10.1093/oso/9780198872221.003.0006

108 BELIEF, IMAGINATION, AND DELUSION

But if cognitive dissent is correct, then the above-listed theories that build the epistemic roles of imagination against the backdrop of cognitive support have been built on quicksand. For if imagination has no space in cognitive architecture, then what does it matter if there are epistemic and psychological phenomena "that can be used to test [cognitive support's] explanatory power and empirical adequacy" (Miyazono and Liao 2016: 235)? The situation would just be like the case of seventeenth-century scientists using phlogiston to explain physical phenomena, all of which crumbled when it was discovered that phlogiston is nonexistent.

The aim of this chapter is to debunk cognitive dissent. My central claim is that if indeed experiential and propositional imagination are by-products of perception and language, respectively, then the relationship between the former must reflect the relationship between the latter. Using two household findings, I argue that this is not so. First, cognitive neuroscience, as supported by perceptual foundationalism, says that there is a double dissociation between perception and language, and, so, they are indirectly connected in cognitive architecture. Second, aphantasia shows that there is a single dissociation between experiential and propositional imagination, and, so, they are directly connected in cognitive architecture. The failure of these household findings to map onto each other, I argue, falsifies cognitive dissent. As a positive spin, I argue that cognitive support succeeds in mapping them onto one another, doing so by rejecting cognitive dissent's claim that experiential and propositional imagination share the same neural substrates with perception and language. In the end, I will have argued that imagination does have its own space in cognitive architecture.[2]

This chapter will proceed as follows. I begin by discussing cognitive support (Section 2), so as to motivate and clarify cognitive dissent (Section 3). Once clarified, I proceed to show how cognitive dissent fails to map the two household findings—i.e., cognitive neuroscience on the relationship between perception and language, and aphantasia on the relationship between experiential and propositional imagination—onto each other (Section 4). In Section 5, I argue that cognitive support succeeds in so mapping them. I conclude in Section 6. But before I begin, let me give one brief clarification.

---

[2] Note that this debate cuts across other debates in the philosophy of imagination, e.g., the debate about whether propositional imagination and supposition are distinct attitudes (e.g., Arcangeli 2017). One can agree or disagree about this issue and still be either a cognitive supporter or dissenter, however. Carruthers (2002, 2006a), a cognitive dissenter, agrees with Nichols and Stich (2003)—who are cognitive supporters—that propositional imagination and supposition are not distinct attitudes. It is also possible for a cognitive dissenter or supporter to take propositional imagination and supposition to be distinct attitudes. A cognitive dissenter would only need to be clear on how the psychological processes dedicated to the formation of propositional imagination are distinct from those dedicated to the formation of supposition. On the flip side, Weinberg and Meskin (2006)—who are cognitive supporters—have already shown how the psychological processes dedicated to the formation of propositional imagination are different from those dedicated to the formation of supposition.

IMAGINATION IN THE ARCHITECTURE OF THE MIND   109

I take it to be clear that this chapter engages with the tradition that there is propositional imagination, even though the tradition has been challenged by a view we might call *cognitive denial* (see, e.g., Langland-Hassan 2012). But in order to be clear about the theoretical status of cognitive dissent, I will occasionally juxtapose it with cognitive denial as we progress.

2. Cognitive Support

Cognitive support says that propositional imagination deserves its own space in cognitive architecture. This is often done in boxology terms, i.e., with boxes and arrows representing mental components and the connections between them, respectively.[3] On this interpretation, cognitive support amounts to saying that there is a box for imagination, which is connected to different mental components. This does not, however, mean that imaginings share a spatial location in the mind, but that they share an important cluster of causal and functional properties that other representation types (e.g., beliefs) lack. Theorists who talk about imagination in boxology terms include but are not limited to Shaun Nichols and Stephen Stich (2003), Jonathan Weinberg and Aaron Meskin (2006), and Susanna Schellenberg (2013).[4] And works that rely on these theories to explain imagination's diverse epistemic roles are plentiful—I listed some in the opening paragraph of Section 1. In short, cognitive support is the dominant position in the literature.

Talk of boxes as representatives of mental attitudes in cognitive architecture is sometimes weakly taken to signify the functional (but not content) distinction between different mental attitudes. For example, the content 'I am wealthy' can be taken up by a belief or an imagining, such that I can simultaneously believe and imagine that 'I am wealthy', although the belief will be truth conducive in ways that the imagining will not be. (See Kind, this volume, for a discussion of the difference between belief and imagination in terms of truth conduciveness.) But by talking in terms of the belief and imagination boxes such that the above belief and imagining are in their respective boxes, which then suggests that they can get connected up to different mental components, the message is clear: even though belief and imagination can take the same content, they sometimes interact with different mental components leading to them having different causal and functional properties, and playing different epistemic and psychological roles. While this way of distinguishing between belief and imagination (as well as other mental

---

[3] Though this boxology framework has been criticized as being unfruitful in theorizing about imagination (see, e.g., Stock 2011), it is integral to the current debate, and, so, I will retain it.

[4] This literature diverges, however. Some (e.g., Nichols and Stich 2003; Weinberg and Meskin 2006) say there is only one imagination box; others (Currie and Ravenscroft 2002) say there are two imagination boxes; a minority (Schellenberg 2013) says there is only one belief/imagination continuum box. See Liao and Doggett (2014), and Miyazono and Liao (2016) for overviews.

110 BELIEF, IMAGINATION, AND DELUSION

attitudes) has helped to simplify matters, there is a stronger notion at work in talk of boxes beyond merely giving a map of the mental vis-à-vis imagination's place therein.

Talk of boxes as representatives of mental attitudes in cognitive architecture is also taken to signify the psychological processes involved in the formation of the representation tokens that get stored inside the boxes. Notably, Nichols and Stich's (2003) cognitive support account describes such a process for imagination. According to them, this process requires the synergized operation of two mental components: an 'imagination generator' that generates and embellishes imaginings, and an 'imagination box' that is a temporary workspace and storeroom where this generation and embellishment occur.[5] These mental components, according to Nichols and Stich, constitute the cognitive architecture of imagination, i.e., they are the psychological mechanisms dedicated to the formation of imagination. In short, they constitute the internal structure of imagination. For clarity purposes, I will refer to the mental components collectively as the 'imagination system'. I will say more about the imagination system in Section 5. For now, it suffices to say that although other cognitive supporters do not explicitly describe an imagination system, I read them as implicitly endorsing Nichols and Stich's account, i.e., their talk of 'cognitive architecture of imagination' entails that some dedicated psychological processes underlie imagination formation.

In this stronger sense, the intention with architecture talk about imagination extends beyond merely giving a map of the mental vis-à-vis the place of imagination therein; rather, it includes the specific kind of mapping involved in allocating imagination such place. This stronger sense is what sets cognitive dissent on edge: it denies that imagination has such a space.

3. Cognitive Dissent

Critiquing Nichols and Stich's cognitive support account, Peter Carruthers gives what I will take to be the core thesis of cognitive dissent. I will quote him at length:

> Now, I doubt whether there is any reason to think that the '[imagination] box' required the creation of any new adaptation. Surely, already-existing working-memory systems could have been co-opted for the job. But the [imagination] generator is another matter. For on this model it looks as if it would have required the creation of a whole new type of propositional attitude (distinct

---

[5] Though Nichols and Stich call the imagination generator, 'script elaborator', I prefer 'imagination generator' because it aligns with my narration. They also postulate another mechanism—the 'UpDater'—which uses relevant beliefs to modify imaginings. I skip the UpDater here because they say it also works in belief formation, and, so, it is not *dedicated* to imagination formation. In addition, as we will see shortly, cognitive dissent also skips it in its criticism of cognitive support.

from either belief or desire, nor reducible to combinations thereof) in order for imaginative thinking [...] to make its appearance in the hominid lineage [...] But actually there is some reason to think that imagination comes in at least two forms, each of which would be provided 'for free' by the evolution of other faculties. First, there is experiential imagination—namely, the capacity to form and manipulate images relating to a given sense modality (visual, auditory, and so on). There is some reason to think that a basic capacity for this sort of imagination is a by-product of the conceptualizing processes inherent in the various perceptual input-systems [...] Second, there is propositional imagination. This is the capacity to form and consider a propositional representation without commitment to its truth or desirability. There is some reason to think that this capacity comes to us 'for free' too, this time with language. (2002: 241–2)

Carruthers sets the stage for cognitive dissent right from the beginning of this passage. He agrees that we have a capacity for "imaginative thinking", which is "distinct from either belief or desire" and not "reducible to combinations thereof". That is, he does not deny that imagination is a distinct mental attitude, and, so, he is not a cognitive denier. Rather, he seems to be pushing for a substantive view about imagination formation, one that is different from what cognitive support says. What view?

By contrasting imagination with belief, Carruthers acknowledges cognitive support's claim that only propositional (i.e., belief-like) imagination is involved in architecture talk. However, his swift transition—which begins from "But actually there is some reason to think that imagination comes in at least two forms" (2002: 241)—shows that he has some misgivings about this claim. Thus, he calls for the inclusion of experiential imagination in architecture talk. But once we include it, he says, we see that experiential and propositional imagination share the same neural substrates with perception and language, respectively, and so, what we need to accommodate in cognitive architecture are perception and language, not experiential and propositional imagination, since the latter will be the by-products of the former (Fig. 6.1). Hence, he says: "the supposer need not be an additional cognitive faculty, with any distinct neural realization" (2002: 242). If we read 'supposer' as 'imagination system', then Carruthers is simply saying that in cognitive architecture, there is no imagination system. There are no psychological processes dedicated to imagination formation. How, then, are imaginings formed?

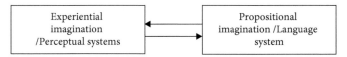

Fig. 6.1 Cognitive dissent.

112 BELIEF, IMAGINATION, AND DELUSION

Since cognitive dissent says experiential and propositional imagination are by-products of perception and language, respectively, it is saying that the psychological processes at work in experiential and propositional imagination formation are those belonging to perception and language, respectively. Think of how there are no mechanisms dedicated to the production of the smoke from your car exhaust; rather, the car engine produces it as a by-product—the mechanisms belong to the car, not the smoke. Thus, in denying that there is an imagination system, cognitive dissent is saying that imagination has no internal structure:

> [In Nichols and Stich's model, imagination] has significant internal structure, sometimes including separate sub-components, innately structured learning mechanisms, and socially acquired information of various sorts [...] But it should be clear that their theory faces problems and challenges that don't exist on my own account, which for the most part, utilizes pre-existing systems and pre-existing connections amongst systems. (Carruthers 2006a: 176, 322–3)

Thus characterized, cognitive dissent is not internally contradictory: it does not countenance imagination as a distinct mental attitude that can be individuated without saying something about the individuation, i.e., without saying how imaginings are formed in ways that distinguish them from other attitudes (e.g., beliefs). Cognitive dissent has a positive thesis about experiential and propositional imagination formation, the thesis is just reductive, reducing it to the psychological processes involved in perceptual and language operations, respectively.

If so, then, like cognitive support, cognitive dissent is a substantive view about the place of imagination in cognitive architecture, differing only in terms of what it means by 'the *place* of imagination'. Put differently, both cognitive support and cognitive dissent talk in terms of the 'cognitive architecture of imagination', but they mean different things by it. Where cognitive support means that imagination has a space in cognitive architecture, cognitive dissent means that imagination lacks any such space. Where cognitive support means that imagination has an internal structure, cognitive dissent means that it lacks any such structure. Where cognitive support means that some psychological processes are dedicated to imagination formation, cognitive dissent means that there are no such dedicated processes.

This then explains why even though Carruthers realizes how cognitive dissent only differs from cognitive support in terms of the place of imagination in cognitive architecture, he nonetheless doubles down on the difference between both views by emphasizing how cognitive support's claim of an internal structure complicates things:

> Taken in one way, there is no inconsistency between [Nichols and Stich's] proposals and [mine]. There is some reason to think that Nichols and Stich don't merely intend their model in this weak way, however [...] We can read

IMAGINATION IN THE ARCHITECTURE OF THE MIND   113

Nichols and Stich's account more robustly and realistically, then—taking their box-and-arrow diagrams to postulate a set of distinct interacting systems, not just as labels for a set of capacities. And read in this way, the account really is in direct competition with my own. Whether or not Nichols and Stich themselves intend their account in this stronger way, I propose to evaluate it in that light.

(Carruthers 2006a: 318–19)

In this way, we can clearly define the difference between cognitive dissent and cognitive denial. Where cognitive denial eliminates imagination as a distinct mental attitude by reducing it to other attitudes, cognitive dissent eliminates imagination as a cognitive structure by reducing it to pre-existing structures. Also, cognitive denial implies cognitive dissent, but not conversely. Once you deny that imagination is an attitude, you *ipso facto* deny that it has an internal structure, but you can deny that it has an internal structure without denying that it is an attitude.

Thus characterized, cognitive dissent is not only plausible but also appealing. For one, it has an explanatory power that matches cognitive support. For example, Carruthers (2006a) uses it to explain our capacity for scientific reasoning, whereas cognitive support has not been so used, although cognitive support has been applied in areas where cognitive dissent has not, e.g., personal identity (Nichols 2008). For another, cognitive dissent seems to have evolutionary support. As Carruthers says, experiential and propositional imagination are "provided 'for free' by the evolution of other faculties" (2002: 241). Put simply, cognitive dissent takes experiential and propositional imagination to be 'evolutionary spandrels', where spandrels are phenotypic or cognitive characteristics that are not direct products of adaptive selection but by-products of the evolution of some other characteristics (Gould and Lewontin 1979).[6]

---

[6] Might this spandrel issue add more weight to the claim that imagination lacks an internal structure? No doubt, it is true that if imagination was not initially selected for its own adaptive value, then that might explain why one would think it lacks an internal structure. How would such an internal structure come about if evolution did not set out to construct it, it might be asked? But as McDermott says, evolution is "more of a question stopper than a question answerer" (2007: 133), and, so, this spandrel question is better treated independently.

There is also another aspect of cognitive dissent I will leave for future consideration. The imagination system, we have seen, refers to the two mental components that (cognitive support says) are involved in imagination formation: the imagination generator and the imagination box (Section 2). But the aspect of cognitive support that questions imagination's internal structure only concerns the imagination generator, i.e., how imaginings are formed/generated. The other mental component, i.e., the imagination box, which represents where imaginings are stored and manipulated is left out, and the aspect of cognitive dissent that concerns it is spelled out in this claim: "Now, I doubt whether there is any reason to think that the '[imagination] box' required the creation of any new adaptation. Surely, already-existing working-memory systems could have been co-opted for the job" (Carruthers 2002: 241). To understand how this claim leads to the conclusion that the imagination box is also not needed, we need to bring in Carruthers (2011, 2013). In those works, Carruthers argues that propositional attitudes are fundamentally unconscious and that they become active and accessible to a wide range of consumer

114 BELIEF, IMAGINATION, AND DELUSION

It might be asked then that if cognitive dissent is this appealing, why is it not being talked about? My suspicion is that, despite its allure, cognitive dissent can easily slip into cognitive support, such that unless carefully disentangled as I have done here, it might not even be apparent that one is a cognitive dissenter. This might, in fact, be true of Carruthers: he may not be aware of the full ramifications of the view he espouses in his (2002) and (2006a). More on this in Section 6. For now, it suffices to say that cognitive dissent might be taken not just as a minority view but also as one that is dying out. I want to offer my voice as a final nail in the coffin.

My argument is simple. Cognitive dissent's view of the place of imagination in cognitive architecture, as depicted in Figure 6.1, is wrong. This is because, given everything we know so far, perception and language are not directly connected in cognitive architecture, but experiential and propositional imagination are. Figure 6.1 wrongly depicts one of these pairs.

4. Against Cognitive Dissent

By putting experiential imagination in the perception box and propositional imagination in the language box, cognitive dissent is saying that the relationship between experiential and propositional imagination mirrors the relationship between perception and language. Two household findings falsify this claim: (i) basic beliefs vis-à-vis double dissociation between perception and language, and (ii) aphantasia vis-à-vis single dissociation between experiential and propositional imagination. First, a quick word about 'dissociation'.

Dissociation is the main tool of cognitive neuropsychology (e.g., Glymour 1994; Lyons 2001), which involves using brain-damaged patients to infer mental structure. It comes in two varieties: single and double. In single dissociation, a lesion is followed by impairment with respect to task A but not task B. Here, the conclusion is that A and B are performed by different systems. But this conclusion is weak because it may just be that B is a more difficult task than A such that the damaged system may yet be involved in the performance of A. In double dissociation, one lesion is followed by impairment with respect to A but not B, while another lesion

---

systems only when they are in the working-memory system. Thus, his point is that once imaginings have been generated as by-products of perception and language, they go on operating in the background until they are placed in the working-memory system. In this way, the working-memory system can do the job of storing and manipulating imaginings, and, so, there is no need for an imagination box. I skip this aspect of cognitive dissent here only because it comes apart from the internal structure question that is my focus. After all, one is about the formation of imaginings, and the other is about their storage and manipulation. In addition, the exact relationship between the working-memory system and the imagination box remains underdeveloped. Does the claim that imaginings only become active and accessible in working memory exclude the possibility of the imagination box? Does the same analysis apply to beliefs, such that there is no belief box as well? Answering these questions here will take us too far afield.

IMAGINATION IN THE ARCHITECTURE OF THE MIND   115

(in a different subject) is followed by impairment with respect to *B* but not *A*. Here, the possibility that one task was simply more difficult than the other is ruled out. In what follows, the notion of double dissociation will be integral to my argument that perception and language are indirectly connected (Section 4.1), and the notion of single dissociation to my argument that experiential and propositional imagination are directly connected (Section 4.2).

4.1 Basicality: Towards Double Dissociation between Perception and Language

Uncontroversially, perception and language are interdependent (Waltz 1978). For example, on the one hand, perception influences language in the McGurk illusion, where visual cues of speech enhance speech perception or even distort it (McGurk and MacDonald 1976), and on the other hand, language influences perception by mediating the motion processing of visual stimuli (Coventry et al. 2013). Though how to characterize this interdependence remains unclear (Klemfuss et al. 2012), we know that it is not in terms of co-functioning, i.e., perception can function without language and vice versa. This is because double dissociation has been reported between perception and language (Kemmerer and Tranel 2000).

Before David Kemmerer and Daniel Tranel's study, it was unclear whether the meanings of English locative prepositions (e.g., *in, on, above, below*) are independent of the representations used for the visuospatial recognition/construction of spatially complex objects. Using two brain-damaged subjects, they report a double dissociation according to which "the meanings of locative prepositions may be language-specific semantic structures that are separate from the mental representations underlying many other kinds of high-level non-linguistic visuospatial abilities" (Kemmerer and Tranel 2000: 393).

This double dissociation would have been blocked if perception and language are directly connected in cognitive architecture: the connection would entail the severance of their interdependence once double dissociation is admitted. If they are directly connected, then any lesion that impairs a perceptual or linguistic task would globalize, which is implausible. For instance, even though 1978JB, one of Kemmerer and Tranel's brain-damaged subjects, has impaired knowledge of locative prepositions, they understand instructions and produce coherent verbal responses.

I do not mean that dissociation is never possible between two directly connected systems, however. Consider face perception and face memory systems. Though they are both components of one system—the face recognition system—which suggests that they are directly connected, it has been shown that they are doubly dissociable (Dalrymple et al. 2014). What is happening here, however, is that since face recognition is developmental, it gets hooked up to other capacities, e.g., the emotion recognition system, as it couples face perception and face memory together. As such, the connection between face perception and face memory is mediated by emotion recognition, even though, taken holistically, as components of face recognition, they are directly connected. But notice how this further clarifies why perception and language are not directly connected—despite their interdependence, they do not couple together to form any larger system.

Consequently, to explain the double dissociation between perception and language without sacrificing their interdependency, cognitive neuroscientists, although they do not say so explicitly, tend to explain the interdependence as mediated by a third system. For instance, Lisa Aziz-Zadeh and colleagues (2006) explain it through the action system; Holger Mitterer and colleagues (2009), through memory systems; Mark Landau and colleagues (2010), through the face recognition system; Loïc Heurley and colleagues (2012), through decision-making about colours; Anthony Dick and colleagues (2014), through behavioural gestures. Representing this third system as 'system x', Figure 6.2 is a rough depiction of the relationship between perception and language in cognitive architecture.

We can see clearly then where Figure 6.1 goes wrong. By putting experiential imagination in the perception box and propositional imagination in the language box, cognitive dissent implies that perception and language are directly connected in cognitive architecture. But as we have seen, this contravenes everything we know so far about the relationship between perception and language. One piece of theoretical evidence that Figure 6.2 is correct is that it subtends one standard epistemological conclusion about perception—namely, perceptual foundationalism.

Perceptual foundationalism is the doctrine that perceptual beliefs are basic or immediately justified, i.e., their justification is not based on any other beliefs (e.g., Pryor 2005). Rendered in cognitive scientific terms, we say that perceptual beliefs are basic because *inter alia* perceptual systems are 'inferentially opaque' (Lyons 2009). Where a system is inferentially opaque if its output beliefs are not the result of an introspectable train of reasoning. For instance, you believe right now that 'you are reading this chapter', and you did not arrive at the belief through some reasoning process; rather, the belief was cognitively spontaneous.

But if perceptual and language systems are directly connected, this cognitive spontaneity will be lost. This is because perceptual systems will take inputs from the language (comprehension) system, which is inferentially non-opaque. When you are at a conference, listening to a philosopher deliver a talk, very little of what they say is cognitively spontaneous for you. You go through an introspectable train of reasoning processes to comprehend the talk. I do not mean that the

Fig. 6.2 Perception and language in cognitive architecture.

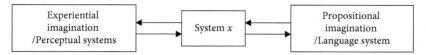

Fig. 6.3 Cognitive dissent updated.

language system is always inferentially non-opaque, however. Sometimes, its outputs are familiar enough to count as general facts (see Lyons 2009: 135). For instance, comprehending that '/ba/ is not /da/' is, arguably, evolutionarily hardwired into our language system such that believing so is now cognitively spontaneous. Simply put, general-fact language beliefs are basic but specific-fact ones are non-basic.

Thus, if perceptual and language systems are directly connected such that they send inputs to each other, then there is no non-arbitrary way of ensuring that perceptual systems do not take specific-fact language beliefs as inputs, which would render perceptual beliefs cognitively non-spontaneous, i.e., non-basic. Thus, unless we are ready to forgo perceptual foundationalism, following cognitive dissent and stipulating a direct connection between perception and language is inimical to our epistemic constitution.

A cognitive dissenter might respond, however, that they would not, in fact, say that experiential imagination and perception on the one hand and propositional imagination and language on the other hand are directly connected. That the connection between the pairs is mediated, as in Figure 6.3, such that perception and language are not forced to be directly connected.

While I agree that perception and language should not be directly connected, I disagree that experiential and propositional imagination should not be directly connected. As I will show, the cognitive dissenter is only trading Scylla for Charybdis.

4.2 Aphantasia: Towards Single Dissociation between Experiential and Propositional Imagination

Since experiential and propositional imagination are species of one genus, it follows that not only are they interdependent, but they are also not mediated by any third system. Recall face perception and face memory, which are directly connected because they are species of one genus. Thus, just as face perception and face memory are grouped in one face recognition system box, so too experiential and propositional imagination should be in the same box.

To see this, consider aphantasia, a psychogenic pathology that impairs voluntarily entertaining mental imagery (de Vito and Bartolomeo 2016). Aphantasia comes in two forms: partial and complete. Partial aphantasia impairs one or more sensory

118 BELIEF, IMAGINATION, AND DELUSION

modalities—"Some can 'imagine' in other modalities, hearing with the mind's ear, for example, but others can't" (Zeman 2016). Complete aphantasia impairs all sensory modalities—"I see what is around me unless my eyes are closed when all is always black. I hear, taste, smell, and so forth, but I don't have the experience people describe of hearing a tune or a voice in their heads" (Watkins 2018: 4)— such that we can say that complete aphantasia impairs experiential imagination. My concern here is complete aphantasia, although I will simply say 'aphantasia'.

Now, aphantasia does not impair propositional imagination. Nicholas Watkins continues:

> [T]he likely effect of aphantasia on me is to increase my reliance on the verbal over the visual and to enhance my interest in the abstract rather than the concrete. I have an ability to jump between concepts very easily, but people have commented that I often forget to explain how these apparently frictionless leaps happened. I think it may have contributed to making me more interested in questions than answers, and problems rather than solutions because I am always aware of the caveats surrounding an idea, and the different possibilities that could be adopted. (2018: 4)

Though Watkins is a physicist, the sort of propositional reasoning he describes here is similar to what philosophers do, in that it involves abstract reasoning within the scope of imagination, i.e., it involves propositional imagination, not mere supposition. We can say then an aphantasic can propositionally imagine even though they cannot experientially imagine. This then informs two very important conclusions about imagination.

First, since experiential and propositional imagination are co-present in healthy subjects, and since aphantasia impairs experiential but not propositional imagination, it follows that, in some cases, experiential imagination is absent but propositional imagination is present. The conclusion here is that propositional imagination can function without experiential imagination. This conclusion is not controversial since both cognitive supporters and cognitive dissenters (but not cognitive deniers since they deny the existence of propositional imagination) agree that propositional imagination is non-experiential, i.e., it does not trade on mental imagery.

Second, since experiential and propositional imagination are co-present in healthy subjects, and since aphantasia impairs experiential but not propositional imagination, it follows that, *arguably*, in all cases, experiential and propositional imagination are always co-present. Why 'arguably'? Because aphantasia is the only known pathology that speaks to a dissociation between experiential and propositional imagination, such that until another pathology that impairs propositional but not experiential imagination surfaces, we have defeasible evidence that experiential imagination cannot function without propositional imagination. Though most cognitive supporters and cognitive dissenters (as well as cognitive deniers since they discountenance propositional imagination) would disagree with this conclusion because they take experiential imagination and propositionality to be mutually exclusive, this orthodoxy has been challenged. One such unorthodox view (Grzankowski 2015) argues that pictures have propositional contents, which then suggests that our engagement with pictures, which trades on mental imagery, will, in some important respect, be propositional. This unorthodox view supports the conclusion that we have defeasible evidence that experiential imagination cannot function without propositional imagination. Perhaps experiential imagination and propositionality are not, after all, contrary to orthodoxy, mutually exclusive.

If so, then the dissociation between experiential and propositional imagination is single. If propositional imagination can function without experiential imagination but experiential imagination cannot function without propositional imagination, then propositional imagination is dissociable from experiential imagination, but experiential imagination is not dissociable from propositional imagination. To sustain this single dissociation, it is best to put them in the same box such that the inability of experiential imagination to function without propositional imagination can be guaranteed, as in Figure 6.4—since the dissociability of propositional imagination from experiential imagination suggests that the former can function independently of the latter, the broken lines depict how propositional imagination need not take inputs from experiential imagination to function.

The cognitive dissenter might say that my argument is conditional, i.e., it relies on what we know so far about pathologies that impair imagination, such that nothing blocks a normative analysis that is not conditional because it considers a futuristic pathology that impairs propositional but not experiential imagination. This normative analysis will, of course, double the dissociation between experiential and propositional imagination such that Figure 6.3 will be correct, i.e., experiential and propositional imagination will indeed belong in the perception and language boxes, respectively. I agree that my argument is conditional, but I have misgivings about normativity in cognitive psychology, not least because it involves novel unsubstantiated problems, e.g., this futuristic pathology (see Elqayam and Evans 2011). Even if we accept this normativity, the cognitive dissenter must still give a non-arbitrary account of system x.

No doubt, the cognitive dissenter can allude to any of the systems I listed earlier that are used to explain the interdependence between perception and language, i.e., any of the action, memory, face recognition, and colour judgement systems (Section 4.2). I don't think this works. We need unity at the functional level of theorizing about the mind, just as we need unity at the biological level. As Shen-Yi Liao and

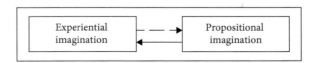

Fig. 6.4 Experiential and propositional imagination in cognitive architecture.

120 BELIEF, IMAGINATION, AND DELUSION

Tyler Doggett put it: "Boxology highlights ceteris paribus psychological laws that hold between different components of the mind" (2014: 272). Simply, system x cannot vary among humans. And settling on one among the four systems won't work either: they must now tell us why that choice is not arbitrary.

In short, as things stand, cognitive dissent cannot give an account of system x, and so it fails to meet its own standard. For if the dissociation between experiential and propositional imagination is single, and the one between perception and language is double, then each pair cannot be in the same box. Cognitive support comes in at this juncture, offering a way out, one that simultaneously retains the single dissociation between experiential and propositional imagination and the double dissociation between perception and language, doing so by offering an account of system x and moving experiential and propositional imagination out of the perception and language boxes, respectively, into the accounted-for-system-x.

5. In Defence of Cognitive Support

According to cognitive support, propositional imagination has its own space in cognitive architecture, i.e., there are psychological processes dedicated to its formation. In Section 2, I characterized these processes as the 'imagination system'. In this section, I will argue that cognitive support can use the imagination system to account for system x. Since the exclusion of experiential imagination from architecture talk is part of what sets cognitive dissent on edge (Section 3), let me begin by bringing it into the fold.

Though details differ, everyone—cognitive supporters, cognitive dissenters, and cognitive deniers alike—agrees that there are psychological processes dedicated to the formation of experiential imagination. For instance, Stephen Kosslyn's (1994) highly influential theory of mental imagery talks about a 'visual buffer' that can be activated without sensory input such that it outputs visual mental imagery. I am licensed then to simply say that the imagination system also includes this visual buffer (and other mental components involved in experiential imagination formation). In this way, we can rename Figure 6.4 as the imagination system.

With the notion of the 'imagination system' thus extended and clarified, I can go about my business. As I've said, my contention is that the imagination system can be system x, i.e., it can mediate between perception and language by relocating experiential and propositional imagination from the perception and language boxes, respectively, into itself. Let's begin by moving experiential and propositional imagination into the imagination system.

The reason cognitive dissent says that experiential and propositional imagination are by-products of perception and language, respectively, such that the former share the same boxes with the latter, is that it takes each pair to map onto the same neural substrate. Experiential imagination and perception share the same neural substrates—namely, the visual, auditory, and so on cortices (although I will talk most in terms of the visual cortex in what follows). Propositional imagination and language share the same neural substrates—namely, the prefrontal cortex. Simply put, cognitive dissent takes cognitive architectures to map onto neural architectures (Section 3). But as Dan Cavedon-Taylor (2021) convincingly argues, this one-one correspondence between cognitive and neural architectures is false, at least for perception and imagery/experiential imagination, and this is sufficient for my purposes. I will rehearse relevant aspects of his arguments here.

According to Cavedon-Taylor, the claim that experiential imagination and perception share identical neural substrates can be challenged on two grounds: methodological and clinical. Methodologically, a large number of the experimental studies on which the claim relies either reported that the visual cortex was not essential in imagery-based tasks or the studies themselves were set up with lenient standards. Clinically, shared neural substrates between experiential imagination and perception imply that impaired imagery functions should not be observed with normal visual functions and vice versa, but they are: there are double dissociations between imagery and normal vision functions both at global course-grained and domain-specific fine-grained levels.

At the global level, congenitally blind people can perform imagery-based tasks (Aleman et al. 2001), and aphantasics have normal visual abilities (Zeman et al. 2015, 2016). One lemma Cavedon-Taylor notes here is that aphantasia has been said to suggest that perception and imagery do not rely upon identical neural substrates and representations (see Bainbridge et al. 2021). At the domain-specific level, impairment of colour imagery despite normal colour perception (De Vreese 1991), and impairment of colour perception despite normal colour imagery (Bartolomeo et al. 1997) have been observed. Thus, Cavedon-Taylor concludes: "The point is that what bears most directly on whether imagery shares a neural substrate with vision and visual experience is whether there are dissociations between the two, and not, crucially, whether they are co-present in healthy subjects" (2021: 7226). One corollary he adds is that it has been argued that circuitry in the prefrontal cortex is the neural substrate of visual mental imagery, rather than areas in the occipital cortex, where the visual cortex is located (Spagna et al. 2021). In fact, as Cavedon-Taylor reports, even Kosslyn, a chief champion of this one-one correspondence, has walked back some of his claims in the face of extant empirical literature (Kosslyn et al. 2006: 151).

If so, then the one-one correspondence that cognitive dissent draws between experiential imagination and perception is false. And this suggests that we should be cautious of inferring identical neural substrates also for propositional imagination and language. After all, it is well known that language relies on more neural substrates than just the prefrontal cortex. For instance, speech perception is processed in the transverse temporal gyrus, located on the upper surface of the temporal lobe that contains the primary auditory cortex.

What all this leads to is that while it is expected that we use neural architectures to explain cognitive architectures, it is a mistake to expect the latter to mirror the former. For if other neural substrates are involved in the formation of perceptual and language representations, then surely, it is not the case that experiential and propositional imagination are by-products of perception and language. For all we know, some other neural substrates are involved in the formation of experiential and propositional imagination but absent in the formation of perceptual and language representations.

It is clear then that the imagination system can get its own box in cognitive architecture without needing to map directly onto any neural substrates; it can spread over different regions. Thus, there need not be any neural substrates dedicated to imagination formation, which is what cognitive dissent is gunning for with its one-one correspondence between cognitive and neural architecture thesis. If so, then we can remove experiential and propositional imagination from the perception and language boxes, respectively, and move them into the imagination system box, slotting the imagination system between the perception and language box as system x. This way, the direct connection between experiential and propositional imagination is sustained (as in Fig. 6.4), and the indirect connection between perception and language is also sustained (as in Fig. 6.2). Cognitive support nicely depicts all this in Figure 6.5.

It is important to reacknowledge that my argument is conditional on two fronts: it relies on (i) aphantasia being the only known pathology that speaks to a dissociation between experiential and propositional imagination and (ii) on what we know so far about the interdependence between perception and language. Earlier, the cognitive dissenter suggested a normative analysis that is not conditional along the lines of (i) in that the analysis will accommodate a futuristic pathology that impairs propositional but not experiential imagination (Section 4.2). I argued then that even if we accept that cognitive psychology is normative, the cognitive dissenter must non-arbitrarily account for system x. Having now argued that the imagination system can be system x, what happens if this futuristic pathology is discovered?

As I have conceded, the dissociation between experiential and propositional imagination will be doubled. So there will be no mismatch if experiential imagination is put in the perception box and propositional imagination in the language box. But there will still be the problem of giving a non-arbitrary account of system x. Perhaps discovering this pathology that impairs propositional but not experiential imagination will open a way for cognitive dissent to provide this account.

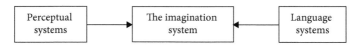

Fig. 6.5 Cognitive support.

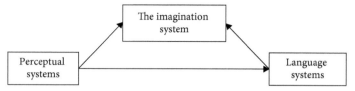

Fig. 6.6 Cognitive support if perception and language are directly connected.

Perhaps not. I am content with this outcome—philosophy should not be infallible, and being revisable in light of new evidence is virtuous. That said, until this pathology is discovered, the available evidence—i.e., aphantasia—speaks only to a single dissociation between experiential and propositional imagination, so the imagination system remains the best candidate for system x.

What about (ii)? What happens if new neuroscientific evidence turns up to the effect that perception and language are, after all, directly connected? My view will still stand. This is because we can expect this new evidence to be compatible with the inferential opacity of perceptual systems, such that perceptual foundationalism subsists—the thesis that perceptual beliefs are immediately justified, though controversial, is widespread and, in my opinion, true. Since sustaining the inferential opacity of perceptual systems requires perceptual systems to not take (specific-fact) linguistic outputs as inputs (Section 4), we can predict that this newly discovered direct connection between perception and language would be such that perceptual systems send inputs to the language system but do not receive inputs from it. Thus, the interdependence between perception and language would now be as a triangle: perception is directly connected to language, but language is mediated by a system x, as in Figure 6.6. Since the imagination system can be system x, it can continue to play its mediator role.

But notice how this new evidence would still confound the cognitive dissenter. Since they say experiential and propositional imagination belong in the perception and language boxes, respectively, and since only perceptual systems must send inputs to the language system despite this new evidence, cognitive dissenters would be saying experiential imagination can function without propositional imagination. But, as I have just reiterated, this depends on a different pathology that impairs propositional imagination but not experiential imagination, which, so far, is non-existent.

6. Conclusion

This chapter was about the place of imagination in the architecture of the mind. I characterized the issue in terms of whether imagination has an internal structure, i.e., whether there are psychological processes dedicated to imagination formation, i.e., whether imagination has a space in cognitive architecture. To clarify this issue, I catalogued three architectural positions about imagination, focusing on the first two: cognitive dissent, cognitive support, and cognitive denial. Cognitive dissent says that experiential and propositional imagination lack internal structures. Cognitive support says that propositional imagination has an internal structure but says nothing about experiential imagination. Cognitive denial says that there is no propositional imagination at all. I then argued that when it comes to whether imagination has an internal structure, cognitive support, not cognitive dissent, is the correct architectural position about imagination, interjecting my argument where necessary with cognitive denial.

Specifically, I argued that cognitive dissent's claim that experiential and propositional imagination belong in the perception and language boxes, respectively, does not align with what we know so far about the interdependence between perception and language, which is that they are not directly connected in cognitive architecture. But experiential and propositional imagination ought to be directly connected due to them being kinds of *imagination*, such that if cognitive dissent is correct, then perception and language are also directly connected. To show that cognitive dissent cannot take respite in saying that experiential and propositional imagination can be indirectly connected, like perception and language, I brought in aphantasia. Aphantasia tells us that there is, so far, only a single dissociation between experiential and propositional imagination, such that it is best to put them in the same box, which suggests that they are directly connected.

My positive thesis showed how cognitive support sustains the direct connection between experiential and propositional imagination and the indirect connection between perception and language. Modifying cognitive support to include experiential imagination in what I call the 'imagination system', I argued that the imagination system can mediate between perception and language without sacrificing the fact that experiential and propositional imagination are species of one genus, and rejecting the one-one correspondence cognitive dissent draws between cognitive and neural architectures. If so, then unless some of our best sciences are wrong, imagination must have an internal structure. Those who say it lacks such a structure will do themselves a world of good if they jump ship and join cognitive supporters. And this brings me to a final point.

Though I have identified Carruthers as the only cognitive dissenter I am aware of, I now want to point out that even though he sets himself up to be read in that light, he does say other things that paint him as a cognitive supporter. In addition to seeing how cognitive dissent can easily slip into cognitive support—though he doubles down on cognitive dissent being a better alternative to cognitive support (Section 3)—he modifies some cognitive support's accounts (Currie and Ravenscroft 2002; Nichols and Stich 2003) to explain why we pretend (Carruthers 2006b). Although he often speaks in a non-committal manner, as though he is offering an account on behalf of the cognitive supporters whose views he is modifying, he, nonetheless, ends up with a cognitive support view, whether or not he intends so. My unsolicited advice, then, is that it would be best if he clarifies his intentions. If he doubles down again, saying that he indeed means to push for a cognitive dissent view, then, given what I have said here, he would be staring down the barrel.

Acknowledgments

Sections 4 and 5 appeared in the Junkyard, but it has been significantly improved since then. I thank those who replied to the blog contribution and engaged me on the topic. I thank David Spurrett, Monique Whitaker, and Matthew Glaser for reading an earlier version of the blog contribution and for their comments. I especially thank Ema Sullivan-Bissett, Nick Wiltsher, and Shen-yi Liao for reading earlier versions of this chapter and providing valuable comments. The two readers for OUP also raised invaluable comments and suggestions, without which this chapter would have been an unreadable blob.

References

Aleman, A., van Lee, L., Mantione, M., Verkoijen, I., and de Haan, E. (2001). 'Visual Imagery Without Visual Experience: Evidence from Congenitally Totally Blind People', *NeuroReport* 12: 2601–4.

Arcangeli, M. (2017). 'Interacting with Emotions: Imagination and Supposition', *The Philosophical Quarterly* 67/269: 730–50.

Aziz-Zadeh, L., Wilson, S., Rizzolatti, G., and Iacoboni, M. (2006). 'Congruent Embodied Representations for Visually Presented Actions and Linguistic Phrases', *Current Biology* 16: 1818–23.

Bainbridge, W., Pounder, Z., Eardley, A., and Baker, C. (2021). 'Quantifying Aphantasia through Drawing: Those without Visual Imagery Show Deficits in Object but not Spatial Memory', *Cortex* 135: 159–77.

Bartolomeo, P., Bachoud-Levi, A., and Denes, G. (1997). 'Preserved Imagery for Colours in a Patient with Cerebral Achromatopsia', *Cortex* 33: 369–78.

Carruthers, P. (2002). 'Human Creativity: Its Cognitive Basis, Its Evolution, and Its Connections with Childhood Pretence', *British Journal for the Philosophy of Science* 53/2: 225–49.

Carruthers, P. (2006a). *The Architecture of the Mind* (Oxford: Oxford University Press).

Carruthers, P. (2006b). 'Why Pretend?', in S. Nichols (ed.), *The Architecture of the Imagination* (New York: Oxford University Press), 89–109.

Carruthers, P. (2011). *The Opacity of Mind* (New York: Oxford University Press).

126 BELIEF, IMAGINATION, AND DELUSION

Carruthers, P. (2013). 'On Knowing Your Own Beliefs: A Representationalist Account', in N. Nottelmann (ed.), *New Essays on Belief: Constitution, Content, and Structure* (Basingstoke: Palgrave Macmillan), 145–65.

Cavedon-Taylor, D. (2021). 'Untying the Knot: Imagination, Perception, and their Neural Substrates', *Synthese* 199: 7203–30.

Coventry, K., Christophel, T., Fehr, T., Valdés-Conroy, B., and Herrmann, M. (2013). 'Multiple Routes to Mental Animation: Language and Functional Relations Drive Motion Processing for Static Images', *Psychological Science* 24/8: 1379–88.

Currie, G. and Ravenscroft, I. (2002). *Recreative Minds: Imagination in Philosophy and Psychology* (New York: Oxford University Press).

Dalrymple, K. A., Garrido, L., and Duchaine, B. (2014). 'Dissociation Between Face Perception and Face Memory in Adults, but Not Children, with Developmental Prosopagnosia', *Developmental Cognitive Neuroscience* 10: 10–20.

de Vito, S. and Bartolomeo, P. (2016). 'Refusing to Imagine? On the Possibility of Psychogenic Aphantasia, a Commentary on Zeman et al. (2015)', *Cortex* 74: 334–5.

De Vreese, L. (1991). 'Two Systems for Colour-Naming Defects: Verbal Disconnection vs Colour Imagery Disorder', *Neuropsychologia* 29: 1–18.

Dick, A., Mok, E., Raja Beharelle, A., Goldin-Meadow, S., and Small, S. (2014). 'Frontal and Temporal Contributions to Understanding the Iconic Co-speech Gestures that Accompany Speech', *Human Brain Mapping* 35/3: 900–17.

Elqayam, S. and Evans, J. (2011). 'Subtracting "Ought" from "Is": Descriptivism Versus Normativism in the Study of Human Thinking', *Behavioural Brain Science* 34: 233–48.

Glymour, C. (1994). 'On the Methods of Cognitive Neuropsychology', *British Journal for the Philosophy of Science* 45: 815–35.

Gould, S. and Lewontin, R. (1979). 'The Spandrels of San Marco and the Panglossian Paradigm: A Critique of the Adaptationist Programme', *Proceedings of the Royal Society B: Biological Sciences* 205/1161: 581–98.

Grzankowski, A. (2015). 'Pictures Have Propositional Content', *Review of Philosophy and Psychology* 6/1: 151–63.

Heurley, L., Milhau, A., Chesnoy-Servanin, G., Ferrier, L., Brouillet, T., and Brouillet, D. (2012). 'Influence of Language on Colour Perception: A Simulationist Explanation', *Biolinguistics* 6/3–4: 354–82.

Kemmerer, D. and Tranel, D. (2000). 'A Double Dissociation Between Linguistic and Perceptual Representations of Spatial Relationships', *Cognitive Neuropsychology* 17/5: 393–414.

Kind, A. (2013). 'The Heterogeneity of the Imagination', *Erkenntnis* 78/1: 141–59.

Klemfuss, N., Prinzmetal, W., and Ivry, R. (2012). 'How Does Language Change Perception? A Cautionary Note', *Frontiers in Psychology* 3/78. https://doi.org/10.3389/fpsyg.2012.00078.

Kosslyn, S. (1994). *Image and Brain: The Resolution of the Mental Imagery Debate* (Oxford: Oxford University Press).

Kosslyn, S., Thompson, W., and Ganis, W. (2006). *The Case for Mental Imagery* (Oxford: Oxford University Press).

Landau, A., Aziz-Zadeh, L., and Ivry, R. (2010). 'The Influence of Language on Perception: Listening to Sentences about Faces Affects the Perception of Faces', *The Journal of Neuroscience* 30/45: 15254–61.

Langland-Hassan, P. (2012). 'Pretense, Imagination, and Belief: The Single Attitude Theory', *Philosophical Studies* 159/2: 155–79.

Liao, S. and Doggett, T. (2014). 'The Imagination Box', *The Journal of Philosophy* 111/5: 259–75.

Lyons, J. (2001). 'Carving the Mind at its (not Necessarily Modular) Joints', *British Journal for the Philosophy of Science* 52: 277–302.

Lyons, J. (2009). *Perception and Basic Beliefs* (Oxford: Oxford University Press).

McDermott, D. (2007). 'Artificial Intelligence and Consciousness', in P. Zelazo, M. Moscovitch, and E. Thompson (eds.), *The Cambridge Handbook of Consciousness* (Cambridge: Cambridge University Press), 117–50.

McGurk, H. and MacDonald, J. (1976). 'Hearing Lips and Seeing Voices', *Nature* 264: 746–8.

Mitterer, H., Horschig, J. M., Müsseler, J., and Majid, A. (2009). 'The Influence of Memory on Perception: It's Not What Things Look Like, It's What you Call Them', *Journal of Experimental Psychology: Learning, Memory, and Cognition* 35: 1557–62.

Miyazono, K. and Liao, S. (2016). 'The Cognitive Architecture of Imaginative Resistance', in A. Kind (ed.), *The Routledge Handbook of Philosophy of Imagination* (New York: Routledge), 233–46.

Nichols, S. (2004). 'Imagining and Believing: The Promise of a Single Code', *The Journal of Aesthetics and Art Criticism* 62/2: 129–39.

Nichols, S. (2008). 'Imagination and the I', *Mind & Language* 23/5: 518–35.

Nichols, S. and Stich, S. P. (2003). *Mindreading: An Integrated Account of Pretence, Self-Awareness, and Understanding Other Minds* (Oxford: Clarendon Press).

Omoge, M. (2021). 'Imagination, Metaphysical Modality, and Modal Psychology', in C. Badura and A. Kind (eds.), *Epistemic Uses of Imagination* (New York: Routledge), 79–99.

Pryor, J. (2005). 'There is Immediate Justification', in M. Steup and E. Sosa (eds.), *Contemporary Debates in Epistemology* (Malden, MA: Blackwell Publishing), 181–201.

Schellenberg, S. (2013). 'Belief and Desire in Imagination and Immersion', *The Journal of Philosophy* 110/9: 497–517.

Spagna, A., Hajhajate, D., Liu, J., and Bartolomeo, P. (2021). 'Visual Mental Imagery Engages the Left Fusiform Gyrus, but not the Early Visual Cortex: A Meta-Analysis of Neuroimaging Evidence', *Neuroscience & Biobehavioral Reviews* 122: 201–17.

Stock, K. (2011). 'Unpacking the Boxes', in E. Schellekens and P. Goldie (eds.), *The Aesthetic Mind* (New York: Oxford University Press), 268–82.

Waltz, D. (1978). 'On the Interdependence of Language and Perception', in D. L. Waltz (ed.), *Theoretical Issues in Natural Language Processing-2* (New York: Association for Computing Machinery and Association for Computational Linguistics), 149–56.

Watkins, N. (2018). '(A)phantasia and Severely Deficient Autobiographical Memory: Scientific and Personal Perspectives', *Cortex* 105: 41–52.

Weinberg, J. and Meskin, A. (2006). 'Puzzling Over the Imagination: Philosophical Problems, Architectural Solutions', in S. Nichols (ed.), *The Architecture of the Imagination: New Essays on Pretence, Possibility, and Fiction* (Oxford: Clarendon Press), 175–202.

Zeman, A. (2016). 'Aphantasia: 10,000 People Make Contact over Visual Imagery', *The Exeter Blog*. https://blogs.exeter.ac.uk/exeterblog/blog/2016/11/08/aphantasia-10000-people-make-contact-over-visual-imagery/.

Zeman, A., Dewar, M., and Della Sala, S. (2015). 'Lives Without Imagery—Congenital Aphantasia', *Cortex* 73: 378–80.

Zeman, A., Dewar, M., and Della Sala, S. (2016). 'Reflections on Aphantasia', *Cortex* 74: 336–7.

7

Believing in Stories

Delusions, Superstitions, Conspiracy Theories, and Other Fairy Tales

Neil Levy

Philosophers typically understand beliefs to be representations with the right direction of fit. My belief that *p* is a state that reflects my take on the world and serves as a map to guide action. This simple account has a lot going for it: it does well in capturing a very large proportion of our exemplars of belief. But it falls short when it comes to a range of unusual cases, as well as a number of common but often overlooked cases.

In many of these cases, people profess to believe a proposition, but their behaviour is puzzlingly inconsistent with their assertion. Take delusions as an example. Subjects with the Capgras delusion assert that someone familiar to them has been replaced by an impostor. But they are often puzzlingly untroubled by the incident. They don't tend to report their wife (e.g.) as missing to the police, or to express worry about her welfare (Bayne and Pacherie 2005). More puzzlingly still, their apparent beliefs may fluctuate over time. DS experienced Capgras delusion for his father, but the delusion remitted when they spoke on the telephone: only the visual percept provoked the delusion (Hirstein and Ramachandran 1997). FE, a sufferer from mirrored-self misidentification (the delusion that the image reflected in the mirror is another person), is an even more dramatic example:

EXAMINER: Who does it look like? Have you seen this person in here before? (*pointing to the reflection of the examiner*).
FE: That's you.
EXAMINER: That's me?
FE: Yes.
EXAMINER: Me, here? (*pointing to herself*) What's my name?
FE: I don't know, oh yes, it's Nora.
EXAMINER: Nora, that's right. So that's me in the mirror?
FE: Yes.
EXAMINER: That's my reflection?

Neil Levy, *Believing in Stories: Delusions, Superstitions, Conspiracy Theories, and Other Fairy Tales* In: *Belief, Imagination, and Delusion*. Edited by: Ema Sullivan-Bissett, Oxford University Press. © Oxford University Press 2024. DOI: 10.1093/oso/9780198872221.003.0007

FE: Yes.

EXAMINER: And who is that? (*pointing to FE's reflection*).

FE: I don't know what you would call him. It makes me a bit sick because he moves about freely with us. I don't be too friendly because I don't see it does him any good. (Breen et al. 2000: 84–5)

FE understands what a mirror is and how it works when he attends to the reflection of another person, but his delusion crowds out the knowledge when he attends to his own reflection.

Delusions are, of course, pathological cases. Monothematic delusions (my focus in this chapter, though it will soon be clear that the scope of the account is broader than that) usually arise as the consequence of brain injury or lesion. It is plausible that these dramatic cases cannot be entirely explained by mechanisms or processes that drive cognition in the absence of mental illness or brain pathology. Nevertheless, they may be *partially* explained by such mechanisms. One reason to think that might be true is that some of the puzzling features of these cases are shared by others that are non-pathological. Consider conspiracy theories.[1]

While there is a range of different theories that are commonly described as conspiracy theories, some of these theories have a content little less bizarre than the content of some clinical delusions (conversely, some genuine delusions seem more akin to ordinary self-deceptive beliefs in their contents: consider Reverse Othello Syndrome, the delusional belief that a romantic partner continues to be faithful). Yet these conspiracy theories appear to be widely accepted. For example, 21 per cent of American survey respondents report believing that vaccines are used to implant tracking chips, chips that will later be activated by 5G networks, and 15 per cent report believing that Covid-19 is a hoax (Schaffner 2020). Do they *really* believe these puzzling claims? As with delusions, one reason to hesitate in ascribing (full) belief is that the behaviour of those who profess such beliefs is often inconsistent with them (see Levy and Ross 2021 for discussion of some other reasons to withhold believing in belief in some cases).

Hugo Mercier (2020) gives multiple examples. In 1969, for instance, a rumour swept the town of Orleans that local Jewish shopkeepers were kidnapping local girls and selling them into slavery. Many people apparently thought it was true. Yet they failed to act as you would think they would if they truly believed it. They

---

[1] David Coady (2007) and Charles Pigden (2007) both urge that we drop the pejorative use of 'conspiracy theories', because conspiracies are all too often real and we risk unjustifiably stigmatizing conspiratorial explanations. However, there is (albeit contested) evidence from psychology and political theory that suggests a unity to what we commonly call conspiracy theories, conspiracy theorists, and the narratives they postulate (for a review, see Douglas et al. 2019; Uscinski and Parent 2014); we need some term to pick out the subject matter of this work.

didn't storm the shops, looking for kidnapped girls. They didn't even report their suspicions to the police. Rather, Mercier reports, they glared at shops owned by those they suspected. A descendant of this rumour lives on today, in the (once again anti-Semitic) fantasies of those who profess to believe the QAnon conspiracy, which also centres on child abuse. Despite the actions of the Capitol Hill rioters, very few of the millions of people who profess to believe the conspiracy take much action. It's not just the bizarreness of the claims or the difficulty of acting on them that block action. Political partisans express divergent assessments of the economy, for example, but their beliefs about economic prospects seem to have little effect on their economic behaviour (see Bullock and Lenz 2019 for review).

In this chapter, I'll advance a novel (and, admittedly, speculative) account which I will suggest helps to explain how people come to sincerely profess beliefs that have little subsequent influence on their behaviour. I'll suggest that the mechanisms we use for understanding counterfactuals dispose us to treat sufficiently satisfying narratives as representations of a way the world just might be. These mechanisms evolved for behaviour, and their outputs remain poised for action control even when we deploy them offline, for constructing fantasies or considering bizarre counterfactuals. Because they're poised for behaviour control, they *feel* real and when the stakes are low—when nothing much hangs on it—we may find ourselves accepting them *as* real. When the stakes rise, our mechanisms of epistemic vigilance are activated and we're unlikely to act on these claims. From delusions to conspiracy theories to partisan cheerleading, we're apt to *say* certain things because they're narratively satisfying (and for that reason engage with machinery that treats representations as real), but most of us are unlikely to act consistently with the stories we tell, at least when something more than speech or a tweet is at stake.

My aim is to (partly) explain pathological cases—delusions—by explicating a mechanism that is also involved in ordinary cases, like mere partisan cheerleading. I'll start with a case in which I hope the reader can recognize herself: superstition. Almost all of us are apt to *entertain* superstitions, even if we don't act consistently with them or even profess to believe them. If I'm right, the same mechanism at work to spectacular effect in delusions and to less florid effect in partisan cheerleading is also at work, in an even more attenuated form, in ordinary superstitions like those that I find myself entertaining.

1. Superstition Without Belief

Many people—myself included—who sincerely claim to be not at all superstitious nevertheless sometimes act, and more often feel, in ways that seem to belie the claim. Here's an example that resonates with me:

132 BELIEF, IMAGINATION, AND DELUSION

My football team is leading 1-0 against a more fancied side, and the game is entering its final 10 minutes. You remark on how well my team is playing. I can't help feeling that's 'tempting fate'. I won't be very distressed. I won't take steps to reverse the jinx and I won't—really—blame you if my side loses. But I have a definite preference that you don't make remarks like that. If you persist in this kind of behaviour, I might avoid watching important matches with you.

I take myself to be entirely disbelieving in jinxes, and I can point to a great deal of behaviour that supports my claim. I will be the first to point out there is no plausible causal mechanism whereby your words (uttered in my lounge room, say, many miles from the match) can affect my team's performance. I would require only a small financial incentive to override my distress (maybe I will happily override it just to demonstrate, to myself perhaps, that I don't believe these things). And my distress won't play a big role in my behaviour. If you are otherwise good company I might put up with your teasing.

I suspect that many readers recognize themselves in this description. Perhaps the specific example doesn't resonate with you, but another superstition has a (tenuous) hold on you. Perhaps you don't actively avoid flying on Friday 13th, but if you could fly the day before at no inconvenience or cost to yourself, you would prefer to do so. Perhaps you don't believe your horoscope contains even a grain of truth, but you read it anyway and find yourself recalling it throughout the day, trying to match what happens to its predictions.

I decisively reject superstition. Standard ways of measuring belief strength will demonstrate just how low my credence in such superstitions is. For example, I'd bet a fair amount of money that your jinx won't actually affect my team's performance. Why do I nevertheless find myself feeling uncomfortable at your words and apt to avoid joining you to watch matches in the future? I suggest that the leakiness of fiction helps to explain the phenomenon. Fiction is leaky in the following sense: when we entertain fictions, *qua* fictions, we are disposed to *feel* the happenings within them as affecting the world outside the story. Fictions co-opt mechanisms for understanding the actual world, and therefore tend to leak into it.

A dissociation between our affective states and our beliefs is a normal and expected (even sought) concomitant of consuming fictions. We're disposed to feel emotions when immersed in fictions. There is a lively debate over the rationality of these emotions (and, relatedly, over their content; see Friend 2016 for discussion). But there is no doubt that we have reactions that in their phenomenology and their functional roles closely resemble the emotions we experience in response to real events. I may feel anxiety at the prospect of an upcoming job interview, and I may experience something phenomenologically similar when I contemplate the obstacles that confront a fictional character. I may feel distressed by the breakdown of the marriage of a close friend and tears may role down my face in the

BELIEVING IN STORIES   133

cinema at the poignant ending of a relationship I know to be fictional. Of course, these affective states do not cause identical behaviour. I do not run from the cinema when I experience fear, or its fictional analogue, for instance. But the states are similar enough phenomenologically and share enough in the way of functional role to justify categorizing them as emotions of the same kind.

While we are familiar with the fact that fictions provoke affective responses in us, it is much less widely appreciated that fictions often lead to us forming and maintaining beliefs about the world outside the story. In many cases, there is nothing troublesome about our coming to have such beliefs. Such formation may be licensed by the conventions of a genre. Historical fiction, for instance, might allow readers to form beliefs about the social mores and political culture of Tudor England. Fictions might allow us to form justified beliefs about human psychology or about counterfactuals (Friend 2006). None of this is troublesome because the beliefs so acquired may be justified. Authors of historical fictions generally attempt to make the background facts about the period and place in which the narrative is set as accurate as possible, and readers are generally aware of this fact. They may therefore justifiably come to believe that Anne Boleyn was beheaded, on the basis of reading *Wolf Hall*. It is widely believed that great novelists in the realistic tradition possess psychological insights into character; these insights might license us in forming beliefs about how character states interact and cause behaviour.[2] In addition, though, we also seem to come to acquire beliefs from fictions in a way that is much harder to justify.

The relevant experiments have typically proceeded as follows.[3] In the experimental groups, participants read a version of an obviously (and explicitly labelled) fictional story, in which assertions are made about the world outside the story. The stories differ in the truth of these statements, so that some participants get a version in which a character states, for example, that mental illness is contagious while others get a version in which they state that mental illness is not contagious (control subjects, meanwhile, read a story in which no claims about the target propositions are made). After a filler task, participants are given a general knowledge quiz, in which they are asked about the target propositions (e.g., is mental illness contagious?). The participants who had read a version containing the false assertion are significantly more likely to agree with it than those who read a version containing the true assertion or who read the control version (this description is based on Prentice et al. 1997; Wheeler et al. 1999 report a replication). Other studies

---

[2] This claim is contestable. If folk psychology is importantly false, then it may be that the psychological patterns we find satisfying in fictions are sometimes or often at variance with the psychology of actual agents. Fiction might give us insight into the structure of folk psychology alone. A mixed view, on which high quality fictions allow for the acquisition of true beliefs about human psychology with regard to certain traits and states and not others, is to my mind plausible.
[3] The discussion of this empirical literature is indebted to the review and discussion in Friend (2014) and Steglich-Petersen (2017).

134 BELIEF, IMAGINATION, AND DELUSION

produced the same results using a slightly different methodology; rather than having the true or false propositions asserted, they are mentioned as peripheral narrative details (e.g., Marsh and Fazio 2006). Again, participants are significantly more likely to accept claims presented in the fiction as true in the real world.

As we saw, beliefs acquired from stories may be justified because stories are typically a reliable source of true information. Creators of fiction import a great deal of background material from the real world, thereby reducing the burden on themselves of having to create a world and the burden on the reader of having to imagine it (Van Leeuwen 2013). Apart from the central facts of the narrative and those that are entailed or implied by those facts, everything in a story is probably imported from the real world. The fact that the fictional world shares its background with the real world, or with how the author takes the real world to be (or have been) makes fiction a good source of information, and readers (implicitly) know this to be the case. In line with this suggestion, readers are less inclined to accept assertions made about the real world when they occur in the context of a story set in a dramatically different setting (Rapp et al. 2014); i.e., when readers lack a good grip on what might have been imported from the real world. With more realistic narratives, when assertions are made in the story, and especially when they are presented peripherally, we are usually entitled to accept them as true in the real world.

However, our disposition to accept fictional claims as true seems broader and deeper than might be explained by our awareness that background facts tend to be imported from the real world. We seem in fact to be *more* inclined to accept claims made in a fiction than identical claims made in a passage presented as factual (Prentice and Gerrig 1999; Strange 2002). Moreover, factors known to reduce acceptance of claims presented as factual do not significantly reduce reliance on claims presented as fictional. Need for cognition is protective against false information in other contexts, but not in the fictional context (Strange 2002). Even when participants are warned that the stories may contain false information (Marsh and Fazio 2006) or when stories are presented slowly to allow for intensive processing (Fazio and Marsh 2008), acceptance of false claims does not decrease. Our awareness that background facts tend to be imported seems unable to explain our heightened credulity when it comes to fiction.

Further, we tend to accept claims presented as fictional even when we have good reason to think that they are *not* imported from the real world. Acceptance may occur when the information is explicitly presented as false, and even when evidence is adduced to demonstrate its falsity. This gives rise to what we might call the debunker's dilemma: attempting to debunk false claims requires repeating them, and repetition increases acceptance (Schwarz et al. 2007). One reason why repetition increases acceptance may be that familiarity is taken as a cue for truth, perhaps because true claims are more likely to be repeated (Weaver et al. 2007). If it is true that we are more likely to accept claims made in an explicitly fictional context than those made in a factual context, however, repetition cannot be the entire explanation. I will suggest that the narrative context itself increases acceptance.

2. Hijacking the Narrative Machinery

We are able to build and understand fictional narratives because we have a suite of mechanisms that allow us to build and assess counterfactuals. These mechanisms are designed to optimize behavioural control by allowing us to weigh options. We can assess the costs and benefits of various possible actions utilizing these mechanisms. In effect, we construct little narratives to decide how to act. How would my boss respond if I asked her for a raise? Would she be more amenable if I approached her late on a Friday? What would the traffic be like were I to take the turnpike? If I accepted that job offer, what would my daily life look like? Every time we deliberate over how to act, we construct a narrative concerning how things might go. Fictions are entertainments that parasitize—or exapt—mechanisms designed for behavioural control.

Evolution, in its parsimony, has led us to use a single network for the offline construction of a range of different kinds of simulations. A single network of brain regions is utilized by episodic memory (memory of past personal experiences), imagining how future situations might play out and many aspects of social cognition. This machinery is put to work in much the same way in imagining counterfactual states of affairs, episodic memory, and the simulation of anticipated events. We might have thought that episodic memory involves the simple retrieval of stored events. In fact, it involves the *reconstruction* of events from stored cues; hence memory retrieval is unreliable and context-sensitive (Schacter 2001). In effect, episodic memory involves *imagining* one's experience of a past state of affairs on the basis of cues, and prospection involves imagining a future state of affairs.[4] Cognitive scientists refer to our capacity to reconstruct the past and construct the future as mental time travel (see Suddendorf and Corballis 2008 for a review of supporting evidence). This machinery is adaptive, because it allows us to utilize stored knowledge to prepare for future contingencies (Suddendorf et al. 2011). The machinery for mental time travel overlaps considerably with the so-called default mode network; the set of mechanisms that are engaged when participants in experiments are doing nothing in particular (Buckner 2010). In this 'resting' state, people engage in undirected daydreaming and fantasy. Engaging in such mind wandering is adaptive, since it is low cost (we

---

[4] Episodic memory, prospection, and imagination should not, however, be collapsed; see Debus (2016) for a discussion of the differences between them.

136 BELIEF, IMAGINATION, AND DELUSION

do it when there's nothing more pressing to do) and it involves the simulation of possible future social encounters and thereby preparation for them.

We should expect the construction of narratives for mere entertainment to use this pre-existing machinery. Evolution is unlikely to build a new mechanism (especially for something that is relatively frivolous—i.e., not directly connected to the business of survival and reproduction) when there's an available mechanism that can be utilized. Just as we utilize mechanisms (including mental mechanisms) designed for reproduction to engage in sex for pleasure, so we utilize mechanisms designed for a very different purpose—the simulation of counterfactuals to decide how best to act—for the construction and consumption of fictions. Fiction wouldn't be satisfying were it not for the fact that it utilizes this machinery. We feel emotions in response to stories because the machinery is linked to motivational mechanisms; mechanisms that attach values to outcomes. Because fiction uses mechanisms designed for behavioural control and for understanding the world, it's not surprising that we are often disposed to find the representations it trades in as describing how the world is or would be were certain events to occur.[5] Because mental time travel is a mechanism for the guidance of behaviour, fictions which parasitize this mechanism dispose us to feel as if the events described are real, and even to behave in ways that are consistent with the content of the fiction.

I suggest it is these mechanisms that explain why your remarks about my team's performance make me feel uneasy and dispose me to act in certain ways. The machinery for the simulation of counterfactuals—our narrative machinery—is activated by your remarks (see Ichino 2020 for a parallel suggestion). A little narrative is suggested to me: a tale of hubris and what is aptly (in this context) called poetic justice. It's noteworthy, here, that this machinery is known to be easily and often automatically triggered. Mind-wandering, for instance, occurs without agents intending it; indeed, when they intend to be engaged in some other task but fail to maintain focus. The ease with which it is triggered allows for the rapid generation of affective responses and dispositions to accept claims from minimal cues. It is unsurprising, then, that your remarks about my team's prospects give rise to anxiety in me. Your remark primes me to retrieve or construct what we might call the jinx narrative.

The jinx narrative is a simple and satisfying one. It is an instance of a common morality tale, one that is probably found in all cultures, in which an overconfident individual gets his or her comeuppance. Perhaps it makes such a satisfying narrative due to our evolved concern with undeserved inequality; this concern

---

[5] Some accounts of beliefs take dispositions to feel appropriately as partially constitutive of believing (Schwitzgebel 2002). These accounts might entail that the generation of a broad and systematic set of affects is sufficient to generate a state that is belief-like; perhaps what Schwitzgebel (2010) calls an in-between belief.

may cause us to find a deep sense of fittingness in the fall of the boastful individual.[6] Alternatively, perhaps it is concern with the character of the individual that makes the narrative satisfying (as suggested by the common notion, dating back to Aristotle, that hubris is a character flaw). Whatever the explanation for the fact, there is evidence that predictions of success automatically generate thoughts about negative outcomes. Jane Risen and Thomas Gilovich (2008) found, for example, that participants judged that an applicant to Stanford who wore a Stanford t-shirt before hearing back from the admissions office was less likely to be accepted than one who did not wear it. In another experiment, participants were asked to judge whether a continuation of a story involving tempting fate (e.g., the student wearing the t-shirt before hearing whether his application was accepted) was logical or not. The dependent measure was participants' reaction times. When the story did not end in the agent getting his or her comeuppance, reaction times were significantly slower, indicating that thoughts of the negative outcome were more accessible to participants. In effect, participants automatically generated a proto-narrative: agent tempts fate; agent gets his comeuppance. Whether they (fully) *believe* that tempting fate leads to an increased probability of being rejected by Stanford, or merely are disposed to respond in ways consistent with that claim, might depend on their antecedent views. If they reject the superstition, then they may come to have the affective dispositions without the (full) belief. Fictional narratives may dispose us to believe when we do not already have content-inconsistent beliefs.

3. Acquiescence in Fictions

An agent believes (or fully believes) a superstition when she accepts the representations it makes salient to her and allows them full access to the mechanisms of behavioural control. She may, for example, accept that *if my friend jinxes my team, it is more likely to lose* and form expectations on that basis. But most of us are at least a little sceptical of at least some superstitions that, nevertheless, trigger proto-narratives in us. We don't (fully) believe the representations they give rise to. Nevertheless, because they generate affective responses that make them *feel* real, we're disposed to treat them as representations of reality, in some contexts and for some purposes. To some degree, we find ourselves *acquiescing* (Risen 2016) in these representations, where acquiescence is not so much acceptance as a failure to resist their influence. The degree of acquiescence varies from context to context;

---

[6] It is widely accepted that prior to the late Palaeolithic, human beings lived in egalitarian groups (see Hayden 2013). Anthropological evidence suggests that egalitarianism was sustained not by a concern for equality but rather by a desire not to be dominated (see Boehm 1999).

138   BELIEF, IMAGINATION, AND DELUSION

for most of us, as the stakes rise we become more vigilant and more likely to resist their influence.

Some of us will be disposed to *say* that the representations such stories give rise to in us are true. Talk is often cheap: nothing much turns on it. For that reason, we're much less careful in what we say than we are in how we act; when talk has little consequences for our lives, we may accept bizarre claims (Mercier 2020). Conspiracy theories make good stories, and we're apt to entertain them, if not take them seriously. When those around us endorse them and the costs of doing so yourself are negligible (or, better yet, when endorsement marks you as being on the right side, as endorsement of QAnon does for Trump supporters), you may well say you believe them. You're less likely to go on to act as if they're true in other ways and in other contexts. Delusions, too, make good stories (Capgras-like scenarios feature in many science fiction movies). Delusions are usually held to be at least partly the result of unusual phenomenology caused, in turn, by a brain lesion (Stone and Young 1997); for example, in Capgras the person fails to experience the usual feeling of recognition associated with perceiving a familiar face. The causal route from phenomenology to endorsement remains unknown, at least in any detail, but part of the explanation may lie in the phenomenology making accessible a matching proto-narrative: the combination of the narrative and the phenomenology that provides evidence for it may dispose the sufferer to acquiesce at least minimally: to *say* they believe it. Whether the person will acquiesce in this way or not will depend on various factors, of course: individual differences in need for cognition, our social setting (which influences the costs of asserting a claim: will I be ostracized, mocked, or rewarded[7]), and so on.

Cultural setting will be important too. In particular, cultural setting will make a significant difference to whether an event or a feeling triggers a particular narrative in an agent, and to the costs of acquiescing in it. Some delusions are 'culture bound'. For example, koro (the delusion that the penis is shrinking) occurs in Indonesia, and in some regions in Africa and China but is almost entirely unknown in Europe (Ungvari and Mullen 1994). Some delusions may not only be culture-bound but also transitory (Hacking 1998). Both the temporal and geographical specificity may be explained (at least in part) by the availability of narratives. A narrative may provide someone with a way of framing and explaining their distress; the fit between narrative and phenomenology or symptoms disposes the person to entertain and rehearse the narrative and subsequently acquiesce in the representations it makes salient. Narratives may also lower the costs of assertion, since the cultural availability of the narrative makes the delusion understandable and perhaps acceptable. The cultural availability of narratives

---

[7] Rewards might include engagement by others such as medical professionals; this might be a significant reward to someone who is incapacitated by a stroke, say, and therefore has few other competing rewards available to them.

BELIEVING IN STORIES   139

certainly goes a long way towards explaining their content: Capgras patients may now see their relatives as robots (think, too, of the recent rise of the alien abduction belief, which may qualify as a genuine delusion; see Sullivan-Bissett 2020 for discussion). Note that phenomenology itself fluctuates, sometimes rapidly (think of the Capgras sufferer who experiences estrangement only in response to seeing his father, not to hearing him). As phenomenology fluctuates, so does the accessibility of the narrative and the pressure it exerts towards acceptance.

As stakes rise, belief tends to fall away. It's easy to acquiesce in the narrative *that the Democrats are kidnapping children* when nothing more significant than sharing a post on Facebook turns on it. But if we're asked to act on it, only a few of us are willing to pick up our assault rifles and go and investigate (as Edgar Welch did, in 2016). We're a lot more epistemically vigilant when the time comes for action and much less likely to acquiesce. Similarly, we may acquiesce in the jinx superstition, but not be willing to bet on it. Of course, many of us fall away yet sooner; we don't get all the way to assertion. Perhaps the inconsistency between our other beliefs is more salient to us, or perhaps our local culture—our friends and families—are unreceptive to such claims, which it would therefore be costly to assert.

Subjects with delusions differ among themselves in how far they acquiesce. Diagnosis depends on assertion: those who experience the phenomenology of Capgras but resist saying that familiar people have been replaced do not merit the label. They get off the bus at the first stop; perhaps there are many people who fail to meet the diagnostic criteria for delusion due to their awareness of the costs of assertion or to being sufficiently high in need for cognition or sufficiently concerned with consistency. Among those people who assert the content of a delusion, the majority appear to be unwilling to act consistently with it.

They retain a grasp of the sheer unlikelihood of the story they tell and may withdraw acquiescence under persistent probing (Bayne and Pacherie 2005). Even when they continue to insist on their delusion, they may acknowledge its unlikelihood and even that they wouldn't believe it in their doctor's shoes (e.g., Young and Leafhead 1996). Their grip on reality and the degree of conflict between it and their delusion helps explain why they don't tend to act in accordance with it even when they acquiesce. Epistemic vigilance is intact (enough) to prevent highly costly action. Of course, some subjects *do* go on to act consistently with their delusions, sometimes to tragic effect. Just as with superstition and conspiracy theories, that's not surprising. The cultural acceptability of the narrative may ensure that the delusion is accepted as a (full) belief for some subjects. Other subjects may have impaired capacities to detect conflict or to engage in reality monitoring, due to their lesion. Different subjects will be motivated to different degrees to seek the approval of those around them, and will differ in how insistent the phenomenology of the disorder is and therefore in how much pressure towards belief the narrative exerts on them.

140 BELIEF, IMAGINATION, AND DELUSION

The account sketched here has a family resemblance to several other accounts of the nature of delusion. In different ways, Gregory Currie and Ian Ravenscroft (Currie 2000; Currie and Ravenscroft 2002) and Philip Gerrans (2014) have each placed imagination at the centre of their own accounts. Currie and Ravenscroft, moreover, precede me in postulating that delusions may arise in part due to ways in which imagination uses the mechanisms of behavioural control. My account diverges from these earlier accounts, however, in appealing only to species-typical mechanisms, functioning as designed within normal limits. The similarities (in bizarreness of content and encapsulation from action control) between monothematic delusions and widespread conspiratorial beliefs should motivate us to look for an account that doesn't require pathology or dysfunction; rather, we should see pathology as explaining the content of the delusional belief and the strength of endorsement.

Currie and Ravenscroft argue that deluded individuals don't believe their delusions: rather, they mistake their imaginings for beliefs. To explain how this might occur they appeal to pathology; specifically pathology in the forward modelling of actions. On an influential account, forward models are used to predict the sensory consequences of our own actions; comparison between the predicted consequences and the actual (sensed) consequences is then available for fine-tuning of action in real time (Frith et al. 2000; Blakemore et al. 2002). Currie and Ravenscroft suggest that these same systems are also used in the offline simulation of actions; that is, their imaginative analogues. There is independent evidence that people with schizophrenia are impaired in their capacity to monitor the motor imagery utilized by such forward models; Currie and Ravenscroft suggest that this deficit may explain why they would mistake their own imaginings for beliefs. This appeal to dysfunction is unnecessary, if I'm right. Mistaking our imaginings for beliefs is an everyday phenomenon, and even those who resist endorsing the implications of our satisfying narratives nevertheless feel their doxastic pull. We don't need to postulate deficit or pathology to explain why people may take themselves to believe sometimes bizarre things, but fail to act consistently with these states: we're built so that if the right narratives are circulating in our local context, we're all apt to do that.

Gerrans's (2014) account seems more promising because it does not require pathology to explain delusion-like thought. He suggests that delusions are produced by the default network: the network of mechanisms involved in the production of narratives concerning the self. Delusions arise when the default mechanism is able to spin a narrative unsupervised by the mechanisms that normally have the role of testing thoughts for consistency and empirical adequacy. Because these mechanisms are hypoactive, or because the default thoughts monopolize processing resources, the essentially imaginative products of the default network come to play an abnormal role in the person's thought and behaviour. Hypoactivity in monitoring mechanisms may arise from pathology, but we all may become sufficiently preoccupied with anxious thoughts for them to capture processing resources.

Gerrans gives the example of an anxious parent who is worried about the whereabouts of his child. The fact that she is out later than she promised generates anxious thoughts about what might have happened, and these anxious thoughts might motivate actions (calling her friends, for instance) designed to relieve the anxiety. Something along these lines is indeed plausible: the parent who can't set aside his worries about his daughter is familiar. But bizarre conspiratorial beliefs (or, at any rate, thoughts that are taken for beliefs) may arise without any such arousing or anxiety-provoking thoughts. My superstitious thoughts illustrate how little credence we need to give to such thoughts and how even when the emotions they provoke are relatively weak they can nevertheless exert palpable pressure in the direction of endorsement.

If this is right, delusions are on a continuum with very familiar experiences, and the puzzling inconsistency that characterizes them is a feature of ordinary experience too. We all, or almost all, experience pressure to acquiescence in the representations that narratives triggered in us make salient. These representations continue to dispose us to feel, and even to act, in certain ways even when we reject them decisively. Superstitions are culture-bound like delusions and therefore have different degrees of grip on us, depending (*inter alia*) on the accessibility of the narratives they trigger in us.[8] Individual differences, in psychological dispositions and in cultural setting, will play a role in whether we acquiesce and to what extent: do we *assert* that the superstition is true; do we go on to act in accordance with it, and in what settings? In the absence of pathology, most of us will get off the bus earlier than the deluded person, but the outlines of the story may be roughly the same across the cases.

4. Objections and Conclusions

We are sometimes disposed to act in ways that appear to conflict with our professed beliefs. These cases are philosophically interesting and have provoked a number of theories (Gendler 2008; Schwitzgebel 2010; Van Leeuwen 2014). It may be that more than one of these theories is (partially) true; one might explain delusions, another phobias, a third implicit biases, and so on. The human mind is complex, and our cognition and behaviour may be caused by a variety of processes. To this already unwieldy mix, I propose adding yet another; one that

---

[8] It is likely that proto-narratives are more or less accessible, such that (other things equal) those that are more accessible generate stronger affect and increased disposition to accept claims than those that are less accessible. Green and Brock (2000) report that the degree of 'transportation' experienced by readers—the degree to which they are caught up in the story—correlates with the extent to which they accept story-consistent claims. Transportation surely depends on many things apart from the extent to which a story jibes with our narrative expectations (for starters, with the skill of the author), but accessibility of narrative may be one of its determinants.

explains some cases by itself, and which may play a role in many more (perhaps by effectively lowering the threshold at which alternative mechanisms are sufficiently powerful to induce belief, or profession of belief). In these cases—I have focused on delusions, superstitions, and conspiracy theories, but the proposal may explain other cases too—we may be disposed to feel and to behave in ways that conflict with our professed beliefs because certain cues trigger proto-narratives in us. Narratives are powerful. Because they utilize machinery for assessing counterfactuals that is designed to produce adaptive behaviour, they dispose us to have story-consistent emotions and even to accept claims made in the fiction. Even minimal cues to stories may break free of the fictional frame and produce behaviour in the real world.

The account I've sketched here is (as I flagged at the outset) rather speculative. While it builds on a great deal of empirical evidence, it depends on certain interpretations of that evidence and these interpretations are contestable. However, most of these interpretations are widely, if not universally, accepted. It is very widely accepted that the mechanisms involved in mental time travel evolved for the purposes of behavioural control and almost as widely accepted that imagination uses these same mechanisms. It is therefore widely accepted that simulation, of the sort that occurs when we process fictions, involves mechanisms that have the function of representing the world (or a way the world might be) for the purposes of guiding action. The further idea that fictions trigger representations that we might go on to endorse under certain conditions is more speculative, but is supported by evidence from psychology that representations are indeed often endorsed by those who process them, even when they are explicitly presented as fictions. Probably the most speculative element of the story is the idea that narratives, or proto-narratives, can be triggered by fairly minimal cues (as in my example of the jinx narrative); that idea is supported by evidence from Risen and colleagues showing that people have a sense of what continuation of a story is most fitting.

A more direct challenge to the account given here might come from evidence that people do not easily confuse attitude types. Even young children rarely confuse imaginings with beliefs (Weisberg 2013). While I have not committed to any particular mechanism, moreover, the account I have given here is most naturally embedded within an interpretivist framework (Carruthers 2011), according to which belief attribution depends on the interpretation of cues, in the first-person case as much as the third-person case. But interpretivist views are controversial; indeed, in this volume Kengo Miyazono argues that such views cannot account for delusions. He gives several reasons why this is so; at the heart of his objection is the claim that the internal evidence available underdetermines attitude type, such that we'd regularly mistake our imaginings for beliefs.

The interpretivist view I've defended elsewhere (Levy 2022) is not vulnerable to this objection, because it is pluralist. It is committed only to the claim that interpretations of the same kinds of evidence that are available in the third-person case (for example, interpretation of behaviour) play a role in self-attribution of

BELIEVING IN STORIES 143

belief, and that we should therefore expect that interpretation also plays a role when it comes to the sensory and phenomenological evidence available only from the first-person perspective. While we are very reliable in self-attribution, there is overwhelming evidence of attitude confabulation, driven by interpretation (see Levy 2021 for summary). Philip Corlett (this volume) provides a neurobiological framework that can smoothly incorporate this model. On his predictive processing account, organisms are engaged in predicting sensory input and updating their model of the world on the basis of disparities between actual and expected input. Corlett provides extensive evidence that top-down expectations and explanatory framework play a role in shaping our predictions and therefore in shaping our model of the world. This account predicts that we will take the world to be in a certain way when sensory input matches predictions; we then self-attribute the corresponding belief disquotationally. Anything that shapes expectations and interpretive framework can therefore shape what beliefs we take ourselves to have. But since these high-level expectations are only one source of evidence, such self-attribution might be tentative and unstable.

The story about stories I've just told not only helps us to understand delusions and the inconsistencies that characterize them, in the sense of providing a sketch of some of the mechanisms that underlie them, it may also help us to understand them from *within*: to grasp what makes them possible and to see their continuity with experiences that are familiar to most of us. If I'm right, delusions are a pathological manifestation of a propensity towards acquiescence to which we are all subject to some degree. The deluded person is not so categorically different from us. Nor is the conspiracy theorist. We share mechanisms that disposes us all to acquiesce in bizarre beliefs, even if most of us resist taking the next step to action. We're story-telling animals, and our stories help to make us who we are.

Acknowledgements

I am grateful to Ema Sullivan-Bissett for helpful comments on an earlier version of this chapter. This chapter has been transformed at her promptings and suggestions. I am also grateful to two readers for Oxford University Press. I am also grateful to the Australian Research Council (DP180102384) for their support.

References

Bayne, T. and Pacherie, E. (2005). 'In Defence of the Doxastic Conception of Delusions', *Mind & Language* 20: 163–88.

Blakemore, S.-J., Wolpert, D. M., and Frith, C. D. (2002). 'Abnormalities in the Awareness of Action', *Trends in Cognitive Sciences* 6: 237–42.

Boehm, C. (1999). *Hierarchy in the Forest: The Evolution of Egalitarian Behavior* (Cambridge, MA: Harvard University Press).

Breen, N., Caine, D., Coltheart, M., Hendy, J., and Roberts, C. (2000). 'Towards an Understanding of Delusions of Misidentification: Four Case Studies', *Mind & Language* 15: 74–110.

Buckner, R. (2010). 'The Role of the Hippocampus in Prediction and Imagination', *Annual Review of Psychology* 61: 27–48.

Bullock, J. G. and Lenz, G. (2019). 'Partisan Bias in Surveys', *Annual Review of Political Science* 22: 325–42.

Carruthers, P. (2011). *The Opacity of Mind: An Integrative Theory of Self-Knowledge* (Oxford: Oxford University Press).

Coady, D. (2007). 'Are Conspiracy Theorists Irrational?', *Episteme* 4: 193–204.

Currie, G. (2000). 'Imagination, Hallucination and Delusion', *Mind & Language* 15: 168–83.

Currie, G. and Ravenscroft, I. (2002). *Recreative Minds: Imagination in Philosophy and Psychology* (New York: Oxford University Press).

Debus, D. (2016). 'Imagination and Memory', in A. Kind (ed.), *The Routledge Handbook of Philosophy of Imagination* (New York: Routledge), 135–48.

Douglas, K., Sutton, R. M., and Cichocka, A. (2019). 'Belief in Conspiracy Theories: Looking Beyond Gullibility', in J. Forgas and R. Baumeister (eds.), *The Social Psychology of Gullibility: Conspiracy Theories, Fake News, and Irrational Beliefs* (New York: Routledge), 61–76.

Fazio, L. K. and Marsh, E. J (2008). 'Slowing Presentation Speed Increases Illusions of Knowledge', *Psychonomic Bulletin and Review* 15: 180–5.

Friend, S. (2006). 'Narrating the Truth (More or Less)', in M. Kieran and D. McIver Lopes (eds.), *Knowing Art: Essays in Aesthetics and Epistemology* (Dordrecht: Springer), 35–49.

Friend, S. (2014). 'Believing in Stories', in G. Currie, M. Kieran, A. Meskin, and J. Robson (eds.), *Aesthetics and the Sciences of Mind* (Oxford: Oxford University Press), 227–48.

Friend, S. (2016). 'Fiction and Emotion', in A. Kind (ed.), *The Routledge Handbook of Philosophy of Imagination* (New York: Routledge), 217–29.

Frith, C. D., Blakemore, S.-J., and Wolpert, D. M. (2000). 'Abnormalities in the Awareness and Control of Action', *Philosophical Transactions of the Royal Society of London B: Biological Sciences* 355: 1771–88.

Gendler, T. S. (2008). 'Alief and Belief', *Journal of Philosophy* 105: 634–63.

Gerrans, P. (2014). *The Measure of Madness: Philosophy of Mind, Cognitive Neuroscience, and Delusional Thought* (Cambridge, MA: MIT Press).

Green, M. C. and Brock, T. C. (2000). 'The Role of Transportation in the Persuasiveness of Public Narratives', *Journal of Personality and Social Psychology* 79: 701–21.

Hacking, I. (1998). *Mad Travelers: Reflections on the Reality of Transient Mental Illnesses* (Charlottesville, VA: University Press of Virginia).

Hayden, B. (2013). *Naissance de l'inégalité: L'invention de la hiérarchie durant la Préhistoire* (Paris: CNRS).

Hirstein, W. S. and Ramachandran, V. S. (1997). 'Capgras Syndrome: A Novel Probe for Understanding the Neural Representation of the Identity and Familiarity of Persons', *Proceedings of the Royal Society of London B: Biological Sciences* 264: 437–44.

Ichino, A. (2020). 'Superstitious Confabulation', *Topoi* 39: 203–17.

Levy, N. (2021). 'Not So Hypocritical After All: Belief Revision Is Adaptive and Often Unnoticed', in H. De Cruz and J. De Smedt (eds.), *Empirically Engaged Evolutionary Ethics* (Cham: Springer), 41–61.

Levy, N. (2022). *Bad Beliefs: Why They Happen to Good People* (Oxford: Oxford University Press).

Levy, N. and Ross, R. (2021). 'The Cognitive Science of Fake News', in M. Hannon and J. De Ridder (eds.), *The Routledge Handbook of Political Epistemology* (New York: Routledge), 181–91.

Marsh, E. J. and Fazio, L. K. (2006). 'Learning Errors from Fiction: Difficulties in Reducing Reliance on Fictional Stories', *Memory & Cognition* 34: 1141–9.

Mercier, H. (2020). *Not Born Yesterday: The Science of Who We Trust and What We Believe* (Princeton, NJ: Princeton University Press).

Pigden, C. (2007). 'Conspiracy Theories and the Conventional Wisdom', *Episteme* 4: 219–32.

Prentice, D. A. and Gerrig, R. J. (1999). 'Exploring the Boundary Between Fiction and Reality', in S. Chailen and Y. Trope (eds.), *Dual Process Theories in Social Psychology* (New York: Guilford Press), 529–46.

Prentice, D. A., Gerrig, R. J., and Bailis, D. S. (1997). 'What Readers Bring to the Processing of Fictional Texts', *Psychonomic Bulletin and Review* 4: 416–20.

Rapp, D. N., Hinze, S. R., Slaten, D. G., and Horton, W. S. (2014). 'Amazing Stories: Acquiring and Avoiding Inaccurate Information from Fiction', *Discourse Processes* 51: 50–74.

Risen, J. L. (2016). 'Believing What We Do Not Believe: Acquiescence to Superstitious Beliefs and Other Powerful Intuitions', *Psychological Review* 123: 182–207.

Risen, J. L. and Gilovich, T. (2008). 'Why People Are Reluctant to Tempt Fate', *Journal of Personality and Social Psychology* 95: 293–307.

Schacter, D. (2001). *The Seven Sins of Memory: How the Mind Forgets and Remembers* (Boston, MA: Houghton Mifflin).

Schaffner, B. (2020). 'QAnon and Conspiracy Beliefs'. https://www.isdglobal.org/wp-content/uploads/2020/10/qanon-and-conspiracy-beliefs.pdf.

Schwarz, N., Sanna, L. J., Skurnik, I., and Yoon, C. (2007). 'Metacognitive Experiences and the Intricacies of Setting People Straight: Implications for Debiasing and Public Information Campaigns', *Advances in Experimental Social Psychology* 39: 127–61.

146 BELIEF, IMAGINATION, AND DELUSION

Schwitzgebel, E. (2002). 'A Phenomenal, Dispositional Account of Belief', *Noûs* 36: 249–75.

Schwitzgebel, E. (2010). 'Acting Contrary to Our Professed Beliefs or the Gulf Between Occurrent Judgment and Dispositional Belief', *Pacific Philosophical Quarterly* 91: 531–3.

Steglich-Petersen, A. (2017). 'Fictional Persuasion and the Nature of Belief', in E. Sullivan-Bissett, H. Bradley, and P. Noordhof (eds.), *Art and Belief* (Oxford: Oxford University Press), 174–93.

Stone, T. and Young, A. W. (1997). 'Delusions and Brain Injury: The Philosophy and Psychology of Belief', *Mind & Language* 12: 327–64.

Strange, J. J. (2002). 'How Fictional Tales Wag Real-World Beliefs', in M. C. Green, J. J. Strange, and T. C. Brock (eds.), *Narrative Impact: Social and Cognitive Foundations* (Mahwah, NJ: Lawrence Erlbaum Associates), 263–86.

Suddendorf, T., Addis, D. R., and Corballis, M. C. (2011). 'Mental Time Travel and the Shaping of the Human Mind', in M. Bar (ed.), *Predictions in the Brain: Using Our Past to Generate a Future* (New York: Oxford University Press), 344–54.

Suddendorf, T. and Corballis, M. C. (2008). 'The Evolution of Foresight: What Is Mental Time Travel and Is It Unique to Humans?', *Behavioural and Brain Sciences* 30: 299–313.

Sullivan-Bissett, E. (2020). 'Unimpaired Abduction to Alien Abduction: Lessons on Delusion Formation', *Philosophical Psychology* 33: 679–704.

Ungvari, G. S. and Mullen, R. S. (1994). 'Koro: The Delusion of Penile Retraction', *Urology* 43: 883–5.

Uscinski, J. E. and Parent, J. M. (2014). *American Conspiracy Theories* (New York: Oxford University Press).

Van Leeuwen, N. (2013). 'The Meanings of "Imagine" Part I: Constructive Imagination', *Philosophy Compass* 8: 220–30.

Van Leeuwen, N. (2014). 'Religious Credence Is Not Factual Belief', *Cognition* 133: 698–715.

Weaver, K., Garcia, S. M., Schwarz, N., and Miller, D. T. (2007). 'Inferring the Popularity of an Opinion from Its Familiarity: A Repetitive Voice Can Sound Like a Chorus', *Journal of Personality and Social Psychology* 92: 821–33.

Weisberg, D. S. (2013). 'Distinguishing Imagination from Reality', in M. Taylor (ed.), *The Oxford Handbook of the Development of Imagination* (New York: Oxford University Press), 75–93.

Wheeler, C., Green, M. C., and Brock, T. C. (1999). 'Fictional Narratives Change Beliefs: Replications of Prentice, Gerrig, and Bailis (1997) with Mixed Corroboration', *Psychonomic Bulletin and Review* 6: 136–41.

Young, A. W. and Leafhead, K. M. (1996). 'Betwixt Life and Death: Case Studies of the Cotard Delusion', in P. W. Halligan and J. C. Marshall (eds.), *Method in Madness: Case Studies in Cognitive Neuropsychiatry* (Mahwah, NJ: Lawrence Erlbaum Associates), 147–71.

PART III
DELUSIONAL EXPERIENCE

8

The Capgras Delusion

An Interactionist Approach Revisited

Garry Young

1. Introduction

It is a trivial truth that, where x denotes a certain person's identity, the proposition <This person is not x> is true of everyone except x. Therefore, when S announces that *this* person—pointing at x—is not x, in the absence of evidence to the contrary, the principle of charity requires us to conclude that S is simply mistaken, rather than, say, delusional or acting with devious intent. This is because the principle of charity would have us assume other things about S (apart from the fact that he is mistaken) such as: (i) in making the claim, S must believe that he is sufficiently acquainted with x, and/or has sufficient knowledge of x, to judge that the person before him is not x, and (ii) he must have drawn on this knowledge when making the determination; it just so happens that he is mistaken for reasons yet to be established. The principle of charity therefore requires us to assume that S believes he has *good reason* for his declaration—that he feels *justified* in his claim—despite his error (Archer, this volume).

Suppose that S's error is pointed out to him. His friends and family tell him that he is mistaken; because the person he claims is not x is in fact x. Indeed, x asserts this herself. Moreover, let us allow that she reveals personal information known only to S and x; yet still S insists that the person before him is not x. In such a situation, it would seem that S not only believes that the person is not x but, given the claims being made, that she is also an impostor. Whatever reason S has for maintaining this belief, it is resistant to revision, at least from the kinds of counterevidence described.

People with the Capgras delusion typically declare that certain persons—close family members, friends, significant others—are not who they claim to be (Capgras and Reboul-Lachaux 1923). A popular example is that of the Capgras husband pronouncing, despite evidence to the contrary, that the woman in front of him—his wife—is not his wife; she is an impostor (Campbell 2001; Coltheart et al. 2010; Ratcliffe 2004). While one may feel less inclined to apply the principle of charity to such a situation, and therefore be less inclined to say that the husband is *simply* mistaken, it nevertheless seems pertinent to ask

Garry Young, *The Capgras Delusion: An Interactionist Approach Revisited* In: *Belief, Imagination, and Delusion*. Edited by: Ema Sullivan-Bissett, Oxford University Press. © Oxford University Press 2024. DOI: 10.1093/oso/9780198872221.003.0008

150 BELIEF, IMAGINATION, AND DELUSION

what reason the Capgras husband has for declaring that his wife is an impostor: for it seems reasonable to assume that he has *a* reason. It also seems reasonable to assume that this reason plays some role in the formation and maintenance of his delusional belief. What, then, does the *subject*—the Capgras husband, in this case—take to be *his* reason for believing that the person in front of him is not who she and others claims she is? What does the Capgras husband consider justifies his (delusional) belief, and how does it fit within the *overall* aetiology of the Capgras delusion?

In posing these questions, it is not my intention to posit the subject's reason, such as it is, as *the* cause of the Capgras delusion; but neither should it be dismissed as causally irrelevant. Instead, my aim is to demonstrate that the subject's reason for believing what he does is intimately tied to his *experiential* content, thereby making his experience causally relevant. Moreover, it is my contention that the subject's reason for *coming to believe* that his wife is an impostor differs from the reason he has for *continuing to believe* it. This is because the subject's experience of his wife prior to embracing the delusional belief differs, markedly, from his experience of her upon accepting it.

Positioning the subject's experience as part of the aetiology of the Capgras delusion is therefore important not just for our understanding of what contributes to the belief's formation *and* its maintenance, but also for our understanding of the transformation that occurs in the nature of the subject's experience as he moves from accepting the belief to maintaining it, and therefore for understanding the mutual effect belief and experience have on each other in the context of the disorder.

The Capgras subject's experience, and how this affects the reason for his belief, may only be one piece of a complex causal puzzle; but it is an important piece, and one that has been neglected in more recent and otherwise innovative accounts of the Capgras delusion (e.g., Coltheart et al. 2010; McKay 2012). A further aim of this chapter, then, is to integrate certain of these innovative characteristics (yet to be discussed) into a revised version of what I have previously called an *interactionist model* of the Capgras delusion (Young 2008). In its original form, the interactionist approach already featured a prominent role for subject experience. It is my view, however, that the *revised* interactionist model has greater explanatory worth than the original, *and* other revisionist models that ignore or relegate the role of personal experience. This is because it is able to incorporate recent innovative thinking about the aetiology of the disorder into its explanatory account, while providing—in fact, restoring to prominence, given the current trend—a role for personal experience. A key component of the revised version is something I am calling *experiential transformation*: a phenomenon that helps explains both the reason the subject has for coming to believe that his wife is an impostor, and his unwillingness to revise this belief.

THE CAPGRAS DELUSION   151

According to the revised interactionist account, the Capgras subject's delusional belief, which I represent throughout using the example of the Capgras husband believing that his wife is an impostor, has the following aetiology:

1. Neurological disruption causes a mismatch within the individual's facial recognition system.
2. A prediction error signal occurs as a result of the mismatch between prediction and outcome within the facial recognition system, resulting in abnormal data O. Abnormal data O co-occurs with an anomalous subject experience (i.e., a sense of unfamiliarity/estrangement towards the putative wife).
3. Candidate hypotheses are presented and, in accordance with abductive reasoning and Bayesian probability, the 'best' explanation—i.e., the stranger hypothesis—is selected to account for abnormal data O *and* the subject's sense of estrangement.
4. The stranger hypothesis enters consciousness, co-occurring with the aforementioned sense of estrangement.
5. The Capgras husband comes to *believe* the stranger hypothesis, and, given the context, infers that the person is an impostor. The delusional belief helps explain the anomalous experience—the sense of unfamiliarity and estrangement—he is experiencing and, in addition to this insight, offers relief from the tension of not knowing what is happening.
6. The accepted (delusional) belief shapes the perception of the woman—his wife—the Capgras husband believes to be an impostor, such that he now perceives an impostor. An experiential transformation has occurred in which the previously perplexing sense of unfamiliarity towards the woman claiming to be his wife is transformed into a *normative* sense of unfamiliarity towards the impostor.
7. The belief and the experience are intimately connected and mutually beneficial, making the delusional belief resistant to revision from external counterevidence.

It is towards a defence of points 1–7 that I now turn.

2. The Traditional Role of Personal Experience

A prominent approach to understanding the Capgras delusion positions the delusional belief as a means of *explaining* an anomalous experience the subject has—typically after a recent brain trauma—whenever he is in the presence of the significant other (Ellis and Young 1990; Maher 1974). Something feels odd, bizarre, 'not quite right' about the woman who looks and acts just like, and indeed claims to be, his wife. The delusional belief is therefore used to close a potential anxiety-inducing explanatory gap that would otherwise exist for the subject (Sullivan-Bissett 2018) between what is said to be the case—that this person is his wife—for which there is some evidence (e.g., her physical similarity, autobiographical and otherwise personal knowledge, the testimony of others) and what he experiences: something odd/not quite right about the woman who claims to be his wife.

Before continuing, it is worth noting that there is another contemporary means of explaining the Capgras delusion that continues to receive attention, known as the endorsement approach (Bayne and Pacherie 2004; Fine et al. 2005; Pacherie 2009; see also Bongiorno 2020, for recent critical discussions). I will postpone discussion on this until the end of the chapter, however (see Section 11). This is because my immediate focus is on revisions to the interactionist account which is *explanationist* in nature. When I do eventually discuss the endorsement approach, it will be to show how a certain key feature—the claim that the Capgras husband perceives his wife *as* an impostor—can be explained without relying on the idea that the experience contains intrinsic 'impostor' properties.

Explanationist approaches present either one or two dysfunctional elements, or *factors*, within their respective accounts. One-factor theorists hold that the process by which the Capgras husband arrives at his delusional belief is not inconsistent with how erroneous but non-delusional beliefs are formed (Gerrans 2002; Maher 1974, 1988; Reimer 2009). The 'single-factor' disruption is not therefore a reference to a breakdown in normal reasoning (Maher 2006) but, rather, neurological damage that is believed to affect one's sense of familiarity (more on this later). It is this that causes the highly unusual and intense experience that the subject's belief is positioned to explain; for such is the nature of the experience— in terms of its intensity and bizarreness—that a delusional belief can be produced to explain it without violating the bounds of normal reasoning. As Brendan Maher explains:

> The delusional belief is not being held "in the face of evidence normally sufficient to destroy it," but is being held because of evidence powerful enough to support it. Where the patient may differ from a normal observer is not in the manner of drawing inference from evidence but in the kinds of perceptual experience that provide the evidence from which the inference is being drawn.
>
> (Maher 1974: 99)

For one-factor theorists, defective reasoning should not be considered the primary protagonist in the formation of the delusional belief; rather, the delusion should be understood as a *reasoned* attempt to make sense of the anomalous experience, or what Philip Gerrans (2000: 116) calls the "deeply disturbing and intractable phenomenal state". Therefore, to understand the Capgras delusion, we must look to the nature and intensity of the phenomenal experience the belief is positioned to explain: for,

THE CAPGRAS DELUSION 153

typically, subjects "begin with a 'feeling' that something is different and then try to find out what has changed" (Maher 1999: 554). What Maher is suggesting is that "the locus of pathology is in the neuropsychology of experience, not in the neuropsychology of deductive or inferential reasoning" (Maher 1999: 551).

Maher's view requires us to embrace the principle of charity when contemplating the Capgras husband's claim. We must acknowledge that the anomalous experience is 'powerful enough' to cause a person engaged in normal, even if not fully rational, processing (i.e., reasoning akin to that which can lead to erroneous but non-delusional beliefs) to conclude that his wife is in fact an impostor. In contrast, two-factor theorists (Davies and Coltheart 2000; Davies et al. 2001; Ellis and Young 1990; Klee 2004; Young and de Pauw 2002) hold that in addition to the aforementioned neurological damage, a second factor, centred around disruption to the subject's belief evaluation system, explains why the delusional belief is accepted, instead of some other less outlandish and therefore more plausible belief, such as the anomalous experience is the result of the Capgras husband's recent brain trauma, or that he has simply fallen out of love with his wife (Corlett, this volume; Gerrans, this volume). To be clear, proponents of the one-factor approach do not deny that the delusional belief is the product of neurologically induced anomalous experience *plus* some other *cognitive* aspect. What they deny is that this other cognitive component is sufficiently abnormal in its functioning to be identified as a second clinical factor.

Addressing whether one needs to posit one or two factors as part of the aetiology of the Capgras delusion and, if two factors, where in the process this occurs (e.g., Coltheart et al. 2010 posit a second-factor deficit in belief evaluation not formation) is not a focus of this chapter. What I have to say on the matter will be postponed until Section 12. Of more immediate interest is the relationship between neurological disruption and the delusional belief, and whether it is the function of the belief to explain the subject's anomalous experience, as more traditional explanationist accounts have argued, or whether it is a product of a mismatch in processing that takes place below conscious awareness. That latter claim is made by Max Coltheart and colleagues' (2010) revisionist model, as well as by others (e.g., McKay 2012). It may, or course, be both, as I intend to argue (although the *reason-giving explanation* the subject provides will only reference the experience).

3. A Disruption Within the Facial Recognition System

Despite their differences, one- and two-factor explanationist accounts have tended to converge on the idea that some form of neurological disruption is the cause of the anomalous experience the subject is motivated to explain. Brian McLaughlin (2009) refers to this as the 'default thesis'. Typically, Hadyn Ellis and Andrew Young (1990) mirror-image model is cited, often in conjunction with Ellis and Michael Lewis's (2001) model of

154 BELIEF, IMAGINATION, AND DELUSION

facial recognition, as a means of illustrating the impact of neurological disruption on normative face recognition functioning; or if not explicitly referenced then certainly contemporary explanations are believed to be compatible with both of these models. In short, disruption to the facial recognition system of Capgras subjects is said to 'mirror' that found in prosopagnosia. As Ellis and Lewis (2001: 149) explain:

> [I]f prosopagnosia is the result of damage to the system responsible for generating conscious face recognition, sometimes leaving an unconscious or covert mechanism intact, then the Capgras delusion might arise when the reverse occurs, that is, an intact overt system, coupled with a malfunctioning covert system.

Simply put, prosopagnosic subjects are unable to recognize, in a conscious sense, familiar faces: a deficit brought about by damage to the ventral route of the visual system. Nevertheless, they exhibit increased skin conductance response (SCR) when presented with a familiar but consciously unrecognized face (Bauer 1984; Tranel and Damasio 1985). The increase in SCR is interpreted as a measure of unconscious (or covert) recognition, made possible by the subject's intact ventral limbic structure (projecting to the amygdala). Damage to these two structures is 'mirror-reversed' in the Capgras subject insofar as the ventral route is intact but not the connecting ventral limbic structure (see Breen et al. 2000, for a more detailed discussion, and also Haxby et al. 2000 and Haxby et al. 2001). Speculation has arisen, although not without contention, over whether there is damage to the ventromedial prefrontal cortex (vmPFC) (see Corlett 2019, for a critical discussion). Whatever the neurological basis, Capgras subjects fail to exhibit increased SCR when in the presence of familiar faces (Ellis et al. 1997; Hirstein and Ramachandran 1997; Brighetti et al. 2007) and, instead, demonstrate emotional hyporesponsiveness (Fine et al. 2005; see also Christodoulou 1976; de Pauw 1994; Feinberg and Shapiro 1989). As a consequence, James Phillips (2002) asserts that Capgras subjects "may recognise the face without the *tone of familiarity*" (p. 61; emphasis added). Similarly, Gerrans (1999) states that the Capgras delusion involves "a form of neurological deficit which damages a discrete capacity to generate *feelings of familiarity*" (596; emphasis added). Ellis and Lewis (2001) likewise describe the Capgras delusion as involving, in part, a "failure to receive a confirmatory *feeling of familiarity*" (p. 152; emphasis added).

A potential problem arises, however, with the claim that whatever is responsible for producing reduced SCR is likewise responsible for the subject's altered experiential state (*qua* a lack of familiarity). Prosopagnosic subjects, who have heightened SCR to familiar faces, do not experience their heightened response in a way that allows them to discriminate familiar faces from unfamiliar ones

(Coltheart 2005).[1] They do not say, for example: "Despite being unable to identify the person in the photograph, I feel I must know them because I am experiencing a feeling of familiarity". If this does not occur in the case of the prosopagnosic subject (as a consequence of that which causes heightened SCR), then why would the Capgras subject experience something approximating a lack of familiarity on account of mirror-reversed neurological damage within the facial recognition system and reduced levels of SCR?

As enticing as reduced SCR is as a measure of neurological disruption in the Capgras subject, what remains unclear is the causal connection between this and the anomalous experiential state the subject is motivated to explain (at least according to more traditional explanationist accounts). As Jakob Hohwy (2004) rightly points out, any alteration in SCR "does not explain the character of the subjective experience" (66); and certainly the subject does not have a 'reduced SCR' experience. Nevertheless, if traditional explanationist approaches are to be believed then the subject has *some pertinent experience* in need of explanation; and both the experience and its alleged anomalousness coincide with reduced SCR, even if an understanding of their causal connection currently evades us.

The troubling matter of explaining the relationship between neurological disruption and experiential content is avoided, however, if we advance the view, as more recent explanationist accounts have done, that the delusional belief is formulated to explain an anomaly that occurs below the level of conscious awareness, and is therefore not something the subject *experiences*. The relegation of the role of experiential content, from that which the subject seeks to explain (*their* explanandum) to an anomaly below conscious awareness, is evident when one compares the description found in Coltheart (2005) with that found in Coltheart and colleagues (2010). First, consider Coltheart (2005: 155):

It is a general principle of cognitive life that we are continually making predictions, on the basis of what we currently know about the world, concerning what will happen to us next. These predictions are normally confirmed. But occasionally they are not, and this calls for an inspection of the database of beliefs about the world, which was used to generate the predictions. The processes of prediction, and of detection of failures of predictions, are all automatic and unconscious. Only when a prediction fails does consciousness get involved; the unconscious system makes some kind of report to consciousness to instigate some intelligent conscious problem-solving behavior that will discover what's wrong with the database and how it should be repaired. A curious phenomenon is that the report from the unconscious to the conscious is sometimes

---

[1] Davies and Egan (2013) speculate over whether Coltheart is correct about this when commenting on a discussion in Young (2008).

156   BELIEF, IMAGINATION, AND DELUSION

underspecified, as when we become aware that there is something different about an old colleague today but are unaware as to exactly what it is (he has shaved off the beard he has had for twenty years).

Now, Coltheart and colleagues (2010 264):

> [T]he first delusion-relevant event of which the patient is aware is the belief "That isn't my wife". Everything that preceded the occurrence of that belief and was responsible for the belief having come about...[is] unconscious. What's conscious is only the outcome that this chain of processes generated: the conscious belief "This person isn't my wife".

In Coltheart (2005), the subject's (*qua* patient's) experience is given a more prominent role. Here, Coltheart seems to be suggesting that more of the problem-solving work is done at the conscious level, or at least that the subject is aware that something 'odd' needs to be explained. There is a failure within the facial recognition system—a mismatch between prediction and outcome that triggers, at the conscious level, some sort of (although quite possibly unspecified) problem-solving activity, equivalent to 'something feels wrong; find out what it is'. In contrast, what Coltheart and colleagues (2010) seem to be proposing is a model in which the problem-solving occurs below conscious awareness. It is not deferred or 'elevated' to the level of consciousness to be resolved; rather, it is resolved before the product of its resolution enters consciousness. Because of this, for Coltheart and colleagues (2010), the first delusion-related event made conscious is not the anomalous experience—as this is not mentioned in the description at all—but, rather, the arrival into consciousness of the delusional belief.

There is some merit to Coltheart and colleagues' (2010) claim. As noted already, we are not conscious of the processes involved in facial recognition, including heightened or reduced SCR (at least *as* heightened or reduced SCR). Moreover, the idea that the means by which the delusional belief is formed involves exclusively unconscious processes avoids having to account for the relationship between attenuated autonomic arousal (as measured by SCR) and anomalous experience. As innovative as this approach is, however, there are problems with it, as I intend to highlight. Before doing so, let us consider Coltheart and colleagues' (2010) revisionist model, and related matters, in more detail.

4. Abnormal Data O

Unlike traditional accounts of the Capgras delusion, Coltheart and colleagues' (2010) revisionist model endorses only part of the default thesis (McLaughlin 2009)—namely, that disruption occurs in the facial recognition system (as presented by

Ellis and Lewis 2001)—such that there is activation of the face recognition unit (FRU) and relevant person identity nodes (PINs), but a lack of activation in the pathway responsible for producing the affective response to a familiar face, a measure of which is heightened SCR. What the model renounces is the claim that the delusional belief is formed in order to explain something the subject is conscious of: namely, an anomalous experience. Instead, it posits that the mismatch within the facial recognition system, between what should occur given the aforementioned activations—namely, a corresponding heightened autonomic response—and what actually occurs—an attenuated response—produces what Coltheart and colleagues (2010) call abnormal data O. Importantly, abnormal data O is processed below the level of conscious awareness.

Coltheart and colleagues' (2010) position draws from, or is certainly compatible with, predictive processing theory and, specifically, in the case of abnormal data O, predictive (or prediction) error.

> Prediction error represents the mismatch between what we expect in a given situation and what we actually experience. By working to reduce this mismatch, we improve our understanding of the causal structure of the world... [A] prediction error is a signal that our understanding of, or belief about, the world must be updated. Furthermore, those stimuli that engender prediction errors become more salient and this will be reflected in greater allocation of attention when they next occur.   (Corlett et al. 2009: 1)

In Young (2014), I argue that for O to be identified as abnormal within the Capgras subject, there must occur a discrepancy between O and some *normative* state of facial recognition (O_n). As Coltheart and colleagues remark: "When you do encounter her [your wife], you [the husband] will *expect* the usual consequences – a response by your autonomic nervous system. But this does not happen" (2010: 263; emphasis added). What might the discrepancy between the expected (what is predicted) and the actual (the outcome on this occasion) look like? *Ceteris paribus*, when in the presence of his wife, the following normative state should arise in the husband's face recognition system. Let us call this version of O the *normative wife* state (O_{nw}).

O_{nw} PIN activation occurs (signifying visual identification) in conjunction with heightened autonomic arousal (as measured by increased SCR).

When in the presence of a stranger, however, the normative state is captured by the following version of O. Let us call this the *normative stranger* state (O_{ns}).

O_{ns} PIN inactivity (signifying no visual identification) is associated with low autonomic arousal (as measured by reduced SCR).

158   BELIEF, IMAGINATION, AND DELUSION

In contrast to both normative states, abnormal data O consists of PIN activity (signifying identification) and attenuated autonomic arousal (associated with a stranger). Consequently, it matches neither normative state O_{nw} nor O_{ns}, resulting in an error signal. Given the state of O and its deviation from O_{nw} and O_{ns}, how might the Capgras husband explain the abnormality: the error signal?

According to Coltheart and colleagues (2010), below the level of conscious awareness, two mutually exclusive hypotheses are compared: the wife hypothesis (H_w) and the stranger hypothesis (H_s), respectively.

H_w This person who looks like my wife and claims to be my wife is my wife.

H_s This person who looks like my wife and claims to be my wife is not my wife.

When considering each candidate hypothesis, the Bayesian approach adopted by Coltheart and colleagues (2010) entails calculating which hypothesis best explains O (the abnormal data). The calculation involves offsetting the prior probability (prior to observing O) of each hypothesis being true against the explanatory power of the hypothesis (the ability of each to make sense of O). Explanatory prowess is a function of how well O is explained by the hypothesis, such that, given the truth of the hypothesis, it indicates the likelihood of O occurring. If a hypothesis explains O well, then the likelihood of it occurring given its truth will be high. As a means of demonstrating Bayes' theorem, Coltheart and colleagues (2010) present their own estimated ratios. The prior probability of H_s they estimate at 1:100, whereas the prior probability of H_w is given the much higher value of 99:100. When prior probability is considered in conjunction with the explanatory power of each to explain O (which includes the estimated likelihood of O occurring if a given hypothesis is correct), Coltheart and colleagues (2010) attempt to demonstrate (relative to each hypothesis available) that given a sufficiently high explanatory power, it is reasonable to select one hypothesis over the other as the most suitable. Thus, whilst the prior probability of the truth of H_s—that the person is in fact a stranger even though she looks just like the subject's wife and claims to be her—may be low (estimated at 1:100), it is nevertheless claimed to have high explanatory prowess because it is more able to explain the abnormality evident in O than the wife hypothesis, despite H_w having an estimated higher *prior* probability of being true. Through the use of Bayesian probability, Coltheart and colleagues (2010) argue that H_s is selected (at the unconscious level) in a manner consistent with normal abductive reasoning by the Capgras husband.

Ryan McKay (2012), however, considers H_s to be "a fantastically unlikely occurrence" (p. 340), and therefore the ratio of 1:100 (original suggested by Coltheart et al.) to be somewhat unrealistic. Instead, he suggests a ratio of 1:3650. When the prior probability of H_s is set at this more realistic (although, by his own admission, still quite generous) level, McKay argues that one could not reasonably expect H_s

to be selected as the most suitable hypothesis. What McKay is suggesting, then, is that the means of selecting H_s is not based on rational processing, but is the product of some form of cognitive deficit (a point I will return to in Section 12).

Deciding whether the selection of H_s is based on a rational calculation or is the product of faulty reasoning seems, in part at least, to depend on assumptions fed into the equation (e.g., whether the probability of the wife being a stranger is 1:100 or the higher but still quite generous ratio 1:3650). Moreover, while Bayes' theorem helps calculate the best fit for an already presented choice (in this case, between H_w and H_s), at least based on our assumptions, it has nothing to say about how we should arrive at the choices presented for selection in the first place. As Matthew Parrott (2021) notes: The reason the Capgras husband's belief strikes us as so bizarre is not that he believes something false (that the person who claims to be his wife is not his wife), or even that it is unjustified given the evidence provided, but that he believes something that is incompatible with the obviously true thing *we expect him to believe*: namely, that she is his wife. For Parrott, then, what remains unclear is how we might explain the underlying mechanism responsible for the *selection* of the set of hypotheses from which the successful 'best fit' hypothesis (to explain abnormal data O) is drawn. The assumption generating this question is that hypothesis (H_s)—"This person who looks like my wife and claims to be my wife is not my wife"—is so improbable as to be, in Cordelia Fine and colleagues' (2005) words, a *non-starter*.

A possible response can be found in Parrott (2016) in which he states, not unreasonably, that when faced with a puzzling situation ("Why is x doing y?" or "Why is this happening?"), we select a candidate hypothesis—what we consider to be the best fit to explain x's current causal connection to y—from a set of hypotheses drawn from our prior experience and understanding of what is epistemically possible in the current situation. Parrott then conjectures that the Capgras subject has an abnormal sense of what is epistemically possible and, for this reason, includes H_s (because it is not impossible) within his set of epistemically possible hypotheses.

I suggest an alternative reason for the inclusion of H_s, but one that is not incompatible with Parrott's conjecture. It is my contention that what contributes to the inclusion of the so-called 'non-starter' hypothesis—as well as its selection as the successful candidate and, ultimately, its acceptance as a delusional belief—is the anomalous experience the Capgras husband is highly motivated to explain. As Maher (2006: 182) notes when delineating components of the *anomalous experience model*: "[T]he experience must be . . . vivid and intense enough to preoccupy the consciousness of the individual while it is happening. In short, it must create a compelling sense of reality". Moreover, given the strangeness of the experience, the subject feels justified in broadening the scope of what he feels is epistemically possible, as he looks to explain what is happening. Again, in the words of Maher: "The individual experiences something that is very much out of the ordinary and

160   BELIEF, IMAGINATION, AND DELUSION

for which there is no immediately obvious explanation. This set of circumstances creates puzzlement, anxiety, and a search for an explanation" (Maher 2006: 181).

Importantly, then, my conjecture, in accordance with Maher, rests on the idea that the selection of H_s should draw on information from outside of the narrow context of a mismatch within the facial recognition system: for, as Neralie Wise (2016) warns, any account that reduces the cause of the delusional belief to just such an event is impoverished because it fails to acknowledge the wider context in which the delusion takes place, including other causally relevant factors. Mindful of Wise's warning, while it is my intention to incorporate abnormal data O and its cause within my explanation of the Capgras delusion, it is not my intention to *reduce* the formation of the delusional belief to this. Instead, I intend to elaborate on how *personal-level* (and therefore conscious) factors, relating to context, contribute to the anomalous nature of the subject's experience, and how this 'anomalousness' influences the selection of the candidate hypothesis and, ultimately, the delusional belief.

As a tentative first step towards restoring the role of anomalous experience within the aetiology of the Capgras delusion, and therefore understanding why neurological damage/disruption and unconscious processes alone are not *sufficient* to account for formation of the delusional belief, in the next section I consider what the Capgras husband's experience would be like if it were the case, as Coltheart and colleagues (2010) maintain (see below), that the first delusion-related event of which the Capgras husband is conscious is the belief "This person is not my wife". Before doing so, recall the description from Coltheart and colleagues (2010: 264) used earlier (repeated, this time, in more detail):

> [T]he first delusion-relevant event of which the patient is aware is the belief "That isn't my wife". Everything that preceded the occurrence of that belief and was responsible for the belief having come about – the stroke, the neuropsychological disconnection, the absence of an autonomic response when the wife is next seen, the invocation of a process of abductive inference to yield some hypothesis to explain this, and the successful generation of such a hypothesis – all of these processes are unconscious. What's conscious is only the outcome that this chain of processes generated: the conscious belief "This person isn't my wife".

5. The Candidate Hypothesis Appearing as an Unbidden Thought

According to Coltheart and colleagues' example, prior to the neurological disconnection (which they attribute to a stroke)—call it t_1—the Capgras husband's face

THE CAPGRAS DELUSION 161

processing system is working normally and so conforms to the normative requirements of O_{nw} when in the presence of his wife, and O_{ns} when in the presence of strangers. At t_2, however—after the disconnection (the stroke)—when the husband is in the presence of his wife, data O no longer conforms to the requirements of O_{nw}. Following Coltheart and colleagues' (2010) model, at time t_1, and at the conscious level, when the husband sees his wife, presumably he is aware of the fact that the person in front of him is his wife. Forming part of his conscious set of background beliefs (*inter alia*) is the belief corresponding somewhat unremarkably to "This is my wife". At t_2, however, all remains the same within the subject's experience except the belief that now enters consciousness and forms part of his background beliefs has changed from "This is my wife" to "This is *not* my wife", and no doubt stands out because of this. Certainly it would be inconsistent with the belief that she looks just like her or sounds like her, acts like her, is wearing her clothes, *claims to be her* (etc.).

Importantly, then, if all else remains the same from t_1 to t_2, it is difficult to understand how the sudden emergence of the delusional belief "This is not my wife" at t_2 could be experienced as anything other than an unbidden thought (Young 2011). The physical features of the Capgras husband's wife are registered by the FRU and PINs in the normal way, thereby producing a normal visual percept of his wife (consciously experienced as such, at least in terms of her physical features), but suddenly the belief (as Coltheart et al. 2010 refer to it) "This is not my wife" 'pops' into his head. What is he to make of this sudden change of belief relative to his other background beliefs when it emerges into consciousness? To reiterate, would the sudden appearance of the belief, with its unprecedented content (from the subject's perspective), not be treated as an unbidden thought?

My point is that the Capgras husband's belief or, as I intend to refer to it in the discussion to follow, *thought* about his wife, suddenly appearing as it does in consciousness, lacks sufficient context. Why should the Capgras husband suddenly believe that the person in his house, wearing his wife's clothes, looking and sounding like his wife, is not his wife? What, in my view, helps contextualize the newly emerged *thought* (i.e., not yet something he believes) is the co-occurring anomalous experience.

To be fair, Coltheart and colleagues (2010) do not deny the existence of an anomalous *conscious* experience. As they remark:

> [T]here is no doubt that people with Capgras delusion do have abnormal (conscious) experiences: Having a stranger living in your house without any explanation is an abnormal experience. So is having some stranger pretending to be your wife. But these experiences are not the cause of the delusion; they are consequences of the delusion.   (p. 264)

162 BELIEF, IMAGINATION, AND DELUSION

What Coltheart and colleagues (2010) have done, however, as the extract above reveals, is turn the anomalous conscious experience (to be clear, not abnormal data O) into a consequence of the delusion, thereby denying its causal contribution. In order to resist this move and, instead, take a further step towards reclaiming a role for *conscious* experience within the aetiology of the Capgras delusion (and in doing so negate the unbidden thought challenge just presented), it is important to delineate the nature of the experience beyond the common-place description, 'anomalous' that is often used (or 'abnormal', as Coltheart and colleagues 2010 refer to it). This I will do, now, in order to understand why the subject's experience is a major feature of *his reason* for embracing the thought "This person is not my wife", and the subsequent inference "she is an impostor", as a (delusional) belief, rather than merely acknowledging it as a consequence of the belief (as Coltheart et al. (2010) maintain); and therefore why it has causal efficacy within the overall aetiology of the Capgras delusion.

6. 'Anomalousness' as a Feeling of Unfamiliarity

In this section, I argue that, on returning to his marital home (for example), the Capgras husband experiences a salient sense of unfamiliarity towards the person who greets him as his wife. In defence of this claim, consider Matthew Ratcliffe (2004) who states that the Capgras husband is *struck* (Ratcliffe's term) by a marital home that is not only bereft of his wife but occupied by an unfamiliar other.

In an attempt to convey what this might be like, Ratcliffe (2004) draws a comparison between the experience of a Capgras husband expecting to see his wife and Sartre's (1969) example of a friend waiting for Pierre to enter the café. Whether you enter a café expecting to meet Pierre or your home expecting to be met by your wife, the experience is structured, Ratcliffe tells us, around the possibility that these people will appear. If they fail to do so, "the experience incorporates an absence into its structure" (Ratcliffe 2004: 38), either in the form of 'Pierre is not here' (if one is in the café) or 'my wife is not here' (if one is at home). In each case, the absence is salient.

The manner in which the Capgras husband interprets the context in which he expects to find his wife but does not is, according to Ratcliffe, equivalent to Pierre's friend continuing to experience the café as a place in which Pierre is absent each time someone other than Pierre enters the premises. There is, however, an important difference between the respective experiences of Pierre's friend and the Capgras husband. In the café example, Pierre is experienced as absent because he *is* absent. This is not the case, of course, with the wife: who continues to be experienced as absent even when she enters the room. This is because "the buzz of recognition" (Ratcliffe 2004: 38) that is integral to one's experience of one's spouse, *as one's spouse*, does not occur. Instead, the Capgras husband is confronted with a sense of unfamiliarity towards her.

THE CAPGRAS DELUSION   163

To help illustrate the salient nature of this unfamiliarity, Ratcliffe introduces his own variation on Sartre's café example, which he claims, in part at least, is phenomenologically equivalent to the unfamiliarity experienced by the Capgras subject.

> I enter a pub in England not expecting to see a certain friend, who I believe to be in Ireland. As I sit down, I see someone waving at me. Even though I perceive him clearly, it is not initially obvious 'who' he is. And then there is the feeling of familiarity. The face transforms, the whole experiential structure changes and takes on an air of familiarity as the face's significance is registered; 'It's him!' Without that sudden experiential reorientation, perhaps he would remain unfamiliar, unrecognised. Imagine an experience that hovers permanently in the state prior to re-orientation. Unfamiliarity is something that experientially strikes one. No inference will circumvent the persistent feeling that 'he is not known to me'.   (Ratcliffe 2004: 39)

According to Ratcliffe, the experiential reorientation brings with it a sense of familiarity that is absent pre-reorientation. But, equally, Ratcliffe wants the *absence* of familiarity to be salient. Yet we experience an absence of familiarity regularly without necessarily being 'struck' by it (e.g., when in a crowd of weekend shoppers, or at the cinema or the theatre). Therefore, when Ratcliffe notices the man waving at him from across the room, yet fails to recognize him as his friend, what has changed from moments earlier—when he may have viewed the man merely as one among many in the pub—is the expectation that comes with this sudden social interaction: "Who is the man waving at me? He seems to know me. Should I know him?" In this context, given the change of expectation brought about by the seeming nature of the encounter, it is not simply that Ratcliffe does not experience the man as a friend (after all, he did not experience him as a friend prior to the hand waving); rather, given the sudden change in context, it is that he now experiences him as unfamiliar, and therefore as not a friend. Ratcliffe is struck *not* by the absence of familiarity but by the salience of his sense of *unfamiliarity*; and it is the salience of *this* experience that we are told equates to the phenomenology underpinning the Capgras delusion.

While I believe the two cases have some commonality, I am not convinced that they represent a useful phenomenologically comparison. When the Capgras husband meets his wife, he is struck by a salient sense of unfamiliarity, but not the same unfamiliarity as Ratcliffe experiences, pre-reorientation. Given the context in which the Capgras husband finds himself—arriving home, say—he expects to be greeted by his wife and, subsequently, to feel a sense of familiarity towards the woman currently smiling at him and attempting to solicit a conversation. But any familiarity he might expect to feel is not simply absent—in the way one would expect it to be absent when queuing with strangers for a takeaway

164   BELIEF, IMAGINATION, AND DELUSION

coffee, or pre-reorientation, in the case of Ratcliffe's friend—it is *missing* and experienced as such. The unfamiliarity the Capgras husband experiences towards the woman currently occupying the marital home, stems from a *loss* of familiarity, not simply a lack of it. The unfamiliarity reveals what is missing[2] because there is an expectation that a sense of familiarity should be present, and it is not.

The origin of the Capgras husband's anomalous experience (neurological disruption aside, for the moment) is rooted in the fact that he does and yet does not *recognize* his wife. Now, clearly, this statement is ambiguous. In what sense is the wife recognized and in what sense is she not? The Capgras husband does not claim that this person is not his wife because she looks nothing like her. There is therefore a sense in which the husband recognizes who the person is *meant* to be, particularly in the context in which she appears; but there is also a sense in which the salient experience of unfamiliarity indicates that he fails to recognize her as *being* the woman that context suggests she should be. There occurs what George Christodoulou (1977) calls a pathological negation of being.

The Capgras husband is confronted with a violation of expectation (just as Pierre's friend was each time someone other than Pierre entered the café). The discrepancy between expectation and reality (at least as the Capgras husband experiences it) produces a salient sense of unfamiliarity towards the person occupying the otherwise familiar surroundings of the marital home. The unfamiliarity perceived is not the result of 'unfamiliarity' properties intrinsic to the experience, however; rather, it is the consequence of the predictive error signal discussed earlier, in the form of abnormal data O, made salient. But not just this. After all, the expectation that it should be his wife that greets him is something the Capgras husband is conscious of, and therefore conscious of being violated (it seems) when he is confronted by the unexpected and salient sense of unfamiliarity towards the person who claims to be his wife.

Of course, it may be difficult for the Capgras husband to describe his experience beyond the feeling that something is wrong. It will likely make for an unusual and even disturbing experience (as Maher originally conjectured); but however troubling it is, it should not yet be described as an 'impostor' experience. This is because the Capgras husband does not yet perceive, and therefore experience, the person stood before him as an 'impostor' (a point I shall return to in Section 10). If the *current* experience is to be articulated, beyond the common-place description, "anomalous", then it is my contention that 'estrangement' (defined as the feeling of being alienated from another person who one expects to have strong positive feelings towards) is as good a term as any for capturing the contextualized sense of unfamiliarity that the Capgras husband suddenly experiences towards his wife.[3]

---

[2] Insofar as the experience contains a sense that something is *missing*, it is similar to the experience Pierre's friend has of the café in the absence of Pierre.

[3] It is also a term used by Gerrans (1999).

THE CAPGRAS DELUSION   165

Unlike the pre-reorientation sense of unfamiliarity Ratcliffe describes feeling towards the man waving at him in the pub, the unfamiliarity the Capgras husband experiences towards the person that context demands *is*, and indeed he recognizes as being *just like*, his wife is more akin to a sudden sense of estrangement. This is because, pre-reorientation, Ratcliffe does not recognize the man at all. There is therefore no conflict between one's recognition of who the person is *meant* to be and one's negation of that person *being* who they are meant to be (as is the case with the Capgras husband), because, for Ratcliffe, there is no conflict of recognition, owing to the fact that there is no recognition at all pre-reorientation. The unfamiliarity experienced by the Capgras husband cannot therefore be phenomenologically equivalent to Ratcliffe's pre-orientation experience in the pub.

Taking stock: The Capgras husband is confronted with a person who looks just like his wife, who claims to be his wife, in a place where he would expect to find his wife. Owing to neurological disruption, a mismatch occurs in the facial recognition system triggering a predictive error signal below the level of consciousness, otherwise known as abnormal data O. In response to this, candidate hypotheses are presented for consideration: H_w and H_s. At the same time, the Capgras husband experiences—is struck by—a salient feeling of unfamiliarity. (All I am committing myself to, here, is the *co-occurrence* of abnormal data O and the subject's sudden feeling of unfamiliarity/sense of estrangement.)[4]

To understand the significance of the subject's sense of estrangement to the selection of candidate hypothesis, H_s, we need to take a step back and reconsider what a hypothesis intended to explain data constitutive of a mismatch in the facial recognition system, *only*, would look like: for it is my contention that, from such a reductionist perspective, it would not be as Coltheart and colleagues (2010) describe (see Section 4).

7. The Need for a Less Reductionist Approach to Hypothesis Selection

We are told, and I have accepted, that abnormal data O is the product of a mismatch in the facial recognition system between a given outcome and what was predicted. If we were to adopt a reductionist approach then, from that

---

[4] What remains unclear, at this stage, is the precise causal mechanism underlying the co-occurrence of the subject's experience: its neurological underpinnings. The view that unconscious processes have an effect on personal experience is not without support. Cleary and Specker (2007), for example, argue that covert autonomic arousal can enter consciousness as a feeling of familiarity or what they call "tartling," which equates to recognition without identification (see Young 2009, for more details). Davies and Egan (2013), for their part, assume that "although the Bayesian inference begins from data that are not available to personal-level consciousness, the result of the inference will determine the content of an experience that presents or represents the world as being a certain way" (Davies and Egan 2013: 713)

166   BELIEF, IMAGINATION, AND DELUSION

perspective, where abnormal data O occurs, because $x \neq W$ and it was predicted that $x = W$, hypotheses must be selected to account for the discrepancy, couched in the 'language' of that discrepancy. In other words, abnormal data O would need to be explained by hypotheses that reflect the available data because they are constrained by it. But such reductionist language is not what Coltheart and colleagues (2010) use to describe the two candidate hypotheses intended to explain abnormal data O. Recall H_s is described as "This person who looks like my wife and claims to be my wife is not my wife". This description goes beyond information processed by the facial recognition system *alone*, and therefore beyond what I would argue is constitutive of a reductionist or narrow perspective. To explain: It is perfectly possible that the person's face could be identified as 'wife' by the facial recognition system, owing to the correct activation of the FRU and PINs; but the hypothesis makes reference to the person *claiming to be the husband's wife* and this goes beyond the narrow context we are discussing.

Davies and Egan (2013: 713) make a similar point: "A module that is dedicated to processing information about faces will have a limited representational 'vocabulary' and the hypotheses that it can 'consider' will be correspondingly restricted". Davies and Egan surmise, however, that hypotheses will also take into account who the person is in relation to other people (e.g., wife, sister, aunt, and so on), who they look like if not identified, or whether they are unknown. In keeping with Davies and Egan's supposition, Coltheart and colleagues' (2010) candidate hypotheses seem to draw on information available from a wider perspective. This being the case, then not only does the *notion* of abnormal data O allow more than just information pertaining to a mismatch in the facial recognition system, it opens up the possibility that candidate hypotheses are being selected to explain an anomaly that is much broader in scope. As part of this wider context, the anomalousness of the subject's experience (how it makes him feel) must be factored into the selection process. Hypotheses would need to be sensitive to the context in which the estrangement was experienced (i.e., they must take into account the woman in the marital home acting like and claiming to be the husband's wife and, importantly, the sense of unfamiliarity the subject is struck by, and the context in which it occurs). There is therefore more to be explained than whether x is or is not W. Such a hypothesis would need to address the following: "If this is my wife then why do I suddenly feel this way?" and "If this is not my wife then what is going on?" These questions are framed using personal-level language and reflect a holistic rather than reductionist approach to the violation of expectation occurring at both the unconscious and conscious levels.

Given that H_s, as presented by Coltheart and colleagues (2010) appears to draw from a wider context than simply information constitutive of a mismatch in the facial recognition system, it is my intention to show how the subject's experience influences the content and selection of H_s because it influences what H_s is required to explain. Moreover, recall that it has been a point of contention whether the selection of H_s is the product of normal (Coltheart et al. 2010) or abnormal (McKay 2012) reasoning. To help resolve this issue, recall that, for Maher (1974), the intensity of the anomalous experience is powerful enough to cause an otherwise rational person—the Capgras husband—to conclude that his wife is an impostor. The subject takes it to be the best explanation for what is happening to him: for why he feels the way he does. Thus, while the subject's delusional belief is said to be the product of an inference that is not dissimilar to those made by non-delusional subjects, it is nevertheless based on experiential content that *is* strikingly dissimilar (Maher 1974, 1992, 2006). Let us examine this claim further.

8. Psychological Inevitability?

More recently, Eisuke Sakakibara (2019) has sought to refine Maher's position. I intend to apply his argument to the successful selection of candidate hypothesis, H_s, while adhering to Wise's (2016) warning not to remove the explanation from its broader context. Sakakibara argues that the Capgras husband's reasoning is only partially intact: for while it remains the case that H_s is able to explain abnormal data O and the anomalous experience, the selection of H_s as the candidate hypothesis that the Capgras husband *comes to believe* does not follow (necessarily) from the occurrence of either of these events (abnormal data O and the anomalous experience; although, of course, the subject is only *conscious* of the anomalous experience and H_s as it enters consciousness as the thought "This is not my wife"). There are, after all, other explanations for abnormal data O and the anomalous experience available (e.g., head trauma). In recognition of this fact, Sakakibara draws a distinction between the reasonableness (as he sees it) of the selection of H_s as *one* of the candidate hypotheses (*qua* collection of possible explanations) and the more irrational *evaluation* of H_s as the best fit to explain the bizarre nature of the sudden experience of estrangement that accompanies the mismatch in the face recognition system. And while he recognizes that the acceptance (not selection) of the hypothesis, as *the* reason above all other reasons for the experience, is epistemically irrational, he nevertheless concedes that, because of the intensity of the experience, it is excusable. In fact, he goes so far as to say that it may be psychologically inevitable that a belief corresponding to the selected hypothesis, H_s, is endorsed (I will have more to say on this and the psychological benefit of the delusional belief in Section 9 when discussing *epistemic innocence* and *delusional atmosphere*). For Sakakibara, the intensity of the experience, and the anxiety it elicits, may induce context-specific performance errors (Gerrans 2001) that distort the subject's evaluation of candidate hypothesis, H_s, resulting in its selection as the most suitable reason-giving explanation available (see Noordhof, this volume, for a different view).

168   BELIEF, IMAGINATION, AND DELUSION

Sakakibara further conjectures that the anxiety produced by the intense experience results in the subject having difficulty maintaining a certain 'distance' from the experience, such that they are unable to look 'inside' themselves to find the cause of the experience's 'anomalousness' (e.g., brought on by the recent brain trauma) and so, instead, look to the other person for the answer: there must be something wrong with *them*. Such is the "intensity of the experience [that it] removes the patient's ability to represent the experience [simply] as an *experience they are having*" (Sakakibara 2019: 178; emphasis added).[5]

Sakakibara's supposition is compatible with a distinction Marga Reimer (2009) draws between the candidate hypothesis as a rational response to the experience and the view that it is the response of a rational agent to the sudden and strange experience that confronts them. In keeping with Sakakibara's claim, it could be that the selection and particularly the acceptance of the candidate hypothesis is the sort of thing an otherwise rational agent would do, *under duress*—owing to the anxiety-inducing experience—without making the process of selection *and* acceptance fully rational.

Understanding the conditions under which H_s emerges as the successful hypothesis involves recognizing the influence of the wider, personal-level, context on the selection process. Moreover, when the thought "This person is not my wife" emerges into consciousness, alongside the subject's sense of estrangement, it is far less likely to be treated as unbidden and is instead more likely to be given credence at the conscious level. The thought gives meaning to the confronting experiential change the Capgras husband has undergone by providing him with a reason for what has happened. The thought is therefore more likely to be accepted not because of the content's proximity to the truth (its verisimilitude)—after all, there are other hypotheses that would trump H_s in this regard—but because of the psychological benefit it delivers to a confused husband seeking answers.

To illustrate this confusion, Sam Wilkinson (2015) asks: How can the Capgras husband justify to another his claim that there is something "odd" or "not quite right" about the person who is supposed to be his wife? How does the subject articulate their sudden feeling of estrangement in a manner that would adequately count as evidence that something is different and wrong; that would persuade the onlooker that *this person*—the Capgras husband's wife—is not who they claim to be? It seems that the onlooker must either take the subject's testimony on trust or fail to believe them. Given that the latter outcome is more likely, the incredulity of others may simply add to the confusion and possibly increase the tension the subject experiences, inadvertently helping to create a delusional atmosphere.

---

[5] Hustig and Hafner (1990) likewise report a correlation between fluctuation and intensity of auditory hallucinations and fluctuation and intensity of delusional belief.

THE CAPGRAS DELUSION   169

9. Delusional Atmosphere

Lisa Bortolotti (2015) argues that certain delusional beliefs, which she refers to as *epistemically innocent*, can nevertheless be of epistemic and psychological benefit to the subject. The belief that one's wife is an impostor has epistemic benefit, it is claimed, despite being grounded on faulty cognition, if it helps avoid an epistemically worse consequence (e.g., the epistemic gap that exists between how the world is said to be and how the Capgras husband experiences the world *as being*, at least regarding his wife). In support of the psychological benefit of the delusional belief (its adaptive function), Shitij Kapur (2003) describes it as acting to *relieve* the patient's (*qua* subject's) mounting anxiety. Andrew Sim's (1995) expresses a similar view (see also Berner 1991; Jaspers 1997) when describing a phenomenon known as *delusional atmosphere*:

> For the patient experiencing delusional atmosphere, his world has been subtly altered: 'Something funny is going on'...When the delusion becomes fully formed, he often appears to accept it with a feeling of relief from the previous unbearable tension of the atmosphere.   (Sims 1995: 109)

> [In fact, it] is easier to bear the certainty of a delusion than the uncertain foreboding of the atmosphere.   (Sims 1995: 112)

Ema Sullivan-Bissett (2018: 938) adds:

> [I]t is in no part the claim of epistemic innocence that subjects forming monothematic delusions are in line with the prescription of epistemic norms, the claim is only that the epistemic route taken is one which has epistemic benefits mediated by psychological ones.

The idea of a delusional atmosphere (or mood) as a precursor to the delusional state is also suggested by Philip Corlett (2010) when seeking to induce a delusional state (temporarily) in a volunteer through the use of ketamine: "We suggest that the present subject was experiencing a particular type of delusional mood that would *lead them to construct* a Capgras' delusion (had the ketamine infusion continued or been administered at a higher dose)" (e2; emphasis added).[6]

For Kapur (2003), the delusional patient's (*qua* subject's) attempt to make sense of what is for him a perplexing and anxiety-provoking situation is usually followed by relief, and even a proclaimed new awareness, as the delusion crystallizes. The

---

[6] See, also, Spitzer (1992) for a discussion on delusional mood and the phenomenology of delusions.

170 BELIEF, IMAGINATION, AND DELUSION

psychological benefit of the delusional belief is that it *appears* to give the patient the power to understand what they are highly motivated to understand (Bortolotti 2016), offering "insight relief" or "psychotic insight" (Kapur 2003: 15).

10. Experiential Transformation

Bortolotti (2016), Kapur (2003), and Sims' (1995) overlapping descriptions are compatible with the idea of *experiential transformation*, whereby the Capgras husband's experience is transformed from an initially salient and perplexing sense of estrangement—contributing to the tension of the delusional atmosphere— into a full-blown 'impostor' experience as the delusional belief takes hold. Experiential transformation also offers insight into what Louis Sass and Elizabeth Pienkos (2013) refer to as "the temporal interdependence [or dia- chronic relationship] of distinct phases or stages in the *development* of the patient's lived world" (632; emphasis in original). For the Capgras husband, accepting the delusional belief that his wife is an impostor alters his perception of her so that she now appears to him *as* an impostor (Corlett, this volume). This transformation can be likened to how one's perception of the *Leeper's Lady* visual illusion is altered depending on whether one is primed to see an old or young woman (Leeper 1935) or, in the case of the *Duck-Rabbit* illusion, a duck or a rabbit.

Analogously, on coming to believe that the woman who claims to be his wife is not his wife, and after inferring from this that she must be an impostor, the Capgras husband's newly acquired belief helps transform his experience from a sense of estrangement—i.e., an initially perplexing and confronting sense of unfamiliarity—into a *normative* sense of unfamiliarity. The delusional belief provides the Capgras husband not only with (alleged) insight into his lived world but, importantly, relief from what went before. After all, unfamiliarity is what one is supposed to experience when living with an impostor. There is now congruence between the Capgras husband's belief about his wife (*qua* the impos- tor living in his house) and the way she appears to him.

Of course, one might object to this move as follows: Given the alleged trans- formative power of belief on experience, why does the Capgras husband not just affirm (or reaffirm) his belief that the person in front of him is his wife in order to have the belief transform his anomalous experience into something less anomal- ous? In response, I would say that a major causal component of the subject's experience is neurological damage (as discussed in Section 3). This remains the case, no matter what he believes. The mismatch in the facial processing system continues unabated. So even if the Capgras husband were able to believe, despite his sense of estrangement, that the person in front of him is his wife, such a belief is not capable of transforming his sudden sense of unfamiliarity into the kind of familiarity he had previously experienced towards his wife;[7] but it is capable of transforming the already existing and, given the context, *perplexing* unfamiliarity into a *normative* unfamiliarity: the kind of unfamiliarity one is expected to experience in the presence of a stranger/impostor.

Experiential transformation helps account for why the delusional belief resists revision. Sakakibara (2019), in keeping with what I have just discussed, describes the anomalous experience as "persistent and omnipresent" (p. 176), at least when confronted with the significant other who is believed to be an impostor. He is agnostic, however, on the matter of whether the "permanently powerful" (Coltheart et al. 2010: 283) anomalous entity is conscious or unconscious. I have argued that co-occurring with the persistent and omnipresent abnormal data O (in the context of the wife) is the subject's troubling *experiential* content; and while I agree that what the subject experiences is powerful, or at least powerful enough to motivate him to explain it, I nevertheless question the extent to which it persists unchanged. Instead, I advocate a transformation in the subject's experience from an initial sense of estrangement to a normative sense of unfamiliarity that accompanies the Capgras husband's perception of his 'impostor' wife.

Acceptance of the delusional belief can bring its own reward, both in terms of relief from the delusional atmosphere and the kinds of benefit advanced by the argument for epistemic innocence. On top of this, the belief can *shape* the ongoing experience such that what was once an uncomfortable feeling of estrangement, from which the subject sought relief, and to close an epistemic gap, is now a normative sense of unfamiliarity. What this means, from the subject's perspective, is that the belief and the experience are not just aligned but intimately linked. The experience validates the belief and the belief authenticates the experience. This is how he is supposed to feel under the circumstances. Why would he seek to challenge such a matchup?

11. Perceiving an Impostor

In contrast to explanationist accounts, endorsement theorists argue that the content of the delusion belief—"This person is not my wife; she is an impostor"—is implicitly contained within the subject's phenomenal experience, thereby removing the explanatory gap between what the subject experiences and what he believes. The Capgras husband's belief that he is in the presence of an 'impostor

---

[7] Turner and Coltheart (2010) report the experiences of a woman with neurological impairment that they speculate has created a first-factor impairment similar to Capgras delusion. When the woman sees her mother, she reports that it does not *feel* like her. The woman does not, however, go on to develop a delusional belief about her mother. The point of this example is that it shows how the woman's belief that this person was still her mother did not alter the experience of something being wrong; of it not *feeling* like her.

172   BELIEF, IMAGINATION, AND DELUSION

wife' is therefore said to be derived (with the help of a bias in his prepotent doxastic response; see Davies and Egan 2013) from his experience of an impostor wife. Critics have been quick to point out, however, that the approach bestows on personal experience sole responsibility for the content of the delusional belief (Young and de Pauw 2002). The *experiential encoding problem*, as it has been called (Bongiorno 2020), arises because the content of the experience does not appear to be 'rich' or 'fine grained' enough to suffice as material from which the delusional belief is derived. Robert Klee (2004) shares this criticism, considering it implausible that "raw perceptual experience contains its own intrinsic thematic content" (p. 26). In other words, it is unlikely that the husband's delusional belief that his wife is an impostor is derived solely from an experience with intrinsic 'impostor wife' properties.

Explanationist approaches, for their part, have tended to offer fairly scant descriptive detail when it comes to personal experience, often referring to it as simply "anomalous". Even Coltheart and colleagues (2010) when talking about patient experience as a consequence rather than a cause of the delusional belief, refer to it in minimal terms (i.e., "abnormal"). The revised interactionist account, in contrast, not only provides more detail than other explanationist approaches on the phenomenal character of the subject's experience but also explains how it is that the Capgras husband comes to experience his wife *as* an impostor, as claimed by proponents of the endorsement approach.

Experiential transformation allows that the subject's experience is initially 'anomalous', insofar as it presents as a sudden and confronting sense of estrangement which the subject is troubled by and so motivated to explain; but, through the acquisition of the delusional belief (as a means of explaining the experience), the experience is transformed into an 'impostor' experience. On coming to *believe* that his wife is an impostor, what the Capgras husband sees when he looks at his wife *is* an impostor. The experiential content does not have intrinsic 'impostor wife' content, however, as the endorsement approach suggests, but neither does it remain as it was (i.e., as a confronting sense of estrangement). The wife is *now* perceived as an impostor (thereby giving a nod to the endorsement approach), but only as a result of the *interaction* between experiential content and belief; rather than on account of any intrinsic properties of the experience.[8]

In short, the belief is first accepted because it explains why the subject feels a sudden sense of estrangement, and therefore provides him with a reason for why things are the way they are (i.e. "This is why I feel the way I do towards this person"). Accepting the belief then helps transform the subject's initial experience into something that he now feels he is able to make sense of and gain insight into (i.e., "The sense of unfamiliarity I feel is how I should feel when in the presence of

---

[8] This claim is in contrast to Bongiorno's (2020) suggestion (speculative proposal) that the Capgras husband perceives an impostor in a metaphorical sense only.

an impostor"). The *reason* the Capgras husband now has for believing that the woman in front of him is not his wife but an impostor is that he perceives her as such: as an impostor.

Thus far, I have presented the case for a revised interactionist model and, in doing so. sought to defend points 1–7 as set out in Section 1. The interactionist approach amounts to a *tentative* two-factor account, for a reason that will be made clear as we progress. In the final section, I will say a little about the second factor I tentatively embrace, and its relationship to the subject's experience.

12. The Second Factor

A well-documented characteristic of the Capgras delusion is that the subject typically resists revising their delusional belief. Why is this? After all, no matter how much the belief and the experience align, or how much relief one might obtain by accepting the delusional belief, given that, at best, the belief is extremely unlikely to be true, and given the sheer weight of evidence against it being true and therefore justified as a belief, one might hope or even expect that the Capgras husband would be motivated to revise his belief. Instead, the belief is entrenched.

As mentioned in Section 2, two-factor approaches posit some form of second-factor cognitive disruption, in addition to the first-factor neurological disruption, to account for the subject's formation of the delusional belief and/or their unwillingness to revise it. Lesions to brain regions associated with belief evaluation have been reported in Capgras patients. R. Ryan Darby and colleagues (2017), for example, identified two areas of neurological disruption in seventeen patients suffering from delusional misidentification (not all of which were Capgras delusion). In addition to lesions located in the left retrospenial cortex (which is associated with familiarity) they reported lesions in the right ventral frontal cortex and anterior insula (associated with violation of expectation and belief evaluation). Similarly, Coltheart and colleagues (2018: 237) report: "[T]he effect of the right DLPFC [dorsolateral prefrontal cortex] abnormality is to impair the normal process of belief evaluation and hence to fail to prevent the thought from becoming a belief". As a way to explain variations found in the site of neurological damage, Darby and colleagues (2017) have proposed a lesion network approach whereby Capgras symptoms can be traced not necessarily to damage to a specific areas of the brain but, rather, to lesions that occur across different sites that are *functionally connected* with belief evaluation.[9]

---

[9] Darby and colleagues' lesion network approach might help explain inconsistencies in the location of the lesion reported in cases of Capgras delusion. Currella and colleagues (2019), for example, after carrying out a meta-analysis of a UK mental health service provider database, identified 34 Capgras cases but found that right hemisphere damage was not predominant (see also Bell et al. 2017, whose findings Currella et al. closely replicate). They also report that a significant minority of cases did not conform to the 'dual route' model.

174   BELIEF, IMAGINATION, AND DELUSION

Given the emerging support for disruption to areas of the brain that are functionally independent (e.g., concerned with familiarity and belief evaluation) in Capgras patients, I favour a two-factor account. I do so tentatively, however, because I recognize the validity of Sullivan-Bissett's (2020) claim that the burden of proof is on the two-factor theorists to establish that the neurological damage identified in Capgras subjects causes *abnormal* reasoning, and therefore justifies the inclusion of a second-factor to the explanatory model. Sullivan-Bissett's point, in accordance with Maher, is that *if* the reasoning that produces delusional beliefs characteristic of the Capgras delusion (although not limited to this disorder) is not outside of the normal range of reasoning error (i.e., not dissimilar to the reasoning found in non-deluded but erroneous belief formation) then, while the neurological damage may have a causal role to play, it does not justify the need for a second factor (Noordhof, this volume). The reason I still favour the two-factor approach, however, is because Sullivan-Bissett's objection is that neurological damage has not been shown to cause abnormal reasoning. She does not go so far as to deny that the damage could have a role to play in the aetiology of the disorder. Because of this—that is, because neurological damage may well be affecting the subject's reasoning to some degree, even if not to an abnormal degree (however that might be distinguished from the range of normal reasoning)—it still constitutes an additional factor that is *contributing* to the Capgras delusion (and possibly other disorders). The fact that neurological damage could be affecting the subject's reasoning, even if it is not sufficient to make the reasoning abnormal, and so could be playing a part in their symptomatology, is reason enough, I contend, to include it as a distinct factor to be considered.

That said, among two-factor theorists, there is disagreement over the precise nature of the cognitive disruption and therefore where in the process it occurs (Davies and Egan 2013). To help articulate my own thoughts on this issue, consider the following comment by Coltheart and colleagues (2011: 284):

> The propositions yielded by abductive inference are not beliefs, but rather hypotheses or candidates for beliefs. For any such proposition to be adopted as a belief, it must be submitted to, and survive, a belief-evaluation process, and it is here that plausibility has a critical role.

There are a few things to consider about Coltheart and colleagues' (2011) comment. First, the hypothesis (or candidate for belief) must be evaluated before it becomes a belief; before the Capgras husband *comes to believe it* (or not). This aligns with Coltheart's view that the second-factor disruption concerns belief evaluation (there is therefore no disruption to the process of candidate *selection*; which follows abductive inference based on Bayesian probability). But what is not clear from the description above is whether the belief evaluation is directed towards a hypothesis/candidate belief of which the subject is conscious. If it occurs below the level of consciousness, and only enters consciousness after being accepted as a belief, then my earlier objection stands regarding the sudden emergence of this belief having the appearance of an unbidden thought in the absence of further context.[10] Also, if it concerns information processed below the level of consciousness, one is left to ponder what the basis of the *evaluation* is, again, given that this would likely be bereft of a broader context. If, on the other hand, it emerges into consciousness as a candidate belief—as a *thought* (as I referred to it in Section 8) to be entertained and evaluated—then, while still potentially having the appearance of an unbidden thought, it would suggest that the *evaluation* draws on personal-level factors (potentially, other things the subject is conscious of). Even so, and to reiterate my earlier criticism, under the conditions described, the conscious evaluation of the candidate belief, in the absence of a co-occurring experiential change (i.e., the sudden sense of unfamiliarity), would appear to be based on nothing that is different in the Capgras husband's lived world. As such, why should a thought that suddenly 'pops' (unbidden) into the subject's head be accepted? For what reason? On the other hand, where the emerging thought provides some meaning to the subject's co-occurring experience then he *has a reason* to believe the content of the thought that suddenly emerges unbidden. Importantly, though, as noted previously, while the co-occurrence of a bizarre and potentially distressing experience (*qua* estrangement) does not necessarily make the evaluation and acceptance of the candidate belief more rational, it does make it psychologically more understandable.

For this reason, like McKay (2012), I favour a second-factor disruption in the form of a bias towards *explanatory adequacy*, whereby one is more willing to accept a hypothesis that explains a *salient piece of evidence* than one that, say, aligns more closely with one's already existing beliefs (Aimola Davies and Davies 2009; see also Levy, this volume). The bias towards explanatory adequacy is not necessarily ubiquitous but, rather, manifests itself, first, as a performance error—a selective disruption to the Capgras husband's reasoning—exacerbated by the unexpected and unnerving feeling of estrangement that he is motivated to explain and, again, as an unwillingness to revise the (delusional) belief that his wife is an impostor. After all, in the latter case, what piece of evidence is more compelling, from the Capgras husband's perspective, than the fact that he now *perceives* an impostor when in the presence of his wife. Evidence that is difficult to refute through mere testimony or other less direct (than his own experience) evidential routes because these alternatives offer little in the way of relief and (alleged) insight into the situation: something the Capgras husband now believes he possesses.

---

[10] To be consistent with comments found in Coltheart and colleagues (2010), in which the (delusional) belief is the first-delusion-related event of which the patient is conscious, the evaluation of the belief would have to occur below the level of consciousness.

13. Conclusion

In presenting my defence of a revised interactionist approach to the Capgras delusion, I hope to have established the important role personal experience plays in the aetiology of the Capgras delusion. The co-occurrence of a (conscious) sense of estrangement, alongside (unconscious) abnormal data O, helps provide a broader context for the selection of the candidate hypotheses, by expanding what the subject considers to be epistemically possible given the current situation. The potential perplexing and anxiety-inducing nature of the experience also provides a reason for him to embrace his bias towards explanatory adequacy (a situation-driven performance error). Moreover, the experiential transformation that occurs after the subject has come to believe that his wife is an impostor illustrates a further role for personal experience that, again shows a bias towards explanatory adequacy. The reason the Capgras husband continues to believe that the person in front of him is an impostor is because that is what he perceives when he looks at her.

References

Aimola Davies, A. M. and Davies, M. (2009). 'Explaining Pathologies of Belief', in M. R. Broome and L. Bortolotti (eds.), *Psychiatry as Cognitive Neuroscience: Philosophical Perspectives* (Oxford: Oxford University Press), 285–23.

Bauer, R. M. (1984). 'Autonomic Recognition of Names and Faces in Prosopagnosia: A Neuropsychological Application of the Guilty Knowledge Test', *Neuropsychologia* 22: 457–69.

Bayne, T. and Pacherie, E. (2004). 'Bottom-Up or Top-Down? Campbell's Account of Monothematic Delusions', *Philosophy, Psychiatry & Psychology* 11/1: 1–11.

Bell, V., Marshall, C., Kanji, Z., Wilkinson, S., Halligan, P., and Deeley, Q. (2017). 'Uncovering Capgras Delusion Using a Large Scale Medical Records Database', *British Journal of Psychiatry Open* 3/4: 179–85.

Berner, P. (1991). 'Delusional Atmosphere', *British Journal of Psychiatry* 159/Suppl. 14: 88–93.

Bongiorno, F. (2020). 'Is the Capgras Delusion an Endorsement of Experience?' *Mind & Language* 35/3: 293–312.

Bortolotti, L. (2015). 'The Epistemic Innocence of Motivated Delusions', *Consciousness and Cognition* 33: 490–9.

Bortolotti, L. (2016). 'Epistemic Benefits of Elaborated and Systematized Delusions in Schizophrenia', *British Journal for the Philosophy of Science* 67/3: 879–900.

Breen, N., Caine, D., and Coltheart, M. (2000). 'Models of Face Recognition and Delusional Misidentification: A Critical Review', *Cognitive Neuropsychology* 17/1–3: 55–71.

Brighetti, G., Bonifacci, P., Borlimi, R., and Ottaviani, C. (2007). '"Far from the Heart Far from the Eye": Evidence from the Capgras Delusion', *Cognitive Neuropsychiatry* 12/3: 189–97.

Campbell, J. (2001). 'Rationality, Meaning and the Analysis of Delusion', *Philosophy, Psychiatry & Psychology* 8/2–3: 89–100.

Capgras, J. and Reboul-Lachaux, J. (1923). 'L'illusion des "Soises" dans un Délire Systématisé Chronique', *Bulletin de la Société Clinique de Médicine Mentale* 11: 6–16.

Christodoulou, G. N. (1976). 'Delusional Hyper-Identification of the Frégoli Type', *Acta Psychiatrica Scandinavica* 54: 305–14.

Christodoulou, G. N. (1977). 'The Syndrome of Capgras', *British Journal of Psychiatry* 130: 556–64.

Cleary, A. M. and Specker, L. E. (2007). 'Recognition Without Face Identification', *Memory and Cognition* 35/7: 1610–19.

Coltheart, M. (2005). 'Conscious Experience and Delusional Belief', *Philosophy, Psychiatry & Psychology* 12/2: 153–7.

Coltheart, M., Cox, R., Sowman, P., Morgan, H., Barnier, A., Langdon, R., Connaughton, E., Teichmann, L., Williams, N., and Polito, V. (2018). 'Belief, Delusion, Hypnosis, and the Right Dorsolateral Prefrontal Cortex: A Transcranial Magnetic Stimulation Study', *Cortex* 101: 234–48.

Coltheart, M., Langdon, R., and McKay, R. (2011). 'Delusional Belief', *Annual Review of Psychology* 62: 271–98.

Coltheart, M., Menzies, P., and Sutton, J. (2010). 'Abductive Inference and Delusional Belief', *Cognitive Neuropsychiatry* 15/1: 261–87.

Corlett, P. R. (2010). 'Capgras Syndrome Induced by Ketamine in a Healthy Subject', *Biological Psychiatry* 68: e1–e2.

Corlett, P. R. (2019). 'Factor One, Familiarity and Frontal Cortex: A Challenge to the Two-Factor Theory of Delusions', *Cognitive Neuropsychiatry* 24/3: 165–77.

Corlett, P. R., Krystal, J. H., Taylor, J. R., and Fletcher, P. C. (2009). 'Why Do Delusions Persist?' *Frontiers in Human Neuroscience* 3/12: 1–9. DOI:10.3389/neuro.09.012.2009.

Currella, E. A., Werbeloffa, N., Hayesa, J. F., and Bella, V. (2019). 'Cognitive Neuropsychiatric Analysis of an Additional Large Capgras Delusion Case Series', *Cognitive Neuropsychiatry* 24/2: 123–34.

Darby, R. R., Laganiere, S., Pascual-Leone, A., Prasad, S., and Fox, M. D. (2017). 'Finding the Imposter: Brain Connectivity of Lesions Causing Delusional Misidentifications', *Brain* 140: 497–507.

Davies, M. and Coltheart, M. (2000). 'Introduction: Pathologies of Belief', *Mind & Language* 15/1: 1–46.

Davies, M., Coltheart, M., Langdon, R., and Breen, N. (2001). 'Monothematic Delusions: Towards a Two-Factor Account', *Philosophy, Psychiatry & Psychology* 8/2–3: 133–58.

178 BELIEF, IMAGINATION, AND DELUSION

Davies, M. and Egan, A. (2013). 'Delusion: Cognitive Approaches, Bayesian Inference and Compartmentalisation', in K. W. M. Fulford, M. Davies, R. G. T. Gipps, G. Graham, J. Sadler, G. Stanghellini, and T. Thornton (eds.), *The Oxford Handbook of Philosophy and Psychiatry* (Oxford: Oxford University Press), 689–728.

de Pauw, K. W. (1994). 'Delusional Misidentification: A Plea for an Agreed Terminology and Classification', *Psychopathology* 27: 123–9.

Ellis, H. D. and Lewis, L. (2001). 'Capgras Delusion: A Window on Face Recognition', *Trends in Cognitive Sciences* 5/4: 149–56.

Ellis, H. D. and Young, A. W. (1990). 'Accounting for Delusional Misidentification', *British Journal of Psychiatry* 157: 239–48.

Ellis, H. D., Young, A. W., Quayle, A. H. and de Pauw, K. W. (1997). 'Reduced Autonomic Responses to Faces in Capgras Delusion', *Proceedings of the Royal Society B: Biological Sciences* 264: 1085–92.

Feinberg, T. E. and Shapiro, R. M. (1989). 'Misidentification-Reduplication and the Right Hemisphere', *Neuropsychiatry, Neuropsychology and Behavioral Neurology* 2: 39–48.

Fine, C., Craigie, J., and Gold, I. (2005). 'Damned If You Do, Damned If You Don't: The Impasse in Cognitive Accounts of the Capgras Delusion', *Philosophy, Psychiatry & Psychology* 12/2: 143–51.

Gerrans, P. (1999). 'Delusional Misidentification as Subpersonal Disintegration', *The Monist* 82/4: 590–608.

Gerrans, P. (2000). 'Refining the Explanation of Cotard's Delusion', *Mind & Language* 15/1: 111–22.

Gerrans, P. (2001). 'Delusions as Performance Failures', *Cognitive Neuropsychiatry* 6: 161–73.

Gerrans, P. (2002). 'A One-Stage Explanation of the Cotard Delusion', *Philosophy, Psychiatry & Psychology* 9/1: 47–53.

Haxby, J. V., Gobbini, M. I., Furey, M. L., Ishai, A., Schouten, J. L., and Pietrini, P. (2001). 'Distributed and Overlapping Representations of Faces and Objects in Ventral Temporal Cortex', *Science* 293: 2425–30.

Haxby, J. V., Hoffman, E. A., and Gobbini, M. I. (2000). 'The Distributed Human Neural System for Face Perception', *Trends in Cognitive Sciences* 4/6: 223–33.

Hirstein, W. and Ramachandran, V. S. (1997). 'Capgras Syndrome: A Novel Probe for Understanding the Neural Representation of the Identity of Familiarity of Persons', *Proceedings of the Royal Society B: Biological Sciences* 246: 437–44.

Hohwy, J. (2004). 'Top-Down and Bottom-Up in Delusion Formation', *Philosophy, Psychiatry & Psychology* 11/1: 65–70.

Hustig, H. H. and Hafner, R. J. (1990). 'Persistent Auditory Hallucinations and Their Relationship to Delusions and Mood', *Journal of Nervous and Mental Disease* 178: 264–7.

Jaspers, K. (1997). *General Psychopathology*, trans. J. Hoenig and M. W. Hamilton (Baltimore, MD: Johns Hopkins University Press).

Kapur, S. (2003). 'Psychosis as a State of Aberrant Silence: A Framework Linking Biology, Phenomenology, and Pharmacology in Schizophrenia', *American Journal of Psychiatry* 160: 13–23.

Klee, R. (2004). 'Why Some Delusions Are Necessarily Inexplicable Beliefs', *Philosophy, Psychiatry & Psychology* 11/1: 25–34.

Leeper, R. (1935). 'A Study of a Neglected Portion of the Field of Learning: The Development of Sensory Organization', *The Journal of Genetic Psychology* 46: 41–75.

McKay, R. (2012). 'Delusional Inference', *Mind & Language* 27/3: 330–55.

McLaughlin, B. P. (2009). 'Monothetic Delusions and Existential Feelings', in T. Bayne and J. Fernández (eds.), *Delusion and Self-Deception: Affective and Motivational Influences on Belief Formation* (New York: Psychology Press), 139–64.

Maher, B. A. (1974). 'Delusional Thinking and Perceptual Disorder', *Journal of Individual Psychology* 30/1: 98–113.

Maher, B. A. (1988). 'Anomalous Experience and Delusional Thinking: The Logic of Explanations', in T. F. Oltmanns and B. A. Maher (eds.), *Delusional Beliefs* (New York: John Wiley & Sons), 15–33.

Maher, B. A. (1992). 'Delusions: Contemporary Etiological Hypotheses', *Psychiatric Annals* 22/5: 260–8.

Maher, B. A. (1999). 'Anomalous Experience in Everyday Life: Its Significance for Psychopathology', *The Monist* 82/4: 547–70.

Maher, B. A. (2006). 'The Relationship between Delusions and Hallucinations', *Current Psychiatry Reports* 8/3: 179–83.

Pacherie, E. (2009). 'Perception, Emotion, and Delusions: The Case of the Capgras Delusion', in T. Bayne and J. Fernández (eds.), *Delusion and Self-Deception: Affective and Motivational Influences on Belief Formation* (New York: Psychology Press), 107–25.

Parrott, M. (2016). 'Bayesian Models, Delusional Beliefs, and Epistemic Possibilities', *British Journal for the Philosophy of Science* 67: 271–96.

Parrott, M. (2021). 'Delusional Predictions and Explanations', *British Journal for the Philosophy of Science* 72/1: 325–53.

Phillips, J. (2002). 'Arguing from Neuroscience in Psychiatry', *Philosophy, Psychiatry & Psychology* 9/1: 61–3.

Ratcliffe, M. (2004). 'Interpreting Delusions', *Phenomenology and the Cognitive Sciences* 3: 25–48.

Reimer, M. (2009). 'Is the Impostor Hypothesis Really So Preposterous? Understanding the Capgras Experience', *Philosophical Psychology* 22/6: 669–86.

Sakakibara, E. (2019). 'Intensity of Experience: Maher's Theory of Schizophrenic Delusion Revisited', *Neuroethics* 12: 171–82.

Sartre, J. P. (1969). *Being and Nothingness*, trans. H. Barnes (London: Routledge).

Sass, L. A. and Pienkos, E. (2013). 'Delusion: The Phenomenological Approach', in K. W. M. Fulford, M. Davies, R. G. T. Gipps, G. Graham, J. Z. Sadler, G. Stanghellini, and T. Thornton (eds.), *The Oxford Handbook of Philosophy and Psychiatry* (Oxford: Oxford University Press), 632–57.

Sims, A. (1995). *Symptoms in the Mind: An Introduction to Descriptive Psychopathology* (London: W. B. Saunders Company).

Spitzer, M. (1992). 'The Phenomenology of Delusions', *Psychiatric Annals* 22/5: 252–9.

Sullivan-Bissett, E. (2018). 'Monothematic Delusion: A Case of Innocence from Experience', *Philosophical Psychology* 31/6: 920–47.

Sullivan-Bissett, E. (2020). 'Unimpaired Abduction to Alien Abduction: Lessons on Delusion Formation', *Philosophical Psychology* 33/5: 679–704.

Tranel, D. and Damasio, A. R. (1985). 'Knowledge Without Awareness: An Automatic Index of Facial Recognition by Prosopagnosics', *Science* 228: 1453–4.

Turner, M. and Coltheart, M. (2010). 'Confabulation and Delusion: A Common Monitoring Framework', *Cognitive Neuropsychiatry* 15/1: 346–76.

Wilkinson, S. (2015). 'Delusions, Dreams, and the Nature of Identification', *Philosophical Psychology* 28/2: 203–26.

Wise, N. (2016). 'The Capgras Delusion: An Integrated Approach', *Phenomenology and the Cognitive Sciences* 15: 183–205.

Young, A. W. and de Pauw, K. W. (2002). 'One Stage Is Not Enough', *Philosophy, Psychiatry & Psychology* 9/1: 55–9.

Young, G. (2008). 'Capgras Delusion: An Interactionist Model', *Consciousness and Cognition* 17/3: 863–76.

Young, G. (2009). 'In What Sense "Familiar"? Examining Experiential Differences Within Pathologies of Facial Recognition', *Consciousness and Cognition* 18/3: 628–38.

Young, G. (2011). 'On Abductive Inference and Delusional Belief: Why There Is Still a Role for Patient Experience Within Explanations of Capgras Delusion', *Cognitive Neuropsychiatry* 16/4: 303–25.

Young, G. (2014). 'Amending the Revisionist Model of the Capgras Delusion: A Further Argument for the Role of Patient Experience in Delusional Belief Formation', *AVANT: Trends in Interdisciplinary Studies* 5/3: 89–112.

9

Cotard Syndrome

The Experience of Inexistence

Philip Gerrans

A 48-year-old man with no medical history, apart from a previous short depressive illness, was seen by a psychiatrist after a self-electrocution attempt. Eight months later, he first told his general practitioner that his brain had died. He further explained that "I am coming to prove that I am dead", that he no longer needed to eat or sleep and was condemned to a kind of half-life, with a dead brain in a living body. He acknowledged that his abilities to see, hear, think, remember, and communicate proved that his mind must be alive: he could not explain how his mind could be alive if his brain was dead, but he was certain that this was the case. Psychotropic treatment had little therapeutic effect and his delusion receded only to return (Charland-Verville et al. 2013: 1997).

The Cotard syndrome or delusion was first described by Jules Cotard in 1880 as the "Delire des Negations". In the popular imagination it is thought of as the belief that the subject has died but it is more accurately described as the belief that the subject has ceased to exist. This belief is often preceded by or associated with beliefs about transformation or disappearance of the body, parts of the body, or of the world itself (Holper et al. 2012). It typically arises in a context of extreme depression but is also associated with a wide variety of neurological conditions ranging from Parkinson's and Alzheimer's to encephalitis (Restrepo-Martínez et al. 2019; Ramirez Bermúdez et al. 2021).

The philosophical interest of the delusion is obvious. Its explanation goes to the heart of the nature of self-awareness. Alexandre Billon (2016) has proposed that the delusion is a belief formed to explain the loss of the sense of "mineness" for experience. In the normal case, experience involves the feeling that the experience belongs to the subject. This feeling is both subtle and constant, a structural feature of experience so that its nature is not apparent to us. It is only in cases where it goes missing or awry that its role in our phenomenology becomes apparent. Billon argues that depersonalization experience, either as a transient episode or a constant feature of life, as in depersonalization disorder, is a case of loss of "mineness". For Billon the Cotard delusion is a belief that explains a pervasive and intractable depersonalization experience.

Philip Gerrans, *Cotard Syndrome: The Experience of Inexistence* In: *Belief, Imagination, and Delusion*. Edited by: Ema Sullivan-Bissett, Oxford University Press. © Oxford University Press 2024. DOI: 10.1093/oso/9780198872221.003.0009

Billon's account, which is clearly the most comprehensive and informed recent philosophical account, integrates the insights of early psychiatrists and philosophers with recent structural accounts of self-awareness and accounts that draw on the cognitive neuroscience of delusion formation. These latter accounts argue that delusions have two factors: anomalous experience (the first factor) and a belief that explains that experience (the second factor). So the two-factor account of Cotard delusion makes depersonalization experience the first factor and the delusion the second factor.

One point to note about such accounts is that they combine a focus on the rationality or irrationality of delusion with an account of the role of precipitating experience. Thus classic two-factor accounts argue that that there is some abnormality in processes of rational belief fixation involved in delusion (Bayne and Pacherie 2005). That abnormality can be characterized epistemically (does the experience provide a good reason for the delusion?) or procedurally (does it involve malfunction of the processes of belief fixation?). A key piece of evidence for a two-factor account is cases in which subjects have *ex hypothesi* similar experience to delusional subjects but do not proceed to develop a delusion. Instead they report that it is "as if p" where p is a delusional content. In such cases the subject is either not treating the precipitating experience as a reason to believe delusional content or is not subject to a malfunction of the processes underlying belief fixation (Coltheart 2010; Coltheart et al. 2010; Coltheart and Davies 2021).

Two-factor accounts were developed to integrate the neuroscience of psychiatric disorder with the clinical profile of psychological symptoms initially for delusions of misidentification (Stone and Young 1997). However in the case of Cotard delusion there are few studies that identify its neural substrates. So the evidential base for a project of identifying a substrate for the sense of mineness and its loss in depersonalization and Cotard delusion was until very recently very slight. However some recent imaging studies have begun to remedy this situation (Restrepo-Martínez et al. 2019). Combining Billon's account with the neuropsychiatric one leads to an integrated account in which insula cortex dysfunction produces the experience of depersonalization, and abnormal reasoning based on prefrontal cortical dysfunction produces the delusional belief. The structure of the integrated account is given in Figure 9.1.

Although this two-factor account is elegant, I shall argue that it is not quite right as an explanation of the experience involved in Depersonalization Disorder (DPD) or the Cotard delusion. Depersonalization experience is not simply the "as if" version of Cotard delusion. Cotard delusion is a metacognitive response to a *syndrome* of experiences of which depersonalization is one aspect (Tomasetti et al. 2020). The account I present is consistent with the idea that *epistemically* the Cotard patient is intact (she knows that her experience cannot license that conclusion as an empirical inference: it is not sufficient reason for a delusion).

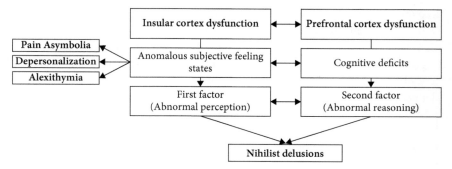

Fig. 9.1 Two-factor model of the Cotard delusion (Gerrans 2023).

However the *processes* by which beliefs about the self are formed are not intact. Not least because these processes are implemented in a distributed hierarchy that is reciprocally modulated by a variety of regulatory systems. The Cotard delusion subject can no longer integrate and regulate signals from these systems in a predictable way. The highest level of the hierarchy, the ability to verbalize and narrate experience, remains intact but it no longer functions as part of a coherent regulatory system because it is unmoored from the hierarchy that normally supports it.

To support this conclusion and explain the difference in experience between Cotard and DPD we need a theory that explains the role of the insula in producing self-awareness (the sense of mineness), its loss in depersonalization and its role in Cotard syndrome. That account is the *active interoceptive inference account of self-representation* (jargon to be explained below) (Friston et al. 2011; Pezzulo et al. 2015; Barrett et al. 2016; Seth and Friston 2016; Barrett 2017) which treats the self as a predictive model (representation) made by the mind to track, predict, and interpret interoceptive (perception of the *internal milieu*) experience. The model has different components, bodily (interoceptive), affective, and narrative that are related in a processing hierarchy. These components of the model have neural substrates. These substrates are not discrete modules but hubs that coordinate distributed processing relevant to their functional roles. The relevant hubs are the posterior insula cortex (interoceptive self), anterior insula cortex (affective self), and default mode network (narrative self). This hierarchical model malfunctions in different ways for different reasons in DPD and Cotard.

Depersonalization experience is a phenomenon in which the affective component of the self-model is deactivated, typically as a dissociative response to stress or trauma. Cotard syndrome is the result of a catastrophic breakdown of the self-model caused by cascading effects of intractable interoceptive dysregulation or *dyshomeostasis* as it has been baptized (Stephan et al. 2016). So the aetiologies of the conditions are different and so are the resultant experiences and metacognitive responses.

One feature of this account is that it does not essentially involve the concept of belief or the related concept of abnormal reasoning on which second-factor

184 BELIEF, IMAGINATION, AND DELUSION

accounts depend. We can explain the Cotard delusion without invoking some kind of epistemic or procedural reasoning failure (Boehme et al. 2014). The subject experiences herself as non-existent because she can no longer model (represent) her experiences as belonging to the persisting entity that regulates her bodily and affective states and whose autobiographical trajectory is recalled, planned, and narrated by the narrative "I".

In the rest of this chapter I first give a more complete characterization of the Cotard delusion. I then present Billon's phenomenological account of the Cotard delusion and the recent neurocognitive account of Ramirez Bermúdez and collaborators (2021). Billon's account is agnostic about mechanisms but Ramirez Bermúdez implicates insula dysfunction as a first factor in the genesis of the delusion. I argue that the best explanation of this role for the insula is that anterior insular functioning is essential for the self-attribution of affective states. I defend this "deaffectualization" account of depersonalization and Cotard delusion against two objections. The first derives from Billon's structural account of mineness together with some interpretations of studies of patients with lesion to the insula. The second is a recent challenge to "deaffectualization" explanations of the Cotard delusion by Martin Davies and Max Coltheart who show that affective experience is present in cases of the delusion. I argue that both these challenges are met by the self-modelling account. In a final section I return to the question of whether a one or two-factor doxastic theory is the best way to interpret the evidence in these cases.

1. The Cotard Syndrome

The Cotard syndrome, or Cotard delusion, is part of a rare psychiatric syndrome named after Jules Cotard who published an extensive description of a case in 1880. It involves a denial of the patient's own body, of her mental states, of feelings and in approximately 60 per cent of cases of their own existence. Billon (2016) classifies symptoms as bodily (desomatization), mental (dementization), and of death and non-existence with the latter perhaps constituting an extreme form. It is also worth noting that some patients retain a degree of insight into the paradoxical nature of claims that they or their body do not exist or have died. Here are three typical reports (all cited in Billon 2016, the most comprehensive historical and philosophical account available).

> She had the constant experience of having no identity or "self" and being only a body without content...she was convinced that her brain had vanished, her intestines had disappeared, and her whole body was translucent.
>
> (Debruyne, Portzky, Van den Eynde, and Audenaert, 2009, p. 197)

> He said "I speak, breathe and eat, but I am dead".
>
> (Nejad and Toofani, 2005, p. 250)

COTARD SYNDROME: THE EXPERIENCE OF INEXISTENCE   185

It was as if it was not me walking, it was not me talking, as if it was not me living...I can look at me, I am somehow bothered by my body, as if it wasn't me, as if I lived on the side of my body, on the side of myself if you like. I don't know how to explain.

(Janet and Raymond, 1898, p. 70) [Note the "as if" locution]

The Cotard delusion is sometimes described as the delusion that the subject has died, although it is better described as a delusion of inexistence ("délire de negation"). The delusion is part of a wider syndrome that includes anomalous bodily experiences. Often these experiences arise in the context of an episode of profound depression. Cotard himself noted the link between acute depression, a negative self-referential pattern of rumination ("le malade s'accuse lui-même"), and the delusion. There is no single or simple neural correlate or aetiology. Cotard delusion has been found in cases of affective disorders and schizophrenia, neurosyphilis, acute encephalitis, subdural haemorrhage, arteriovenous malformations, brain neoplasms, migraine, Parkinson's disease, semantic dementia, cerebrovascular disease, and epilepsy, among others (Mendez and Ramírez-Bermúdez 2011; Ramirez-Bermúdez et al. 2010; Sahoo and Josephs 2018).

The following describes a case arising in the context of anti NMDAR encephalitis. This patient was the subject of one of the recent and rare imaging studies of this disorder.

After claiming to be dead, Mr. A, a 19-year-old man, was referred to the National Institute of Neurology and Neurosurgery of Mexico, because of psychotic and catatonic symptoms. According to his mother, one month before admission, his appetite had diminished, he barely slept at night and, during the day, he stayed withdrawn and silent. Mr. A would complain about his body, saying that his tendons had dried up and that his organs, particularly his heart, were getting bigger. He would speak of an internal haemorrhage: all his organs had been torn apart. Mr. A began to insist that he was dead: *"I can no longer feel the blood flowing through my veins"*. This assertion did not deprive him of looking for sharp objects to cut his neck and forearms, he tried on multiple occasions to commit suicide. Gradually, his behaviour became disorganised: he began to urinate on his clothes, refused to eat, and his verbal production diminished to mutism...

Four days after he received his fifth session of plasma exchange, his alertness improved, but psychotic symptoms remained. When asked how he felt, he answered: *"I do not have feelings because I am dead...All human beings will be dead"*. He added that he had a "right-sided" heart and that it had stopped.

The patient was transferred to the neuropsychiatric unit. Over the following days, catatonic symptoms continued to improve (BFCRS score of 8/21), but nihilistic delusions persisted unchanged: *"I am dead, among other human beings. This is*

186 BELIEF, IMAGINATION, AND DELUSION

like a program where I am dead". The patient claimed to be a dead person among the corpses under the earthquake debris. Doctors and nurses were part of a game whose objective was to cover up his death.

(Restrepo Martinez et al. 2019: 471–72)

As we noted above, the authors of this study proposed a two-factor account of Cotard delusion in which the first factor is an anomalous experience caused by insula dysfunction. If we combine their account with Billon's we get the idea that the first factor is a sense of depersonalization that produces an "as if" version of the Cotard delusion. In other words "it feels 'as if' I do not exist". The second factor is a failure of reasoning that leads the subject to "endorse" or take the content of experience at face value.

2. Depersonalization Experience as the First Factor in Cotard Delusion

According to Billon, the precipitating experience is depersonalization, which he characterizes as loss of the experience of "mineness". Mineness is a phenomenological term of art but it refers to the sensation that an experience belongs to the subject. Another way to put this is to say that all experiences have "subjective character" or "sense of presence". The experience is subtle and elusive, a constant background to other experience so that we only notice it when it is absent. As Billon says:

their ubiquity also implies that we normally lack the contrast cases needed to spot the regular presence of these features. (Billon 2016: 379)

Billon's characterization of mineness rehearses that of one of the pioneers of phenomenology who explicitly linked it to depersonalization:

Every psychic manifestation, whether perception, bodily sensation, memory, idea, thought or feeling carries this particular aspect of 'being mine' of having an 'I' quality, of 'personally belonging', of it being one's own doing. This has been termed personalisation. If these psychic manifestations occur with the awareness of not being mine ... we term them phenomena of depersonalisation.

(Jaspers 1962: 121)

Billon's account of mineness is a structural account that treats is as a form of "self-location". Self-location allows one to feel that a representation is actual, present, and mine (part of *my* life trajectory through a world I am engaging with rather than a free-floating Humean experiential atom).

Billon's account is not a mechanistic one, so it is not proposed as an explanation of the role of neural correlates. If we accept a broad consensus that hypoactivity of the insula, especially right anterior insula is a neural correlate of depersonalization experience then we can ask how insula activity contributes to the experience of "mineness" in normal and pathological conditions. Ideally the structural account should be consistent with such an empirically based account.

3. Interoceptive Active Inference and Self-Awareness

The most persuasive account of the role of the insula in self-awareness and its loss integrates the theories of A. D. Bud Craig, Anil Seth, and Mauricio Sierra with predictive processing theories of bodily self-representation (Craig 2009a, 2009b, 2010; Joffily and Coricelli 2013; Limanowski and Blankenburg 2013; Seth 2013; Seth and Tsakiris 2018). On this view the self is an *avatar*, a model or representation made by the mind to integrate, predict, and manage endogenously generated states. Because we have no direct access to fundamental bodily processes we need system-level representations that treat complex hierarchical interactions that maintain organismic integrity as properties of a simple unified persisting entity. For example we cannot directly affect cell metabolism when energy is depleted, but we can rest, an action that programs the innumerable microprocesses required to replenish energy. The feeling of tiredness is an interoceptive state that allows the subject to regulate the organism by managing fatigue. As Descartes (1985), who had an interoceptive theory of the phenomenology (not the metaphysics) of subjective experience, said:

> Through these sensations of pain, hunger, thirst, etc., nature also teaches me that I am present in my body not merely as a sailor is present in his ship, but rather that I am very closely joined and as it were intermingled with it, so that I compose a single thing with it. (Descartes 1985: 56)

The key point here is that the brain attributes these interoceptive (basic internal bodily) experiences to a persisting unified entity. This is an obligatory cognitive strategy. Just as the mind integrates exteroceptive information by populating the world with objects, interoceptive information is attributed to a unified persisting entity and felt as such giving rise to a basic bodily sense of self.

This basic bodily sense of self subtends an affective sense of self (the subject of emotional states and feelings) as well as sensorimotor and agential senses of self. These experiences are integrated and interpreted, reported and communicated at a conceptual level by the narrative "I". The narrative "I" provides a symbolic/linguistic representation of the integrated hierarchy as a simple unified entity. In the normal case, the narrative "I" is subtended by the integrated hierarchy of bodily and affective processes whose trajectory it tracks, predicts, interprets, and communicates (Hohwy and Michael 2017; Letheby and Gerrans 2017).

Thus on the predictive processing view, the self is an avatar, a model or representation manoeuvred through bodily and affective state space by the brain as a *proxy* for the constellation of processes whose integration and regulation is necessary to maintain organismic integrity against inevitable entropic forces. Unless a living system can model its functioning as belonging to a unified persisting entity it will degrade and disintegrate (Joffily and Coricelli 2013; Corcoran and Hohwy 2017).

Perhaps the most important form of self-modelling is affective. By acting to reduce negative affect and produce or prolong positive affect, we optimize organismic functioning. For example, we cannot directly change cortisol levels but we can act to reduce feelings of stress and anxiety. Not only that but humans have the capacity to reflect and plan, so we can act to produce or prolong positive effect in the future at different time scales. In order to do this we need a form of affective forecasting that predicts (however imperfectly) how we will feel given future contingencies (Joffily and Corricelli 2013; Fernandez Velasco and Loev 2021). The organism takes the action that optimizes bodily/affective experience and in the process refines a model of the self whose experiences signal regulatory success or failure (Friston et al. 2013; Kirchhoff et al. 2018; Limanowski and Friston 2018; Lyon et al. 2021).

Interoceptive and affective states have a common basis in allostatic (action to optimize internal body states in context) regulation. However, they are subtly different and the architecture of the mind reflects that difference. Affective processes *reinterpret* interoceptive states according to emotional context to allow us to feel them, not just as overall states of the body, but as states that inform us of emotional significance in the form of affective experience. This emotional *transcription* of interoceptive signals integrates the interoceptive signal with information about the emotional salience of the situation and the subject's history. It is in that sense that emotional processes are forms of interoceptive active inference (Barrett and Simmons 2015; Barrett et al. 2016; Barrett 2017; Kleckner et al. 2017). They provide higher-level interpretive and regulatory models that allow changes in bodily state to be felt as affective experiences.

Still higher levels of self-modelling, narrative or conceptual, interpret and predict affective states. In the end, without affective experience we are an organism to whom the world and its own states, as represented by our battery of cognitive faculties, no longer matter.

The fatigue of depression and its morphing into disconsolate apathy provides a nice case study of the role of hierarchical interoceptive active inference. Fatigue is an adaptive state designed to restore depleted subsystemic function. If, however, fatigue is intractably sustained, the result will be a persistent homeostatic/allostatic error signal experienced as a characteristic interoceptive state: weariness and

COTARD SYNDROME: THE EXPERIENCE OF INEXISTENCE   189

exhaustion. The active inference hierarchy will exploit higher levels of self-modelling to interpret and contextualize these interoceptive signals (Barrett et al. 2016; Friston 2018; Velasco and Loev 2020). Initially, such models predict restoration consequent on rest. If, however, rest does not work, tiredness and distress will increase. Ultimately the self will be modelled as unable to control basic states and to act efficaciously in the world. Bodily state is now felt as apathy and anhedonia, and possibly anxiety at the prospect of exertion. At the level of narrative self-representation, thoughts of hopelessness and inadequacy interpret this experience. As Klaas Stephan and colleagues put it in their predictive processing account of fatigue and depression:

> belief of failure at one's most fundamental task—homeostatic/allostatic regulation—...arises from experiencing enhanced interoceptive surprise. We suggest that fatigue is a (possibly adaptive) initial allostatic response to a state of interoceptive surprise; if dyshomeostasis continues, the belief of low allostatic self-efficacy and lack of control may pervade all domains of cognition and manifests as a generalized sense of helplessness, with depression as a consequence.   (Stephan et al. 2016)

This hierarchical nature of interoceptive processing and affective processing is reflected in cytoarchitecture (Barrett and Simmons 2015). Sections of the posterior insula cortex (PIC) take primary interoceptive afferents and integrate those representations to coordinate basic regulatory functions. The PIC, for example, integrates values of allostatic variables such as blood pressure and hydration as well as nociception (bodily damage). Although it is not the only channel for bodily signalling, its role as a primary integrative hub of interoceptive afferents makes PIC a crucial substrate of the experience of material me (Medford and Critchley 2010; Nelson et al. 2010; Moayedi 2014).

The anterior insula cortex (AIC) is specialized to re-represent and integrate information about body state to allow us to feel the significance of interoceptive states as affects. AIC sits at the apex of the so-called "salience system", the neural hierarchy that signals whether and how information matters to the organism. In order to perform its role, it must communicate with emotional processing hubs that coordinate representation of emotional significance (for example the presence of danger, immediate and concrete, or long-term and non-specific, in the case of the emotion of fear). Thus, the AIC is activated by perception of emotionally salient/self-relevant scenarios. Its activity allows us to feel the emotional significance of events. It is also active in scenarios in which we reflect on past events or anticipate the future, allowing so-called mental time travel to be imbued with affective significance. Thus, AIC activity can also provide the affective texture for anticipation and recollection as well as online sensory processing (Craig 2009a, 2009b; Terasawa et al. 2013).

190 BELIEF, IMAGINATION, AND DELUSION

This leads some affective neuroscientists to treat experience produced by AIC activation as a form of higher-order bodily representation that represents the integrated functioning of the organism *evaluated against emotionally salient goals creating a sense of self in the process.* As Bud Craig (2009a) puts it:

> The integration successively includes homeostatic, environmental, hedonic, motivational, social, and cognitive activity to produce a 'global emotional moment,' which represents the sentient self at one moment of time.
>
> (Craig 2009a: 1934)

Craig's idea is that the AIC plays a key role in transforming interoceptive signals integrated by the PIC into representations of states of an affective self. It determines whether I experience fatigue as mere tiredness requiring sleep or as part of an episode of depression.

The AIC is an integrative hub of processes that transform a bodily into an affective signal, in the process transforming what would otherwise be a pure bodily feeling into an affective/emotional one. The AIC communicates with hubs of emotional processes to convert the neural signal representing interoceptive information into a neural signal representing the emotional significance of that information for the organism. Thus, I describe the processing relationship between AIC and PIC as *emotional transcription* (Gerrans 2020, 2022). This transcription creates the crucial affective dimension of self-modelling. Without it, we could navigate the world using other dimensions, agential, narrative, sensorimotor, and bodily in order to optimize organismic functioning. However, we would lack a way to experience the *significance* of our interactions with the world.

This is not a claim that the AIC is a discrete or modularized substrate of self-representation and affect. Rather, its integrative role, connecting low- and high-level emotional processing and interoception and in the generation of affective experience, makes it an important hub of processing that enables us to feel the significance of events as affective states. The mind models fluctuations in resultant affective states by attributing them to a continuing entity: the thing that experiences the emotional ups and downs. Affective me is that entity. And a good candidate for its neural substrate, given its role as a hub of self-referential processing, is the AIC.

4. Depersonalization Experience and the Insula

The idea that the AIC is the substrate of affective self-modelling fits with studies of (relatively) selective damage or hypoactivity of AIC in disorders of depersonalization. In depersonalization disorder, patients report phenomenology such as the following:

COTARD SYNDROME: THE EXPERIENCE OF INEXISTENCE   191

I do not feel I have a body. When I look down I see my legs and body but it feels as if it was not there. When I move I see the movements as I move, but I am not there with the movements. I am walking up the stairs, I see my legs and hear footsteps and feel the muscles but it feels as if I have no body; I am not there. I am sensing that my face and body are not there at all—almost invisible. I see my hands and my body doing things but it does not feel like me and I am not connected to it at all. I don't feel alive in any way whatsoever. I don't feel a thing except for hot or cold; maybe hunger. Even if I touch my face I feel or sense something but my face is not there. As I sense it I have the need to make sure and I rub, touch, and hurt myself to feel something. I touch my neck for instance with my hand but it doesn't feel like my hand touching my neck. I can't feel me touching my own body.... When I move and walk and talk I feel nothing whatsoever. I exercise but don't feel I am doing anything, just my muscles but not my body moving, its madness not to feel myself move, talking...

(Sierra 2009: 28)

The mechanism is hypothesized to be spontaneous inhibition of AIC by the ventrolateral prefrontal cortex (Medford et al. 2006; Medford and Critchley 2010; Medford 2012; Sierra et al. 2012; Medford et al. 2016). This is consistent with clinical theories that treat depersonalization as a dissociative phenomenon produced by emotional inhibition. The core of the account is that higher level regulatory systems deactivate the anterior insula in order to reduce or remove a distress response. Thus Sierra states that:

depersonalization represents an anxiety-triggered 'hard-wired' inhibitory response intended to ensure the preservation of adaptive behaviour during situations normally associated with overwhelming and potentially disorganizing anxiety.   (Sierra 2009: 70)

The result is affective flattening or deaffectualization while cognition, perception, and the cognitive and expressive aspects of emotion remain intact. Of course, given the integrative role of the AIC and its dense multidirectional coupling and functional connectivity, there may be no unique cause of anterior insula hypoactivity. It could be the case that the AIC is not receiving interoceptive afferents from lower levels or has lost connectivity with systems that appraise those signals for emotional relevance. In any case, if the AIC is not active the result is that most dimensions of self-representation, bodily, agential, sensorimotor, and narrative are intact, but the agent does not feel as if any of the resultant experiences belong to her. The reason is that the AIC is no longer functioning to allow her to feel the significance of bodily changes evoked by her passage through the world (Gerrans 2020 2023).

It is worth emphasizing that this is a *dissociative deaffectualization* account of depersonalization experience that depends implicitly on a role for self-modelling.

192 BELIEF, IMAGINATION, AND DELUSION

It is not just that the subject feels no affective reaction (for example to physical or psychological abuse) but that the mind continues to predict affective reaction in that context. It is the violation of that prediction that makes the subject feel as if she is not present in the experience.

5. Two Objections to Deaffectualization Accounts of DPD and Cotard Delusion

Billon is very clear that mineness cannot be an affective phenomenon and therefore deaffectualization cannot explain depersonalization experience. His main reason for rejecting the affective account is that both DPD and Cotard seem to present us with cases of loss of mineness *for emotion*. That is patients will say that they have an episode of fear or anger that nonetheless feels as if it is not theirs. If affective experience is part of the essence of emotion it should not be possible to have an experience of emotion without affective tone. Similarly, if affect is part of the essence of emotion and the basis of mineness it follows that forms of cognition such as abstract thought should lack mineness, since they can be experienced without affect. Clearly, however, solving equations does not produce depersonalization experience.

But Billon does not rely on such conceptual points. He points to the clinical reports like that of Paul Schilder who wrote:

> The objective examination of such patients reveals not only an intact sensory apparatus, but also an intact emotional apparatus. All these patients exhibit *natural affective reactions* in their facial expressions, attitudes, etc.; so that it *is impossible to assume that they are incapable of emotional response.*
> (Schilder 1935: 120, cited in Sierra 2012: 25; my italics)

If this is correct then the dissociative deaffectualizaition account of loss of mineness in DPD is in trouble.

Interestingly, however, in the same passage Schilder wrote:

> The emotions likewise undergo marked alteration. Patients complain that they are capable of *experiencing* neither pain or pleasure; love and hate have perished with them.   (Schilder 1928, cited in Sierra 2012: 26; my italics)

In this passage Schilder suggests that patients no longer *experience* emotions, even though they have "intact emotional apparatus and natural affective reactions". This looks inconsistent with the previous passage.

However, if we distinguish affective experience *qua feeling* from other aspects of an emotional episode these passages are consistent. Emotional episodes include

COTARD SYNDROME: THE EXPERIENCE OF INEXISTENCE   193

sensorimotor responses, autonomic and visceral reactions, action tendencies, higher level cognition, *and* affective response produced by emotional transcription of interoceptive signals. In a prototypical episode these components synchronize in a characteristic way according to the way a situation is evaluated (appraised in the preferred terminology of emotion theorists).

The dissociative deaffectualization explanation was that it results from the unpredicted loss of the felt/affective aspect of emotion. It is consistent with this account that other sensory and behavioural aspects remain intact. The DPD patient continues to recognize the emotional salience of situations: her basic appraisal mechanisms are intact (there is no suggestion that the appraisal hubs, the amygdala and vmPFC are impaired) and initiate the automatic bodily and behavioural responses. However, due to hypoactivity in the AIC she does not feel the significance of those changes and it is the dissonance between absence of predicted feeling, cognition, and action which makes her feel "as if" she is an automaton performing actions which are not really hers. This is consonant with the description by a patient of Ludovic Dugas who first described the disorder.

> I only feel anger from the outside, *by its physiological reactions.*
>
> (Dugas and Moutier 1911: 121; my italics)

Billon's main reason for rejecting the affective account is the dissociation between affective feeling, cognition, bodily response, and behaviour in DPD. But this dissociation is explicable if these are dissociable components of emotional processing. Deactivation of the anterior insula, the hub of affective transcription, explains the relatively selective loss of mineness in virtue of loss of predicted affect.

The very same considerations apply to some cases cited as counterexamples to the idea that insula hypoactivity produces deaffectualization and loss of the sense of mineness. For example patient R seems to retain affective responses and a self-awareness. As Carissa Philippi and colleagues put it:

> R is a conscious, self-aware, and sentient human being despite the widespread destruction of cortical regions purported to play a critical role in SA, namely the insula, anterior cingulate cortex, and medial prefrontal cortex.
>
> (Philippi et al. 2012)

However, the forms of self-awareness manifested by R are semantic and cognitive: mirror self-recognition and autobiographical knowledge for example. Once again these abilities are not dependent on the *feeling* of mineness or self-awareness.

Another objection to deaffectualization accounts comes from Davies and Coltheart (2021) who argue that Cotard delusion is not characterized by lack of affect. Their argument is part of a general argument against "deaffectualization" theories of the first factor of Cotard delusion (of which I was formerly a

194 BELIEF, IMAGINATION, AND DELUSION

proponent) (Gerrans 2000). On these theories, loss of affect in Cotard delusion is not produced by dissociation but arises progressively as part of extreme depression. This "depressive deaffectualization" theory was in fact first proposed by Cotard himself, noting the connection with what would now be called depression.

Such deaffectualization theories, whether depressive or dissociative, are incomplete because deaffectualization alone is insufficient for depersonalization. If I read about a situation that evokes no affect in me I do not feel depersonalized. Secondly, deaffectualization theories do not explain why loss of affect would not be reported simply as a feeling of flattened affect rather than loss of a sense of mineness or presence. The self-modelling theory fills this gap. The self-model predicts characteristic affective experience and uses those predictions to steer the organism through the world. When those predictions are unpredictably and intractably violated the organism feels as if experiences are not hers anymore. A parent who sees a delighted child and feels nothing has to account for that feeling of unwanted detachment.

A second challenge to deaffectualization theories comes from Davies and Coltheart (2021) who point out as part of their argument against deaffectualization theories of Cotard delusion that the delusion is not always characterized by total loss of affect. They present seven case studies in which patients "experienced various emotions including anxiety, fear, guilt, distress, euphoria and worry" (Davies and Coltheart 2021: 496). So, as they say, a pure deaffectualization theory of the first factor in Cotard delusion confronts a range of counterexamples.

However, it is hard to retain both the idea that depersonalization is the first factor in Cotard delusion and the idea that deaffectualization is not part of the delusion. Recall that according to Sierra and collaborators depersonalization is a consequence of deaffectualization caused by insula hypoactivity. If this is right then deaffectualization causes depersonalization (in paradigm dissociative cases) which is the first factor in Cotard delusion. But according to Davies and Coltheart, Cotard delusion does not essentially involve deaffectualization. What then *is* the first factor in Cotard delusion? Or, not to beg the question in favour of two-factor accounts, what is the precipitating anomalous experience in Cotard delusion if it is not depersonalization caused by deaffectualization?

6. Disintegration of the Self-Model

While it is clear that depersonalization is part of Cotard syndrome it also seems that the syndrome is characterized by a wider network of interrelated bodily symptoms. It also seems clear that Cotard delusion is not essentially dissociative. Although affective transcription and self-modelling are impaired, the aetiology is not selective inhibition as a dissociative response but disintegration of the self-modelling hierarchy.

COTARD SYNDROME: THE EXPERIENCE OF INEXISTENCE   195

Support from this idea comes from a combination of imaging studies and recent interoceptive theories of depression (Paulus and Stein 2010; Barrett et al. 2016). An example is Stephan and colleagues (2016) who use the example of fatigue to develop the concept of dyshomeostasis. Imagine for example being unable to sleep properly for weeks or months. Such dyshomeostasis can be the result of internal homeostatic failure, or intractably stressful physical or social environments or, very likely, a combination. Whatever the precise pathway, the idea is that when the subject cannot regulate basic biological functioning such as sleep the consequences cascade through the control hierarchy. The first stage is at the level of interoceptive self-modelling:

> the emitted control actions cannot reduce interoceptive surprise, a metacognitive interpretation ensues that leads to the subjective feeling of fatigue.
>
> (Stephan et al. 2016: 21)

At higher levels the subject tries cognitive and behavioural strategies to reduce fatigue. However, all strategies fail, which teaches the subject that no matter what the subject does she cannot control her*self* at the most basic level:

> an agent's experience of enduring dyshomeostasis signals a fundamental lack of mastery and control (over bodily states and thus survival) which may generalize, from the allostatic domain to other cognitive domains that are crucial for self-evaluation, planning and action selection.   (Stephan et al. 2016: 17)

This is essentially a bottom-up account of the cognitive aspects of depression: thoughts of failure, worthlessness, and inefficacy are consequent on basic failures of bodily self-regulation. Thus intractable fatigue becomes apathy, misery, and "sickness behaviour" and cognition reflects systematic failure in thoughts of failure hopelessness and worthlessness. Stephan and colleagues don't describe the architecture that produces depressive symptoms as a result of dyshomeostasis but they propose that the insula is a key component of a control hierarchy that progressively re-maps interoceptive signals with the result that high-level metacognitive states such as depressive beliefs are a "consequence not a cause" of lower level representational processes.

This model postulates a control hierarchy that links one form of allostasis, energy regulation, to depressive symptoms. But there are numerous pathologies that can induce dyshomeostasis, including cancers, chemotherapy, and, tellingly, autoimmune diseases. In the latter cases the dysregulation can be even more pervasive and resistant to regulation than fatigue. Patients discussed by Ramirez Bermúdez and colleagues had a form of encephalitis that attacks the NDMAR regulatory system, a pervasive basic neural function. They describe a patient, Mr A whose admission to hospital was preceded by feelings of physical and mental weakness following the Mexico City earthquake. His symptoms included:

headaches, insomnia, decreased appetite, irritability, auditory and visual hallucinations, delusions, and prolonged periods of mutism, and aggressive behaviour
toward himself and others. He also became paranoid, believing that his family
wanted to harm him . . .

fluctuating levels of consciousness with periods of psychomotor agitation,
inattention, and disorientation.

autonomic instability and catatonic features, including motor excitement alter-
nating with immobility, mutism, staring, and posturing.

(Ramirez Bermúdez et al. 2021: 65)

In other words he experienced a catastrophic and chaotic failure across the
hierarchy of systemic regulation. In such a situation there is *no* adequate bodily
model that predicts the consequences of regulatory action and no predictable
transcription of such symptoms that allows affective experience to serve as a
regulatory proxy. The subject cannot model herself as someone whose bodily
and affective states are predicted by, and responsive to, her regulatory actions.

Ramirez Bermúdez and colleagues incorporate the theoretical proposals of Seth
and Craig to argue that the insula is a hub of affective processing and substrate of
self-awareness lost in depersonalization. They use these proposals to interpret the
results of imaging studies of Cotard syndrome in which a consistently reoccurring
theme is insula hypoactivity, "the neural basis of a first factor necessary for the
development of nihilistic delusions" (Joffily and Coricelli 2013: 5). Their discussion mentions another imaging study of a case of Cotard delusion following
extensive atrophy of insula cortex, "demonstrating the central role of insular
cortex in self-perception and its ability to produce Délire des negations through
dysfunction" (Chaterjee and Mitra: e53).

As well as insula dysfunction, Ramirez Bermúdez and colleagues implicate the
default mode network (DMN) in the genesis of the delusion. A role for the DMN
was identified in a PET study by Charland-Verville and colleagues in 2013 of a
classic case of a man referred to psychiatric services after an electrocution attempt.
This man had almost complete atrophy of the DMN (Charland-Verville et al.
2013). Ramirez Bermúdez and colleagues in their imaging studies noted hypoactivity of the DMN and its role in "integrating information from multiple sources,
including autobiographical memory and interoceptive processes, suggesting an
active role of the DMN in the neural construction of the self" (Neurocase 5). This
role for the DMN reflects its activation in a wide variety of self-referential activities
such as rumination, episodic memory, planning, imagination, and dreaming. On
some views it is a substrate of the narrative "I". The DMN is connected to both hubs
of the appraisal hierarchy and to the insula cortex. It is an integrative hub that allows
the subject to experience affectively-inflected experiences as episodes in the life of
a temporally extended and unified self. As Christopher Davey and colleagues put it:

The DMN therefore coordinates a sense of self that spans cognitive abstractions about the self with a more grounded awareness of the state of the body.

(Davey and Harrison 2018: 279)

Interestingly however Ramirez Bermúdez and colleagues did not include the DMN in their two-factor model, partly because it was not a target of their imaging studies. However, its role in self-awareness and self-referential processing is well established.

Although the evidence is slight at present for a role for the DMN in Cotard delusion, hypoactivity in that network is consistent with the self-modelling account. The best way to conceptualize the role of the DMN is at the top level of the self-modelling hierarchy. It assembles and associates information necessary for the subject to experience herself in episodes of autobiographical thought. It communicates with hubs of appraisal and insular circuitry to allow narratives to be felt as affectively salient and hence imbued with mineness. As such, if the default network is disconnected from the more basic forms of bodily/affective selfhood and from secondary appraisal, then the ability to represent the self as an embodied entity with a past and future will be compromised.

On this view cascading bottom-up damage to the hierarchical self-model will effectively hollow it out. The narrative "I" becomes disembodied and if the DMN is disabled or impaired then the ability to construct an autobiographical trajectory is also lost. Jean, a patient studied by Young and Leafhead, described herself as "just a voice and if that goes I won't be anything... if my voice goes I will be lost and I won't know where I have gone" (Young and Leafhead 1996 157).

7. Factors in Delusion Formation

My aim here is not to argue against two-factor accounts in general but to suggest that conceptualizing Cotard in terms of two factors might be misleading because it requires that depersonalization experience and the first stage of the Cotard delusion are essentially the same. I agree that in delusion, experience is "taken at face value" so to speak and I also agree that in Cotard delusion the syndrome of which it is a part *includes* depersonalization experience. However, we should resist the idea that DPD is the "as if" version of Cotard. The panoply of bodily and cognitive symptoms in the syndrome—rotting, translucency, disappearance, the sense that the mind and person herself are disappearing combined with the aetiologies of depression, trauma, or low-level malfunction—seem to differentiate the experience from DPD. The experience in DPD does seem to be essentially dissociative, to deactivate affective transcription while sparing (to a greater or lesser degree) the other bodily and cognitive processes. At the same time the self-modelling account is also consistent with the idea that depersonalization experience could overlap with other bodily and interoceptive dysfunctions precisely because the insula cortex, like other components of the model is a hub of horizontal and vertical regulatory processes not a discrete module.

Another reason to distinguish depersonalization and the precipitating experience of Cotard delusion is that the "as if" formulation of the two-factor approach suggests that the essential difference between Cotard delusion and DPD is that the Cotard patient lacks the ability to reason about the anomalousness of her condition as a result of damage to mechanisms of belief evaluation. For example Bhaskar Chatterjee and Nayan Mitra (2015), like Ramirez Bermúdez and Billon argue that depersonalization caused by experience is taken at face value in the Cotard delusion as a result of failure of a belief evaluation system caused by malfunction of dorsolateral prefrontal circuitry. The subject hence accepts a delusional belief that reflects the content of experience. But, as with many delusions, that does not seem to be quite the case. The inability to override the delusion coexists with rational insight. Vanessa Charland-Verville and colleagues' patient is just one of many:

> He acknowledged that his abilities to see, hear, think, remember and communicate proved that his mind must be alive: he could not explain how his mind could be alive if his brain was dead, but he was certain that this was the case.
> (Charland-Verville et al. 2013)

This is not an "as if" report but it does show a degree of rational insight as do many patients. However, Pierre Janet's patient specifically used the "as if" locution:

> It was *as if* it was not me walking, it was not me talking, *as if* it was not me living . . .
> I can look at me, I am somehow bothered by my body, as if it wasn't me, *as if* I lived on the side of my body, on the side of myself if you like. I don't know how to explain.   (Janet and Raymond 1898: 70)

This suggests that right prefrontal dorsolateral deactivation does not lead to inability to reason about experience or that Cotard delusion consists in simply taking "as if" experience at face value, without the ability to detect inconsistency with background knowledge. And when we focus on the syndrome rather than the content of the delusion description of the phenomenology it also suggests that the experience of Cotard delusion involves a wider range of bodily anomalies than the loss of affective transcription in DPD.

It seems clear that the self-model has disintegrated even though traces of its high-level narrative structure remain. So the patient who now experiences her body as a disintegrating and dysregulable panoply of sensations has to say something. She is in fact correctly reporting that she does not exist where "she" refers to the representation that she normally relies on to regulate herself though life. The delusion reports that experience. A proponent of the second-factor view

COTARD SYNDROME: THE EXPERIENCE OF INEXISTENCE   199

might still reasonably claim that what needs explaining is why it is that the subject does not ultimately *override* the delusion even if its content does reflect experience.

What we might call classic second-factor theories argue that the failure to override or replace the delusion reflects a failure of a metacognitive capacity for "reality testing", "belief evaluation", or rational insight. Typically this failure is associated with dorsolateral prefrontal hypoactivity. Precisely how to conceive of the role of that dorsolateral prefrontal circuitry is a tricky question. If we import folk psychological conceptions of rational belief fixation we may end up focusing on the apparent failures of reasoning in delusion. I do not disagree that that the patient is reasoning abnormally measured against canonical standards of rationality (although it is by no means clear what Bayesian or logical reasoning demands of a patient in Mr A's situation). However, conceiving of the delusion as a "failure of reasoning" is a folk psychological interpretation of the patient's phenomenology rather than the definition of a cognitive process. It does not map well to the role of the insula and default mode network in the genesis of the delusion. Equally to try and resuscitate the patient's rational capacities by saying that they are reasoning *normally* on the basis of anomalous experience endorses the idea that a key *explanandum* here is the apparent failure of rational insight.

I think that attention to the genesis of the delusion suggests that the problem here is a failure of *regulation*, rather than representation or reasoning. In that context reference to metacognition should emphasize its role in cognitive and behavioural control rather than epistemic evaluation. Metacognition refers to a suite of abilities that can be flexibly integrated to deal with problems that cannot be solved by lower level processes. Sometimes these metacognitive processes can be coordinated to establish the truth of propositions as a form of high-level cognitive control but it is not clear that the Cotard patient's problem lies there. It seems more likely that massive and intractable dysregulation across the control hierarchy has rendered her a spectator to her own disintegration. Paul Noordhof suggests in this volume that attention may be a key to understanding how "a subject can recognize the *relevance* of evidence against the delusory belief and yet retain it" (Noordhof, this volume). The idea is that anomalous experience dominates attentional resources leaving the subject only able to sporadically focus on the epistemic aspects of her condition. When she does so she is able to realize that the delusion is not rational by procedural standards. However, the anomalous experience ultimately commands attentional (and I would say other executive functioning) resources making stable belief revision impossible. The subject cannot restructure functioning of her cognitive economy to reflect her abstract propositional knowledge. Another way to put this in the framework I have outlined is to say that active inference is effectively disabled for subjects with the Cotard delusion. Technically active inference is the accumulation of evidence to confirm a model that predicts the consequences of (ultimately) regulatory activity.

200 BELIEF, IMAGINATION, AND DELUSION

But the Cotard patient has no such model available. And she is unable to take any activity that would create and sustain an alternative model. Noordhof pitches his attentional account as part of an argument against two-factor accounts that ultimately explain delusion in terms of a metacognitive abnormality. As he points out, the monopoly of cognitive resources by anomalous experience may not differentiate delusional from non-delusional subjects. When a subject has "anomalous, striking, or traumatic experiences", "They can be overly inclined to attend to these experiences" (Noordhof, this volume) with cascading effects for resource allocation across the mind. I agree but I think ultimately that the active inference framework displaces emphasis on the normality or otherwise of reasoning and belief fixation in delusion. The reason is that it inverts the relationship between reasoning and representation and regulation.

References

Barrett, L. F. (2017). 'The theory of constructed emotion: an active inference account of interoception and categorization'. *Social Cognitive and Affective Neuroscience* 12(1): 1–23.

Barrett, L. F., K. S. Quigley, and P. Hamilton (2016). 'An active inference theory of allostasis and interoception in depression'. *Philosophical Transactions of the Royal Society B: Biological Sciences* 371(1708): 20160011.

Barrett, L. F. and W. K. Simmons (2015). 'Interoceptive predictions in the brain'. *Nature Reviews Neuroscience* 16(7): 419–29.

Bayne, T. and E. Pacherie (2005). 'In defence of the doxastic conception of delusions'. *Mind & Language* 20(2): 163–88.

Billon, A. (2016). 'Making sense of the Cotard syndrome: insights from the study of depersonalisation'. *Mind & Language* 31(3): 356–391.

Billon, A. (2017). 'Mineness first: three challenges to the recent theories of the sense of bodily ownership'. In F. De Vignemont and A. J. T. Alsmith (eds.), *The Subject's Matter: Self-Consciousness and the Body* (Cambridge, MA: MIT Press), 189–216.

Boehme, S., W. H. R. Miltner, and T. Straube (2014). 'Neural correlates of self-focused attention in social anxiety'. *Social Cognitive and Affective Neuroscience* 10(6): 856–62.

Charland-Verville, V., M. A. Bruno, M. A. Bahri, A. Demertzi, M. Desseilles, C. Chatelle, A. Vanhaudenhuyse, R. Hustinx, C. Bernard, L. Tshibanda, S. Laureys, and A. Zeman (2013). 'Brain dead yet mind alive: a positron emission tomography case study of brain metabolism in Cotard's syndrome'. *Cortex* 49(7): 1997–9.

Chatterjee, S. S. and S. Mitra (2015). '"I do not exist": Cotard syndrome in insular cortex atrophy'. *Biological Psychiatry* 77(11): e52–e53.

Coltheart, M. (2010). 'The neuropsychology of delusions'. *Annals of the New York Academy of Sciences* 1191(1): 16–26.

Coltheart, M. and M. Davies (2021). 'Failure of hypothesis evaluation as a factor in delusional belief'. *Cognitive Neuropsychiatry* 26(4): 213–30.

Coltheart, M., P. Menzies, and J. Sutton (2010). 'Abductive inference and delusional belief'. *Cognitive Neuropsychiatry* 15(1–3): 261–87.

Corcoran, A. W. and J. Hohwy (2017). 'Allostasis, interoception, and the free energy principle: Feeling our way forward'. In M. Tsakiris and H. De Preester (eds.), *The Interoceptive Mind: From Homeostasis to Awareness* (Oxford: Oxford University Press), 272–92.

Craig, A. (2009a). 'Emotional moments across time: a possible neural basis for time perception in the anterior insula'. *Philosophical Transactions of the Royal Society B: Biological Sciences* 364(1525): 1933–42.

Craig, A. D. (2009b). 'How do you feel – now? The anterior insula and human awareness'. *Nature Reviews Neuroscience* 10(1): 59–70.

Craig, A. (2010). 'The sentient self'. *Brain Structure and Function* 214(5–6): 563–77.

Davey, C. G. and B. J. Harrison (2018). 'The brain's center of gravity: how the default mode network helps us to understand the self'. *World Psychiatry* 17(3): 278–9.

Davies, M. and M. Coltheart (2022). Cotard delusion, emotional experience and depersonalisation. *Cognitive Neuropsychiatry*, 27(6): 430–46.

Debruyne, H., M. Portzky, F. Van den Eynde, and K. Audenaert (2009). 'Cotard's syndrome: a review'. *Current Psychiatry Reports* 11(3): 197–202.

Descartes, R. (1985). *The Philosophical Writings of Descartes*. Trans. J. Cottingham, R. Stoothof, and D. Murdoch (Cambridge: Cambridge University Press), 56.

Dugas, L. and F. Moutier (1911). *La Dépersonnalisation* (Paris: Félix Alcan). http://www.biusante.parisdescartes.fr/histmed/medica/cote?79749.

Feinstein, J. S., S. S. Khalsa, T. V. Salomons, K. M. Prkachin, L. A. Frey-Law, J. E. Lee, D. Tranel, and D. Rudrauf (2016). 'Preserved emotional awareness of pain in a patient with extensive bilateral damage to the insula, anterior cingulate, and amygdala'. *Brain Structure and Function* 221(3): 1499–511.

Fernandez Velasco, P. and S. Loev (2021). 'Affective experience in the predictive mind: a review and new integrative account'. *Synthese* 198(11): 10847–82.

Friston, K. (2018). 'Am I self-conscious? (Or does self-organization entail self-consciousness?)'. *Frontiers in Psychology* 9: 579.

Friston, K., J. Mattout, and J. Kilner (2011). 'Action understanding and active inference'. *Biological Cybernetics* 104(1–2): 137–60.

Friston, K., P. Schwartenbeck, T. Fitzgerald, M. Moutoussis, T. Behrens, and R. J. Dolan (2013). 'The anatomy of choice: active inference and agency'. *Frontiers in Human Neuroscience* 7: 598.

Gerrans, P. (2000). 'Refining the explanation of Cotard's delusion'. *Mind & Language* 15(1): 111–22.

Gerrans, P. (2020). 'Pain asymbolia as depersonalization for pain experience: an interoceptive active inference account'. *Frontiers in Psychology* 11: 523710.

Gerrans, P. (2023). 'A vessel without a pilot: bodily and affective experience in the Cotard delusion of inexistence'. *Mind & Language* 38(4): 1059–80.

Hohwy, J. and J. Michael (2017). 'Why should any body have a self?' In F. De Vignemont and A. J. T. Alsmith (eds.), *The Subject's Matter: Self-Consciousness and the Body* (Cambridge, MA: MIT Press), 363–92.

Holper, L., N. Kobashi, D. Kiper, F. Scholkmann, M. Wolf, and K. Eng (2012). 'Trial-to-trial variability differentiates motor imagery during observation between low versus high responders: a functional near-infrared spectroscopy study'. *Behavioural Brain Research* 229(1): 29e40.

Janet, P. and F. Raymond (1898). *Névroses et idées fixes*, vol. 2 (Paris: Félix Alcan).

Jaspers, K. (1962). *General Psychopathology* (Manchester University Press).

Joffily, M. and G. Coricelli (2013). 'Emotional valence and the free-energy principle'. *PLoS Computational Biology* 9(6): e1003094.

Kirchhoff, M., T. Parr, E. Palacios, K. Friston, and J. Kiverstein (2018). 'The Markov blankets of life: autonomy, active inference and the free energy principle'. *Journal of The Royal Society Interface* 15(138): 20170792.

Kleckner, I. R., J. Zhang, A. Touroutoglou, L. Chanes, C. Xia, W. K. Simmons, K. S. Quigley, B. C. Dickerson, and L. Feldman Barrett (2017). 'Evidence for a large-scale brain system supporting allostasis and interoception in humans'. *Nature Human Behaviour* 1(5): 0069.

Letheby, C. and P. Gerrans (2017). 'Self unbound: ego dissolution in psychedelic experience'. *Neuroscience of Consciousness* 2017(1): nix016.

Limanowski, J. and F. Blankenburg (2013). 'Minimal self-models and the free energy principle'. *Frontiers in Human Neuroscience* 7: 547.

Limanowski, J. and K. Friston (2018). '"Seeing the dark": grounding phenomenal transparency and opacity in precision estimation for active inference'. *Frontiers in Psychology* 9: 643.

Lyon, P., F. Keijzer, D. Arendt, and M. Levin (eds.) (2021). 'Basal cognition: multicellularity, neurons and the cognitive lens'. Special issue of *Philosophical Transactions of the Royal Society B: Biological Sciences* 376(1821).

Medford, N. (2012). 'Emotion and the unreal self: depersonalization disorder and de-affectualization'. *Emotion Review* 4(2): 139–44.

Medford, N. and H. D. Critchley (2010). 'Conjoint activity of anterior insular and anterior cingulate cortex: awareness and response'. *Brain Structure and Function* 214(5–6): 535–49.

Medford, N., B. Brierley, M. Brammer, E. T. Bullmore, A. S. David, and M. L. Phillips (2006). 'Emotional memory in depersonalization disorder: a functional MRI study'. *Psychiatry Research: Neuroimaging* 148(2): 93–102.

Medford, N., M. Sierra, A. Stringaris, V. Giampietro, M. J. Brammer, and A. S. David (2016). 'Emotional experience and awareness of self: functional MRI studies of depersonalization disorder'. *Frontiers in Psychology* 7: 432.

Mendez, M. F. and J. Ramírez-Bermúdez (2011). 'Cotard syndrome in semantic dementia'. *Psychosomatics* 52(6): 571.

Moayedi, M. (2014). 'All roads lead to the insula'. *Pain* 155(10): 1920–1.

Nejad, A. G. and K. Toofani (2005). 'Co-existence of lycanthropy and Cotard's syndrome in a single case'. *Acta Psychiatrica Scandinavica* 111(3): 250–52.

Nelson, S. M., N. U. F. Dosenbach, A. L. Cohen, M. E. Wheeler, B. L. Schlaggar, and S. E. Petersen (2010). 'Role of the anterior insula in task-level control and focal attention'. *Brain Structure and Function* 214(5–6): 669–80.

Paulus, M. P. and M. B. Stein (2010). 'Interoception in anxiety and depression'. *Brain Structure and Function* 214(5–6): 451–63.

Pezzulo, G., F. Rigoli, and K. Friston (2015). 'Active inference, homeostatic regulation and adaptive behavioural control'. *Progress in Neurobiology* 134: 17–35.

Philippi, C. L., J. S. Feinstein, S. S. Khalsa, A. Damasio, D. Tranel, G. Landini, G., K. Williford, and D. Rudrauf (2012). 'Preserved self-awareness following extensive bilateral brain damage to the insula, anterior cingulate, and medial prefrontal cortices'. *PloS One* 7(8): e38413.

Ramirez-Bermúdez, J., L. C. Aguilar-Venegas, D. Crail-Melendez, M. Espinola-Nadurille, F. Nente, and M. F. Mendez (2010). 'Cotard syndrome in neurological and psychiatric patients'. *Journal of Neuropsychiatry and Clinical Neurosciences* 22(4): 409–16.

Ramirez Bermúdez, J., P. Bustamante-Gomez, M. Espínola-Nadurille, N. E. Kerik, I. E. Dias Meneses, M. Restrepo-Martínez, and M. F. Mendez (2021). 'Cotard syndrome in anti-NMDAR encephalitis: two patients and insights from molecular imaging'. *Neurocase* 27(1): 64–71.

Sahoo, A. and K. A. Josephs (2018). 'A neuropsychiatric analysis of the Cotard delusion'. *Journal of Neuropsychiatry and Clinical Neurosciences* 30(1): 58–65.

Schilder, P. (1935). *The Image and Appearance of the Human Body* (London: Kegan Paul).

Seth, A. K. (2013). 'Interoceptive inference, emotion, and the embodied self'. *Trends in Cognitive Sciences* 17(11): 565–73.

Seth, A. K. and K. J. Friston (2016). 'Active interoceptive inference and the emotional brain'. *Philosophical Transactions of the Royal Society B: Biological Sciences* 371(1708): 20160007.

Seth, A. K. and M. Tsakiris (2018). 'Being a beast machine: the somatic basis of selfhood'. *Trends in Cognitive Sciences* 22: 969–81.

Sierra, M. (2009). *Depersonalization: A New Look at a Neglected Syndrome* (Cambridge: Cambridge University Press).

Sierra, M. and A. S. David (2011). 'Depersonalization: a selective impairment of self-awareness'. *Consciousness and Cognition* 20(1): 99–108.

Sierra, M., N. Medford, G. Wyatt, and A. S. David (2012). 'Depersonalization disorder and anxiety: a special relationship?' *Psychiatry Research* 197(1): 123–7.

Stephan, K. E., Z. M. Manjaly, C. D. Mathys, L. A. E. Weber, S. Paliwal, T. Gard, M. Tittgemeyer, S. M. Fleming, H. Haker, A. K. Seth, and F. H. Petzschner (2016). 'Allostatic self-efficacy: a metacognitive theory of dyshomeostasis-induced fatigue and depression'. *Frontiers in Human Neuroscience* 10: 550.

Stone, T. and A. W. Young (1997). 'Delusions and brain injury: the philosophy and psychology of belief'. *Mind & Language* 12(3–4): 327–64.

Terasawa, Y., M. Shibata, Y. Moriguchi, and S. Umeda (2013). 'Anterior insular cortex mediates bodily sensibility and social anxiety'. *Social Cognitive and Affective Neuroscience* 8(3): 259–66.

Tomasetti, C., A. Valchera, M. Fornaro, F. Vellante, L. Orsolini, A. Carano, A. Ventriglio, M. Di Giannantonio, and D. De Berardis (2020). 'The "dead man walking" disorder: an update on Cotard's syndrome'. *International Review of Psychiatry* 32(5–6): 500–9.

Young, A. W. and K. M. Leafhead (1996). 'Betwixt life and death'. In H. John and M. Peter (eds.), *Case Studies of the Cotard Delusion. Method in Madness: Case Studies in Cognitive Neuropsychiatry*, 147–71.

10
Delusions and Everyday Life

Douglas Lavin and Lucy O'Brien

In this chapter we will consider a series of questions with the aim of framing, in a distinctive way, the nature of delusion as a topic for philosophical reflection. We aim to do this without presupposing, or taking as given, any particular theory of mind. The underlying purpose is to get away from the 'psychological attitude' approach framing current philosophical discussion. This approach asks what kind of attitude is a delusion—a belief or an imagination? Something else? We aim instead to shift attention to the question of the 'object' of delusions. What is delusion *of*? What is the *intentional object* of this condition of mind? This effort is motivated in part by a suspicion that much of the current discussion of the nature of delusion, and the importance of understanding it, proceeds against a background of presuppositions that distort it.

We think that the significance of this distortion lies beyond a disruption to our understanding of delusions; it also results in a failure to connect delusory thought with ordinary forms of thinking that are ubiquitous in the difficulties and failures faced by reflective humans in everyday life. It is a striking fact about the philosophical discussion of delusion that there is little said of the fact, and pervasiveness, of fantasy and magical thinking, etc. in human life, let alone its sometimes seemingly systematic character. On our view, a pervasive aspect of being human is that we think in ways that cannot be captured by the presuppositions of the 'psychological attitude' approach.

1. The Psychological Attitude Approach

Delusions come in very different kinds, and are experienced by individuals with different forms of neurological damage, and different kinds of cognitive lives. Monothematic delusions (such as Capgras, Cotard, Erotomania) are usually experienced by people with otherwise typical or unremarkable cognitive lives. Other delusions occur more often in the context of schizophrenia or other severely uncircumscribed cognitive disruption. Despite these differences, much of the literature on delusion proceeds on the assumption that it can be more or less clear about what the relevant content of a given delusion is. In the case of Capgras it is the representation that 'my wife is an impostor', and in the case of Cotard it is

Douglas Lavin and Lucy O'Brien, *Delusions and Everyday Life* In: *Belief, Imagination, and Delusion*. Edited by: Ema Sullivan-Bissett, Oxford University Press. © Oxford University Press 2024. DOI: 10.1093/oso/9780198872221.003.0010

the representation that 'I am dead' or 'I do not exist'. Or in the case of paranoid delusions that the 'CIA are following me'. In the case of erotomanic delusions the content proposed is that 'He loves me'—maybe even that 'He can read my mind'. For somatic delusions the content may be that 'My skin is crawling with lice', or that 'That arm attached to my body is not mine'. Let any of these contents be represented by the proposition *p*.

With the content supposedly settled, the hard work is then directed at the business of working out what *kind* of an attitude to that content a delusory attitude could be. Probably the most popular, although also most contested, suggestion is that delusions with these contents are *beliefs* (Bayne and Pacherie 2005; Bortolotti 2010). But if they are beliefs, it is asked, how come they are *so* irrational and based on entirely insufficient evidence, if any evidence at all. It is then usually suggested that there is a kind of evidence—an anomalous experience—that the deluded person is responding to, and forming her belief on the basis of. It is widely accepted, however, that even given an anomalous experience, to believe one is dead, or does not exist, say—while speaking—is still a highly irrational and puzzling thing to do.[1] For one to believe that this woman in one's sitting room is not one's wife but someone who looks just like her and has been substituted for her, requires the setting aside of enormous amounts of contrary evidence. For us to make sense of a belief being formed on the basis of the anomalous experience, the anomalous experience had better have a fairly decisive character. The experience is usually characterized as a disturbed or unusual affective response. In these cases, to one's body or to one's wife. Most theorists committed to delusions being beliefs themselves argue that that will unlikely be enough, and that some further irrationality over and above the anomalous evidence would be required. One-factor views (for example that of Noordhof and Sullivan Bissett 2021) will appeal to a normal range of irrationalities and two-factor theorists to some bias in information processing, performance error, or deficit in belief evaluation.[2] In either case the deluded subject is the victim of things feeling strange coming together with a reasoning capacity that fails in that instance. Other theorists, for example, Matthew Parrott (2019), argue that that will still be not enough. We can think of belief formation in most cases of deluded belief as having two aspects and we can worry about irrationality in relation to either. There is the aspect of hypothesis formation—the hypothesis that, I am dead, say. There is then also the question of how come the subject believes the hypothesis— takes herself to have evidence in support of it. Perhaps if a subject is *forced* to

---

[1] Something that the subject who has the delusion will often recognize. 'He acknowledged that his abilities to see, hear, think, remember, and communicate proved that his mind must be alive: he could not explain how his mind could be alive if his brain was dead, but he was certain that this was the case' (Gerrans, this volume).

[2] Noordhof (this volume) suggests that conscious attention captured by anomalous experience can be enough to explain the formation of delusory beliefs.

consider whether she is dead we can make sense of her condition by appealing to a combination of peculiar experience and rational or critical deficit. However, it remains mysterious what the basis was for the subject to select that hypothesis, rather than the myriad other ones open to her: that she is affectively numb, depressed, or partially paralysed, and so on.

The basic puzzle is that delusory subjects seem to be in a position readily to know that the proposed contents of their delusions are false. If their delusions are beliefs, that makes them very puzzling. Of course, what it is for an attitude to be a belief is much disputed. One thing, however, that most disputants agree upon is that our beliefs can be true or false, and that the norms that govern beliefs are, or are connected to, truth norms—we believe correctly if our beliefs are formed in a way that secures alethic values.[3] The difficulty in making sense of delusions as a kind of belief comes from the fact that we struggle to see delusions as a kind of attitude that aims, in one way or another, at the accurate apprehension of facts, as an attitude that is correct only if is true.

So maybe the relevant attitudes taken towards the agreed delusory contents are not belief attitudes. Maybe they are some other kind of attitude? Maybe they are, others suggest, attitudes of imagination: the deluded subject does not believe that they are dead, that their wife is an impostor, rather they imagine that they are dead or their wife is an impostor (Currie 2000)? Their weirdness and disconnection from evidence would not be such a problem, it is reasoned, if they were attitudes of imagining. Imagining that something is the case is not constrained by evidence in the same way. If delusions were 'imaginings that' two things will strike us.

First, if delusions are 'imaginings that' why are they such a *problem* for the person who suffers from them, and for those around them? We all imagine weird and irrational things being the case, and express our imaginings for our amusement, inspiration, to give voice to our desires. The thought that puts weight behind the idea that delusions are beliefs is that in expressing their delusions a subject is expressing how things *really are* for them—they are not engaged, knowingly at least, in a game of play or make-believe. Subjects expressing their delusions will importune others to take them seriously, to believe them.[4] So, if the attitude we take towards delusory contents is an attitude of imagination it becomes puzzling why they are expressed with such sincerity and seriousness.

Second, imaginings on this proposal can still be said to be true or false—what one is imagining can correspond to a state of reality or not. If I imagine that I am dead, in so doing, if I am a self-conscious human adult, I know that the state of affairs being imagined is the state of affairs in which I am dead—and that that state of affairs is inconsistent with the truth that I am alive. Evidence in favour of my

---

[3] We do not intend to give a theory of belief and belief norms here—just to utilize the idea that their correctness is determined in relation to their truth or falsity.

[4] 'You don't believe me, no one believes me' (Patient U. Case History, Carano et al. 2014: 350).

208 BELIEF, IMAGINATION, AND DELUSION

being alive counts against the possibility that I am now dead. (Indeed, one might think that we have decisive evidence, in virtue of the fact that we are imagining, that if we are imagining being dead, what we are imagining is false.)

Of course, those who argue that a delusion is an imagination have lots they can say about both aspects of what is *prima facie* puzzling. They could take delusions to be imaginations that the subject mistakes for a perception or a belief, as Gregory Currie (2000) does. Or they may have something expansive to say about the nature of states of affairs we can take attitudes to. Or they may be able to deploy something like Neil Levy's idea of acquiescent sayings (this volume, Section 3) to explain the seeming seriousness of expressions of delusion. However, our point is not that there are things that we might be able to add to the suggestion that delusions are belief or imagination attitudes, towards truth-evaluable contents that make the suggestion fit better with the phenomena. The puzzles we have raised go no further than those that have been recognized by those who defend a belief theory of delusion, or an imagination theory of delusion. Our point is that before we start more elaborate theory construction we should be sure that we have started in the right place in our theorizing.

Similarly, what if we were to wonder whether the attitude is one of desiring that, or supposing that, or wondering whether? In adopting any of these options we commit ourselves to trying to make sense of what we described as the sincerity and seriousness of delusions, in the expression of which a subject is communicating 'how things really are for them', and to there being an attitude to a content that is either true or false, correct or incorrect, accurate or inaccurate, and which can be the object of other attitudes—beliefs, imaginations, etc.—committal or not.

2. Expressions of Delusions

It is important to remember that our topic is the nature of delusion, and not the nature of delusive utterances. We have every reason to think that many subjects undergo delusory experiences without verbalization, without expressing their experiences in communicative speech. It is in the task of trying to make their suffering intelligible to others that those undergoing delusions offer expressions of their state aimed at being intelligible. And given that pathological delusions are not widespread, most of us have no first-person experience of them; we know them only through the verbal expression of them reported by subjects, in turn reported by psychiatrists. Verbal reports are particularly suited to communication of matters of fact. There are many experiences—especially sensory and emotional ones—that are hard to put into words. Moreover, many of these verbal expressions are not spontaneous, but are the result of conversations with a probing psychiatrist. These reports then get relayed, very often in *oratio obliqua* form, by philosophers and psychologists. So, there are multiple points at which we may get distortion of the phenomenon and its most natural spontaneous expression.

DELUSIONS AND EVERYDAY LIFE   209

Nevertheless, we want to step back and do a little descriptive work—looking at the common examples of the verbal expressions of the delusions we are trying to make sense of. It will be become obvious that such utterances, although in some ways very varying in theme and content, point towards some underlying patterns.

Having considered the pathological cases we will widen our search and look at more common verbal expressions of what we can call everyday delusions. There are remarkable similarities in theme and topic of the everyday and the pathological case. We will look in particular at common expressions of love and grief. This allows us to ask—from a perspective in which we have first-person knowledge of the delusion we are indulging in, and giving expression to—what we might be doing in saying such things.

Let us then turn to some verbal expressions of pathological delusion. The first thing to acknowledge is that there is a vast amount of potential data that we could look at, and that our aims here are not to provide any kind of empirical analysis or review—quantitative or qualitative—of the data on delusion expression. We are rather going look again at typical examples theorists give of what subjects with delusions 'say'. It is worth underlining the fact that many papers on delusions give very few, and often no, direct quotations of patients experiencing delusions but instead offer *oratio obliqua* reports on 'what they believe'. But here are the sorts of things subjects are supposed to say:

Cotard syndrome: 'I am dead', 'I do not exist'

Capgras syndrome: 'That is not my spouse. It is an impostor'

Anton syndrome: 'I can see' [when tested as blind]

Erotomania: 'Tom Hardy loves me; he is sending me secret messages'

Mirror Self Identification: 'That is not me in the mirror. It is my sister'

Delusional parasitosis: 'My skin is crawling with lice'

Asomatognosia: 'That arm [attached to my body] is not mine'

Somatoparaphrenia: 'That arm [attached to my body] is not mine, it is my mother's'

Solipsism Syndrome: 'The world beyond me does not exist'

Paranoid Delusions: 'They are spying on me'

Thought insertion: 'Someone is putting thoughts in my head'[5]

---

[5] Thanks to a reader for Oxford University Press for raising the question of how hallucinations might fit with our account of delusions. Our topic here is delusion, rather than hallucination. We realize, however, that the distinction is not always as sharp a one as our way of proceeding might suggest. Our example of delusional parasitosis ('my skin is crawling with lice') makes that clear: that sentence can be used to express a sensory hallucination, as well as be evidence of a delusion. We also

210 BELIEF, IMAGINATION, AND DELUSION

In fact, of course, one rarely gets just one sentence on its own from a patient engaged in delusory thinking. We often see patients uttering a series of sentences, often repeated, struggling to put into words how things seem for them. When one does get longer verbatim reports the extent to which expressions of delusions are often also expressions of extreme distress becomes obvious. Here, for example, is a longer verbatim report from a patient suffering Cotard syndrome:

> You don't believe me, no one believes me... I have lost everything... I don't have anything now... I lost my spine... I don't have the mind, I don't have it anymore... there's nothing to do... no one can do anything... I can't cry because I don't have tears, I never had them... I don't have lungs, I don't have an intestine, I'm empty! I can't walk... I don't have legs, I can't eat... all my teeth fell off, I can't go to the bathroom... because everything is connected... ... My whole body has become empty and petrified... I've lost everything... Kill me, I'm useless, I don't want to suffer anymore. Even God cannot do anything for me...
>
> (Carano et al. 2014, Patient U. Case History, p. 350)

We want now to make some naïve observations about the sentences that report the kinds of primary delusions that we are looking at.

First, consider how we would actually respond to such utterances, were they directed at us by a subject, in the contexts in which such utterances tend to be made. It seems unlikely that our response would be to consider whether to accept or not accept what seems to have been said to us by the subject. Taken as assertions of statements of fact, using English, as ordinary English speakers use it, what is being said seems out of the question—if not, impossible—and surely known to be so by the uttering subject. We would not generally receive such utterances as expressions of acts of thinking that were liable to being true or false, correct or incorrect, depending on the facts being described. As John Campbell points out, if we did that we would surely wonder whether the subjects mean something different to what we mean by the terms they are using.[6] Maybe we would do that, or we might wonder whether, even if they are using words in ordinary English, as we do, they are putting those words into service in some other way.

Second, and relatedly, even if we were to set out to either accept or reject what is being said, it is hard to see how we could conceive of the activity of settling the matter. What kind of proof or evidence might we think that the uttering subject

---

acknowledge that sensory hallucinations may give rise to specific kinds of delusion, and that delusions may give rise to sensory hallucinations. We look forward to thinking further about this, but very crudely we are inclined to think of sensory hallucinations as involving the abnormal exercise of our sensory capacities which can be deployed veridically or not, and of (most) delusions as involving the abnormal exercise of our self-conscious affective capacities which are valuative, rather than concerned with veridicality.

[6] See Campbell (2001: 90).

DELUSIONS AND EVERYDAY LIFE   211

has, that it is for us to see the strength of, or to undermine? It is not clear that there is such a thing as evidence or proof on which an act of thinking of that type could even conceivably be correct or well grounded.[7] In a characteristically insensitive style, Wittgenstein makes something like this observation in *On Certainty* (1969):

> 159. If someone said to me that he doubted whether he had a body I should take him to be a half-wit. But I shouldn't know what it would mean to try to convince him that he had one. And if I had said something, and that had removed his doubt, I should not know how or why.

We would not use the slur, nor take such an attitude towards these patients—we hope—but we would take them to be someone suffering an abnormal disruption to ordinary ways of being. We might try to empathize with them: to try to imagine what their experience would have to be like for those to be the words that they reach for in order to communicate how things are for them. But we would not interrogate them on their grounds, nor try to persuade them to change their mind—not only out of sensitivity to their plight, but because we would not know 'what it would mean' to do those things.

Might it be said that this is true for some of the cases, but not all? It is after all not impossible or not provable that Tom Hardy loves the subject suffering erotomania, that the patient has lice on their skin, or that the mob are out to get the subject suffering from paranoid delusions. (As Joseph Heller is supposed to have put it 'just because you're paranoid does not mean that they aren't after you'.) That is true. If fact psychiatrists will very occasionally face the diagnostic difficulty that their patient is not in fact delusional but is in a very unusual circumstance— they are anxious and paranoid because they have good reason to believe that someone is out to kill them.[8] The interesting question here is what we would be doing if we carried out an investigation of whether it is likely that anyone is out to kill the patient, and whether the patient has evidence that that is the case. Would our answer, in itself, be determinative of whether the patient's thinking is delusory or not? Our suggestion is that in such an investigation we would rather be seeking indirect evidence to try to settle what *form of thinking* our patient is engaged in—a form of thinking directed at a putative state of affairs, and for which truth and falsity determine correctness or incorrectness, or rather a form of thinking in

---

[7] In this we agree with Archer (this volume) that we do not make sense of such cases by looking for epistemic reasons.

[8] A doctor we know, on a psychiatry rotation, was called on to offer a judgement on the question of whether a prison patient was suffering from paranoia. He said that the patient told him that he was in prison for assaulting a woman whose family were a criminal gang with prison contacts, and who were plotting to get the prison guards to kill him. As the doctor said, 'I needed a private investigator to make a reliable diagnosis'.

212 BELIEF, IMAGINATION, AND DELUSION

which a subject is suffering from a disrupted sense of themselves. Or indeed a form of thinking that has come to involve both of these elements.[9]

This leads us to the third feature of the expressions of delusion we started with: the reports all involve the first person in some guise. In each case the delusion is a delusion either about the subject's relation to herself, or about her relation to another or 'the world'. We suggest that this reflects a feature, often expressed by psychiatrists, but which sometimes get left behind in philosophical literature, that delusions are a disrupted or distorted form of self-awareness on the part of the subject, and as such concern the way in which a subject relates to and is aware of herself.[10] It may seem as though Capgras, for example, or erotomania, or certain paranoid delusions rather have another subject as their object—the spouse, Tom Hardy, or the spy. However, in these delusions also the others figure as they are in relation to the subject—as a stranger to her or impostor in her life, as a person who loves her, or as someone spying on her. The experience of Capgras is also often the experience of another assuming familiarity, or rights of intimacy or access to the subject herself.[11] On some putative explanations of Capgras the affective disruption occurring is the same as in Cotard—a failure to feel others in one's sense of oneself. The disruption is a disruption to a form of self-awareness the subject has when she thinks of herself as the object of awareness of the other. In the case of nihilistic or other delusions that involve 'the world', delusions that 'the world does not exist', or that 'the world has nothing in it for me', it is again clear that the world is the object of the delusion in so far as it is the world for the subject: either that there is no world beyond the subject, or it is an alien or barren or repelling world.

The further thing to notice is that many of the cases involve not just one condition, or another, of the subject and her situation in relation to others and her world, but a concern with the existence, or status of the existence, of the subject, others, and her world. In many cases delusions do not correspond to general questions about what properties the subject of the delusion has. These subjects are not deluded about whether they have a Ford or a Bugatti, or whether their spouse has brown or blond hair. They are deluded about whether they, or

---

[9] A referee for this volume raised the very interesting question of whether these need be mutually exclusive forms of thought. There seems no reason to say that they must be. In fact, one of the fruits of our discussion may turn out to be that we can use the distinct forms of thinking identified to throw light on each other, and to make sense of complex forms of thinking where they interact.

[10] Gerrans does not leave this behind: 'If affect is completely flattened, the taken-for-granted background of stable selfhood will be disrupted' (1999: 604). Nor does Billon in his 'Making Sense of the Cotard Syndrome: Insights from the Study of Depersonalisation' (Billon 2016). See also Gerrans (this volume) for an articulation of the kind of disruption to experience of self that may be involved in Cotard's syndrome, and for a resistance to the idea that we need to appeal to abnormal evidential reasoning to explain the delusion.

[11] Note that in cases of 'stranger Capgras' the strangers are often police, or doctors, and people with particular entitlements to access the private world of the patient. Patients do not generally think their neighbour or work colleague's spouse has been replaced by an alien.

DELUSIONS AND EVERYDAY LIFE   213

parts of them exist, whether there is the other subject, or their world. We suggest that these are expressions of extreme—sensory, affective, emotional—disruption to the subject's relation to herself—whether as the only object, or also through her relation to another, or to her world.

3. Expressions of Everyday Delusional Thinking

Belief theorists about delusion often describe themselves as committed to a 'continuity', as opposed to a 'discontinuity', approach to delusion. Delusions are states of mind to be understood as continuous with other ordinary beliefs: the subjects are just in a peculiar position, with peculiar rational tendencies, with peculiar evidence. We want to advertise ourselves as committed to a different, and we think in many ways more important, continuity: the continuity between the delusory thinking of the ill patient, and the delusory thinking that disrupts, and is expressed in most human lives. As we remarked at the outset, it is a striking fact about the philosophical discussion of delusion that there tends to be little said of fantasy and magical thinking in human life. We think that connecting our discussion of delusions with more everyday delusory thinking will bring into view a continuity between pathological delusions and our everyday experiences. We think this is important both philosophically—its gets the phenomenon more properly into view in a way that does not distort it—and interpersonally, and so clinically—it enables us to draw on our own self-reflective resources not just to comfort or correct, but better to understand how things might be for the deluded patient.

So, let us now consider some familiar everyday expressions of everyday delusions. To keep our discussion under control, and to focus on experiences that mirror the kinds of delusions we have been looking at, we will focus on the kind of fantastical and impossible locutions we use in trying to communicate our love and grief.[12]

Here are some common, widely uttered, expressions of grief:

'I have lost a part of me'

'There is a hole in me where he was'

'There is a hole in the world where he was'

'He was my world'[13]

'I have lost the whole world'

[12] We might have considered expressions of shame: 'In my experience of shame, the other sees all of me and all through me, even if the occasion of shame is on my surface – for instance my appearances; and the expression of shame' (Williams 1993: 89) or pride: 'fit to burst'. Or extreme sadness or depression.
[13] Or more poetically, 'He was my North, my South, My East, My West...' (Auden).

214   BELIEF, IMAGINATION, AND DELUSION

'His being gone is killing me'

'My heart, my body, is breaking'

'I am broken'

'I have no future, my world has ended'

'My life is over'

Here are some common, widely uttered, expressions of love:

'He is part of me now'

'He has changed my world'

'The two of us are one'[14]

'He is my world'

'He is my life'

'I am alive because of him'

'I am now whole'

'He has put me back together'

'I only started living when I met him'

'If he dies I will die'

These utterances—of love and grief—reflect each other, and the reflection is not
an accident. As Nick Cave puts it in remarks he made after the death of his son: 'It
seems to me that if we love we grieve. That's the deal. That is the pact.' And that
which love does for us—indeed *to* us—grief rips away.

How do, and indeed how should, we respond to expressions of love and grief of
this kind?[15] Of course, these are sentences that *can* be assessed as true or false. And
on a straight reading almost every one of them is manifestly false. However, it is
not just politeness, or pointlessness, that stops us responding to the grieving widow
'No, your life is not over, and is unlikely to be anytime soon given your health and
life expectancy'. 'No, he was no part of you – and no part of you is now missing – he
was an organically independent animal, as are you'. Or to the lover 'No, you two are
not one – consider, she went to work, and you are still here. There is, granted, a
single abstract object – a set – with both of you as members – but neither you nor
she is the set, nor are you identical to each other'. To respond in that way would be
to miss what the grieving or loving subject is up to in uttering those sentences. That

---

[14] Or more poetically, 'Our two souls therefore, which are one / Though I must go, endure not yet /
A breach, but an expansion / Like gold to airy thinness beat' (Donne, 'A valediction forbidding
mourning').

[15] Shengold's discussion of Freud on love (1995: Chapter 6) is helpful in bringing out the extent to
which love gives rise to delusional thinking.

is not to say, that in uttering these sentences, the subjects are not trying to convey how things actually are for them in their love or grief. If you said to the bereaved person: 'I am so sorry, is that really how things are?', they may very well say 'yes, it is'.

Perhaps, it might be suggested, that as interlocutors, we could engage in an exercise in compassionate understanding as part of which we might reinterpret the words uttered in these sentences so that they *do* express meanings that would enable us to take the utterances as statements of fact the truth of which could assessed by both parties?[16] However, to undertake such an exercise would be to assume that we—the subject expressing their love or loss in these ways, and I the hearer—merely lack a shared vocabulary as a result of which the subject is forced to redeploy ordinary English in the expressions of the truths they wanted to convey. The implication would be that this lack of shared vocabulary in turn forces me into an exercise in translation in relation to a newly minted meaning.

This, however, does not seem to be what is going on. Our problem seems to be that how things really are for the loving or grieving subject does not admit of a vocabulary that is neutral between the subject orientated towards herself and the other in an attitude of love or loss—and the subject aiming to understand how things are for one in that condition. The subject expressing her grief by saying 'I am broken' is not offering information about a state of the world that speaker and hearer could both agree or disagree on the evidence for. She offers these fantastical, peculiar, false descriptions—because they best communicate, even with their *ordinary meanings*, an aspect of the condition of her self-conscious-ness—as distorted, disrupted—in her love and loss.

Our claim is not, of course, that pathological delusions, of the kind we referred to earlier, are the same as, or indeed similar to, the everyday delusions of subjects in extreme emotional states that disrupt their sense of themselves and their relation to the others or the world. Our claim is that we should approach those delusions, and their expression with a similar mode of understanding. We should consider that (i) the subjects are trying to convey how things actually are for them; (ii) that the subjects are stretching the limits of ordinary language in the expression of their delusions, but not inventing a new one; (iii) that they are not offering information about a fact of the world that obtains independently of the type of their orientation towards it.

We think making room for such an approach requires looking a bit more closely at the supposed object of a delusion, and the distinction we started with: between the supposed content of the delusion and delusory way of thinking about such a content.

---

[16] We are indebted here to the approach to understanding another that Lear takes in *Radical Hope* (2006) when he tries to make sense of Plenty Coups' utterance 'After this nothing happened', made after the destruction of the Crow Nation.

216 BELIEF, IMAGINATION, AND DELUSION

4. What Are Delusions About?

The psychological attitude approach assumes a framework on which delusions are attitudes towards distinctly understood prior contents. The attitude might be formed in a particular and peculiar way, and be abnormally situated in relation to the subject's other attitudes and capacities, but the delusion is a given attitude to a given truth-evaluable content. We can see from the way in which the belief approach has developed in the literature that we get increasingly complex accounts designed to preserve the attitude–content link, trying to make it seem possible and plausible that an adult normal human being with standing beliefs can come to believe with certainty contents which they are manifestly in a position to know to be false. Indeed, in the cases in which a subject has insight into their condition they *do know and say* that the sentences they sometimes utter when they express their delusion are false. We move from the one-factor view—the anomalous experience, to the two-factor view—anomalous experience and rational recklessness or deficit, to the three-factor view—anomalous experience, abnormal hypothesis selection, rational recklessness or deficit. Even so, the assumption that these complexities concern how it is that a subject comes to stand in a given attitude to a given independent content remains unexamined.

One thing that may make us suspicious of the way of approaching the topic is that there is, in this way of setting up, no obvious impediment to there being delusions about almost anything at all. An experience of almost anything can be unexpected or anomalous, and if they are experiences that are had by individuals with the cognitive architecture implicated by the best account of the formation of the kind of attitude that makes for delusion, then we have no reason not to expect that the subject will have a delusion. There seems to be no deep reason to expect delusions to have a distinctive subject matter. We could have delusions that emeralds are red, that dogs steal old men's whiskers, that tea bags have orange paint in them, or that the oceans are full of silver thread. However, these kinds of absurd irrational commitments to how the world might be are not like the delusions we started with. Those delusions seem to have a distinctive kind of subject matter. The kind of delusory thinking that we take to be our topic is not any old absurd, irrational, or neurotic thinking.

We may be able to get some help here from Philippa Foot's discussion of what it is to think about something as 'good'. She is concerned to resist a view of such thinking as involving two separable elements—what she calls 'statements of facts' on the one hand, and 'evaluations' on the other. On such a view an evaluation is not "connected logically with the factual statements on which it is based" (1958: 83). This way of setting things up, she complains, would, if it were right, have the consequence of allowing varieties of thinking about goodness that are unrecognizable as such. The assumed separation of fact and evaluation allows that:

DELUSIONS AND EVERYDAY LIFE   217

> One man may say that a thing is good because of some fact about it; and another may refuse to take that fact as any evidence at all, for nothing is laid down in the meaning of 'good' which connects it with one piece of 'evidence' rather than another. It follows that a moral eccentric could argue to moral conclusions from quite idiosyncratic premises; he could say, for instance, that a man was a good man because he clasped and unclasped his hands, and never turned N.N.E. after turning S.S.W. He could also reject someone else's evaluation simply by denying that his evidence was evidence at all.   (Foot 1958: 84)

She insists, in contrast, that there is no way of understanding what it is to commend something, to evaluate it as good "without fixing the object to which [it is] supposed to be attached. Without first laying hands on the proper object of such things as evaluation, we shall catch in our net either something quite different, such as accepting an order or making a resolution, or else nothing at all" (1958: 86). We will, in other words, lose the subject matter of evaluation if we do not start by 'laying our hands' on its proper object.

We think we are in something of the same situation with our topic here: that we need to reorientate the discussion and try to lay our hands on the proper object of delusory thinking. As we saw above, the topic of delusory thinking has been approached on the assumption that we have the question of the 'statements of facts' on the one hand—the contents of our delusions—and the subjects standing in a deluded or other relation to that fact, on the other. On such a view there is no internal connection between the attitude involved in delusory thinking and the objects of such thinking. One could just as well—if the evidence allowed it—have that object of one's thinking be the content of a well-evidenced non-delusory belief, say.

In relation to thinking about goodness, Foot asks, what she calls the 'crucial' question: "Is it possible to extract from the meaning of words such as "good" some element called "evaluative meaning" which we can think of as externally related to its objects?" (1958: 85). We think a crucial question in thinking about delusory thinking is to ask 'Is it possible to extract from the meaning of words such as "delusory" some descriptive element which we can think of as externally related to its objects?' We suspect that a positive answer to that question is untenable. To understand what it is to suffer from a delusion of the kinds we started with we need to understand what the proper objects are to which it is attached.

So, what are the proper objects of delusions and in what way are they inseparable from the mode of their apprehension in delusions? Well, it is obvious by now that, on the simplest version of our view, the object of a delusion is the subject herself. However, to say only that is to say something too simple. If we are right in taking delusions to be felt as disruptions of self-consciousness then the right object of the delusion is not only the subject, but the subject's *relation* to herself. The subject of a delusion does not only stand in a relation to herself—she also stands in

218 BELIEF, IMAGINATION, AND DELUSION

a relation to her *relation* to herself—a relation that can also be determined by the ways in which she relates to other subjects and to her world.

We want to suggest the following as a framework for thinking about delusions. First, we suggest taking the delusion to be an emotional or affective phenomenon. It is not, on our view, a product or consequence of being in a deluded state that one suffers, is agitated, or feels disruption. The delusion *is* the suffering, agitation, or disruption. Second, we suggest taking delusion to involve an affective response that encodes the significance of the subject's current conscious relation to herself. On our view, many of the standard cases of delusion encode the significance to a subject of their disrupted self-consciousness. As such they are forms of self-consciousness that are second order in nature: forms of affective self-consciousness that encode the subject's apprehension of the significance of ways in which she is conscious of herself.

Let us unpack what we mean here a little. To do that let us go back to simpler emotional responses that encode the significance of her situation for a subject. Consider fear, which we understand as an experience that encodes the experiencing subject's relation 'as threatened' by the thing that the subject fears. Take, for example, a subject's fear of something presented to her in visual perception—a snarling dog, say. We will not properly characterize such fear if we think of the fear as involving only the dog, or its snarling, or indeed its dangerousness. The fear also, and at the same time, involves the subject herself. She fears the dog, as we might put it, on her own behalf. As Sartre puts it: "The emotional subject and the object of the emotion are united in an indissoluble synthesis" (1985: 57). To fear the dog—to feel that the dog is dangerous—is at the same time and inextricably to feel herself threatened. Moreover, it is not to feel the conjunction that the dog is dangerous, and that she, herself, is threatened. The emotion is rather a recording of the significance of the subject's *relation* to the dog, capable of activating both expressions of the relation to others, and behaviour congruent with the subject's aims and well-being.[17] The experience of fear is not—on this way of thinking—a representation of how things are, a propositional attitude that is capable of being true or false.

Now consider the fact that, for a self-conscious subject, her fear will—in relating the subject to the significance of the *relation* that she stands in to the dog—also put her in a relation to herself as the subject for whom the significance of the relation *is significant*. She experiences herself as someone that feels threatened. The significance of that reflexive relation can be recorded differently for her—her relation to herself as feeling fearful may lead to further fear, even panic, or self-disgust—or instead to calm resolve, or perhaps excitement. The experience of herself that records the significance of the relation of 'feeling fearful' is again not

---

[17] For a fuller account of this way of thinking of emotions as having relations the subject stands in as their primary 'objects' see O'Brien (n.d.).

a propositional attitude that can admit of evidence, can be true or false, and the object of other attitudes.

Consider now a subject who, for whatever cause—brain lesion, trauma, depression, ingesting psilocybin—experiences herself in a way that is anomalous, peculiar, painful, disturbed, or disrupted. The disruption may attach particularly to her experience of herself in relation to others, or to her own body, or her own thoughts. In any case the relation that she stands in to herself is disrupted and experienced as abnormal. And this disruption may lead to a more complex form of self-conscious experience—a form of self-consciousness that also involves the not feeling herself as she is habituated to. Such an experience—depending on its basis—can be a form of self-consciousness that also incorporates her experience of relation to others and her world.

If we look back to the patterns that emerged from our consideration of the verbal expressions of delusions, unreliable as we think they are at fully delineating the phenomenon, we have evidence that, in one way or another, a core aspect of delusive experience is a disruption to the sense of self, sometimes in relation to the other. Taking one of the most extreme cases—that of Cotard syndrome—it arises in cases of extreme depression where the subject experiences herself as without many of the normal bodily affects. Her lack of affect in her consciousness of herself gives rise to a terrible alienating affective self-consciousness that makes her feel as if she were dead or did not exist. She has the distressing experience of losing her normal sense of herself.[18]

If what we have said above about delusory experiences is right, they have distinctive objects: the subject's experiential relation to herself. Self-consciousness, if you will. These are not, however, propositional contents of any kind that may be true or false, believed or not believed, supposed or imagined, that we may know or not know. They are expressions—often agonizing and painful ones—of a subject's affective self-awareness of distortions to the orientation that a subject has towards themselves. They are forms of self-awareness that stand in contrast to those that are normally operative in a subject engaged in the business of living a practical life. These distortions of self-consciousness may have many sources—from within the subject's own body or from the felt relations to others, or the subject's environment—but their significance is encoded in forms of a responsive affective self-consciousness.

We think that this more complex form of self-consciousness—incorporating both the subject's first order experienced relation to herself, and her second order relation to herself as so experiencing herself—offers a hypothesis for where to start looking if we want to make sense of what a subject is giving expression to when she utters the kinds of things we have seen those who experience delusions utter.

---

[18] See Gerrans (1999), and Gerrans, this volume.

It offers a hypothesis that has advantages over the psychological attitude approach—not least that it can be used also to illuminate the kinds of everyday delusions we find in the disruption to our forms of self-consciousness brought on by love and grief.

5. Delusions in Relation to Framework or 'Hinge' Judgements

Wittgenstein in *On Certainty* points us towards a body of truths that he thinks we believe groundlessly, and that have the character that, roughly speaking, all of us know them if any of us know them:

> 100. The truths which Moore says he knows, are such as, roughly speaking, all of us know, if he knows them.
>
> 101. Such a proposition might be e.g. "My body has never disappeared and reappeared again after an interval".[19]

The kind of thing that is being claimed is inseparable from the possibility of my rationally not believing it.

> 155. In certain circumstances a man cannot make a mistake. ("Can" is here used logically, and the proposition does not mean that a man cannot say anything false in those circumstances.) If Moore were to pronounce the opposite of those propositions which he declares certain, we should not just not share his opinion: we should regard him as demented.
>
> 156. The difficulty is to realize the groundlessness of our believing.

Some—we have in mind particularly Campbell (2001) here, but also Jacob Ohlhorst (2021)—have taken some of the immunity or irrelevance of evidential thinking to delusional thinking, that we have also remarked on, as reason to wonder whether, for the deluded subject their delusions function as framework, or 'hinge', judgements, in the way the non-deluded treat their opposites as framework judgements. The victim of a delusion might seem to offer up utterances as commitments they have without evidence, as commitments that organize whatever else they might claim, and as such should we not treat them as bearing the same kind of relation to their claim 'I am dead', say, as we bear to the claim 'I am alive'? Well in a way. But not in quite the way the framework, or 'hinge', theorists mean it.

---

[19] And later, in 252, he writes 'it isn't just that I believe in this way that I have two hands, but that every reasonable person does'.

We agree that Wittgenstein's remarks in *On Certainty* are very suggestive. However, we think that what they show is that there are kinds of thinking, in relation to which, there are two ways to go wrong, each with its own departure from normality or sanity. We think that the subject of the delusion goes wrong in denying the undeniable, in denying the presuppositions of their form of life, and that we as theorists of delusions go wrong in taking what is at issue to be a matter to be established on the basis of evidence. The subject of the delusion *does* depart from the framework, our joint framework. They depart from a framework and may try to give evidence for their departure, as we may try to give evidence for our adherence. However, the deluded person departs from the framework, not by instituting a new one in which things go aright again—the thing about frameworks, is that you cannot just institute a new one—but by going wrong, denying the undeniable. Wittgenstein remarks:

> 467. I am sitting with a philosopher in the garden; he says again and again 'I know that that's a tree', pointing to a tree that is near us. Someone else arrives and hears this and I tell him: 'This fellow isn't insane. We are only doing philosophy'.
>
> 468. Someone says irrelevantly 'that's a tree'. He might say this because he remembers having heard it in a similar situation, he was struck by the tree's beauty and the sentence was an exclamation ... And now I ask him 'How did you mean that?' and he replies 'it was a piece of information directed at you'. Shouldn't I be at liberty to assume that he does not know what he is saying, if he is insane enough to want to give me this information?

This affinity between a 'fellow who is insane' and the person doing philosophy, who is not insane can be played out in relation to a number of claims:

I can see that [visually presented] tree

I have two hands

I exist

Other people exist

My wife has not been replaced by an impostor

The world exists

There is a future

There was a past before any event I experienced happened.

What Wittgenstein suggests is that in relation to each, one can err in thinking them not true (as might the fellow who is insane) or err in thinking taking them to be 'pieces of information' in relation to which we can take an attitude of them being true, on the basis of excellent evidence. One can err in thinking that one's wife has been replaced by an impostor, but can also err in concluding, and offering as 'a piece of information directed' at another, the thought that the evidence is squarely against one's wife having been replaced by an impostor. Both stand in contrast to the person who says, struck by the tree's beauty, 'that's a tree', or to the person who says, struck by his love of his wife, 'that's my wife'.

We think that the person who has a delusion 'goes wrong', but not because their evidence about the nature of reality points in a different way from ours. Whether we judge 'I am alive' or the deluded person judges 'I am dead', or we judge 'that is my wife' or the deluded person judges 'that is an impostor who has replaced my wife' what is meant is inseparable from, and an expression of, the condition of our affective self-consciousness—neither of us offers evidence, and all of us could go wrong were we to. Judgements of this kind, if made, are normally not evidence-based hypotheses about the nature of the world at all, they are affective judgements that are expressions of self-consciousness. The deluded person 'goes wrong' in virtue of their relation to themselves 'going wrong'. Those of us who 'go right' do so in virtue of being more fortunate in the form of our self-consciousness: at that moment we feel to be ourselves and our orientation towards ourselves feels normal. Of course, we rarely in fact say 'I am alive', 'the world exists', or 'my wife has not been replaced by an impostor': our normality is unremarkable.

The philosopher goes wrong in thinking that were someone to say these things they *must* be giving expression, not to their form of self-consciousness, but to an attitude towards the nature of reality based on 'pieces of information', and so insists that they offer evidence that they are alive, and not dead, that their wife has not been replaced by an impostor, that there is a future. It may be that the philosopher may properly ask us, two philosophers, what warrant we could offer for the claims 'I exist', 'my co-author has not been replaced by an impostor', 'there is a future'. We leave a proper treatment of that question for another occasion—but for now we want to suggest the reply 'I am okay'.

References

Bayne, T. and Pacherie, E. (2005). 'In Defence of the Doxastic Conception of Delusions', *Mind & Language* 20/2: 163–88.

Billon, A. (2016). 'Making Sense of the Cotard Syndrome: Insights from the Study of Depersonalisation', *Mind & Language* 31/3: 356–91.

Bortolotti, L. (2010). *Delusions and Other Rational Beliefs* (New York: Oxford University Press).

Campbell, J. (2001). 'Rationality, Meaning and the Analysis of Delusion', *Philosophy, Psychiatry & Psychology* 8/2: 89–100.

Carano, A., De Berardis, D., Cavuto, M., Ortolani, C., Perna, G., Valchera, A., Mazza, M., Fornaro, M., Iasevoli, F., Martinotti, G., and Di Giannantonio, M. (2014). 'Cotard's Syndrome: Clinical Case Presentation and Literature Review', *International Neuropsychiatric Disease Journal* 2/6: 348–55.

Currie, G. (2000). 'Imagination, Delusion and Hallucinations', *Mind & Language* 15/1: 168–83.

Foot, P. (1958). 'Moral Beliefs', *Proceedings of the Aristotelian Society New Series* 59: 83–104.

Gerrans, P. (1999). 'Delusional Misidentification as Subpersonal Disintegration', *The Monist* 82/4: 590–608.

Lear, J. (2006). *Radical Hope: Ethics in the Face of Cultural Devastation* (Cambridge, MA: Harvard University Press).

Noordhof, P. and Sullivan Bissett, E. (2021). 'The Clinical Significance of Anomalous Experience in the Explanation of Monothematic Delusions', *Synthese* 199: 10277–10309.

O'Brien, L. (n.d.). *Pervious to Others* (unpublished manuscript).

Ohlhorst, J. (2021). 'The Certainties of Delusion', in L. Moretti and N. Jang Lee Linding Pedersen (eds.), *Non-Evidentialist Epistemology* (Leiden: Brill), pp. 211–29.

Parrott, M. (2019). 'Delusional Possibilities', *Canadian Medical Association Journal* 191/31: E867–8.

Sartre, J.-P. (1985). *Sketch for a Theory of the Emotions* (London: Methuen).

Shengold, L. (1995). *Delusions of Everyday Life* (New Haven, CT: Yale University Press).

Williams, B. (1993). *Shame and Necessity* (Berkeley, CA: University of California Press).

Wittgenstein, L. (1969). *On Certainty* (Oxford: Basil Blackwell).

PART IV
DELUSIONS, BELIEF, AND EVIDENCE

11

Why Do You Believe That?

Delusion and Epistemic Reasons

Sophie Archer

1. Introduction

At the very end of his 'On the Aim of Belief', David Velleman (2000: 281) says:

> Aren't there people who believe that they are Napoleon? (People other than Napoleon, I mean.) Don't such people have a belief that isn't regulated for truth?

> I think the answer is that it isn't literally a belief. I suspect that we tend to apply the term 'belief' in a figurative sense to phantasies for which the subject doesn't or cannot have countervailing beliefs. When someone is said to believe that he is Napoleon, he actually has a phantasy to the effect; but on the question of who he is, a phantasy is all he has. He is somehow incapable of reality-tested cognitions of his identity. The phantasy of being Napoleon is thus what he has instead of a belief about his identity; and in this sense it is his belief on the topic, just as a cardboard box on the sidewalk may be his house by virtue of being what he has instead of a house.

> If you ask me, however, a cardboard box on the sidewalk isn't really a house. And a phantasy of being Napoleon isn't really a belief.

Setting aside Velleman's positive claim here—that a delusion that p is a phantasy that p—let's address his negative one—that a delusion that p is *not* a belief that p. The issue has been much discussed in more recent times, no more so than by Lisa Bortolotti (e.g. 2010, 2012; Bortolotti and Broome 2008), who has argued extensively that most delusions *should* be counted as beliefs that p, on a continuum with ordinary (non-pathological) irrational beliefs.

In this chapter, I will consider one specific case of delusion and use it to help sharpen our concept of belief. In §2, I will motivate and elaborate on this narrowing of focus. In §3, I will argue that the person involved in the case of delusion I have in mind does not have a subjective epistemic reason on the basis of which to hold the belief attributed to them. I will maintain though that this is *not* why they do not believe the content of their delusion. As I will explain in §4,

---

Sophie Archer, *Why Do You Believe That? Delusion and Epistemic Reasons* In: *Belief, Imagination, and Delusion.*
Edited by: Ema Sullivan-Bissett, Oxford University Press. © Oxford University Press 2024.
DOI: 10.1093/oso/9780198872221.003.0011

228 BELIEF, IMAGINATION, AND DELUSION

there do seem to be cases of ordinary beliefs held on the basis of no subjective epistemic reason. Rather, in §5, I will argue that the person in the case of delusion I am considering does not believe the content of their delusion because they do not satisfy what I will call the 'Anscombean Condition'. This condition has it that, even if one does not hold one's belief on the basis of a subjective epistemic reason, one must nonetheless give application to the question, 'Why do you believe that?' (where this question is understood as requesting an epistemic reason(s)).

2. Narrowing the Focus

Bortolotti resists the conclusion that *all* delusions are beliefs, which foregrounds the first main difficulty with the general question regarding whether someone deluded that *p* believes that *p*: delusions vary wildly. Some standard distinctions regarding types of delusion will immediately give a sense of this variety. Delusions are often classified as either 'polythematic' or 'monothematic'. In polythematic cases, one has a number of delusions on several (often interrelated) themes, such as persecution and alien control, for example (Bortolotti 2022). Monothematic delusions, on the other hand, sometimes have a highly specific topic: that one's partner has been replaced by an impostor, as in Capgras syndrome for example. Relatedly, delusions are often classified as 'circumscribed' or 'elaborated'. A circumscribed delusion can remain thoroughly isolated from the rest of one's thinking and behaviour, whereas an elaborated delusion is more integrated into these. Polythematic delusions are usually (though not always) elaborated but monothematic delusions can be either. Someone with a circumscribed delusion that their partner has been replaced by an impostor could make no effort to find them, failing to report them missing to the police, for example. Whereas, if their delusion were elaborated, they might be extremely concerned about where the impostor came from, what they are up to, how their *real* partner might be attempting to communicate with them, etc.

The question as to whether someone deluded that *p* believes that *p* is also vexed along its other dimension. The term 'belief' is used in such multifarious ways, that it is not at all obvious that we have a unitary concept to encompass them all, for which we can provide necessary and sufficient conditions. Even when we restrict ourselves to propositional belief (belief-that), it remains important to specify further. In this chapter, I will not be concerned with any use of the term 'belief' which, broadly speaking, might be considered synonymous with 'faith'. Furthermore, though it is common to speak of human infants and some non-human animals as having 'beliefs', I will only be interested here in the beliefs of cognitively mature human beings.[1] And, given how different one delusion can be

---

[1] It is important to note here that the fact that we are developmentally and evolutionarily continuous with human infants and non-human animals respectively does not itself entail that our beliefs are

DELUSION AND EPISTEMIC REASONS   229

from the next, rather than ask whether all delusions are beliefs in this sense, my aim will be to try to better understand such beliefs, via consideration of one particular case of delusion.

The case I will think about is discussed by Bortolotti and Matthew Broome (2008: 829):

> A man believes his wife is unfaithful to him because the fifth lamp-post along on the left is unlit.   (Sims 2003: 119)

I will assume that the "because" here is meant as a rational, not a causal one. The claim being made is not that the man's belief that his wife is unfaithful to him is simply *caused* by the fifth lamp-post along on the left being unlit. Rather, the claim is that this is the man's *reason*, on the basis of which he believes that his wife is unfaithful to him. More specifically, the idea is that it is his *epistemic* reason. Furthermore, let's imagine that the claim is that this is the *sole* epistemic reason on the basis of which the man believes that his wife is unfaithful to him. Now, this cannot be quite the right way of putting it, of course. Every epistemic reason functions against a certain background, some aspects of which will reasonably be identified as additional, perhaps 'support-ing', epistemic reasons. In this case, there would be his having a wife and their having a certain history together, etc., for example. What I mean when I suggest that we imagine it is his sole epistemic reason is that we imagine that he does not have a story (however far-fetched) about the relationship between the lamp-post and his wife's fidelity. He does not believe that a friend of his is attempting to warn him that his wife is meeting a lover by putting out the light in the lamp-post, for example. The case, as we are understanding it, does not involve any further articulation of this kind.

Some will baulk at this point. Is this not a highly unrealistic construal of the case? Are there *ever* cases of delusion akin to this in real life? (Even if the man fails to *express* his case, this does not establish that he does not have one.)[2] In response, one thing to mention is that Bortolotti and Broome (2008: 829–30) consider such a version of the case (versus one in which the man *does* have a story about the connection between the lamp-post and his wife's fidelity) and seem to take it to involve belief in the sense I am interested in nonetheless. Regardless, my primary interest here is in charting the bounds of belief so, when push comes to shove, it would not matter to me whether such a case of delusion were ever actual. It can be understood as an imagined case that I am using as a test for our concept of belief.

---

essentially the same as theirs. Such developmental/evolutionary continuity cannot be pointed to then to undermine an initial focus on the beliefs of cognitively mature human beings. See Boyle (2017) for a full development of this idea.

[2] Thanks to Esther Yadgar and Ema Sullivan-Bissett (the editor of this volume) for each, individu-ally, pressing me on this point. See also Lavin and O'Brien's chapter in this volume, especially their §2.

230 BELIEF, IMAGINATION, AND DELUSION

3. Fidelity and Lamp-Posts

I will begin by asking whether the state of the lamp-post could be this man's epistemic reason on the basis of which he believes that his wife is unfaithful to him.[3] First, we need to draw upon the familiar distinction between what we might call the 'objective' and 'subjective' senses of such 'epistemic reasons'. An objective epistemic reason for believing that p, as I will be understanding it, is a fact, independent of p, that counts in favour of the truth of p.[4] A subjective epistemic reason on the basis of which someone believes that p, on the other hand, is a fact (or something which the person *takes* to be a fact), independent of p, that the person *takes* to count in favour of the truth of p, whether or not it really does. So, the two can coincide. And, indeed, in the good case, they do. But subjective and objective epistemic reasons can also come apart—I can take something to count in favour of p's truth—and therein believe something on the basis of a subjective epistemic reason—even though it does *not* count in favour of p's truth—I do not have an objective epistemic reason for believing it.

Now, it is surely uncontroversial that this man does not have an objective epistemic reason for believing that his wife is unfaithful to him. We can all readily agree that, objectively speaking, the fact that the fifth lamp-post along on the left is unlit does not count in favour of the truth of his wife's infidelity, with no further story connecting the two. The luminosity of the lamp bears no direct rational relationship to his wife's fidelity whatsoever.

The more interesting question is of course whether the man believes that his wife is unfaithful to him on the basis of a subjective epistemic reason. Does he take the state of the lamp-post to count in favour of the truth of the idea that his wife is unfaithful to him, even though it does not? Putting the question this way, and indeed my formulation regarding what it is to have a subjective epistemic reason, put a lot of pressure on the idea of *taking* something to count in favour of p's truth. What is this? 'To *take* something to be such and such' is really a philosopher's turn of phrase. In ordinary English, we would probably say something more like, 'to think that it is'. But in order for this to be roughly synonymous with 'taking it to be' here, it would have to be understood that this 'thinking that it is' need not be conscious and nor is it an additional belief one must hold. One need not hold the separate belief that R counts in favour of the truth of p for R to be a subjective epistemic reason on the basis of which one believes that p. Rather, the idea is that it is internal to R's being a subjective epistemic reason on the basis of which one believes that p that one thinks that R counts in favour of p's truth. Another rough

---

[3] Just as my interest is in the beliefs of cognitively mature human beings and I am not assuming these to be essentially the same as those of human infants and non-human animals, so too, mutatis mutandis, for epistemic reasons.

[4] Of course, it is controversial that reasons are facts. But, as far as I can see, nothing I say in this chapter depends on their being so, so I will simply assume that they are for the sake of argument here.

DELUSION AND EPISTEMIC REASONS   231

substitute for 'taking something to be such and such' here, I think, is 'understanding it to be such and such', where again this need not be conscious, and nor is it a separate state to having the subjective epistemic reason itself. One difficulty with 'understand' in this context is that it can be heard as factive.[5] Hearing it this way, one could not *understand* that something is a certain way unless it were in fact so. So, one could not *mistakenly* understand something to count in favour of the truth of *p*, on pain of contradiction. However, there is a way to hear 'understand' where it does permit mistakes. I can have a mistaken understanding of something that nonetheless can be contrasted with a failure to have any kind of understanding of it at all: "That was my understanding, though I see now where I went wrong". Even so, one might think that introducing the notion of understanding, even if permissively construed in this way, raises the bar. We might be more ready to admit that the man does not *understand* the state of the lamp-post to count in favour of his wife's infidelity than we are to admit that he does not—confusedly—think that it does, or take it to. For the sake of argument then, let's stick with the latter two formulations.

Now, the man has cited the state of the lamp-post as counting in favour of the idea that his wife is unfaithful to him. Assuming he is not being insincere, is this not sufficient for his thinking that it is, or taking it to be?[6] I think we should grant that, in general, there is a strong presumption that when, on the basis of what is apparently first-personal self-knowledge, one asserts that one takes something to count in favour of the truth of *p*, one does.[7] But this presumption is a defeasible one. One does not need to be a radical sceptic about the possibility of first-personal self-knowledge to think that it is fallible.[8]

But why deny him the particular thought that the state of the lamp-post counts in favour of his wife's infidelity? One way of getting at the difficulty with doing so is to point to the fact that he has no way of specifying *what it would be* for this thought to be true.[9] He has no way of specifying what it would be for the state of the lamp-post, considered on its own in the sense I have outlined, to count in favour of his wife's infidelity. Now, again, 'specifying' can, I think, be heard as factive. In which case, he could not specify what he needs to, given that the state of the lamp-post, considered on its own in the relevant sense, does *not* count in favour of the truth of his wife's infidelity. But, as with 'understanding', we can hear 'specifying' more permissively. And, I think, even more permissively than 'understanding' what it would be for the state of the lamp-post, considered on its own in the relevant sense, to count in favour of his wife's infidelity. Let's grant that in order to be able to specify what it would be for the thought to be true, the man

---

[5] Thanks to Marie Van Loon for her question here.   [6] Compare Ichino in this volume.
[7] Thanks to Ema Sullivan-Bissett for pushing me here too.
[8] See e.g. Moran (2001), especially Chapter 1, for further discussion here.
[9] Thanks to Hans-Johann Glock, who suggested this way of putting the point to me, which is inspired by Wittgenstein (1969).

232   BELIEF, IMAGINATION, AND DELUSION

need only be able to offer a mistaken, *and perhaps even fairly confused*, elaboration of what this would involve. The problem is that it seems that he could not do even this. What *could* he, even somewhat coherently, think or say about this matter? Note that the demand is not that he be capable of offering a further subjective epistemic reason for thinking that the state of the lamp-post counts in favour of the truth of his wife's infidelity. Rather, it is just that he be capable of providing some kind of articulation as to what it *would* be for this connection to be actual. Could we even grant him a thought with truth-apt content in this case, if it were not for his having such an ability?

Unable to offer such a specification, on my view, the man has no subjective epistemic reason to believe that his wife is unfaithful to him. Bortolotti and Broome (2008: 830) also acknowledge that:

> Some would claim that a very bad reason for a belief ceases to be a reason for the belief altogether... [and] the lamp-post being unlit would seem to bear no meaningful relation whatsoever with whether a spouse is faithful, if no additional explanation is offered.

But Bortolotti and Broome do not think that having a subjective epistemic reason on the basis of which to hold a belief is necessary for holding it. On their view, the man could believe that his wife is unfaithful to him, without doing so on the basis of any subjective epistemic reason. Let's turn now to this possibility.

4. Believing on the Basis of No Subjective Epistemic Reason

One might think that you cannot take something to be *true*, in the way you do when you believe it, without doing so on the basis of a subjective epistemic reason(s).[10] It is your subjective epistemic reasons, which are your guide (however faulty) to truth. They are what mediate between you and how things are, so to speak. So, how could you form a view about how things are without them? How could you take something to be true as you do when you believe it—just like that— on the basis of nothing? You do not have that kind of *direct* access to truth. And what is more, you know it.

---

[10] The precise nature of the relationship between belief and truth is, of course, mired in controversy. Williams (1973: 136) infamously claims that, "beliefs aim at truth". But the claim is infamous because even though there seems to be something undeniably right in this vicinity, it has proved notoriously difficult to articulate precisely what that is. Indeed, the Velleman (2000) passage, with which we began, comes from a piece that forms part of a large literature attempting to do just this. I will not try to articulate this relationship here but will rather simply rely on the intuitive line of thought in the text for a moment.

The problem with affirming this line of thought is that there do seem to be examples of ordinary beliefs, which are apparently held on the basis of no subjective epistemic reason.[11] Consider your basic logical belief that, 'Everything is self-identical', for example. Simply in countenancing this proposition—that everything is self-identical—you affirm it as true, in the kind of way one does when one believes something. Or, to put it another way, insofar as you understand the concepts involved, you cannot *fail* to believe that everything is identical to itself. There is no independent consideration one need offer in favour of thinking that this proposition is true. It simply shows up to you in and of itself as such.

Another (quite different) example of apparently believing that p on the basis of no subjective epistemic reason involves non-episodic memory. Take Alvin Goldman's (1967: 370) example of recalling that 'Abraham Lincoln was born in 1809', without remembering anything about why one believes this to be so. In this case, it seems that one believes that Abraham Lincoln was born in 1809, purely *in virtue of* remembering it.[12] Again, one has no subjective epistemic reason on the basis of which one believes this. In this case, the proposition simply shows up *as remembered*.

Now, there is of course lots more that could be said about both such kinds of case (and others besides) of believing that p on the basis of no subjective epistemic reason.[13] But suffice it to say here that, unless all such cases can be explained away, we have not yet established that the man in the delusion case does not believe that his wife is unfaithful to him. He could simply believe this on the basis of no subjective epistemic reason. His could be a case of believing that p, comparable in this respect to those I have just considered, of believing that everything is self-identical, or that Abraham Lincoln was born in 1809. However, I will now argue that there is an even more basic condition on believing (than doing so on the basis of a subjective epistemic reason), which the man in the case of delusion I am considering fails to satisfy.

5. The Anscombean Condition

I will call this more basic condition the 'Anscombean Condition'. It requires that, even if one does not hold one's belief on the basis of a subjective epistemic reason, one nonetheless gives application to the question, 'Why do you believe that?', in the relevant sense. That is, one gives application to the question, 'Why do you believe that?', as seeking epistemic reasons, rather than a causal explanation. When it comes to intentional action, Elizabeth Anscombe (1963: 9) says:[14]

---

[11] Thanks to Matthew Boyle for discussion of beliefs held on the basis of no subjective epistemic reason.

[12] See Burge (1993) here.   [13] I plan to do so in future work.

[14] See Moran (2001: 127), Hieronymi (2008: 359), and Boyle (2009: 137) for precedents when it comes to invoking Anscombe's remarks about intentional agency in understanding belief.

234 BELIEF, IMAGINATION, AND DELUSION

What distinguishes actions that are intentional from those which are not? The answer that I shall suggest is that they are the actions to which a certain sense of the question "Why?" is given application; the sense is of course that in which the answer, if positive, gives a reason for acting.

Anscombe (1963: 25) continues:

The question is not refused application because the answer to it says there is *no* reason, any more than the question how much money I have in my pocket is refused application by the answer 'None'.

So, giving the 'Why?'-question application does *not* mean acknowledging that it is a conceptual necessity on acting intentionally/believing that one do so on the basis of the relevant type of reason in every case. Indeed, it does not even mean acknowledging that one rationally *should* act intentionally/believe on the basis of the relevant type of reason in every case. In the limiting cases of each it might be entirely rationally legitimate that one's answer be the equivalent of, "Just because". What giving the 'Why?'-question application *does* mean is conceiving of it as appropriate that one be asked for the relevant type of reason, insofar as the phenomenon in question is, *in general*, one to which this question applies (even if there are none in this particular case). A nice way of putting the point when it comes to belief is that to give application to the 'Why?'-question is to grant that, for any belief, there is some set of subjective epistemic reasons the believer holds it on the basis of, but one possible set of subjective epistemic reasons is the empty set.[15]

Now, basic logical truths are interesting in this context insofar as it is not clear that there is any epistemic reason one *could* give in support of one's recognition that everything is self-identical, for example.[16] Such cases are different from those involving non-episodic memory, of course. It is certainly *possible* to believe that Abraham Lincoln was born in 1809 on the basis of a subjective epistemic reason(s): one simply *happens* not to in the kind of case I was imagining above. But I think we can allow that, whether the lack of subjective epistemic reason(s) is contingent or not, the believer can give application to the 'Why?'-question in granting that the state in question is, in general, one to which this question applies.

Let's now consider what *failing* to give application to the 'Why?'-question might involve. In *Brideshead Revisited* (1945: 86), Evelyn Waugh's character Sebastian is asked:

---

[15] This mode of expression was suggested to me by Matthew Boyle.
[16] Arguably, there is something to be said from a coherentist perspective, but I cannot explore the issue here, of course. See Hale (2002) for an interesting discussion.

DELUSION AND EPISTEMIC REASONS   235

"But, my dear Sebastian, you can't seriously *believe* it all".

"Can't I?"

"I mean about Christmas and the star and the three kings and the ox and the ass".

"Oh yes, I believe that. It's a lovely idea".

"But you can't *believe* things because they're a lovely idea".

"But I do. That's how I believe".[17]

Sebastian's offering of "It's a lovely idea" in response to the implied 'Why?'-question here is an interesting example of failing to give it application. He *is* offering a reason for believing that the Christmas story is true. But it is the wrong kind of reason. What is striking is of course that it is an *aesthetic* (or perhaps moral), rather than an epistemic, reason. It is nonetheless analogous to a way of failing to give application to the 'Why'-question, which Anscombe explicitly notes—by offering a causal explanation rather than a rational one. When it comes to the Christmas story, one might fail to give the 'Why'-question application with something like, "Well, I was raised a Catholic". Offering this causal explanation amounts to failing to grant the fittingness of the request for an epistemic reason, just as offering an aesthetic or moral reason instead of an epistemic one does. And both types of refusal to give application to the 'Why?'-question when it comes to 'believing' the Christmas story are, of course, in keeping with my earlier exclusion of faith from my subject matter in this chapter.[18]

Another way of failing to give application to the 'Why?'-question in the case of intentional action, according to Anscombe (1963), is insofar as one answers with the equivalent of either, "I was not aware that I was doing that" or, "Oh, yes, I observed I was doing it". In some cases, this seems right: if one is in either of these alienated postures with respect to one's action, it is not an intentional action. Anscombe (1963: 51) provides a convincing example in which someone is asked, "Why are you ringing the bell?" and replies, "Good heavens! I didn't know I was ringing it!" We can imagine them accidentally leaning on the bell, for example, and not realising that they are the one causing it to ring. However, there are other kinds of cases, involving repression, where it is less clear that someone who is not consciously aware that they are doing something is not doing so intentionally. Consider a person who is self-deceived that their partner is not having an affair. They might avoid visiting certain locations, without being consciously aware that this is what they are up to. Nonetheless, arguably, this avoidance is

---

[17] Thanks to Mark Wrathall for suggesting this example to me.
[18] See Wittgenstein (1938/1967) on the inappropriateness of asking for epistemic reasons in support of religious claims and Ichino in this volume for an expression of scepticism regarding the doxastic status proper of religious 'belief'.

236   BELIEF, IMAGINATION, AND DELUSION

intentional—they are unconsciously aiming to avoid discovering their partner with their partner's lover.[19]

Analogously, it seems that we need to make space for repressed beliefs. Consider the repressed belief that one does not deserve love, for example. When asked why one believes this, one might behave exactly as if one rejected the question, "I don't believe that!" But such behaviour should not itself be considered constitutive of rejecting the 'Why?'-question, quite apart from concerns about accommodating repressed belief. Imagine a simple case of deception, for example. When asked, "Why do you believe the regime will fall?", you might very well behave as if you reject the question, "I don't believe that . . . Sir!" But this does not entail that you do not privately give the question application, of course. Likewise, in a case of intentional action one does not want discovered, one might behave as if one fails to give the 'Why?'-question application, but this does not entail that one does not: "Why are you attempting to access government files?"

So, one's verbal (and other external) behaviour should only ever be considered *indicative* as to whether one gives the 'Why?'-question application, not constitutive of this. Nonetheless, there is, of course, a significant difference between cases in which one is attempting to deceive,—"I don't believe the regime will fall!"—and cases in which one's belief is repressed. In the former, one consciously gives the 'Why?'-question application. One merely attempts to hide this from public view. When it comes to repressed beliefs though, one does not consciously give the 'Why?'-question application. One unconsciously does so. But what does this mean?

As with the case in which one is trying to deceive, I think this can be understood dispositionally to some extent, in the sense that, in both cases one *is* disposed to behave verbally as we would expect—to respond to the 'Why?'-question by providing subjective epistemic reasons, or, in the limiting case, with the equivalent of "Just because". In both cases, one's dispositions to behave in such ways are blocked. In the case in which one is attempting to deceive, they are blocked by one's desire to deceive. In the case in which one's belief is repressed, they are blocked by whatever means that one's belief is repressed in the first place—one's anxiety surrounding the topic, for example. But, just as consciously giving the 'Why?'-question application is not merely possessing a set of dispositions, neither is unconsciously doing so. It is holding the state in question, albeit unconsciously, on the understanding that it is fitting that one be asked for an epistemic reason(s) in its favour. It is this which distinguishes it as an unconscious *belief*.

Now, there is much more to say about what is involved, in general, in giving the 'Why?'-question application, when it comes to belief. For now though, I hope I have said enough to render it a plausible condition on believing that *p*. Even

---

[19] See Davidson (1986) for a classic account of self-deception as intentional.

DELUSION AND EPISTEMIC REASONS   237

though one can believe that p, in certain limiting cases, on the basis of no subjective epistemic reason, if one fails to even give application to the question as to why one believes that p, the idea that the state in question is a belief has reached the point of incoherence.

Let's return to our case in hand of delusion. In §3, I argued that the man in this case cannot properly be conceived as taking the state of the lamp-post, considered on its own as described, to count in favour of the truth of the claim that his wife is unfaithful to him. And hence he does not have a subjective epistemic reason on the basis of which to believe that his wife is unfaithful to him. This, I argued, is because he has no way of specifying what it would be for the thought that the state of the lamp-post bears this relation to his wife's infidelity to be true. But does he not, at least, give application to the 'Why?'-question, even if he has no epistemic reason to offer in response?

Imagine the man being asked, "Why do you believe that your wife is unfaithful to you?" He answers, "Because the fifth lamp-post along on the left is unlit". (And he has no elaboration to offer.) Even if he is not answering the question by genuinely providing a subjective epistemic reason in response, is he not giving it application? Is he not *trying* to provide an epistemic reason, thus evidencing the fact that he grants that the question applies? Here we might contrast him with the character of Sebastian in *Brideshead Revisited*. Sebastian fails to give the 'Why?'-question application. But Sebastian is clearly not *trying* to provide an epistemic reason in response. He is fully aware that what he is offering is an aesthetic and/or moral consideration—hence the interest, or affectation (depending on your perspective), of his response.

It is fair to say that the man in our case is *not* 'fully aware' that what he is offering is not an epistemic reason. But I think we should resist the characterization of him as trying to provide one. Again, I think that our concept of someone's attempting to do something can tolerate a certain amount of confusion on their behalf. But conceiving of him as trying to provide an epistemic reason is like thinking of someone who whacks a dartboard with a carrier bag as trying to shoot a bullseye with an arrow. Even if this person reports that they are trying to shoot a bullseye with an arrow, they are not. Again, they do not have unassailable authority here. Given his confusion over the relationship between the luminosity of the lamp-post and his wife's fidelity, meaningful engagement with the 'Why?'-question is currently out of his reach. As things stand, just as he apes having a subjective epistemic reason, he merely apes giving application to the 'Why?'-question.

6. Conclusion

In this chapter, I have used one case of delusion as a test for our concept of belief. I have asked whether it is possible for a man deluded that his wife is unfaithful to him to *believe* this to be the case when, absent insincerity, his response to the question, "Why do you believe that?" is simply, "The fifth lamp-post along on the left is unlit". In §3, I argued that this consideration concerning the lamp-post should not be understood as the man's subjective epistemic reason, on the basis of which he believes his wife to be unfaithful to him. Nonetheless, as I argued in §4, it is possible to hold a belief on the basis of no subjective epistemic reason, such as when one recalls something to be the case, without remembering why one thinks this. However, in §5, I argued that the man does not believe that his wife is unfaithful to him because he does not meet what I have called the 'Anscombean Condition' on belief. This is an even more basic condition on believing that *p* than the idea that one must do so on the basis of a subjective epistemic reason. The Anscombean Condition has it that, even if one does not hold one's belief on the basis of a subjective epistemic reason, one must nonetheless give application to the question, 'Why do you believe that?' (where this question is understood as requesting an epistemic reason(s) in response). I argued that, given the man in our example's confusion over the relationship between the state of the lamp-post and his wife's fidelity, he should not properly be considered even to give application to this question. Someone's confusion can itself debar them from believing that something is the case.

Acknowledgements

Thanks to an audience at Zurich University, Matthew Boyle, Lucy Campbell, Alexander Greenberg, Joseph Schear, Ema Sullivan-Bissett, and Mark Wrathall.

References

Anscombe, G. E. M. (1963). *Intention* (Ithaca, NY: Cornell University Press).

Bortolotti, L. (2010). *Delusions and Other Irrational Beliefs* (Oxford: Oxford University Press).

Bortolotti, L. (2012). 'In Defence of Modest Doxasticism About Delusions', *Neuroethics* 5: 39–53.

Bortolotti, L. (2022). 'Delusion', *The Stanford Encyclopedia of Philosophy* (Summer 2022 Edition), Edward N. Zalta (ed.), https://plato.stanford.edu/archives/sum2022/entries/delusion/.

Bortolotti, L. and Broome, M. (2008). 'Delusional Beliefs and Reason Giving', *Philosophical Psychology* 21/6: 821–41.

Boyle, M. (2009). 'Active Belief', *Canadian Journal of Philosophy* 39/1: 119–47.

Boyle, M. (2017). 'A Different Kind of Mind?', in K. Andrews (ed.), *The Routledge Handbook of Philosophy of Animal Minds* (New York: Routledge), 109–18.

DELUSION AND EPISTEMIC REASONS   239

Burge, T. (1993). 'Content Preservation', *The Philosophical Review* 102/4: 457–88.

Davidson, D. (1986). 'Deception and Division', in M. Cavell (ed.), *Problems of Rationality* (Oxford: Clarendon Press), 199–212.

Goldman, A. (1967). 'A Causal Theory of Knowing', *The Journal of Philosophy* 64: 357–72.

Hale, B. (2002). 'Basic Logical Knowledge', *Royal Institute of Philosophy Supplement* 51: 279–304.

Hieronymi, P. (2008). 'Responsibility for Believing', *Synthese* 161/3: 357–73.

Moran, R. (2001). *Authority and Estrangement: An Essay on Self-Knowledge* (Princeton, NJ: Princeton University Press).

Sims, A. (2003). *Symptoms in the Mind* (Amsterdam: Elsevier).

Velleman, D. (2000). 'On the Aim of Belief', in D. Velleman, *The Possibility of Practical Reason* (Oxford: Oxford University Press), 244–81.

Waugh, E. (1945). *Brideshead Revisited: The Sacred and Profane Memories of Captain Charles Ryder* (Boston, MA: Little, Brown).

Williams, B. (1973). 'Deciding to Believe', in B. Williams, *Problems of the Self* (Cambridge: Cambridge University Press), 136–51.

Wittgenstein, L. (1938/1967). 'Lectures on Religious Belief', in C. Barrett (ed.), *Lectures and Conversations on Aesthetics, Psychology and Religious Belief* (Berkeley: University of California Press), 53–72.

Wittgenstein, L. (1969). *On Certainty* (Oxford: Basil Blackwell).

12

The Paradox of Delusions

Are Deluded Individuals Resistant to Evidence?

Nicholas Furl, Max Coltheart, and Ryan McKay

A wise man... apportions his beliefs to the evidence – David Hume
(1748/2007: 80)

Paradigmatically "wise" individuals apportion their beliefs to the data they receive from the world—when this evidence changes, they change their minds accordingly. However, real people don't always use new evidence to optimally update their beliefs,[1] which are notoriously susceptible to various endogenous biases and distortions. In the most extreme cases—*delusions*—people appear to depart radically from the tenets of rational belief.

Delusions are archetypal symptoms of madness or mental illness (Jaspers 1913) and feature in an array of psychiatric and neurological disorders. In many cases, delusions form part of a wider condition known as psychosis, and can be accompanied by other manifestations of disrupted evidence processing, such as hallucinations. Schizophrenia is perhaps the most well-known disorder associated with psychosis and delusion. Among other things, deluded individuals may claim that they have died or ceased to exist, that their thoughts are being broadcast to others, or that their skin has become infested with parasites. As delusions can have devastating consequences in terms of suffering and impaired social and psychological functioning, many researchers have attempted to characterize and explain them.

The idea of "delusion" feels intuitive and clinicians certainly attest to the reality of the affliction. Yet scholars over the years have struggled to agree on a consistent and complete definition for "delusion" (Bortolotti et al. 2016; Coltheart et al. 2011; David 1999). According to the dominant psychiatric conception, delusions are

---

[1] In other words, real people are not always appropriately *sensitive* to evidence. Ichino (this volume) distinguishes such "sensitivity to evidence" from "appeals to evidence". People (including deluded individuals) may be cognizant of the normative expectation that beliefs should be underpinned by evidence—and thus may *appeal* to evidence to justify their beliefs—but they may nevertheless be insufficiently responsive (*sensitive*) to relevant evidence. Archer (also this volume) discusses cases where the evidence individuals appeal to fails to constitute a subjective (let alone objective) epistemic reason for belief.

Nicholas Furl, Max Coltheart, and Ryan McKay, *The Paradox of Delusions: Are Deluded Individuals Resistant to Evidence?*
In: *Belief, Imagination, and Delusion*. Edited by: Ema Sullivan-Bissett, Oxford University Press.
© Oxford University Press 2024. DOI: 10.1093/oso/9780198872221.003.0012

THE PARADOX OF DELUSIONS   241

beliefs that are insufficiently responsive—indeed, impervious—to counterevidence (Arnold 2016). For example, the American Psychiatric Association (2013) defines delusions as beliefs that are "firmly held despite...evidence to the contrary" (p. 819) and as "fixed beliefs that are not amenable to change in light of conflicting evidence" (p. 87). This characterization of delusions is faithful to a venerable psychiatric tradition dating back to Karl Jaspers (1913), who proposed *incorrigibility* as a central criterion of delusions (together with certainty and impossibility or falsity of content).

Incorrigibility may be a prominent feature of delusions but is not, by itself, sufficient to define them. Many beliefs about commonplace things are relatively fixed and not easily amenable to change and yet are not delusions because they are rooted in solid evidence from prior experience. For example, individuals are typically accustomed to having other people walk behind them, who are incidentally minding their own business. A rational person who notices someone walking behind them would not consider that person any different from the others previously experienced, nor would they radically change their beliefs about other people based on that single experience. However, a deluded individual might ignore all such prior experiences and instead conclude, on the basis of this single piece of evidence, that the CIA must be following them. In other words, in addition to incorrigibility, another key feature of delusion is that a minimal amount of experience too easily displaces prior beliefs.

But how can this be? How can deluded individuals have beliefs that cannot be changed by counterevidence but yet are adopted on the basis of too little evidence? We observe that many of the scientific studies in this field have historically adopted a position on one side or the other of this contrast. As per the dominant psychiatric conception, some studies indicate that individuals with delusions possess some trait that disposes them to rely inflexibly on their existing beliefs and to be less influenced by new experience than healthy people. But other evidence and theoretical work suggests that deluded individuals are disposed to neglect their prior convictions and to be unduly swayed by weak evidence. We outline these respective bodies of work below.

1. Integration of Evidence and Prior Belief:
Computational Approaches

Much of contemporary psychology and neuroscience views belief formation as a process by which new evidence (bottom-up information) interacts with prior belief (top-down expectation). The recent surge of "computational psychiatry" studies have formalized this basic idea into explanations for delusions. Computational psychiatry aims to model the brain's computations, and—like cognitive neuropsychiatry before it (Halligan and David 2001)—to understand

242 BELIEF, IMAGINATION, AND DELUSION

psychiatric abnormalities (aberrant perceptions, behaviours, and beliefs) in terms of pathologies in normal cognitive and neuroscientific processes (Adams et al. 2016). In addition to using behavioural and neuroscientific empirical methods, studies in computational psychiatry often test theories against the data using formal mathematical models. Typically, these models offer meaningful theoretical quantities ("free parameters") that can be estimated in individual participants by model fitting—that is, finding the values of the free parameters that can predict the participants' behaviour as closely as possible. In the models we discuss below, these free parameters typically map onto theoretical concepts related to the relative influence of prior beliefs and new evidence (Fletcher and Frith 2009).

Computational theories of delusion in psychosis are primarily rooted in the notion of *dopaminergic prediction error learning*. Symptoms of psychosis, and especially delusions, appear to be managed to a degree by anti-psychotic medications that antagonize (block the actions of) the neurotransmitter dopamine, which is found in regions of the midbrain and striatum (Deserno et al. 2016). The computations related to belief that are carried out by dopaminergic neurons are relatively well understood. In their foundational work, Wolfram Schultz and colleagues (1997) show that dopaminergic neural responses in the midbrain signal prediction errors, consistent with a computational reinforcement learning model known as a temporal difference (TD) model. Importantly, prediction error signals in the TD model are computed by weighting prior belief against new evidence. Using these prediction error signals, TD models (and other, similar, formal reinforcement learning models) learn which cues predict future rewards. Beliefs are updated and refined based on this subtraction between the actual reward (evidence) and its prediction (expectation from prior belief). The fundamental finding is that, before any learning, the response rate of dopaminergic neurons increases in the presence of an unpredicted reward. This response increase is considered a positive prediction error signal, because it signals there was more reward than expected (the actual reward minus the predicted reward is positively valued). Later, after many trials in which a cue always precedes this reward, the dopaminergic neurons stop positively responding to the reward (i.e., they stop signaling prediction error), as the reward is now predictable from the cue. The actual reward minus the expected reward at this time is now zero and this is reflected in the reduced magnitude of the prediction error signal. Interestingly, however, in both dopaminergic neurons and in the TD model, the positive prediction error signal shifts backwards in time to appear following the cue itself (the first unpredicted sign that the reward is coming) instead of the reward. Moreover, if the predicted reward fails to appear following the cue, then the neurons *decrease* their response rate. This is a negatively-valued prediction error because the actual reward is less than the predicted reward. The prevailing view now is that anti-psychotic medications that block dopamine binding correct some abnormality in this dopaminergic prediction error learning.

The formation of beliefs, whether beliefs about reward or more general beliefs, is often formulated in a Bayesian framework (Sterzer et al. 2018). Bayesian formulations of belief formalize and enshrine the process of updating prior beliefs based on evidence. The Bayesian framework conceives of beliefs as probability density functions. Because the variance of a belief's probability density function expresses the degree of uncertainty about the belief, the precision (inverse of this variance) is taken as confidence in a belief. Before new evidence is considered, a pre-existing belief is embodied by a prior-belief probability density function or "prior distribution". Bayes' rule then governs how a "posterior distribution" (updated belief) is optimally derived from the conjunction of a prior belief and a "likelihood distribution" (which encodes the new evidence and the uncertainty in it). Crucially, the relative influence of the prior and likelihood over the posterior depends on their precisions. If the evidence has a distribution with high precision and the prior does not, the posterior may be shifted a great deal towards the evidence. However, if the prior-belief distribution has high precision, then the evidence would need to be quite extreme for the posterior to be much different from the prior.

One of the most popular algorithmic implementations of this Bayesian framework is hierarchical predictive coding (Adams et al. 2013; Fletcher and Frith 2009; Notredame et al. 2014; Sterzer et al. 2018). This formulation makes explicit a link between the Bayesian formalization of belief formation and prediction error learning (e.g., in dopaminergic neurons; Heinz et al. 2019). In predictive coding, top-down signals represent predictions, or prior beliefs. Bottom-up signals represent the prediction error, or difference between the evidence and the prior. In the hierarchical variety of predictive coding, each level attempts to predict the input from the level below it, requiring a convergence across levels. In delusions, it is assumed that the precision of either the evidence or the prior distribution is abnormally high. If the distribution associated with top-down (prior) predictions has a greater precision than it should (i.e., confidence in the prior is great), then the system will be resistant to learning from evidence and will persist in its existing beliefs. Conversely, if the distribution associated with bottom-up prediction error has a greater precision than it should, the system will learn too quickly from evidence and make hasty, unwarranted changes in belief based on stimulus noise.

Bayesian predictive coding introduces a framework where researchers can characterize explanations for delusions as involving inappropriate precision on either the prior or likelihood, leading presumably to rigid beliefs or easily swayed beliefs. For the most part, such explanations have been expressed in the form of verbally-described speculations (Fletcher and Frith 2009). Researchers are only just starting to formally fit and compare some limited versions of the Bayesian hierarchical predictive coding models to tasks that might be related to delusions (e.g., Adams et al. 2012; Katthagen et al. 2018; Powers et al. 2017).

244   BELIEF, IMAGINATION, AND DELUSION

2. Deluded Individuals Form Inflexible Beliefs: The Bias Against Disconfirmatory Evidence

The standard psychiatric definition of delusions emphasizes that, to be a delusion, a prior belief should be inflexible, even in the face of considerable counterevidence. Several paradigms have been developed, which assume that such delusions arise from a general trait possessed by deluded individuals, that would be detectable not just in their deluded behaviour but also in suitably designed laboratory tasks that tap into this trait. For example, a number of studies have provided evidence that deluded individuals exhibit a *bias against disconfirmatory evidence* (BADE; Woodward et al. 2006). In the titular BADE task, participants read a series of scenarios (see Fig. 12.1 for an example). Each scenario unfolds sequentially via a succession of clues. After each clue is presented, participants rate the plausibility

---

Clue 1: *Jenny can't fall asleep*

    Interpretation 1: *Jenny is nervous about her exam the next day* (lure)

    Interpretation 2: *Jenny is worried about her ill mother* (lure)

    Interpretation 3: *Jenny loves her bed* (absurd)

    Interpretation 4: *Jenny is excited about Christmas morning* (true)

Clue 2: *Jenny can't wait until it is finally morning*

    Interpretation 1: *Jenny is nervous about her exam the next day* (lure)

    Interpretation 2: *Jenny is worried about her ill mother* (lure)

    Interpretation 3: *Jenny loves her bed* (absurd)

    Interpretation 4: *Jenny is excited about Christmas morning* (true)

Clue 3: *Jenny wonders how many presents she will find under the tree*

    Interpretation 1: *Jenny is nervous about her exam the next day* (lure)

    Interpretation 2: *Jenny is worried about her ill mother* (lure)

    Interpretation 3: *Jenny loves her bed* (absurd)

    Interpretation 4: *Jenny is excited about Christmas morning* (true)

Fig. 12.1 The BADE Task. Participants are presented with a sequence of clues. After each clue appears, participants rate the plausibility of competing interpretations of the scenario.

THE PARADOX OF DELUSIONS   245

of competing interpretations of the scenario. As additional information is revealed, an initially unlikely ("true") interpretation gains in plausibility, while initially plausible ("lure") interpretations become less plausible. Consistent with the dominant psychiatric conception, deluded individuals continue to favour initially tempting interpretations as evidence against those interpretations mounts (see McLean et al. 2017, for a recent meta-analysis, i.e., a study aggregating the results of earlier studies).

3. Are Deluded Individuals Better at Using Prior Belief to Perceive Ambiguous Stimuli?

The strength of prior belief versus evidence has been assessed by asking participants to judge ambiguous stimuli, with the goal of showing that there is an underlying tendency in delusion-prone individuals to leverage overly strong prior beliefs—at least stronger than those evinced by control participants. For example, in a study comparing control participants with individuals with early psychosis or psychosis-proneness, participants attempted to detect human figures in ambiguous two-toned images (Teufel et al. 2015). Surprisingly, control participants were *less* accurate in detecting these figures, presumably because they were less able to use prior belief about the content to resolve the ambiguity.

In other uses of ambiguous stimuli, Schmack, Sterzer, and their colleagues used varieties of noisy, incoherent, or otherwise ambiguous motion stimuli in a series of studies and found evidence both for and *against* the influence of a strong prior over perception in participants with traits associated with delusions, depending on whether the task involved relatively high- or low-level beliefs. In one version of this task, participants were led to believe that special goggles would allow them to detect a particular motion direction in a display where the motion was in fact ambiguous. Schmack and colleagues (2013) reported that sub-clinical delusion-proneness in the general population (measured with the Peters et al. Delusion Inventory; Peters et al. 1999) predicted greater use of prior belief (knowledge about the glasses) to bias visual motion perception. However, these authors found what appear on the surface to be contrasting results when this task was repeated in a study of schizophrenia patients. On the one hand, when patients were compared to controls, the delusion-prone group was less biased. On the other hand, when the schizophrenia group was considered alone, the biasing effect of prior belief about the glasses was positively associated with self-reported positive psychosis symptoms (Schmack and colleagues 2017).[2] Although these results appear difficult to reconcile, a highly similar pattern reappeared in another study of schizophrenia

---

[2] Here and in various other studies of schizophrenia we cite, some of the participants in the clinical group may not have been delusional because not everyone diagnosed with schizophrenia has delusions. This limits the ability of such studies to inform theories of delusions.

246 BELIEF, IMAGINATION, AND DELUSION

patients, using a variant of the task where prior expectation was induced using repeated perceptual experience (Schmack et al. 2015), and perception of rotation in ambiguous motion displays was probed. In another study the authors (Stuke et al. 2019) used tone pitch in perceptual and cognitive variants of their task to manipulate prior expectation either of motion direction in an ambiguous display or, in a parallel task variant, the majority colour of fish in a lake (similar to the beads task, described below). On only the perceptual task variant, subclinical delusion-proneness was *less* associated with biasing effects of prior expectation. So strong prior theory receives variable support, possibly depending on whether a task is relatively cognitive or perceptual in nature. As will be discussed further in the future directions section below, the authors describe hierarchical interactions between different levels within a predictive coding framework to explain their findings (Sterzer et al. 2018).

4. Can a Strong Prior Explain both Delusions and Hallucinations?

In psychosis (e.g., schizophrenia), delusions are often accompanied by hallucinations. Especially in individuals experiencing paranoia, hallucinations (e.g., hearing voices) can be inextricably linked to associated delusions (e.g., believing others are monitoring one's thoughts). Hallucinations are misperceptions (e.g., visual, auditory) which, like delusions (misbeliefs), involve content that is not supportable by evidence from external stimuli. Some authors (e.g., Corlett et al. 2019) propose a theory of hallucinations that mirrors that of the strong prior theory of delusions. When strong perceptual expectations (overly precise priors) meet relatively noisy (imprecise) incoming sensory data (likelihood), the prior dominates, distorting perception and leading in extreme cases to a percept in the absence of any corresponding input from the world.

As we are primarily concerned here with delusions, we will not comprehensively review the empirical literature implicating strong priors in hallucinations (although we acknowledge the parsimony of any candidate theory that might explain hallucinations and delusions by a common cause; see Corlett et al. 2019, for a more complete review). However, most such studies, like many of those we have already cited, have examined patient populations for which hallucinations and delusions are highly comorbid (e.g., patients with schizophrenia). In such studies, it can be exceedingly difficult to disentangle whether a laboratory finding is caused by a trait that gave rise to delusions or hallucinations or both. We will therefore focus here on one recent study which separately examined the role of priors in hallucinations and in psychosis more generally.

In this study, Albert Powers and colleagues (2017) examined a unique sample that included individuals who either did or did not hallucinate voices and who did or did not have a psychosis diagnosis. All four groups of participants (and especially those who hallucinate voices) were likely to falsely report a sound presented in noise (i.e., "conditioned hallucinations") after a training period that set up an *a priori* expectation that the sound would be paired with a visual checkerboard stimulus. The authors then fit to the participants' tone detection judgements a Bayesian hierarchical Gaussian filter (HGF) model (Mathys et al. 2011). Because HGF is a hierarchical model, it has one (lowest) level, the states of which encode the presence of tones and checkerboards. The model also has a second (middle) level that attempts to predict the first level states and learns from prediction errors the contingencies of the tone and checkerboard. At this interaction between the first and second levels, the authors estimated for each participant the balance of prior to evidence as a free parameter. This model also has a third (highest) level, special to the HGF, that attempts to predict the contingencies at the second level and learns how they change in time. The values computed at this level are known as "phasic volatilities" and represent how much the model believes the contingencies between checkboard and tone are changing at any given moment. This model yielded results that supported the strong prior theory of hallucinations: When detecting tones, participants who hallucinate voices were more influenced by their prior beliefs about the presence of the tone than those who don't hallucinate voices, which led to more false perceptions of the tones in the former group.

The authors also analyzed the states of the model that arise from the fitted models and, in doing so, found a different effect that arises for psychosis generally, independent of whether participants also hallucinate voices. On average, the phasic volatilities (belief that contingency between checkerboard and tone is changing) were lower in those with psychosis than those without. Indeed, the authors write "Subjects with psychosis were significantly less sensitive to the changes in contingency as the task progressed. Psychotic symptoms are often associated with pathological rigidity" and that the "findings in psychotic patients may reflect a strong prior that contingencies are fixed. On the other hand, they could reflect a weak prior on volatility. These beliefs were not associated with hallucinations but rather psychosis more broadly. Under chronic uncertainty, secondary to consistent belief violation, it may be adaptive to resist updating belief" (Powers et al. 2017: 600).

The HGF provides a promising new method for reaching conclusions about the strength of prior versus evidence and, moreover, introduces volatility as a related factor that might explain belief rigidity. Yet, these conclusions remain preliminary. Although another study from this research group also used HGF and the same conditioned hallucinations task to produce similar findings—individuals at risk for psychosis used both a stronger prior and perceived lower volatility than control participants (Kafadar et al. 2020). Further studies of paranoia, using variations on this modelling method, have associated paranoia with an expectation that the environment is more changeable (Reed et al. 2020). Two further studies have now shown *increased* (rather than decreased) perceived volatility connected with psychosis, one (Cole et al. 2020) in a relatively small sample ($N = 13$) of individuals clinically at high-risk for psychosis and the other

(Deserno et al. 2020) in a larger sample (N = 46) of schizophrenia patients. Both studies manipulated volatility using instrumental learning tasks that implemented reversals of which stimuli predict rewards. Thus, the data gained from HRF models to date remain confined to too few studies. More studies are needed (1) to resolve the conflicting findings, (2) to clarify to what extent any inferences about volatility can be extended beyond psychosis generally to delusional symptoms per se, and (3) to directly compare hallucinations and delusions and conclude whether they result from the same or different computational mechanisms.

5. Deluded Individuals Are Overly Responsive to Evidence: The Beads Task

Next, we will review studies that link deluded beliefs with undue influence of evidence (i.e., failure to adequately use prior belief to temper the influence of evidence over belief learning). Indeed, underweighting of prior belief in favour of new evidence or feedback appears to be a motif across diverse task types. This motif has already previously been reviewed from various perspectives (Adams et al. 2013; Adams et al. 2016; Bansal et al. 2018). We cover here some prominent illustrative examples, with recognition that they represent only the tip of an iceberg of wider literature. In this section, we begin with the beads task. In later sections, we will move on to several other illustrative examples of empirical findings and then we will turn to larger theoretical frameworks, which explain delusions in terms of evidence overweighting. Collectively, this body of work is difficult to reconcile with the perspective motivated in the above sections, in which evidence appears downweighted in favour of pre-existing belief.

One of the most influential findings to propagate the idea that delusions relate to over-receptivity to evidence is that deluded individuals "jump to conclusions". In a seminal study (Huq et al. 1988), an experimenter drew pink or green beads from a hidden urn; after each draw, participants could attempt to infer the majority bead colour in the urn (i.e., pink or green), or choose to view a further bead. Delusional participants required fewer draws before making this decision than did control participants, with nearly half of the deluded sample deciding on the basis of seeing just a single bead. Many subsequent studies using this "Draws to decision beads task" have documented "jumping to conclusions" (JTC) in delusional and delusion-prone samples (for recent meta-analyses see Dudley et al. 2016; McLean et al. 2017; Ross et al. 2015; So et al. 2016).

Interestingly, the notion of "jumping to conclusions" itself exemplifies the conceptual paradox of delusions (compare: U2's "running to stand still"). After all, "jumping to conclusions" is a term of dual epistemic disapprobation—somebody that has "jumped to a conclusion" has erred both in that they have reached a conclusion before they *should* have done (being overly credulous), and in that they have reached a conclusion *at all* (being overly rigid). Nevertheless, the most widespread interpretation of JTC is the former, i.e., JTC is construed as reflecting a general tendency for the affected individuals to overweight evidence (in this case, bead colours) and therefore to form beliefs based on less evidence than other individuals do.

"Graded estimates" is a second variant of the beads paradigm, and studies employing this variant also suggest oversensitivity to evidence in the delusion-prone. Participants view a sequence of beads and report their beliefs about the majority urn colour after each successive bead, in the form of a probability estimate. Here, delusion-prone individuals "over-adjust" to beads that contradict the currently favoured hypothesis. That is, when deluded individuals view a single pink bead following a sequence of green beads, they will adjust their probability estimate in favour of pink more so than other individuals do (Garety et al. 1991; Rodier et al. 2011). These findings are often taken to indicate that deluded individuals overweight the evidence value of currently presented beads, relative to prior beliefs about the majority colour of the urn (e.g., Evans et al. 2015; van der Leer et al. 2017).

Despite the clear influence of this paradigm on the study of delusions, the interpretation that JTC must rely on a general trait for evidence overweighting that also feeds into delusions is not so clear cut (Evans et al. 2015). Although JTC has been replicated many times (Dudley et al. 2016), it may not be tolerant to changes in design. JTC in psychosis has persistently failed to replicate when conducted in brain imaging environments (Andreou et al. 2018; Krug et al. 2014; Rausch et al. 2014), although healthy participants in the scanner draw fewer beads than optimal (Furl and Averbeck 2011). A recent paper (Baker et al. 2019) reported that, far from jumping to conclusions, their sample of schizophrenia patients (half of whom were medicated) drew *more* beads, when they had more severe delusions. However, these authors did not report a simple increase in draws as a function of delusion severity. Instead, their healthy participants drew roughly the same as the high delusion patients (i.e., both groups appeared to draw less than the low delusion patients). And, this pattern arose only when there was a 60/40 colour split in the urn and not in other conditions. In another paper that has recently brought the draws-to-decision beads task into question (Tripoli et al. 2021), the authors examined a large sample of 817 first-episode psychosis patients and 1294 controls. Using the Baron and Kenny method (1986), they showed that the influence of psychosis on JTC was strongly mediated by IQ. Their conclusion was that whatever trait gives rise to JTC (and perhaps, then, also to delusions) was a manifestation of a more general impairment. Nevertheless, a second large sample study (Henquet et al. 2022) with 1261 schizophrenia patients, 1282 siblings of those patients, and 1525 healthy controls, showed that group membership could be successfully predicted from an interaction between the degree of JTC and

250   BELIEF, IMAGINATION, AND DELUSION

delusion severity, even when adjusting for cognitive ability. Meanwhile Justin Sulik and colleagues (2023) found, in a large general population sample ($N = 1002$), that the relationship between delusional ideation and JTC disappeared when low quality (inattentive/low-effort) responses were removed from the data set; raising the prospect that the vaunted JTC effect in delusion-prone individuals may be related to inattention. The jury is thus still out as to whether, and to what extent, JTC stems from a highly selective trait that is specific to evidence-based belief formation.

The JTC bias, even if confirmed to be a robust and selective phenomenon, can still be explained by theories other than simple evidence overweighting. The draws-to-decision version of the beads task, computationally, can be solved if the agent prospectively estimates the reward value to be gained by continued evidence sampling and uses this value as a threshold against which to compare the reward expected from stopping and deciding now (Averbeck 2015; Baker et al. 2019; Bowler et al. 2021; Furl and Averbeck 2011; Hauser et al. 2018; Moutoussis et al. 2011; van der Leer et al. 2015). If participants use such a "threshold crossing" decision mechanism to solve the beads task, then there are at least two other possible causes of JTC. First, JTC could arise from an overly liberal decision threshold, a possibility for which there is some evidence (e.g., Moritz et al. 2007; Evans et al. 2015). That is, if participants feel that drawing more beads would not be informative, they would stop drawing even if they had not accumulated much evidence so far. Michael Moutoussis and colleagues (2011) demonstrated a second possible explanation for JTC by fitting computational models to the bead-drawing behaviour of schizophrenia patients and controls. They found that drawing behaviour was best predicted when responses were more noisy in the schizophrenia group. Thus decision noise can also explain JTC, in addition to the liberal threshold and evidence over-weighting accounts. In the end, despite the popularity and influence of the beads task, conclusions about evidence overweighting may not be so straightforward. However, there are other sources for the evidence overweighting conception of delusions, which we turn to next.

6. Deluded Individuals Are Overly Responsive to Evidence: Other Empirical Examples

Dan Joyce and colleagues (2013) took a model-based approach to estimate relative contributions of prior belief versus new evidence to decision making when schizophrenia patients played games of "rock-paper-scissors" against a computer. To succeed at the game one must continually update prior beliefs about the computer's gameplay using new evidence, so that patterns in the computer's moves can be learned, predicted, and exploited. The reinforcement learning model these authors fit to the data indicated that although the patients and controls did not differ in how they weighed new evidence, the patients' prior belief decayed too quickly. Because healthy control participants' prior beliefs remained influential for longer, they were better able to exploit their computer opponents than the patients could.

Compared to non-deluded individuals, deluded individuals who use imprecise (weak) prior beliefs to make predictions should show decreased neural responses when prediction errors should be larger, because neurons that signal prediction error would be less able to detect deviations from prior belief. Indeed, patients with schizophrenia show a weakened mismatch negativity (Turetsky et al. 2007), an electroencephalographical auditory evoked response that is interpreted as a signal of violations of prior predictions. In healthy participants, this response occurs 100–250 milliseconds after an "oddball" stimulus, which deviates from a sequence of identical stimuli. The relationship of the mismatch negativity with symptom severity is more complicated, however. On a behavioural level (Dzafic et al. 2020), errors in estimating stimulus occurrence probabilities in the mismatch negativity task are related to severity of subclinical psychosis symptoms measured using the Prodromal Questionnaire (Loewy et al. 2005). Although this suggests that psychosis severity could relate to the *perception* of oddball stimuli, the *neural response* to these oddballs in the form of the mismatch negativity may not be so strongly related to delusional symptoms (Erickson et al. 2017). Nevertheless, delusion-related symptoms might still relate to neural responses to oddballs, albeit for the P300, a later-occurring oddball response (Turetsky et al. 2009).

Preference for sensory evidence over prior belief also appears to render individuals with psychosis resistant to some perceptual illusions. In these cases, they perceive sensory evidence "as-is", without interference from prior belief. In the well-known hollow-mask illusion (Schneider et al. 1996), for example, healthy participants perceive a concave facial impression (or the 2D projection of one) as convex, due to prior expectation that faces are convex; while patients with schizophrenia are not susceptible to this illusory convexity.[3] Interestingly, the hollow-mask illusion and the mismatch negativity discussed in the previous paragraph both involve application of prior belief to *perceptual inference* (e.g., participants judge the convexity of a face or the pitch of a tone), rather than the kinds of *high-level beliefs* that traditionally characterize delusions (e.g., the CIA is reading my thoughts).

We next turn to some prominent theories that propose that the inferential systems of deluded individuals are unduly biased towards sensory evidence.

---

[3] Conversely, Langdon and colleagues (2006) studied a delusional patient who seemed especially prone to visual illusions (e.g., insisting the lines in the Mueller-Lyer illusion were different lengths even when given the opportunity to measure the lines with a ruler).

7. Deluded Individuals Are Overly Responsive to Evidence: Corollary Discharge Theory

There is another illusion that healthy individuals experience but patients with schizophrenia do not. We present this "force-matching illusion" (Shergill et al. 2005) as illustrative of a wider theoretical framework—corollary discharge theory—that predicts that some psychoses are associated with an abnormally weak use of prior belief. The motor system generates "efference copies", representations of actions (e.g., eye movements, hand grips), that can be used by other sensory systems to produce predictions about the sensory consequences of actions (i.e., in "forward models"). One type of efference copy, the "corollary discharge", is specifically used to inhibit or negate sensation caused by self-action (i.e., "sensory attenuation"). Thus, during sensory attenuation, the brain contrasts prior belief about an action (i.e., predictions based on corollary discharge) against incoming sensory evidence about the action. This contrast results in suppression of the sensations (evidence) by the predictions (prior).

Individuals with schizophrenia lack a force-matching illusion because their sensory attenuation (suppression of sensory evidence by prior belief) is disrupted. In the force-matching illusion, participants use their fingers to press with a force that matches another self-generated force. Healthy individuals cannot accurately sense a self-generated force. Because of sensory attenuation, they perceive self-generated forces to be weaker than externally-generated forces of the same magnitude. Schizophrenia patients, who do not use prior beliefs about their motor actions to attenuate their sensations, can counter self-generated forces more accurately than healthy individuals.

Some authors view the failure of sensory attenuation in schizophrenia on the force-matching task to be a laboratory example of a more general trait, which also causes some hallucinations and delusions, such as paranoia (Frith and Dolan 1997). Indeed, several examples of failure to predict and suppress the sensory consequences of actions have been empirically linked with severity of hallucinations and delusions (Bansal et al. 2018). These data are explained by some versions of corollary discharge theory that attempt to explain hallucinations and delusions under a common framework (Brower et al. 2017). Specifically, in schizophrenia patients, sensations of self-actions, broadly construed to include even "internal actions" like thoughts, inner speech, and intentions, are not attenuated as self-actions should be, and so they are perceived as caused by external agents. According to this view, this feeling of external agency over self-generated sensations gives rise to auditory hallucinations such as voices (Heinks-Maldonado et al. 2007), as well as to delusions (Malassis et al. 2015), including delusions that self-generated (internal or external) speech is generated by external agents (Bansal et al. 2018) and other "delusions of control" (Frith 2005).

THE PARADOX OF DELUSIONS   253

8. Deluded Individuals Are Overly Responsive to Evidence: Aberrant Salience and Dopaminergic Prediction Error

Shitji Kapur (2003) suggested that dysregulated dopamine transmission in deluded individuals leads to an aberrant attribution of salience to the contents of their experience; their delusions represent an attempt to make sense of such aberrantly salient experiences. This proposal echoes Brendan Maher's earlier suggestion that delusions arise when individuals employ normal reasoning processes to try to explain intense and anomalous phenomenological experiences: "the locus of the pathology is in the neuropsychology of experience" (Maher 1999: 551).

Kapur's perspective is in large part motivated by the success of dopaminergic antipsychotics in treating psychosis and was originally formulated for the case of schizophrenia (Kapur 2003). As described above, dopaminergic activity in the midbrain and striatum is thought to drive learning of new beliefs about the reward values of actions based on reward prediction errors (Schultz et al. 1997). Thus, in the years since Kapur's theoretical proposal, many studies have sought evidence for aberrant salience in the form of abnormal dopaminergic reward prediction error signals. Such studies test whether indiscriminant dopaminergic signaling leads some predictable information (information that is not in fact informative and should not drive new learning) to appear overly salient, thereby driving new learning of associations that are, in fact, spurious. Effectively, this account is one of over-reliance on evidence. In practice, an agent should weight evidence highly only if it deviates strongly from prior expectation (i.e., has a strong prediction error) and thus prior belief should be instrumental in determining the weighting of evidence. In contrast, if all evidence appears equally "salient" and can drive new learning, then prior belief is being applied weakly. When ordinary experiences that should be predictable from prior belief gain "salience", then beliefs can drift out of line with reality (Heinz et al. 2019).

Functional magnetic resonance imaging (fMRI) studies provide evidence for abnormal prediction error signaling in psychosis. Philip Corlett and colleagues (2007) reported that, compared to typical controls, first-episode psychosis patients showed reduced midbrain responses (believed to be dopaminergic) associated with causal association learning and reduced right frontal responses to events that violated expectations (cf. Griffith et al. 2014). Florian Schlagenhauf and colleagues (2009), in a study of schizophrenia patients, found abnormal responses to omission of expected reward in medial prefrontal cortex and striatum. Jonathan Roiser and colleagues (2013) examined individuals at ultra-high risk of psychosis (who were presumably in a prodromal state) and found that they were more likely to expect reward from irrelevant (poorly predictive) stimuli than controls. Moreover, control participants' explicit ratings of the salience of irrelevant stimuli were better correlated with their ventral striatal responses than were those of the at-risk individuals. Thus, at-risk individuals

254   BELIEF, IMAGINATION, AND DELUSION

appear more susceptible to learning from irrelevant evidence and this could arise from indiscriminate dopaminergic signaling.

Other studies have used computational models to quantify prediction errors (i.e., reinforcement learning). Graham Murray and colleagues (2008) showed that, compared to typical controls, first-episode psychosis patients, in addition to choosing stimuli that led to reward less accurately, also showed abnormally large prediction error responses to neutral stimuli (not associated with any rewarding outcome) in the midbrain and striatum. Liana Romaniuk and colleagues (2010), studying schizophrenia patients, obtained a similar pattern in the midbrain, except using an aversion, rather than reward, conditioning paradigm. Anna Ermakova and colleagues (2018) reported weaker associations with prediction error for responses in midbrain and right prefrontal cortex in first-episode psychosis patients compared to controls. Teresa Katthagen and colleagues (2018) used a Bayesian model to compute a precision-weighted prediction error for stimuli that varied in their relevance for predicting reward. In schizophrenia patients, such prediction error signals in the nucleus accumbens of the ventral striatum (where dopaminergic neurons are present) were associated with decision biases towards irrelevant stimuli (i.e., aberrant salience).

Although there is compelling behavioural and neuroscientific evidence for the aberrant salience framework, it is unclear how to explain other evidence, discussed above, that sometimes the delusion-prone overuse prior belief. Notably, the aberrant salience framework does not, without some modification or clarification, directly predict belief incorrigibility. If an individual succumbs to aberrant salience continuously over time (e.g., years), then one might expect that newly-experienced stimuli would always be driving inappropriate new learning (and delusions) that would continually "overwrite" previous aberrant learning (and delusions) and so beliefs would continually drift as new irrelevant associations proliferate with time. This is a rather different phenomenon than the fixed and incorrigible nature of the delusions that patients experience.

9. Two-Factor Theory and Responsiveness to Evidence

The two-factor theory of delusions (Coltheart et al. 2011) was developed to explain delusions (in particular, monothematic delusions; Coltheart 2013) arising in the context of neuropsychological disorders. The theory holds that anomalous experience represents a first factor that furnishes the content of delusions—the nature of the experience determines the theme of the delusion. Table 12.1 depicts this. The delusions outlined in the third column of the table violate fundamental biological and physical principles (i.e., commonplace and firmly-held prior beliefs about the world)—their content is bizarre. Nevertheless, each delusion has a key feature to recommend it: each delusion is a high-level inference that putatively *explains* the aberrant lower-level inference (first factor) in the table's second column. For example, the belief that one has a swarm of bees flying about inside one's skull (Southard 1912; Maher 1988) would *explain* a loud buzzing sound in one's head—a buzzing sound is just what one would expect if the belief were true (Coltheart et al. 2010). Likewise, the belief, known as Capgras delusion, that a loved one has been replaced by a physically identical impostor would explain why an individual appears physically identical to a loved one yet feels unfamiliar (Darby et al. 2017); and the conviction that one has previously experienced an event that is currently unfolding (a delusional form of déjà vu known as déjà vecu; Turner et al. 2017) would explain why the event feels so familiar.

In many such cases, there is some salient low-level evidence (e.g., a buzzing sound; an anomalous sense of familiarity or unfamiliarity), evidence that the delusional belief in question—though at odds with many background beliefs—accommodates. The two-factor theory thus incorporates Maher's aforementioned insight about the connection between the content of delusions and the content of relevant experiences. Where two-factor theorists part company with Maher is that whereas Maher viewed delusions as stemming from an essentially normal response to abnormal experiences, two-factor theorists suggest there is also something abnormal about the response. Two-factor theory thus implicates not one but two neurocognitive impairments: the first (e.g., cochlear damage, precipitating tinnitus) accounts for the content of the delusion (e.g., "there are bees in my head"), and the second explains why a belief with that content is adopted and maintained.

In brief, the reason two-factor theorists claim a second factor is necessary for delusions to develop is because there are cases where the presumed first factor is present but where a delusion is absent (see fourth column of Table 12.1).[4] To illustrate using the bees-in-the-head example, the authors of one prevalence study estimated that about thirty million Americans suffer from tinnitus (Kochkin et al. 2011), yet the belief that one's head is filled with live bees is extremely rare. So, while a noise in one's head may be a prerequisite for the bees-in-the-head delusion to develop, it is unlikely to be sufficient.

But what does the second factor actually involve, and what does the nature of this factor imply about how deluded individuals respond to evidence? The second factor has been characterized in different ways even by authors of this chapter. Max Coltheart, for instance (e.g., Coltheart et al. 2010; Coltheart and Davies 2021), has proposed that the second factor involves a failure to reject delusional hypotheses in the face of disconfirmatory evidence. Ryan McKay (2012), in contrast, has argued that the second factor involves a bias towards adopting beliefs that explain salient

---

[4] Noordhof and Sullivan-Bissett (2021) argue that this dissociation (if real) is not sufficient justification for a second factor. Noordhof (this volume) suggests that deluded individuals are simply more inclined than non-deluded individuals to give "attentive consciousness" to the contents of their experience.

Table 12.1 Anomalous perceptions generated by neuropsychological impairments and associated delusions

Putative neuropsychological impairment	Anomalous perceptual evidence generated by neuropsychological impairment	Delusion (that explains the anomalous evidence)	Cases where the neuropsychological impairment appears to be present but delusion is absent
Damage to the tiny sensory hair cells (cilia) in the cochlea of the inner ear	Anomalous buzzing sound (tinnitus)	Bees in head delusion	Tinnitus is a common audiological symptom, rarely accompanied by delusions
Dysfunction in the neural circuitry subserving the experience of facial familiarity	Familiar individuals feel unfamiliar	Capgras (impostor) delusion	A patient who had undergone neurosurgery to treat intractable epilepsy subsequently reported that her mother felt unfamiliar (but did not adopt the Capgras delusion) (Turner and Coltheart 2010)
Disruption of temporal lobe recognition systems	Sensation that a sequence of current events has been lived through before	Déjà vecu (delusional déjà vu)	Non-delusional déjà vu is common
Autonomic system over-responsive to faces	Even the faces of strangers produce autonomic responses	Frégoli delusion (the belief that one is pursued by familiar others disguised as strangers)	Patient experiences faces of strangers as highly familiar (Negro et al. 2015; Vuilleumier et al. 2003)
Autonomic system under-responsive to all stimuli	No emotional response to one's environment	Cotard delusion (the belief that one is dead)	Pure autonomic failure: patient is not autonomically responsive to any stimuli (Heims et al. 2004; Magnifico et al. 1998)
Mirror agnosia (loss of knowledge about how mirrors work)	Mirrors are perceived as windows	Mirrored-self misidentification (delusion that the person in the mirror is a stranger)	Other cases of mirror agnosia (Binkofski et al. 1999)
Failure of computation of sensory feedback from movement	Voluntary movements are no longer perceived as voluntary	Delusion of alien control	Haptic deafferentation: patient gets no sensory feedback from any actions performed (Fourneret et al. 2002)
Damage to motor area of brain controlling arm	Left arm is paralysed; patient can't move it	Somatoparaphrenia (denial of ownership of the arm)	Hemiplegia without associated delusions

pieces of evidence.[5] So, while McKay has construed the second factor as involving over-responsiveness to (first-factor) evidence, Coltheart has construed the second factor as involving under-responsiveness to evidence that disconfirms the hypothesis adopted to *explain* the first-factor evidence. For Coltheart, therefore, people with delusions are both over-responsive *and* under-responsive to evidence: being overly swayed by (a certain kind of) experiential evidence *and also* insufficiently swayed by (disconfirmatory) evidence. We leave it to our future selves (or others) to reconcile these diverging construals of the second factor.

10. Future Directions

In this review we have examined prevailing assumptions about delusions and deluded individuals. As we have outlined, the existing research evidence reveals a fundamental puzzle concerning the manner in which deluded individuals integrate new experiences with their prior beliefs. The puzzle is this: How can patients with delusions be both inflexibly reliant on prior belief and easily swayed by new evidence?

This conundrum is not new, but has been amplified in the popular theoretical guise of computational psychiatry (Adams et al. 2016). Nevertheless, casting the problem of delusions in computational terms has attracted criticism (Williams 2018) and has yet to produce a consensus solution. In closing, we briefly mention some ideas that remain to be confirmed or falsified empirically.

- Some proponents of hierarchical predictive coding have offered a speculative solution to explain how some tasks appear to favour the strong prior account while other tasks show oversensitivity to new evidence (Adams et al. 2016; Corlett et al. 2019; Sterzer et al. 2018). Each level of a predictive coding hierarchy is affected bottom-up by a prediction error specific to that level, which arises from the mismatch between that level's input from its preceding level and prior belief derived from its succeeding level. These authors speculate that abnormalities at one level (e.g., more perceptual levels) could "subtend" different kinds of imbalances at other levels (e.g., higher, more cognitive levels), with behaviour on a given task governed by the levels engaged by that task. As yet, these kinds of hierarchical interactions have not been directly observed to occur in implemented computational models, nor have they been verified for human participants by fitting computational models to human task behaviour.

---

[5] More recently, Miyazono and McKay (2019) suggested that the second factor involves overestimation of the precision of the abnormal prediction error generated by the first-factor impairment.

- In an earlier section we reviewed research using the HGF that could estimate, from human patient behaviour, their perceived "volatility", a mechanism that controls how they respond to changes in the contingencies of their environment. These models allow the preference for evidence versus prior to dynamically adapt as event contingencies in the environment change. Although the preliminary evidence we reviewed above has been conflicting to date, future work may explain how beliefs can be malleable at one time and rigid at another. Abnormalities in volatility processing have already been observed for other disorders, such as anxiety (Browning et al. 2015) and autism (Lawson et al. 2017).
- Longitudinally, sensitivity to evidence versus prior might change over time. Theoretically, aberrant salience has been especially associated with the pro-dromal stages of psychosis (Kapur 2003), in which beliefs may be more malleable. Once delusional beliefs become established on the basis of insufficient evidence, then the character of psychosis may change, rendering the new beliefs incorrigible. This, and other closely-related accounts of how susceptibility to evidence might change due to the progression of psychosis (Corlett and Fletcher 2021), remain to be fully tested empirically. Jardri and Denève (2013) have formally described a hierarchical neural network model that, they claim, can account for both hallucinations and delusions. In this model, psychosis arises from an imbalance in excitation/inhibition, which allows predictions and prediction errors to become self-reinforcing through unchecked network reverberation. The authors have used this model to explain the behaviour of schizophrenia patients on a modified version of the beads task (Jardri et al. 2017).

All these ideas require further theoretical development and empirical study. Work on delusions continues apace, but researchers will need to solve the puzzle we have highlighted here if they are to provide a fully satisfying explanation of these perplexing and distressing symptoms.

References

Adams, R. A., Huys, Q. J. M., and Roiser, J. P. (2016). Computational psychiatry: Towards a mathematically informed understanding of mental illness. *Journal of Neurology, Neurosurgery, and Psychiatry* 87: 53–63.

Adams, R. A., Perrinet, L. U., and Friston, K. (2012). Smooth pursuit and visual occlusion: Active inference and oculomotor control in schizophrenia. *PLoS One* 7/10: e47502.

Adams, R. A. Stephan, K. E., Brown, H. R., Frith, C. D., and Friston, K. J. (2013). The computational anatomy of psychosis. *Frontiers in Psychology* 4: 47.

American Psychiatric Association (2013). *Diagnostic and Statistical Manual of Mental Disorders*, 5th edition. Washington, DC: American Psychiatric Association.

Andreou, C., Steinmann, S., Leicht, G., Kolbeck, K., Moritz, S., and Mulert, C. (2018). fMRI correlates of jumping-to-conclusions in patients with delusions: Connectivity patterns and effects of metacognitive training. *Neuroimage: Clinical* 20: 119–27.

Arnold, K. (2016). Is delusional imperviousness a backfire effect of being disbelieved? *Psychosis* 8/4: 369–71.

Averbeck, B. B. (2015). Theory of choice in bandit, information sampling and foraging tasks. *PLoS Computational Biology* 11: e1004164.

Baker, S. C., Konova, A. B., Daw, N. D., and Horga, G. (2019). A distinct inferential mechanism for delusions in schizophrenia. *Brain* 142: 1797–812.

Bansal, S., Ford, J., and Sperling, M. (2018). The function and failure of sensory predictions. *Annals of the New York Academy of Sciences* 1426: 199–220.

Baron, R. M. and Kenny, D. A. (1986). The moderator–mediator variable distinction in social psychological research: Conceptual, strategic, and statistical considerations. *Journal of Personality and Social Psychology* 51: 1173–82.

Binkofski, F., Buccino, G., Dohle, C., Seitz, R. J., and Freund, H. J. (1999). Mirror agnosia and mirror ataxia constitute different parietal lobe disorders. *Annals of Neurology* 47: 553–4.

Bortolotti, L., Sullivan-Bissett, E., and Gunn, R. (2016). What makes a belief delusional? In I. Mac Carthy, K. Sellevold, and O. Smith (eds.), *Cognitive Confusions: Dreams, Delusions and Illusions in Early Modern Culture* (pp. 37–51). Cambridge: Legenda.

Bowler, A., Habicht, J., Moses-Payne, M. E., Steinbeis, N., Moutoussis, M., and Hauser, T. U. (2021). Children perform extensive information gathering when it is not costly. *Cognition* 208: 104535.

Brower, R., Wang, H. R., Bansal, S., and Joiner W. M. (2017). Using corollary discharge and predictive coding to understand false sensations and beliefs. *Biological Psychiatry: Cognitive Neuroscience and Neuroimaging* 4: 770–2.

Browning, M., Behrens, T. E., Jocham, G., O'Reilly, J. X., and Bishop, S. J. (2015). Anxious individuals have difficulty learning the causal statistics of aversive environments. *Nature Neuroscience* 18: 590–6.

Cole, D. M., Diaconescu, A. O., Pfeiffer, U. J., Brodersen, K. H., Mathys, C. D., et al. (2020). Atypical processing of uncertainty in individuals at risk for psychosis. *Neuroimage: Clinical* 26: 102239.

Coltheart, M. (2013). On the distinction between monothematic and polythematic delusions. *Mind & Language* 28/1: 103–12.

Coltheart, M. and Davies, M. (2021). Failure of hypothesis evaluation as a factor in delusional belief. *Cognitive Neuropsychiatry* 26/4: 213–30.

Coltheart, M., Langdon, R., and McKay, R. (2011). Delusional belief. *Annual Review of Psychology* 62: 271–98.

Coltheart, M., Menzies, P., and Sutton, J. (2010). Abductive inference and delusional belief. *Cognitive Neuropsychiatry* 15: 261–87.

Corlett, P. R. and Fletcher, P. (2021). Modelling delusions as temporally-evolving beliefs. *Cognitive Neuropsychiatry* 26/4: 231–41.

Corlett, P. R., Forga, G., Fletcher, P. C., Alderson-Day, B., Schmack, K., and Powers III, A. R. (2019). Hallucinations and strong priors. *Trends in Cognitive Sciences* 23/2: 114–27.

Corlett, P. R., Murray, G. K., Honey, G. D., Aitken, M. R. F., Shanks, D. R., et al. (2007). Disrupted prediction-error signal in psychosis: Evidence for an associative account of delusions. *Brain* 130: 2387–400.

Darby, R. R., Laganiere, S., Pascual-Leone, A., Prasad, S., and Fox, M. D. (2017). Finding the imposter: Lesions causing delusional misidentifications are characterized by a unique pattern of brain connectivity. *Brain* 140: 497–507.

David, A. S. (1999). On the impossibility of defining delusions. *Philosophy, Psychiatry, & Psychology* 6: 17–20.

Deserno, L., Boehme, R., Mathys, C., Katthagen, T., Kaminski, J., et al. (2020). Volatility estimates increase choice switching and relate to prefrontal activity in Schizophrenia. *Biological Psychiatry: Cognitive Neuroscience and Neuroimaging* 5: 173–83.

Deserno, L., Schlagenhauf, F., and Heinz, A. (2016). Striatal dopamine, reward, and decision making in schizophrenia. *Dialogues in Clinical Neuroscience* 18: 77–89.

Dudley, R., Taylor, P., Wickham, S., and Hutton, P. (2016). Psychosis, delusions and the "jumping to conclusions" reasoning bias: A systematic review and meta-analysis. *Schizophrenia Bulletin* 42: 652–65.

Dzafic, I., Randeniya, R., Harris, C. D., Bammel, M., and Garrido, M. I. (2020). Statistical learning and inference is impaired in the nonclinical continuum of psychosis. *Journal of Neuroscience* 40: 6759–69.

Erickson, M. A., Albrecht, M., Ruffle, A., Fleming, L., Corlett, P., and Gold, J. (2017). No association between symptom severity and MMN impairment in schizophrenia: A meta-analytic approach. *Schizophrenia Research: Cognition* 9: 13–17.

Ermakova, A. O., Knolle, F., Justicia, A., Bullmore, E. T., Jones, P. B., et al. (2018). Abnormal reward prediction-error signalling in antipsychotic naive individuals with first-episode psychosis or clinical risk for psychosis. *Neuropsychopharmacology* 43: 1691–9.

Evans, S. L., Averbeck, B. B., and Furl, N. (2015). Jumping to conclusions in schizophrenia. *Neuropsychiatric Disease and Treatment* 11: 1615–24.

Fletcher, P. C. and Frith, C. D. (2009). Perceiving is believing: A Bayesian approach to explaining the positive symptoms of schizophrenia. *Nature Reviews Neuroscience* 10: 48–58.

Fourneret, P., Paillard, J., Lamarre, Y., Cole, J., and Jeannerod, M. (2002). Lack of conscious recognition of one's own actions in a haptically deafferented patient. *Neuroreport* 13: 541.

THE PARADOX OF DELUSIONS 261

Frith, C. (2005). The neural basis of hallucinations and delusions. *Comptes Rendus Biologies* 328: 169–75.

Frith, C. and Dolan, R. J. (1997). Brain mechanisms associated with top-down processes in perception. *Philosophical Transactions of the Royal Society of London B: Biological Sciences* 352: 1221–30.

Furl, N. and Averbeck, B. B. (2011). Parietal cortex and insula relate to evidence seeking relevant to reward-related decisions. *Journal of Neuroscience* 31/48: 17572–82.

Garety, P. A., Hemsley, D. R., and Wessely, S. (1991). Reasoning in deluded schizophrenic and paranoid patients: Biases in performance on a probabilistic inference task. *Journal of Nervous and Mental Disease* 179: 194–201.

Griffiths, O., Langdon, R., Le Pelley, M. E., and Coltheart, M. (2014). Delusions and prediction error: Re-examining the behavioural evidence for disrupted error signalling in delusion formation. *Cognitive Neuropsychiatry* 19/5: 439–67.

Halligan, P. W. and David, A. S. (2001). Cognitive neuropsychiatry: Towards a scientific psychopathology. *Nature Reviews Neuroscience* 2: 209–15.

Hauser, T. U., Moutoussis, M., Purg, N., Dayan, P., and Dolan, R. J. (2018). Beta-blocker propranolol modulates decision urgency during sequential information gathering. *Journal of Neuroscience* 38: 7170–8.

Heims, H. C., Critchley, H. D., Dolan, R., Mathias, C. J., and Cipolotti, L. (2004). Social and motivational functioning is not critically dependent on feedback of autonomic responses: Neuropsychological evidence from patients with pure autonomic failure. *Neuropsychologia* 42: 1979–88.

Heinks-Maldonado, T. H., Mathalon, D. H., Houde, J. F., Gray, M., Faustman, and Ford, J. M. (2007). Relationship of imprecise corollary discharge in schizophrenia to auditory hallucinations. *Archives of General Psychiatry* 64: 286–96.

Heinz, A., Murray, G. K., Schlagenhauf, F., Sterzer, P., Grace, A. A., and Waltz, J. A. (2019). Towards a unifying cognitive, neurophysiological, and computational neuroscience account of schizophrenia. *Schizophrenia Bulletin* 45: 1092–100.

Henquet, C., van Os, J., Pries, L. K., Rauschenberg, C., Delespaul, P. et al. (2022). A replication study of JTC bias, genetic liability for psychosis and delusional ideation. *Psychological Medicine* 52/9: 1777–83.

Hume, D. (1748/2007). *An Enquiry Concerning Human Understanding.* Oxford: Oxford University Press.

Huq, S. F., Garety, P. A., and Hemsley, D. R. (1988). Probabilistic judgements in deluded and non-deluded subjects. *The Quarterly Journal of Experimental Psychology A* 40: 801–12.

Jardri, R. and Denève, S. (2013). Circular inferences in schizophrenia. *Brain* 136/Pt 11: 3227–41.

Jardri, R., Duverne, S., Litvinova, A. S., and Denève, S. (2017). Experimental evidence for circular inference in schizophrenia. *Nature Communications* 8: 14218.

Jaspers, K. (1913). *General Psychopathology*, trans. J. Hoenig and M. W. Hamilton. Baltimore, MD: Johns Hopkins University Press.

Joyce, D. W., Averbeck, B. B., Frith, C. D., and Shergill, S. S. (2013). Examining belief and confidence in schizophrenia. *Psychological Medicine* 43: 2327–38.

Kafadar, E., Mittal, V. A., Strauss, G. P., Chapman, H. C., Ellman, L. M., et al. (2020). Modeling perception and behavior in individuals at clinical high risk for psychosis: Support for the predictive processing framework. *Schizophrenia Research* 226: 167–75.

Kapur, S. (2003). Psychosis as a state of aberrant salience: A framework linking biology, phenomenology, and pharmacology in schizophrenia. *American Journal of Psychiatry* 160: 13–23.

Katthagen, T., Mathys, C., Deserno, L., Walter, H., Kathmann, N., et al. (2018). Modeling subjective relevance in schizophrenia and its relation to aberrant salience. *PLoS Computational Biology* 14: e1006319.

Kochkin, S., Tyler, R., and Born, J. (2011). Marketrak VIII: The prevalence of tinnitus in the United States and the self-reported efficacy of various treatments. *Hearing Review* 18/12: 10–26.

Krug, A., Cabanis, M., Pyka, M., Pauly, K., Walter, H., et al. (2014). Investigation of decision-making under uncertainty in healthy subjects: A multi-centric fMRI study. *Behavioural Brain Research* 261: 89–96.

Langdon, R., Cooper, S., Connaughton, E., and Martin, K. (2006). A variant of misidentification delusion in a patient with right frontal and temporal brain injury [Abstract]. *Neuropsychiatric Disease and Treatment* 2/Suppl 3: 8.

Lawson, R. P., Mathys, C., and Rees, G. (2017). Adults with autism overestimate the volatility of the sensory environment. *Nature Neuroscience* 20: 1293–9.

Loewy, R., Bearden, C. E., Johnson, J. K., Raine, A., and Cannon, T. D. (2005). The prodromal questionnaire (PQ): Preliminary validation of a self-report screening measure for prodromal and psychotic syndromes. *Schizophrenia Research* 79: 117–25.

McKay, R. (2012). Delusional inference. *Mind & Language* 27/3: 330–55.

McLean, B. F., Mattiske, J. K., and Balzan, R. P. (2017). Association of the jumping to conclusions and evidence integration biases with delusions in psychosis: A detailed meta-analysis. *Schizophrenia Bulletin* 43/2: 344–54.

Magnifico, F., Misra, V. P., Murray, N. M. F., and Mathias, C. J. (1998). The sympathetic skin response in peripheral autonomic failure: Evaluation in pure autonomic failure, pure cholinergic failure and dopamine-hydroxylase deficiency. *Clinical Autonomic Research* 8: 133–8.

Maher, B. A. (1988). Anomalous experience and delusional thinking: The logic of explanations. In T. F. Oltmanns and B. A. Maher (eds.), *Delusional Beliefs* (pp. 15–33). New York: Wiley.

Maher, B. A. (1999). Anomalous experience in everyday life: Its significance for psychopathology. *The Monist* 82: 547–70.

THE PARADOX OF DELUSIONS 263

Malassis, R., Del Cul, A., and Colins, T. (2015). Corollary discharge failure in an oculomotor task is related to delusional ideation in healthy individuals. *PLoS One* 10: e0134483.

Mathys, C., Daunizeau, J., Friston, K. J., and Stephan, K. (2011). A Bayesian foundation for individual learning under uncertainty. *Frontiers in Human Neuroscience* 5: 39.

Miyazono, K. and McKay, R. (2019). Explaining delusional beliefs: A hybrid model. *Cognitive Neuropsychiatry* 24/5: 335–46.

Moritz, S., Woodward, T. S., and Lambert, M. (2007). Under what circumstances do patients with schizophrenia jump to conclusions? A liberal acceptance account. *British Journal of Clinical Psychology* 46: 127–37.

Moutoussis, M., Bentall, R. P., El-Deredy, W., and Dayan, P. (2011). Bayesian modelling of jumping-to-conclusions in delusional patients. *Cognitive Neuropsychiatry* 16: 422–47.

Murray, G. K., Corlett, P. R., Clark, L., Pessiglione, M., Blackwell, A. D., et al. (2008). Substantia nigra/ventral tegmental reward prediction error disruption in psychosis. *Molecular Psychiatry* 239: 267–76.

Negro, E., D'Agata, F., Caroppo, P., Coriasco, M., Ferrio, F., et al. (2015). Neurofunctional signature of hyperfamiliarity for unknown faces. *PLoS One* 10/7: e0129970.

Noordhof, P. and Sullivan-Bissett, E. (2021). The clinical significance of anomalous experience in the explanation of monothematic delusions. *Synthese* 199: 10277–309.

Notredame, C. E., Pins, D., Deneve, S., and Jardri, R. (2014). What visual illusions teach us about schizophrenia. *Frontiers in Integrative Neuroscience* 8: 63.

Peters, E. R., Joseph, S. A., and Garety, P. A. (1999). Measurement of delusional ideation in the normal population: Introducing the PDI (Peters et al. delusions inventory). *Schizophrenia Bulletin* 25: 553–76.

Powers, A. R., Mathys, C., and Corlett, P. R. (2017). Pavlovian conditioning-induced hallucinations result from overweighting of perceptual priors. *Science* 357/6351: 596–600.

Rausch, F., Mier, D., Eifler, S. E., Esslinger, C., Schilling, C., et al. (2014). Reduced activation in ventral striatum and ventral tegmental area during probabilistic decision-making in schizophrenia. *Schizophrenia Research* 156: 143–9.

Reed, E. J., Uddenberg, S., Suthaharan, P., Mathys, C. D., Taylor, J. R., et al. (2020). Paranoia as a deficit in non-social belief updating. *Elife* 26/9: e56345. https://doi.org/10.7554/eLife.56345.

Rodier, M., Prévost, M., Renoult, L., Lionnet, C., Kwann, Y., et al. (2011). Healthy people with delusional ideation change their mind with conviction. *Psychiatry Research* 189/3: 433–9.

Roiser, J. P., Howes, O. D., Chaddock, C. A., Joyce, E. M., and McGuire, P. (2013). Neural and behavioral correlates of aberrant salience in individuals at risk for psychosis. *Schizophrenia Bulletin* 39: 1328–36.

264 BELIEF, IMAGINATION, AND DELUSION

Romaniuk, L., Honey, G. D., King, J. R. L., Whalley, H. C., McIntosh, A. M., et al. (2010). Midbrain activation during Pavlovian conditioning and delusional symptoms in schizophrenia. *Archives of General Psychiatry* 67: 1246–54.

Ross, R. M., McKay, R., Coltheart, M., and Langdon, R. (2015). Jumping to conclusions about the beads task? A meta-analysis of delusional ideation and data-gathering. *Schizophrenia Bulletin* 41: 1183–91.

Schlagenhauf, F., Sterzer, P., Schmack, K., Ballmaier, M., Rapp, M., et al. (2009). Reward feedback alterations in unmedicated schizophrenia patients: Relevance for delusions. *Biological Psychiatry* 65: 1032–9.

Schmack, K., Gòmez-Carrillo de Castro, A., Rothkirch, M., Sekutowicz, M., Rössler, H., et al. (2013). Delusions and the role of beliefs in perceptual inference. *Journal of Neuroscience* 33: 13701–12.

Schmack, K., Rothkirch, M., Priller, J., and Sterzer, P. (2017). Enhanced predictive signalling in schizophrenia. *Human Brain Mapping* 38: 1767–79.

Schmack, K., Schnack, A., Priller, J., and Sterzer, P. (2015). Perceptual instability in schizophrenia: Probing predictive coding accounts of delusions with ambiguous stimuli. *Schizophrenia Research: Cognition* 2: 72–7.

Schneider, U., Leweke, F. M., Sternemann, U., Weber, M. M., and Emrich, H. M. (1996). Visual 3D illusion: A systems-theoretical approach to psychosis. *European Archives of Psychiatry and Clinical Neuroscience* 246: 256–60.

Schultz, W., Dayan, P., and Montague, P. R. (1997). A neural substrate of prediction and reward. *Science* 275: 1593–9.

Shergill, S. S., Samson, G., Bays, P. M., Frith, C. D., and Wolpert, D. M. (2005). Evidence for sensory prediction deficits in schizophrenia. *American Journal of Psychiatry* 162: 2384–6.

So, S. H.-W., Sie, N. Y.-F., Wong, H.-L., Chan, W., and Garety, P. A. (2016). "Jumping to conclusions" data-gathering bias in psychosis and other psychiatric disorders: Two meta-analyses of comparisons between patients and healthy individuals. *Clinical Psychology Review* 46: 151–67.

Southard, E. E. (1912). On the somatic sources of somatic delusions. *The Journal of Abnormal Psychology* 7/5: 326–39.

Sterzer, P., Adams, R. A., Fletcher, P., Frith, C., Lawrie, S. M., et al. (2018). The predictive coding account of psychosis. *Biological Psychiatry* 84: 634–43.

Stuke, H., Weilnhammer, V. A., Sterzer, P., and Schmack, K. (2019). Delusion proneness is linked to a reduced usage of prior beliefs in perceptual decisions. *Schizophrenia Bulletin* 45/1: 80–6.

Sulik, J., Ross, R. M., Balzan, R., and McKay, R. (2023). Delusion-like beliefs and data quality: Are classic cognitive biases artefacts of carelessness? *Journal of Psychopathology and Clinical Science*. doi:10.1037/abn0000844

Teufel, C., Subramaniam, N., Dobler, V., Perez, J., Finnemann, J., et al. (2015). Shift toward prior knowledge confers a perceptual advantage in early psychosis and psychosis prone individuals. *Proceedings of the National Academy of Sciences USA* 112/43: 13401–6.

Tripoli, G., Quattrone, D., Ferraro, L., Gayer-Anderson, C., Rodriguez, V., et al. (2021). Jumping to conclusions, general intelligence, and psychosis liability: Findings from the multi-centre EU-GEI case-control study. *Psychological Medicine* 51/4: 623–33.

Turetsky, B. I., Bilker, W. B., Siegel, S. J., Kohler, C. G., and Gur, R. E. (2009). Profile of auditory information-processing deficits in schizophrenia. *Psychiatry Research* 165: 27–37.

Turetsky, B. I., Calkins, M. E., Light, G. A., Olincy, A., Radant, A. D., and Swerdlow, N. R. (2007). Neurophysiological endophenotypes of schizophrenia: The viability of selected candidate measures. *Schizophrenia Bulletin* 33/1: 69–94.

Turner, M. and Coltheart, M. (2010). Confabulation and delusion: A common monitoring framework. *Cognitive Neuropsychiatry* 15: 346–76.

Turner, M. S., Shores, E. A., Breen, N., and Coltheart, M. (2017). Déjà vecu for news events but not personal events: A dissociation between autobiographical and non-autobiographical episodic memory processing. *Cortex* 87: 142–55.

van der Leer, L., Hartig, B., Goldmanis, M., and McKay, R. (2015). Delusion-proneness and 'jumping to conclusions': Relative and absolute effects. *Psychological Medicine* 45/6: 1253–62.

van der Leer, L., Hartig, B., Goldmanis, M., and McKay, R. (2017). Why do delusion-prone individuals "jump to conclusions"? An investigation using a non-serial data gathering paradigm. *Clinical Psychological Science* 5/4: 718–25.

Vuilleumier, P., Mohr, C., Valenza, N., Wetzel, C., and Landis, T. (2003). Hyperfamiliarity for unknown faces after left lateral temporo-occipital venous infarction: A double dissociation with prosopagnosia. *Brain* 126: 889–907.

Williams, D. (2018). Hierarchical Bayesian models of delusion. *Consciousness and Cognition* 61: 129–47.

Woodward, T. S., Moritz, S., Cuttler, C., and Whitman, J. C. (2006). The contribution of a cognitive bias against disconfirmatory evidence (BADE) to delusions in schizophrenia. *Journal of Clinical and Experimental Neuropsychology* 28: 605–17.

13

Irrationality and the Failures
of Consciousness

Paul Noordhof

One dimension along which it is tempting to characterize some mental disorders is irrationality. The two ways of understanding the irrationality of delusion in particular are in terms of epistemic rationality and procedural rationality (Bayne and Fernández 2009: 3–5). The former focuses on the extent to which a delusory belief involves a departure from what the subject has epistemic reason to believe, where epistemic reasons are those that bear on the truth of what is believed (e.g., the content of other beliefs or perceptions).[1] The latter concerns the improper functioning of the processes of belief formation. There are obvious connections between the two ideas but they are distinct. Some would allow that procedural rationality may include errors of epistemic rationality such as the conjunction fallacy (for fallacy, see Tversky and Kahneman 1982: 90–8; for inclusion see Bayne and Fernández 2009: 5). I don't want to go that far. However, procedural rationality may include belief formation that either can't be justified, for example, inductive beliefs, or the incorporation of pragmatic reasons, or influences upon confidence thresholds, such as those involved in wishful thinking supportive of an agent's self-esteem. Each of these, for example, may be given some kind of evolutionary defence.

It is typical to think that delusion lies at the extreme end of one or other of these types of irrationality, and to take this as a distinctive feature of this kind of mental disorder (e.g., Mele 2009: 64; Hirstein 2006: 214–15; for further discussion see Noordhof and Sullivan-Bissett 2023: Section 5.4). However, it is a mistake to take delusion to lie at the extreme. Setting aside those cases of delusion that involve self-deception, self-deception generally involves greater epistemic irrationality and/or more significant procedural irrationality. Quite general features of self-deception and delusion have been misunderstood and, rather than indicating

---

[1] In her chapter in this volume, Sophie Archer distinguishes between objective and subjective epistemic reasons. The characterization I have given here falls between them. They are subjective in that the contents need not be facts but rather something presented to, or taken to be true by, the subject. They are objective in the sense that, it is not a matter of whether the subject takes them to bear on the truth of what is believed but whether they do bear on the truth of what is believed (Archer, this volume).

Paul Noordhof, *Irrationality and the Failures of Consciousness* In: *Belief, Imagination, and Delusion.* Edited by: Ema Sullivan-Bissett, Oxford University Press. © Oxford University Press 2024. DOI: 10.1093/oso/9780198872221.003.0013

that delusion is at the extreme end, support the conclusion that self-deception is a more plausible candidate for the extreme. With Ema Sullivan-Bissett, I have argued this for different understandings of self-deception in an earlier work (Noordhof and Sullivan-Bissett 2023: Section 5.4). In this chapter, I will focus on a particular type of self-deception and its implications for this debate.

The argument will proceed as follows. In Section 1, I identify a feature, of a particular type of self-deception, that is taken to support the idea that the self-deceived are less irrational than those suffering from delusions: the self-deceptively favoured belief is threatened when it is the object of conscious attention along with the psychological history that led up to its adoption. The feature is mistakenly taken to show that the self-deceived are not lost to reason in the way that the deluded are. There is likewise a natural diagnosis of why bringing the psychological history of the belief to consciousness is threatening for the self-deceived, namely that they become aware of how their belief is unsupported by legitimate grounds or, indeed, that there are considerations against the belief. This may be thought to be a relatively unexceptional observation about the nature of consciousness but, in fact, I will argue that something more interesting is at work.

In Sections 2–4, I argue that a key means by which *epistemic* reasons for a belief that p result in the formation of the belief is through conscious attention. In brief, the argument runs as follows. A central process of belief formation is doxastic deliberation. The latter is appropriately characterized as involving conscious deliberation concerning what belief to have, a deliberation that has two distinctive features: transparency and uncontrollability. The explanation of these two features lies in the nature of conscious attention: it makes manifest the attractiveness of being disposed to act upon what we take to be true and the unattractiveness of being disposed to act upon what we take to be false. To establish the last point, I consider the explanations traditionally offered of the two distinctive features, and find them wanting. The principal explanation of the instability of self-deception appeals to this feature of conscious attention.

Once the role of conscious attention is established, Section 5 considers the implication for the respective irrationality of self-deception and delusion. Many monothematic delusions derive from anomalous experiences that draw the subject's attention. They are a consequence of the epistemic weight that attending consciously gives to what is presented as true along with a difficulty in attending specifically to things that don't have the same impact upon our attention. These are mundane features of normal subjects. There may be grounds for thinking that those with monothematic delusions are less able than some normal subjects to attend consciously to the epistemic reasons they have outside of those supported by experience but this is a fault we find across the range of subjects without clinical delusions.

By contrast, the distinctive instability of the self-deceptively favoured belief reveals the substantial epistemic and procedural irrationality involved. The focus

268 BELIEF, IMAGINATION, AND DELUSION

of attention away from what would undermine the self-deceptively favoured belief reveals the subject's evaluation of the reasons in favour of having the belief being wanting, either epistemically or pragmatically, and departure from this assessment. The instability of the belief, and the diversion of conscious attention from its proper role in doxastic deliberation, indicates the procedural irrationality involved.

1. Theoretical Irrationalities

People are prone to various kinds of theoretical irrationality. One is wishful thinking in which subjects believe that p because they want p to be true. Often the desire that p is true causes the belief by adjusting the confidence levels for believing that p or rejecting its negation (Trope et al. 1997: 112–23). Hypotheses that lower one's self-esteem would have to meet higher confidence levels for evidence before they are accepted. Some understand self-deception on this model, adding that the favoured belief must be false or that the self-deceived have evidence the self-deceptively favoured belief is false (e.g., Szabados 1973: 202, 205; Mele 1987a: 14; Mele 1987b: 135; Mele 2001: 73–4; for more on its irrationality compared with delusion, see Noordhof and Sullivan-Bissett 2023: Section 5.4). My focus is on a kind of self-deception distinctively different in, at least, two ways.

One way is that the self-deceptively produced belief may be the result of an intention rooted in evidence against, or even a contradictory belief to, the favoured belief. I have defended the possibility of such cases elsewhere (Noordhof 2009). The main focus of my argument will be on the second distinctive feature of self-deception: its essential instability. The self-deceptively favoured belief, or some weaker form of cognitive endorsement of a favoured content such as avowing to oneself, is the result of a psychological history that has the potential to undermine the belief, for example cognizance of the evidence against the favoured belief, a belief in the opposite of the favoured belief, an intention to have the favoured belief, etc. The instability concerns this psychological history and may be characterized as follows.

(a) The subject, S, fails to attend consciously in a certain way, W, to either the evidence against the, standardly, motivationally favoured proposition that she cognitively endorses, or some element of the psychological history characteristic of the self-deception behind the cognitive endorsement of the motivationally favoured proposition.

(b) If the subject were to attend consciously in way W to both the, standardly, motivationally favoured proposition and either the evidence against it or the psychological history (whichever applied from clause (a)), the, standardly,

IRRATIONALITY AND THE FAILURES OF CONSCIOUSNESS 269

motivationally favoured proposition would no longer be believed. This kind of instability is not to be assimilated to either the attribution of conflicting behaviour due to conflicting beliefs or the existence of 'nagging doubts' about a motivated belief one has unless the latter is a sign of the instability characterized (cf. Graham 1986: 227; da Costa and French 1990: 183–5; Lynch 2012).

I use the phrase 'attend consciously' to allow the discussion to remain neutral on two issues, as well as to single out a distinctive phenomenon. The issues are whether there can be consciousness without attention or attention without consciousness. If William James is right that "Focalisation, concentration of consciousness" are of the essence of attention, then the formulation could have been in terms of attention (James 1890: 403–4). However, there are attention effects—for example, in the case of blindsight subjects focusing on the region in which they claim to be phenomenally blind—which have been taken to show that attention may be non-conscious concerning the content of what is attended to. Involuntary direction of attention to unconscious cues suggests that the attending, as opposed to the content of what is attended to, need not be conscious either (Kentridge et al. 1999: 1810; for criticism, see De Brigard and Prinz 2010: 54–6). Equally, there is some evidence that the content of phenomenal consciousness can exceed what is attended to (Lamme 2003; for criticism see De Brigard and Prinz 2010: 56–8). Talk of attending consciously picks out the relevant phenomenon with the only risk being that the phrase is in some respect redundant. I qualify 'attend consciously' by 'in way W' to rule out possible cases in which the attention is too brief or sloppy (Noordhof 2009: 62–3).

The distinctive instability of self-deception suggests a shortcut to the question of the respective levels of irrationality involved in self-deception and clinical cases of delusion (hereafter, 'delusion') which might otherwise rest upon detailed examination of a range of cases. Delusion is often seen as a particularly strong form of theoretical irrationality whose hallmark is that the instability is no longer there (e.g., Graham 1986: 227; da Costa and French 1990: 183–5; Hirstein 2006: 214, 215; Mele 2009: 64; Funkhouser 2019: 125). What accounts for the difference? One suggestion is that the subject with a delusion that p no longer has the belief in the opposite belief. But as I have suggested above, not all cases of self-deception involving instability may have this character. Subjects with delusions may still be faced with the evidence that favours the opposite belief to that which is their delusion. Indeed, it is often taken to be part of the definition of delusion that subjects have the delusory belief in the face of the evidence. In which case, it is natural to suppose that what is different about the case of delusion is that the subject's relation to *principles of rationality* is different from the case of self-deception. They either fail to be committed to the principles of rationality that non-deluded subjects are committed to or fail to apply these principles (for a suggestion along these lines see Noordhof 2009: 69–71).

Both options just canvassed are ways of capturing the idea that delusion involves losing grip on reality and, following on from this, that delusion is (as I remarked) much worse than self-deception. It captures well how delusion is typically clinically characterized (Funkhouser 2019: 124). For example,

> A false belief based on incorrect inference about external reality that is firmly sustained despite what almost everybody else believes and despite what constitutes *incontrovertible and obvious proof or evidence to the contrary*
>   (DSM-IV, American Psychiatric Association 2000: 821)

or even DSM-V's more laconic 'fixed beliefs that are not amenable to change in light of conflicting evidence' (DSM-V, American Psychiatric Association 2013). Self-deception, by contrast, is taken to involve subjects still committed to, or aware of, the application of principles of rationality but trying to avoid the way in which they undermine the self-deceptive belief that the subject favours. I will argue that this is a misunderstanding of the contrast. As I have argued elsewhere with Sullivan-Bissett, subjects with delusions remain no less committed to principles of rationality than the normal range of non-deluded subjects but the support for their delusory beliefs is more secure (Noordhof and Sullivan-Bissett 2021; Noordhof and Sullivan-Bissett 2023). By contrast, the self-deceived really are seeking to flout or avoid the upshot of these principles. Before we get to this point, we need to understand more about the nature of doxastic deliberation and the role of conscious attention in it.

2. The Two-Faced Character of Belief and Two Distinctive Features of One Face

Beliefs have a functional, or causal, role that is both essential to, and distinctive of, them. The role breaks down into two elements. The first is the downstream motivational role characterized by beliefs' contribution to action, along with the desires, intentions, and other emotional states with which beliefs interact. The second is the formative role informed by the alleged connection between belief and truth.

Some have argued that other mental states may have the same motivational role as beliefs. David Velleman's example is of a child imagining being an elephant (Velleman 2000: 255–63). However, the imagining plays the same motivational role in limited contexts. For example, imagining you're an elephant doesn't involve worrying about the transition into being an elephant, and how this will affect one's future life (Noordhof 2001: 253). Beliefs are the most context insensitive state that are the basis of our actions. That doesn't mean that there are no contexts in which beliefs may fail to play their expected motivational role—for

IRRATIONALITY AND THE FAILURES OF CONSCIOUSNESS   271

example, some cases of self-deception and delusion—but this just shows that their *expected* motivational role is conditional upon standardly envisaged contexts rather than these special cases (Bayne and Pacherie 2005: 181, 184 make a similar move).[2] There is no need to appeal to non-doxastic states instead in these cases.[3]

If belief does have a distinctive motivational role, then we don't need to appeal to its formative role to distinguish beliefs from other states like imagining. Nevertheless, the connection with truth is independently plausible. Understanding how this should be characterized is the basis for the argument I am developing.

A central part of belief's formative role relates to doxastic deliberation. Doxastic deliberation is the process of *conscious* belief formation guided by reasons for belief. Doxastic deliberation needn't involve the concept of belief because forming a belief doesn't require the representation of that belief. This is reflected in one of the distinctive features of doxastic deliberation: (formative) *transparency*—the idea that the question of whether to believe that p is settled by the question of whether p (Shah 2003: 447). Transparency concerning the *formation* of beliefs is distinct from transparency concerning their *self-ascription*, namely in considering whether I believe that p, I consider whether p is true, although Nishi Shah explicitly took the name from Richard Moran's discussion of the latter (Moran 1994; Moran 2001; Shah 2003: 476, fn. 1). If doxastic

---

[2] In his contribution to this volume, Kengo Miyazono highlights a subject with Capgras delusion who does not believe that his wife (whom he believes is replaced by an impostor) is in danger, refuse to live with the impostor or look for his missing wife. There are a number of things to say about this type of case. First, it is compatible with the position I defend here that some cases of delusion need not involve belief. However, second, when a subject has Capgras delusion, they are often in a situation in which they have other health issues which makes it hard for them to act, have no leads to go on as to where their loved one may be, are surrounded by people who say the individual is their loved one, have the assurance of experiencing their voice (which in contrast to anomalous visual experience) does not convey that the loved one is an impostor, and so on. One could take all of these as indicating that the subject does not really believe that their loved one has been replaced by an impostor but equally one can take them as providing a special context in which the expected motivational role of the belief does not come into play. Everyday life is littered with illustrations of cases where people fail to act upon their beliefs, or draw the inferences they should. Finally, there are often good grounds for attributing belief in the delusory content. For example, a particular case that Miyazono cites in which the subject 'never became angry or aggressive' to the impostor, was 'quite pleased to see her' and 'addressed her in a very gentle way' is also one in which 'he was obviously worried about her', 'left the house and went looking for her in the streets' and 'urged her to go with him to the police to report Wilma's disappearance' (Lucchelli and Spinnler 2007: 189). This was all in the context of the onset of dementia. The motivation for attributing a belief takes the evidence for, or against, the belief in the round.

[3] In her chapter in this volume, Sophie Archer argues that there are certain possible cases of delusion whose distinctive states would fail what she dubs Anscombe's condition for beliefs, namely, that the subject takes epistemic reasons to be relevant to the question of why they believe that p. The case she has in mind is of a subject who believes that their wife is unfaithful because the fifth lamp-post on the left is unlit and who has no story about why this is a relevant consideration. It is questionable whether the correct characterization of beliefs need this additional element (Anscombe's condition) if their motivational role is otherwise distinctive. If they do, then it either provides a qualification to the motivational role (namely, that the beliefs may not have consequences for action on occasions when contradicted by a relevant epistemic reason) or suggests that, in addition to formative role, we need to recognize something that may not be involved in belief formation but in their persistence.

272   BELIEF, IMAGINATION, AND DELUSION

deliberation involved a subject evaluating what were the reasons for, as they conceived of the situation, *the belief that p* rather than the reasons for *p*, then doxastic deliberation would essentially involve the concept of belief. Formative transparency reflects how we understand doxastic deliberation.

Shah claims that transparency reflects subjects' grasp of the concept of belief regarding its connection to truth (Shah 2003: 467–8). There are significant problems with this claim. First, if the nature of belief may be captured by its motivational role alone, then it need be no part of a subject's grasp of the concept of belief that it involves a connection to truth. Second, even if the nature of belief involves a link to truth, there is no reason to think that a subject's concept of belief will reflect this or, even if it did, the subject would always have this feature of their concept of belief to the fore when they think about what to believe (as Shah seems to suppose; Shah 2003: 468–9). People make conceptual errors all the time. Philosophers are often inclined to take something to be part of our concept of such and such, other philosophers disagree, and one prosecutes the other for making a conceptual error. I'm not endorsing this way of thinking about philosophical disagreement but an implication of it is that any appeal to the concept of such and such to explain a particular persistent feature of some aspect of our mental lives is going to require an explanation of why conceptual error doesn't occur here on a regular basis or why conceptual error doesn't vitiate the explanation offered. Third, some cases of self-deception plausibly involve the intention to believe that p because of a recognition of the unattractiveness of the truth of not-p. Unlike doxastic deliberation, this involves the concept of the belief that p (in the specification of what the subject intends to do) (contrary to what Shah seems to suppose; Shah 2003: 467). Yet, this doesn't make such self-deception impossible. Of course, it is open to Shah to deny such self-deception is possible, but that is a cost. Later we will see that even setting aside these points, the normative approach that Shah favours cannot explain transparency. So there is no inference from successful explanation back to a view of doxastic deliberation in which transparency is the expression of the grasp of the concept of belief concerning its relationship to truth.

Transparency is not generally taken to be a contingent feature of *doxastic deliberation* that may not hold for other creatures (Shah 2003: 468). While some writers seem to take it as just a psychological fact about us, the apparent contingency they attribute to transparency concerns more whether they think that *non-epistemic* reasons for belief can have weight somehow in belief formation outside doxastic deliberation (e.g., Foley 1993: 16–18). Thus, transparency is taken to *support* the view that the only reasons relevant in doxastic deliberation are epistemic reasons in favour of the truth of p rather than, for example, pragmatic reasons in favour of having the belief that p which, while false, is in some way consoling (Shah 2003: 464, 468; Steglich-Petersen 2006: 503). Call the latter claim about reasons the *exclusivity thesis*.

IRRATIONALITY AND THE FAILURES OF CONSCIOUSNESS 273

It is not obvious that transparency supports the exclusivity thesis. That would depend upon whether subjects suppose that the only reasons in favour of p being the case could be epistemic reasons for p. It is familiar feature of discussion in the political arena, as well as some aspects of our personal life, that we offer reasons for p based upon the *unacceptability* of p not being true. I'm not claiming that we are rational to take into account these reasons but simply that they do seem to have weight to subjects in some cases. Illustrative examples would be that various groupings have an equal distribution of talents because of *the discrimination that would otherwise occur*, that punitive action of a certain kind is successful in curtailing the prevalence of certain behaviour because *otherwise people would get away scot-free*, or that a close friend is innocent of a charge because *taking their guilt to be a fact would be a betrayal* (for some discussion, see Noordhof 2003). These pragmatic reasons are taken to bear on the truth of p without actually providing grounds for p being true. Recognition of these cases does not throw into question transparency but just the support that the exclusivity thesis may derive from it. Transparency contains two elements and the connection between them is not a straightforward as may first appear. The first is the idea that deliberation over whether to be in a mental state turns on the question of what bears on the content of that state. The second is whether what bears on the content of the state, in the case of belief, are solely epistemic reasons for the content as the exclusivity thesis claims in the case of belief. This will become relevant later when, for example we discuss Kieran Setiya's position and formulate the preferred alternative.

A second, and potentially related, feature of doxastic deliberation is expressed by the uncontrollability thesis. It is the claim that *unmediated* conscious belief production is impossible, often dubbed 'believing at will' (Williams 1970). More explicitly, the following is not metaphysically possible ('I' standing for any subject).

(1) I form the conscious intention to believe that p now,
(2) as a result of having this intention, I believe that p now without there being any mediating act of mine which helps to produce this belief, or the support of evidence for p or p being otherwise presented as true, or a belief that by believing that p, I make p true,
(3) the intention and the belief stand in the same relation to each other as intention and action do in the case of intentional actions (Noordhof 2001).

This needs a bit of unpacking. My intention to believe that p now may be a result of a desire to believe that p and the formulation leaves open whether this desire is a reason for belief. All that is excluded is that this desire, and resulting intention, result in a belief that p in the way indicated by (3) with certain exceptions set out in (2).

274   BELIEF, IMAGINATION, AND DELUSION

The second condition excludes the following four types of cases. First, I intend to believe that my arm is raised and, by raising my arm, have the belief that my arm is raised. Raising my arm is a mediating act, as is taking a belief pill to have a belief. Second, suppose that I am told that in the next room there is conclusive evidence in favour of p. I may not have the belief that p as a result of the testimony that there is this conclusive evidence (e.g., if my interlocutor is Boris Johnson). But I could intend to form the belief by going into the room and seeing the evidence for myself. We shouldn't rule out this type of case by denying that beliefs so formed would be something I *do* because the means to forming the belief are insufficiently reliable. That would set the bar for actions being the reliable outcome of the means too high (cf. Mele and Moser 1994: 57–65 for a discussion of some of the relevant issues). As it turns out, the belief is formed by a reliable process but I just didn't know this. Equally, it is plausible that we can sometimes believe at will where the evidence is sufficient so that it is permissible to believe that p and also to withhold belief that p ('equipollent cases') (Roeber 2019: 847–8). Both of these types of cases are set to one side by the 'support of evidence for p' element. Fourth, there are cases of self-fulfilling beliefs. I may believe that I will succeed in doing something and make that belief true by the power of positive thinking. If I know Jemima, a generous neuroscientist is monitoring my brain, I may believe that I will receive £10 from her or believe that Jemima will believe that I have that belief, and either way make the belief true. If I believe in the power of positive thinking, or in the brain scanner and Jemima's generosity, then I can form the relevant beliefs if I want to (for the brain scanner case, see Peels 2015: 529). These qualifications to the uncontrollability thesis are widely noted (e.g., Hieronymi 2009: 150).

The third condition involves the recognition that an intention may produce a belief in deviant ways. For example, suppose I intend to believe that you will give me a present, you find out that I have this intention to believe, and you enlist a neurosurgeon to tamper with my brain and produce a belief in me. The causal chain runs from the intention to the belief but is not a case of belief at will in the relevant sense even if the connection is a reliable one. This illustrates the general point that the causal chain should not be deviant.

The uncontrollability thesis so characterized is the rejection of a particularly strong version of voluntarism about belief. That is the idea that one can control one's belief in the same way one can control one's raising of one's hand or thinking a thought (see, for example, Adler 2002: 56, for this characterization). Some will argue that the characterization of the uncontrollability thesis excludes too much. There are cases of believing at will that fail to meet the conditions. Rik Peels argues that self-fulfilling beliefs show that belief is susceptible to the will since we can, in those cases, decide to believe or not believe depending upon what we want (Peels 2015: 538–40). We can quibble about the characterization but the issue, for my discussion, is how to account for the uncontrollability thesis so

IRRATIONALITY AND THE FAILURES OF CONSCIOUSNESS 275

characterized. It captures an important way in which the will is hamstrung in the case of belief. While it is true that, in the absence of an epistemic reason now in favour of p, we may choose to believe that p or not-p, this is only possible when we believe that, *as a result of the choice*, there will be an epistemic reason in favour of what we believe. It is plausible that this is what people had in mind all along and the issue was simply obscured by formulating it in terms of whether somebody could form a belief that p independent of an epistemic reason for p at the time of willing.

Spinozan theories of belief present another potential complication. According to them, believing that p is the default for any kind of representing or presenting that p (Gilbert et al. 1990: 601–2; Mandelbaum 2014: 61–3). Perceiving or, most relevantly, imagining that p is believing that p. Since imagining that p can be done intentionally, and without mediation, believing that p can be done likewise (Levy and Mandelbaum 2014: 27–8). In noting this consequence, its proponents have distinguished between a thin notion of belief for which it is true and belief as understood by philosophers involving states which, in principle, persevere upon evaluation. The uncontrollability thesis would more naturally concern the latter. It is an open question whether the evidence cited in favour of Spinozan theories supports recognizing a thin notion of belief, as opposed to some other kind of representational state, given that there are clear differences between the functional role of such states and the motivational role we might plausibly attribute to belief. The theory defended at the end of the chapter accounts for some of the features that are mentioned to motivate the claim that the representational states are genuinely beliefs. But, as far as the key claim about imaginings is concerned, the earlier remarks about the relative context insensitivity of belief provides a basis for resisting the claim that imagining is believing. Recognition that imaginings may be inferentially promiscuous in a similar way to beliefs does not imply that they approach the context insensitivity of beliefs (cf. Mandelbaum 2014: 84; Sullivan-Bissett 2019: 641).

The question is whether the features of doxastic deliberation identified can be explained by appealing to theories about the relationship between belief and truth. There are three extant accounts of the connection: normative, agent-teleological, and biological-teleological accounts. I will argue that none of them can, although it is clear that they have been offered as explanations of these features (transparency: Shah 2003: 448; Steglich-Petersen 2006: 499; uncontrollability thesis: Velleman 2000: 245; Shah and Velleman 2005: 504–5). Their approaches to these two features are usefully discussed together. The connection between the failure to explain the transparency thesis and failure to explain the uncontrollability thesis is relatively straightforward. Given that subjects have no control over the way the world is, aside from the ways we have excluded in the statement of the uncontrollability thesis, if belief formation is transparent, it would seem that they cannot believe at will. Failure to explain the transparency of belief may go over to failure

276   BELIEF, IMAGINATION, AND DELUSION

to explain the uncontrollability thesis. I will then consider specific explanations of the uncontrollability thesis that draw on two features: the nature of action and the implications of Bernard Williams's talk of full consciousness (Williams 1970). These are also inadequate. Instead, the two features can be explained by recognizing the particular character of attending consciously.

3. Three Failed Explanations of Transparency and the Uncontrollability Thesis

3.1 Agent-Teleological Theories

Agent-teleological theories take subjects' controlling intentions (or desires) as the basis for beliefs having the *aim* of accepting a proposition p only if p is true (Velleman 2000: 254; Steglich-Petersen 2006: 515–16; Steglich-Petersen 2009: 546). If a subject intended to accept that p, whether or not p is true, due to pragmatic reasons, the subject would not have the controlling truth-aimed intention. If beliefs are states with the constitutive aim of truth, then accepting p without that truth-aimed intention would not be believing. That's the candidate explanation of why doxastic deliberation has the two features identified. Unfortunately, it doesn't work.

One problem concerns the relationship between the controlling truth-aimed intention and the weaker idea of a truth-regulated mechanism. Appeal to the latter enables action-teleologists to explain how beliefs can arise when a controlling truth-aimed intention is absent: for example in sub-conscious processes of perception and inference, wishful thinking, and self-deception. Denying that beliefs occur in such cases is implausible given that they have the distinctive motivational role of beliefs. As Asbjørn Steglich-Petersen acknowledges, the truth-regulated mechanism should be relatively weak if the products of wishful thinking and self-deception are to be counted as beliefs (Steglich-Petersen 2006: 502, 515–16). But then the truth-regulated mechanism isn't strong enough to explain the transparency of doxastic deliberation ('the teleologian's dilemma', Shah 2003: 464). If the truth-regulated mechanism is a weak dispositional condition of being minimally responsive to evidence relating to p while still allowing pragmatic reasons to play a role, the truth or falsity of p doesn't settle the question of whether to believe that p. This point is independent of the question I raised earlier about whether transparency supported exclusivity because some pragmatic reasons are taken to bear on the truth of a proposition. The present issue is whether there may be a reason to believe that p which does not bear upon p's truth. The weak mechanism of truth-regulation described above allows this to be a possibility.

The success of the agent-teleological explanation of transparency is going to rest, as a result, on the appeal to a controlling truth-aimed intention to

IRRATIONALITY AND THE FAILURES OF CONSCIOUSNESS   277

characterize doxastic deliberation. But this won't get past the difficulty. Even if attributing an intention to do A requires that the subject is reliably able to do A, this is not sufficient to rule out pragmatic reasons sometimes playing a role in doxastic deliberation (for a reliability condition of intention attribution see Mele and Moser 1994: 52–65). Reliability does not imply invariability.

So what should be added to an appeal to a controlling truth-aimed intention in doxastic deliberation to rule out pragmatic reasons being operative? It is tempting to appeal to the fact that doxastic deliberation involves consciousness. However, unless there is a necessary connection between the controlling truth-aimed intention and consciousness, that would mean that the explanation of the features of doxastic deliberation doesn't come from the controlling truth-aimed intention.

Perhaps the thought is that, *in being conscious*, we will be aware of our intention and doxastic deliberation will display the features of transparency and uncontrollability. There is no reason to suppose that this is the case. Even if being conscious of the truth-aimed intention helps the intention to be operative, that does not exclude the possibility that pragmatic reasons could be considered and rejected as opposed to just seeming irrelevant. Indeed, by situating the aim of belief at the agent level, the agent-teleological approach invites the objection that an agent typically is able to weigh one aim against another. Even if some of the goods at which we aim are incommensurable with each other, we can still choose to go for one rather than another. In the case of the formation of belief, the aims might be believing the truth against believing a comfortable falsehood. Yet, it seems that doxastic deliberation is exclusive. It doesn't involve weighing the truth against other aims. In which case, taking truth to be an aim of beliefs in this way doesn't explain transparency (Owens 2003: 295–300). For example, why can't a subject intend to believe that p only if p but when they find out that they will have to abandon the belief that they are a fundamentally decent person, they abandon the intention and end up retaining the belief for pragmatic reasons? Suppose it is argued that if the subject did that, then they wouldn't be forming the belief. Beliefs must follow from controlling truth-aimed intentions (e.g., Shah and Velleman 2005: 504–6). The problem is that, not only does this give rise to difficulties in the case of wishful thinking and self-deception but it can't explain transparency. If a subject considers pragmatic reasons for a belief but ends up rejecting them and forming the belief as a result of the controlling truth-aimed intention, their doxastic deliberation is still not transparent. Suppose it is argued that we are only conscious of forming a belief that p by non-observational knowledge of the controlling truth-aimed intention. Then the objection just raised is an objection against this position. We wouldn't cease to be conscious of forming a belief by abandoning the controlling intention in favour of another aim of belief formation.

It is important to recognize that the objection from weighing ends is not answered by pointing out that there might be occasions when, for pragmatic reasons, a subject elects not to find out the truth on a particular subject, for

278　BELIEF, IMAGINATION, AND DELUSION

example, the teacher who decides not to find out which of their pupils broke the window because they would have to punish them (Steglich-Petersen 2009: 403). The controlling truth-aimed intention is not that the subject find out the truth no matter what but rather that pragmatic reasons can't outweigh the fact that a particular proposition is false. Equally, if a subject sets things up so that they later falsely believe something good about themselves on the basis of misleading evidence, this doesn't demonstrate that they have weighed the aim of truth against some other pragmatic end in the appropriate sense. At this point, the subject doesn't have the controlling truth-aimed intention. The objection was that if a subject has an aim, not just whether they are considering whether to have an aim, then it should still be possible for the subject to weigh that aim against other aims they have. Actions generally allow the weighing of other aims during the course of them. For example, if I am reaching out to turn a door handle to open a door and I'm suddenly made aware that it has been wired to give me an electric shock, I can stop the action in mid flow. That is not the case with regard to doxastic deliberation over what belief to have. Even if I'm suddenly aware of the fact that evidence supports a belief it would be damaging for me to have, I can't change course and it is this fact that needs explaining (for more discussion see Sullivan-Bissett and Noordhof 2013, 2017).

One final defence of an agent-teleological approach to belief turns the focus onto the subject's commitments when they end up believing that p. The idea is that believing that p is being answerable to reasons bearing upon whether p. Pragmatic reasons do not settle the question of whether p is true and so only go towards bringing oneself to believe that p. In bringing oneself to believe that p, one is not committed to being answerable for p (Hieronymi 2006: 62–3, calls them 'extrinsic reasons'). For this reason, Pamela Hieronymi argues, we can't actually believe that p as a result of pragmatic reasons. This is a candidate explanation of transparency. Forming a belief that p cannot be an action (and so are not things that we can believe at will) because actions are done for pragmatic reasons whereas forming a belief that p involves making oneself committed to be answerable for p (the content of the belief) upon which pragmatic reasons generally do not bear (Hieronymi 2009: 158–66). Only epistemic reasons (her 'evaluative' reasons) are relevant. The exception would be the belief that this belief is worth having (Hieronymi 2009: 161, fn. 22). In brief, we can't become committed to p on the basis of reasons that don't settle the question of p for us (Hieronymi 2009: 165).

The proposal appeals to a richer notion of belief than that understood in terms of motivational role alone. Thus, a limitation of the approach is that it cannot explain why deliberation leading up to such a state (we may call that doxastic$_{mrstate}$ deliberation) displays the two identified features. However, even on its own terms, the proposal faces problems.

First, the constitutive aim is characterized in terms of a necessary condition, the intention to believe that p only if p. This is wise because we would not want a subject to clutter their minds with all kinds of trivial beliefs (if their intention,

IRRATIONALITY AND THE FAILURES OF CONSCIOUSNESS   279

instead, was to believe p if p). The commitments that a subject who ends up believing that p incurs do not change the picture. They are answerable to epistemic reasons for and against p but this does not rule out a role for pragmatic reasons in believing that p so long as the necessary condition is met. In which case, even if we have an explanation of the uncontrollability thesis, we have no explanation of transparency.

Second, subjects are committed to, and answerable for, self-deceptive beliefs. By the nature of the case, these commitments apply even though self-deceptive beliefs are not formed by considering epistemic reasons alone. So we cannot derive the characteristic role of epistemic reasons in doxastic deliberation from claims about what a subject is committed to and answerable for. Of course, it is open to Hieronymi to claim that we cannot form a belief in full consciousness in the way that we do in the case of self-deceptive beliefs. But this, now, is an assertion of that for which we were seeking an explanation. It doesn't drop out of what a subject is committed to.

Linguistic acts underline the point just made and highlight a third problem. When we assert that p, we are committed to the truth of p, and are answerable for this assertion, because a constitutive aim of assertion is truth or knowledge (we can remain neutral). Yet we can assert that p to deceive people for sound pragmatic reasons. Of course, assertion is one thing and belief is another but the fact that they share the same constitutive aims and involve the same commitments suggests that we can't appeal to them to explain why doxastic deliberation is transparent and the uncontrollability thesis holds of it.

Of course, it is possible for Hieronymi to deny that we are really committed to what we assert in the cases where we have pragmatic reasons for so doing. Instead, we are pretending to be committed and hoping to fool people by the pretence. But this suggests that commitment is too slippery a notion to give us real explanatory purchase on the phenomena we are seeking to explain. After all, we might reasonably insist that somebody who asserts p is genuinely committed to p being the case, even if they haven't properly considered whether p, because they should and will be held to account. The suggestion that there is an internal sense in which they are not really committed relies upon the fact that, generally, we can't believe that p for pragmatic reasons rather than explaining why we can't.

3.2 Normative Approaches

The only plausible truth norm is

You are permitted to believe that p if and only if p.

Evidence that this is what normativists have in mind is that they have characterized the norm in terms of the prescription to believe that p only if p is true and

280 BELIEF, IMAGINATION, AND DELUSION

suggested that prescriptions involve only permissions (Shah 2003: 470–1; Shah and Velleman 2005: 519). There remains the possibility that they should formulate the norm in terms of obligation. There are, at least, two considerations against that.

First, if we ought to believe anything that is true, our mind will be cluttered with beliefs. Even if this is restricted to those issues upon which we focus, for example, the number of blades of grass in Regent's Park and all the implications of that fact, we still end up with the obligation to have a potentially infinite number of beliefs (Bykvist and Hattiangadi 2007: 279). The permissibility formulation reflects Gilbert Harman's plausible clutter avoidance meta-principle on principles of belief revision (Harman 1986: 15).

Second, there is the case of blindspot propositions of the form p and I don't believe that p. I would be under the obligation to believe the corresponding blindspot proposition for every true proposition I don't believe and end up with a false belief for each (Bykvist and Hattiangadi 2007: 281–4).

If the norm related to truth is the permissibility norm characterized above, then this norm allows, indeed requires, non-truth connected reasons to settle whether to believe that p. No matter how much evidence there is in favour of p, or how p is independently compelling, all that follows is that a subject is permitted to believe that p. In which case, it follows that it cannot explain transparency.

We can put the argument like this.

(1) If a subject's epistemic reasons R_1, R_2, R_3, for p entail that p, then S is permitted to believe that p (from the truth norm).

(2) There are no epistemic reasons in addition to R_1, R_2, R_3 for p, such that if S is apprised of them, S is not just permitted but obliged to believe that p (from the truth norm).

(3) Epistemic reasons for p are the only reasons recognized by the norm of truth.

(4) The question of whether to believe that p is not settled by it being permissible to believe that p.

(5) In doxastic deliberation, we do settle whether to believe that p.

Therefore

(6) The appeal to the norm of truth does not explain transparency.

The first premise applies the truth norm to a particular circumstance in which a subject, who is doxastically deliberating may find themselves. I'm assuming that they wouldn't be deliberating over whether to believe that p if they already believed that p but that entailment of p by other reasons is as good as the subject's position is likely to be in such deliberating. The second premise points out that, if entailment of p gives rise to permission to believe, things aren't going to get any

IRRATIONALITY AND THE FAILURES OF CONSCIOUSNESS   281

stronger, and move the subject to being obliged to believe, with additional epistemic reasons for p. The third premise draws out an implication of the norm of truth, namely that epistemic reasons are the only reasons that bear on whether p. (4) expresses a plausible negative condition on what counts as settling a question. It is not enough that a certain answer is permissible. (5) excludes the possibility that the norm of truth shows that nothing is ever settled in doxastic deliberation. This enables us to conclude that the normative approach cannot explain transparency given the characterization of the truth norm. Or, to put it another way, transparency suggests that the nature of the norm of truth should be otherwise than it is but it can't be. So transparency cannot be explained in terms of the norm of truth. The mistake was to assume that if no other reasons could count in favour of a belief that p, than reasons for p, that would be sufficient to explain transparency.

A second argument in favour of the inadequacy of the normative approach shows that the existence of pragmatic norms of belief formation has not been successfully excluded. In which case, the candidate account of transparency fails. The argument runs as follows.

(1) There are pragmatic norms concerning whether we should *produce* beliefs *indirectly* by other means than doxastic deliberation.
(2) The direct/indirect distinction is not normatively significant.
(3) There are pragmatic norms relating to belief formation.
(4) If the norms relevant for belief are to explain transparency, there are no pragmatic norms concerning belief formation.

Therefore,

(5) The norms relevant to belief don't explain transparency.

If somebody offers you £1 million to believe that the number of blades of grass on your lawn is even, then there is a pragmatic reason in favour of *having the belief*. It would considerably further your interests whereas the epistemic down-side of having the belief is minimal. The belief is not a substantial one and it may be true for all you know. So there is a case in favour of there being a pragmatic reason in favour of producing, at least, one belief. There are, of course, many cases of this type. Setting aside general scepticism about the connection between reasons and norms that would vitiate the whole normative approach, if there is a prag-matic reason in favour of *producing* a belief, it is plausible that there is a pragmatic norm concerning this production in, at least, the following sense. There is a permission to believe that p that is, at least, partly a result of the subject being possessed of a reason for having the belief in question. I say 'partly' to allow for possibility that there must always be an epistemic element too. For example, it

282   BELIEF, IMAGINATION, AND DELUSION

may be permissible to believe that p in virtue of the pragmatic reason so long as there is no epistemic reason to believe that not-p.

This, by itself, doesn't mean that there is a pragmatic reason *for the belief*. The question of whether there is depends upon the significance of the claim that, in the case of belief, the pragmatic reason only bears on the production of the belief by indirect means. By contrast, epistemic reasons seem to result in belief without any mediation being required. In other areas, pragmatic reasons may bear upon an upshot although it is only produced indirectly. For example, there might be a pragmatic reason to please your head of department but you will only do that by taking on a collection of tasks nobody could conceivably want to do otherwise. That doesn't mean that the pragmatic reason doesn't apply to pleasing your head of department. Whether something can be achieved directly or indirectly isn't normatively significant as far as the application of the pragmatic reason is concerned. This is what premise (2) asserts (for further support, see Rinard 2015: 212–14; Leary 2017: 538–9; Rinard 2017: 135–6).

It might be argued that the key is not the indirect character of the production of belief but rather the fact that belief is not an action and, therefore, not something that pragmatic reasons can bear on or, indeed, something that can be constrained by norms of any sort. I have some sympathy with this line of thought but it is not helpful to the proponent of the normative approach. The normative approach seeks to explain transparency in terms of the failure of pragmatic reasons to apply. The response just made suggests that this is, in turn, to be explained in terms of whether something counts as an action or not. In which case, it is not the application of norms but the point about action that both explains transparency and is in need of explanation. In any event, the fact that it is permissible to please your head of department is not vitiated by your head of department's pleasure being a state rather than an action.

Premise (4) articulates the connection between a normative approach's explanation of transparency and denying that there are pragmatic norms relating to belief formation. Even if permission to believe that p by epistemic reasons is required, whether to believe that p cannot be settled by epistemic reasons alone. Pragmatic reasons have a role to play contrary to what transparency suggests (Leary 2017: 541 suggests otherwise). The normative insignificance of the distinction between direct and indirect production of an outcome vitiates the normative approach in general.

In one respect, the uncontrollability thesis may be easier to explain for the normativist's approach. The permissibility norm only permits belief in p if p is true. So if p is false, then belief in p is not permitted and, the argument runs, we cannot will that we believe that p. Doxastic deliberation does not have to be transparent for this explanation to be available. If norms had determinative weight with the subject, then this would explain why they couldn't believe at will.

IRRATIONALITY AND THE FAILURES OF CONSCIOUSNESS   283

To see why it is ineffective as an explanation of the uncontrollability thesis, it is helpful to compare a normative approach in this area with moral norms. Consider the following plausible characterization of the relationship between your moral belief about what you ought to do and your motivation.

If you ought to do A/believe you ought to do A, and are practically rational, you will be motivated to do A.

Moral norms are often taken to override non-moral norms and yet it is possible for agents to act immorally. The connection between what you ought to do, or believe you ought to do, and what you are motivated to do and, thus, how you act, is qualified by the practical rationality of the moral agent. We noted earlier that a plausible characterization of the epistemic norm is

It is permissible to believe that p if and only if p.

To bring out the parallel, suppose that you believe that it is impermissible to believe that p. A standard case would be when your evidence is sufficient to establish that not-p. Whether you believe that p will depend upon whether you are theoretically rational. There are circumstances in which you may not be. One example is Thomas Scanlon's case of the untrustworthy friend (Scanlon 1998: 35–6). You have sufficient evidence to believe that they are untrustworthy yet, when you are with them, their apparent sincerity and protestations of affection lead you to believe that they are trustworthy on a certain matter. This case can be understood in different ways. It could be a straightforward case of wishful thinking. Alternatively, it can be a genuine case of epistemic akrasia in which, although the apparent genuineness constitutes a consideration in favour of believing that they are trustworthy, this evidence is outweighed by the evidence that they are untrustworthy. Yet, you irrationally base your belief on the outweighed evidence. Either way, the important point is that belief about what you are normatively constrained not to believe is insufficient to establish that it is not possible to form that belief. It is just that, if you do, you are theoretically irrational. Without an explanation of how epistemic norms are more forceful than moral norms, there is no way of making a normative explanation of the uncontrollability thesis work. In their explanation of the uncontrollability thesis, Shah and Velleman appeal to what is involved in doxastic deliberation having the aim of truth addressed in 3.1.

3.3 Biological-Teleological Theories

The biological-teleological account starts with the idea that, in the past, our belief-producing mechanisms were selected because they produced true beliefs. These

284   BELIEF, IMAGINATION, AND DELUSION

beliefs, along with a creature's desires, are part of the normal explanation of actions that satisfied the desires in question. Satisfaction of creatures' desires explained why these creatures proliferated by passing on their genes. Beliefs have a derived relational proper (i.e., its own) function from the selection history just described. The function is *derived* from the function of the belief-producing mechanisms since particular beliefs may be novel and have no evolutionary history. The function is *relational* in the sense that the creature, who has the belief, is adapted to the environment in which their action is successful (Millikan 1984: 39). In the present case, the relation would be to the circumstances in the environment that hold when the belief is true. The *normal explanation* citing the belief is an explanation of how they carry out their proper function (Millikan 1984: 2, 33–4).

Doxastic deliberation is part of the normal conditions—those that figure as part of the normal explanation—in which true beliefs are produced. Doxastic deliberation is transparent because a subject having the disposition to settle the question of whether they should believe that p by settling the question of whether p produces true beliefs leading to successful action (Sullivan-Bissett 2018: 3467–8). Call this the *transparency disposition.*

By placing their emphasis on explaining the presence of the transparency disposition by evolutionary selection, proponents of the biological-teleological approach underline the fact that there are, at least, two types of explanation of transparency. The first focuses on how the nature of doxastic deliberation makes it transparent. The agent-teleological and normative accounts are attempts to provide the first type of explanation. The second focuses on explaining the presence of the transparency disposition. Part of the explanation of the latter might appeal to something about the nature of doxastic deliberation—and so draw on an explanation of the first type—but the main focus is on how something with that character is present in the first place (Sullivan-Bissett 2018: 3467–8).

Given the failures of the agent-teleological and normative accounts, it is natural for proponents of the biological-teleological approach to limit their response to the first type of explanatory question to the claim that there are certain neurological structures as a result of which, when a subject considers the question whether to believe that p, they just consider whether p is true. The shift to the sub-personal at this point avoids having to answer questions about pragmatic norms or how different aims than truth fail to have application to doxastic deliberation (Sullivan-Bissett 2018: 3453, 3469–70). However, avoiding these questions should not be mistaken for an explanatory advance and an analogous issue recurs within the context of the appeal to selective history that is taken to answer the second explanatory question. There are reasons to be sceptical about whether evolutionary selection would favour a neurological structure that grounds the transparency disposition. Additional explanatory material is needed which raises many of the issues we have already identified for previous accounts.

IRRATIONALITY AND THE FAILURES OF CONSCIOUSNESS   285

The first concerns the balance of the utility of true beliefs against other ways in which beliefs may be useful, for example, to maintain sufficient self-esteem to be able to act effectively, avoid psychologically distressing beliefs, and so on. Both sorts of beliefs can be grouped under the general category: beliefs that make successful action more likely. Some will be relevant to the success of a particular action, others will be the background for the success of a particular type of action, or action in general. Recognition of these competing ways in which beliefs may support successful action, as a result of which creatures so acting may successfully pass on their genes, need not undermine the biological basis for the transparency of doxastic deliberation but it presents a challenge.

The proponent of a biological-teleological approach may argue that there are two distinct neurological structures involved in belief formation. The neurological structure relating to doxastic deliberation is transparent because it is unaffected by the considerations in play for the second mechanism behind belief formation (e.g., Sullivan-Bissett 2018: fn. 22, pp. 3467–8). The problem is that since their subject matters overlap—true beliefs about oneself are useful—how do potential conflicts between the results of these mechanisms get resolved and which takes priority. Either this is done at a sub-personal level or a personal level. Proponents of the biological-teleological approach may suggest that this is done at the sub-personal level because this preserves their explanation of the transparency disposition but they fail to explain why this is plausible from the biological-teleological perspective, and exactly how it works.

Perhaps a more plausible way of resolving the issue of true beliefs against beliefs useful in other respects is to argue that there is a single mechanism for arriving at true beliefs that is adjusted by confidence thresholds for p and not-p derived from pragmatic factors. Thus, the reason why subjects tend to have beliefs that support their self-esteem is because the threshold for believing that they are competent is set low and believing that they are not competent is set high (see e.g., Trope et al. 1997: 126–7). That doesn't explain how this was the evolutionarily preferred solution or why transparency is preserved but it provides a basis for seeking to resolve the issue. One consequence of this suggestion is that it abandons the attempt to understand the connection between belief and truth (as opposed to the useful) by a straightforward appeal to the biological function of beliefs.

The need for a promissory note here may be acknowledged and the emphasis placed on the success of the biological-teleological approach in providing an explanation of the second type, namely the causal explanation of neural structures instantiating the transparency disposition. This brings to me second problem facing the biological-teleological theory: malfunction.

When we attribute a function to a particular mechanism as a result of an evolutionary history, there is always the possibility that the mechanism will have the function and yet fail to function appropriately. The typical example is the heart that has the function of pumping blood around the body and yet can fail in various

286 BELIEF, IMAGINATION, AND DELUSION

ways to do this. If the process of doxastic deliberation has the function of producing true beliefs, then this should fail in various ways. The question is why doesn't this process fail in one of the following two ways: first, take non-epistemic reasons in favour of a certain belief (and thus, the process would not display transparency); second, at times, enable a subject to produce a belief at will.

It can't be argued that the reason why there are no malfunctions of the relevant types is that true beliefs are so important to survival. It is conceded that they are not always important and, anyway, having a beating heart is very important too. And yet we come across malfunctions relating to the heart and other essential organs. The charge is that the proponent of the biological-teleological approach has no explanation of the presence of the transparency disposition and the inability to believe at will. The evolutionary story can only explain something weaker: a neurological structure of belief formation resulting in enough true beliefs for the survival benefits to accrue. The absence of these kinds of malfunction indicates that a standard evolutionary story does not apply.

A tempting response would be to say that we do have malfunctions of doxastic deliberation. That's what occurs in self-deception and wishful thinking. But this doesn't fit the bill for a number of reasons. First, they don't seem to display either of the two malfunctions we specified, for example, consciously taking pragmatic reasons into account in doxastic deliberation. Second, they might either be the result of the *proper functioning* of the second process of belief formation recognized or that process malfunctioning (if the two neurological structure response was adopted). They are not obvious cases of the *malfunctioning* of the first process: doxastic deliberation. Indeed, proponents of the biological-teleological approach face a dilemma. If they suggest that there are cases of malfunctioning of doxastic deliberation involving the influence of pragmatic factors, then they have to deny that they can account for the transparency disposition and inability to believe at will. On other hand, if they say that, when there is malfunctioning of this kind, then we don't have doxastic deliberation, then they haven't explained how doxastic deliberation may involve malfunctioning. Instead they're explaining how belief formation more generally may involve malfunctioning. In which case, the challenge stands.

4. Action, Full Consciousness, and the Uncontrollability Thesis

Up until this point, we have considered explanations of the uncontrollability thesis that may be derived from explanations of transparency. In developing my own proposal, it is helpful to turn our focus to the uncontrollability thesis.

It may seem that the explanation of the uncontrollability thesis is straightforward and doesn't need to appeal to any of the theories we have specified. Unlike raising one's arm, or imagining a pink elephant, believing something is not an action. Beliefs are *states* with a certain causal profile. So there is no reason to think that we need some specific explanation over and above the observation that only actions are something we can do at will.

This is a mistake. The uncontrollability thesis is neutral over whether belief is an action and, if belief is not an action, still identifies something that needs to be explained. The claim is that it is not possible that there is an action that involves intention relating to the state of belief in a way that is characteristic of an action. Many actions are characterized in terms of a terminating state, consider the previous example of making my head of department happy or the simple action of putting a plate on a table. The thesis is neutral over whether we call this candidate action culminating in the state of belief: believing, forming a belief, judging, or something else. The question is why can't our intentions be related to such a state in the way distinctive of action.

Both in Williams's formulation of the uncontrollability thesis and my characterization of it, there is talk of full consciousness. Williams writes:

> If I could acquire a belief at will, I could acquire it whether it was true or not. If in full consciousness I could will to acquire a 'belief' irrespective of its truth, it is unclear that before the event I could seriously think of it as a belief, i.e. as something purporting to represent reality. At the very least, there must be a restriction on what is the case after the event; since I could not then, in full consciousness, regard this as a belief of mine, i.e. something I take to be true, and also know that I acquired it at will.   (Williams 1970: 58)

The conscious element is important because, as we have already noted, self-deception of the kind identified in Section 1 may have the structure of believing at will. The suggestion is that believing at will can only occur, if at all, in the absence of consciousness (Adler 2002: 59). With regard to the discussion of the theories we have considered earlier, although reference to consciousness occurred in the characterization of doxastic deliberation, the explanatory significance of this was not explored. We focused on whether the theories could account for features of doxastic deliberation so characterized and found that they could not.

There are broadly three approaches to the explanatory role of consciousness, and specifically full consciousness. According to the first approach, consciousness is the vehicle of operation of other factors. For example, if you're fully conscious of the norms that govern belief formation or the aim of belief formation, then these norms or aims will make themselves felt more. Whereas, if you are not conscious, you may fail to take them into account. Our earlier discussion demonstrates that appeal to consciousness in the first way doesn't help with the theories discussed so far since none of the features identified helped to explain the character of doxastic deliberation an essential feature of which was that it is a *conscious* process.

288   BELIEF, IMAGINATION, AND DELUSION

According to the second approach, appeal to consciousness works with certain plausible constraints on action to explain why we cannot believe at will. I will argue in what follows that the original promise of such theories is not borne out. According to the approach I favour, the appeal to full consciousness actually shows something about consciousness over and above how it may be a vehicle of operation of other factors.

One appeal to the interaction between consciousness and action focuses upon what we must believe if we intend to do A. Setiya argues that if a subject is doing A intentionally, then they either believe that they are doing A or else doing A by doing some other action A* that they believe that they are doing (Setiya 2008a: 41). In forming a belief, we become progressively more confident that p until we hold that p. The problem with believing at will is that we would be becoming progressively more confident that p while believing that we are not justified in doing so given, in the key case, p lacks evidential support. This is what Setiya takes to be impossible (Setiya 2008b: 42–6).

One problem with Setiya's position is that he assumes that, in intentionally becoming more confident, one has got to articulate to oneself the conditions that make this a case of believing at will, namely that one is becoming more confident *while believing that one is not justified in becoming more confident*. There is no reason why this should be part of the content of the intention. It does not fall out of his condition on what is involved in doing A intentionally. All that is required for this condition is that you intend to have the belief while, in fact, it is the case that you don't have the evidence to support it. Equally, if you don't appreciate that you lack evidence, it is no failure of full consciousness that you don't. Full consciousness requires that, if we appreciate our situation, we are conscious of it. Full consciousness is not omniscience about the circumstance of our action. It is as if Setiya is providing an explanation for why we think we cannot believe at will rather than why we can't.

A final problem is that an explanation of why a subject cannot believe at will shouldn't rest on the assumption that they must be rational in their action. We know people can act irrationally and any appeal to rationality at this point is liable to assume the phenomenon it is seeking to explain. But once this is recognized, it is apparent that subjects can become increasingly confident—as an act of will— that p and yet realize that p is not justified. Their confidence in p comes from elsewhere, for instance, it is simply something that must be believed due to the painfulness or unacceptability of failing to believe that p (Hieronymi 2009: 180–1).

A related proposal rests upon the assumption that subjects who form a belief at will, as a result of a pragmatic reason for believing that p, would have to have a break in the conscious production of their action to shift from the perspective in which they fail to believe that p, but have a pragmatic reason for believing that p, to that in which they focus on whatever grounds would enable them to believe that p. These might include *selectively* focusing on particular epistemic reasons

IRRATIONALITY AND THE FAILURES OF CONSCIOUSNESS   289

for p which are, in the wider situation in which the subject finds themselves, insufficient for p. The break in consciousness is taken to be incompatible with something counting as an action (Scott-Kakures 1994: 93–6; for further discussion see Noordhof 2001: 249, fn. 2; Radcliffe 1997).

The problem is that this is an implausible condition on action generally. Consider the subject who is trying to complete a golf swing successfully. If you asked the subject to make sure that they focused upon how each element of their action related to the reason that led to them engaging in the action in the first place, the action is unlikely to be successful. Successful action plausibly requires breaks in its conscious production. In which case, the fact breaks would have to occur in the case of believing at will cannot be a reason why believing at will is not possible. This reinforces the point made earlier about the normative insignificance of direct versus indirect action. Even if the only way we could form a belief involves deliberately focusing on, or choreographing, evidence in its favour, this would not establish that the result wasn't a belief formed at will with the breaks in consciousness required for its success between the prior pragmatic reason and subsequent epistemic reasons the focus on which resulted in the belief. We might not have fluent performance of such belief-forming actions but it is hard to maintain that the reasons for them cannot be counted as reasons for believing that p (for further discussion, see Rinard 2019: 774–5). Once indirect cases are conceded and breaks in consciousness allowed in cases of successful direct action, the explanation for why there can't be direct cases of conscious belief formation fails.

The second main way of trying to combine consciousness and action into an explanatory package focuses on the end result. Keith Frankish's idea is that it is not possible to believe at will because

> For any proposition p, it is impossible to believe in full consciousness both that one consciously believes that p and that one's belief is unsupported and deviant.
> (Frankish 2007: 532)

A belief is deviant if it is produced by our desires or intentions rather than our recognition of the epistemic reasons in favour of the truth of the belief. The putative end state is self-undermining as a result of which the target belief cannot be formed. He is not arguing that one cannot directly form a belief at will if one thinks of the belief one is trying to form as unsupported and deviant because, as he notes, that is too close to an assertion of the phenomenon he is seeking to explain. The claim is rather that, if one finds oneself in such a state, then full consciousness of how it was produced would undermine it (Frankish 2007: 532).

The difficulty for Frankish's proposal is that it is not plausible that the end state is self-undermining. It is a familiar fact that the following Moore sentence is impossible to believe, although not a contradiction:

290 BELIEF, IMAGINATION, AND DELUSION

p and I do not believe that p.

and it is plausible that the weaker statement that

p and there is sufficient reason to believe that not-p

is impossible to believe because the justification one has for self-attributing the belief that p, which one expresses by 'p', would imply that there is not a sufficient reason to believe that not-p.

However, Frankish's characterization of the end state is not to be assimilated to either of these. Full consciousness that one's belief is unsupported, and has been caused by, say, an intention to believe that p, need not be self-defeating if it seems to you that the proposition believed is true. We are familiar with having beliefs for which we no longer remember the reasons (Harman 1986: 41, as Frankish acknowledges Frankish 2007: 531). In those cases, so long as we believe that we did have reasons at one point, and there are no reasons against the belief now, it may be rational to retain the belief. In the case of believing at will, we don't believe that we once had reasons for the belief. That may be enough to make it rational to adjust one's belief. But the content of what we end up believing may still strike us as true. Beliefs can strike us as independently plausible, even though we have a deviant path to them of which we are aware. Consciousness of the belief as having a suspect history, unless this history implies that there is sufficient reason to *disbelieve* the target proposition, is guaranteed to be self-undermining (for illustration of some cases see Noordhof 2003; see also Rinard 2019: 775–6).

The difficulties identified with approaches appealing to the interaction between consciousness and action seem terminal. They appeal to features of the process or end state that are inadequate to explain the phenomena. Instead, we should look seriously at the idea that the two features of doxastic deliberation identified demonstrate something about the character of a particular type of consciousness. Conscious attention makes manifest the attractiveness of being disposed to act upon what is presented as true (rather than what is comfortable to believe (say)) and unattractiveness of being disposed to act upon what is not presented as true.

When I say 'being disposed to act' what I am adverting to is the attractiveness of being in a state with the motivational role of belief or judgement. My talk of presented as true is supposed to cover the case of perception—in which, by being in a perceptual state, one perceives O being F (where p is that O is F)—and the case of inference from prior beliefs with the content that $E(p)$—in which one believes or judges that $E(p)$ and $E(p)$ is sufficient evidence for p. It does not imply that 'true' is part of the content of the states I described but just picks out a class of states with a certain relation to the content that p. When something seems true perceptually but we have evidence of which we are convinced against it (e.g., cases

IRRATIONALITY AND THE FAILURES OF CONSCIOUSNESS   291

of visual illusion), I take it that the content of perception is not presented as true for the subject.[4]

I remain neutral on what may count as sufficient evidence for p. I assume that if E(p) entails p, then E(p) is sufficient evidence for p. However, something short of entailment may also count as sufficient evidence for p and this may vary because of pragmatic factors relating to the subject's interests. Sufficient evidence for p should not be characterized in terms of the obligation to believe p given what I have argued earlier regarding the proper characterization of the truth norm. However, there are some grounds for allowing its characterization in terms of a wide scope permission—namely that the following is a permitted combination of states: having the belief that E(p) and having the belief that p—so long as the holding of this wide scope permission allows for relativization to the practical interests of the agent.

A necessary condition upon conscious attention making manifest the attractiveness of being disposed to act upon what is presented as true is that, as result of such attention, the subject has the overwhelming desire to be in this dispositional state. Conscious attention to the absence of p being presented as true has the result that the subject has the overwhelming desire not to be in the state in question. In terms of the framework I have defended elsewhere, the attractiveness (or value) of being disposed to act upon what is presented as true is represented by being disposed to desire to believe that p (Noordhof 2018: 98–107). The key aspect of conscious attention making manifest the attractiveness of being disposed to act upon what is presented as true is that it provides the circumstances in which this disposition to desire to believe is manifested in an overwhelming desire to believe that p. The role it plays is brought out by the failures we have identified with previous accounts.[5]

First, the overwhelming character of these desires explains how other ends that we desire fail to be weighed in the process of doxastic deliberation in which we consciously attend to what is presented, or not presented, as true. The puzzle identified for action-teleological accounts is, in fact, evidence for this feature of conscious attention.

'Making manifest the attractiveness of being disposed to act upon what is presented as true' is thus not to be understood as being conscious of whatever attractiveness is possessed by being disposed to act upon what is presented as true. Rather, the idea is that conscious attention gives determinative weight to the attractiveness of this. The attractiveness of other things—for example, being disposed to believe what is presented as comfortable to believe—is set to one side.

---

[4] Thanks to Julia Langkau for pointing out the need for this clarification.
[5] I'm grateful to Fabrice Teroni, Julien Deonna, and Roberto Keller for the line of question that prompted me to think further about this (in chronological order of questioning I believe).

292   BELIEF, IMAGINATION, AND DELUSION

'Set to one side' is importantly different from the attractiveness being reduced or silenced. When we look at the evidence for an uncomfortable belief that p, it is not that we no longer see any attraction in believing that not-p. Indeed, we can even recognize that in a certain sense we ought to believe that not-p. For example, suppose the evidence favours a negative assessment of a friend's abilities. We may feel that we ought to believe in their abilities (even if this feeling that we ought to is mistaken) because that is what friends are for. So the claims aren't silenced and, if we say that they are reduced, then this carries the mistaken suggestion that the obligation to have a positive view of their negative abilities no longer seems as important. Instead, the attraction of believing in line with the evidence—the desire to be disposed to act upon what is presented as true—is overwhelming so that the other claims, by comparison, seem irrelevant. Transparency and the uncontrollability thesis are consequences of this feature of conscious attention.

Second, while, we have allowed that there are both pragmatic and epistemic norms relating to truth, the latter is only a permissibility norm. Conscious attention to sufficient evidence for p has two consequences. First, it is not possible to believe not-p no matter what the pragmatic reasons in favour of not-p are. Conscious attention gives no weight to them because the attractiveness of believing that p is made manifest over all alternatives. Second, although the norm only gives permission, conscious attention makes acting upon that permission attractive at the expense of alternatives. Making manifest the attractiveness of being disposed to act upon what is presented as true takes the permission to believe that p (expressed by the norm of truth) and changes it into a desire. Conscious attention, in effect, helps answer the question of why, if epistemic norms are only permissions, we end up believing anything at all.

In the case of the uncontrollability thesis, if you are attentively conscious of not-p (either presented in perception or in judgements or beliefs that E(not-p)), then you will only be motivated to judge or believe that not-p and, thus, you will not be able to intend to judge or believe that p. Suppose the situation instead is that you have no presentation of the truth of not-p. In that case, you won't be able to will that p because conscious attention makes manifest, in the same way, the unattractiveness of being disposed to act upon what is not presented as true overwhelms whatever the attraction is of believing that p. In this case, the failure to represent p being presented as true as attractive to believe, results in an overwhelming desire to believe that not-p.

In the case of transparency, the overwhelming character of the desires that are the result of conscious attention explains why the question of whether to believe that p in doxastic deliberation is settled by the question of whether p. The characterization of doxastic deliberation in terms of consciousness rather than conscious attention might suggest that there will be cases of doxastic deliberation in which the question of whether to believe that p is not settled by the question of whether p. Pragmatic reasons may seem to have some weight. However, when a

IRRATIONALITY AND THE FAILURES OF CONSCIOUSNESS   293

subject focuses on the question of whether to believe that p, the issue becomes the centre of their conscious attention. As a result, only reasons that bear on the question of whether p have weight.

The approach may be developed within a biological-teleological framework. Doxastic deliberation involving conscious attention may explain the instantiation of the transparency disposition and be part of a normal explanation of belief formation. True beliefs are not guaranteed but their formation is only concerned with whether or not they are presented as true and this makes belief formation sufficiently reliable. When doxastic deliberation involves conscious attention on the question of whether p, then we don't have a case of malfunctioning belief formation. However, belief formation may malfunction in various ways, most salient of which are those cases in which a subject fails to attend consciously to the question of whether p. The mistake in the development of the biological-teleological approach mentioned earlier is to identify the wrong target for the attribution of biological function and fail to recognize the independent explanatory contribution that identification of the properties instantiated when there is no malfunction may play. Once this explanatory contribution is recognized, there is no need for evolutionary considerations to involve an explicit appeal to truth as opposed to usefulness. Whether an evolutionary story can be told of the presence of conscious attention in a properly functioning process of doxastic deliberation remains to be seen. The plausibility of my proposal doesn't depend upon it.

As I have already noted, a subject's interests may have an impact on the confidence thresholds for believing that p and believing that not-p. This allows for a pragmatic influence upon doxastic deliberation but not in a way that qualifies the claim that it is transparent. From the perspective of the view developed here, the influence is felt with regard to the way in which conscious attention on whether p is presented as true results in an overwhelming desire to believe that p. In low stakes situations, what counts as p being presented as true may be less demanding than in high stakes situations, with consequent impact on whether the overwhelming desire is formed.

Earlier I noted that there were occasions when it seems unacceptable to believe not-p because of the moral implications of doing so, partisanship or loyalty, and p is presented as true independent of the evidence for p. Presentation as true in such cases is a complex of factors. It would be a mistake to take p to be a priori true or self-evident in the sense that contemplation of p (independent of evidence for it) is sufficient to be entitled to believe that p. P just seems plausible in the light of the unacceptability of believing other than p and, often, in addition emphasis on how the evidence for not-p could hold without not-p being true. Although the plausibility possessed by p is insufficient in itself for belief that p, in the context described, p is presented as true.

It is a familiar fact that we have some beliefs where we have forgotten the reasons for why we have them. Even if we are attentively conscious to this

294   BELIEF, IMAGINATION, AND DELUSION

situation, we don't seem to lose the belief. Why don't we lose them on the grounds that the unattractiveness of believing something that is not presented as true is made manifest to us? The answer is that what we remember is presented as true either in itself or because we believe that we did have good reasons for what we remember although we, now, do not know what they were. Harman's principle of conservatism

> One is justified in continuing fully to accept something in the absence of special reason not to (for example, positive belief that one's reasons were no good)
>
> (Harman 1986: 39, 46)

explains how the observations about conscious attention work in such cases.

5. Consequences for Delusion and Self-Deception

In Section 1, I identified an essential feature of a particular kind of self-deception: an instability characterized in terms of what would happen if we attend consciously to the psychological history that led up the favoured belief, or other cognitive endorsement, of self-deception. By contrast, except for those cases of monothematic delusion that involve self-deception mentioned below, cases of monothematic delusion do not display the same instability. The orthodox view of the significance of this difference is that the lack of instability in the case of delusion displays a subject's deeper departure from rationality. Instead, I suggested that most cases of delusion involved a lesser departure from rationality than that involved in self-deception.

From the discussion in Sections 2–4, we see that conscious attention has a key role in the explanation of two features of doxastic deliberation: transparency and the uncontrollability thesis. Self-deceivers avoid having their beliefs formed by doxastic deliberation and, more generally, avoid conscious attention having the psychological history behind the belief as its focus along with the belief. Self-deceivers, sometimes intentionally, avoid the epistemic reasons they have recognized against the self-deceptively favoured belief being given the weight that they are given when a subject attends consciously to them.

As I have noted, when there are strong pragmatic reasons in favour of the product of self-deception, this doesn't have to be irrational overall. However, when self-deception takes this character, it typically doesn't involve the instability characterized but just influences the confidence thresholds for believing the target proposition p, and its negation, in a way closer to wishful thinking (Mele 2001). Subjects don't take these pragmatic reasons as counting in favour of the self-deceptively favoured belief. Instead, the pragmatic reasons operate as part of an integrated process of doxastic deliberation, preserving the features of transparency

IRRATIONALITY AND THE FAILURES OF CONSCIOUSNESS 295

and the uncontrollability thesis, by adjusting the thresholds that relate epistemic reasons to the overwhelming desire they generate. It is plausible that these cases of self-deception would be procedurally rational. However, the stronger form of self-deception involves significant procedural irrationality because the pragmatic reasons neither appropriately outweigh the epistemic reasons, nor operate on the confidence thresholds, but rather result in the subject turning their attention away from epistemic reasons that are against the self-deceptively favoured belief with resulting instability.

Some cases of delusion are plausibly characterized as self-deception displaying the distinctive instability, for example, a form of anosognosia involving the denial of hemiplegia (Ramachandran 1996: 348, 355; Noordhof and Sullivan-Bissett 2023: 15). Even here, the motivational elements seem to be different from more typical cases of self-deception. These cases of delusion involve an inhibition of an inhibitor to the self-deceptively favoured beliefs rather than something more deliberately, although unconsciously, planned (Noordhof and Sullivan-Bissett 2023: 16). The question remains what we should say about cases of delusion that don't involve the distinctive feature of self-deception.

While there may be, in theory, cases of delusion that involve subjects who are no longer committed to the principles of evidential reasoning that give rise to the distinctive instability of self-deception, the cases of monothematic delusion we come across do not display this lack of commitment. Instead, the instability is absent because subjects don't have the suppressed belief that is contrary to the delusory belief or have a basis for their delusory belief in experience. A key part of many, potentially all, monothematic delusions is that the subject has anomalous experiences that their delusory belief is an attempt to make sense of. Thus, in contrast to the self-deceived, subjects with delusions aren't trying to avoid having certain experiences that undermine the favoured belief. The experiences in question support the belief.[6]

---

[6] Archer's discussion focuses on a subject who believes that his wife is unfaithful because the fifth lamp-post to the left is unlit without any further explanation of why the fact about the lamppost supports the verdict. The case seems to be an Othello delusion. If that's right, I question whether the description is accurate of the subject's overall situation. Even if it is, it does not qualify the conclusion I'm drawing here about monothematic delusions in general since they typically don't have the character Archer describes. There are also questions about Archer's overall argument that subjects with such delusions don't take epistemic reasons to be relevant to their belief. First, granting that the lamp-post experience fails to present an epistemic reason for the subject to believe that his wife is unfaithful, and the subject is not responsive to this fact, it still might be the case that the subject unconsciously recognizes epistemic reasons to be relevant for their belief (something Archer allows in the self-deception case, p. 236) by citing the fact about the lamp-post. Unconscious recognition of something may manifest itself inappropriately. The simple fact that some ground is cited for a belief (even if what is cited doesn't count as an epistemic reason) can be evidence of the recognition. Second, Archer's grounds for rejecting the subject as taking the content of the experience as an epistemic reason is that, absent a story, it displays too much confusion on the part of the subject to take the lamp-post experience as counting in favour of the belief (Archer, this volume, p. 237). However, Archer allows

296 BELIEF, IMAGINATION, AND DELUSION

On the assumption that the anomalous experiences are conscious experiences, then what they present is going to be the object of conscious attention. The fact that attending consciously to what is presented as true by experience gives them an additional weight in the formation of belief suggests a straightforward explanation of why subjects with delusions have the beliefs that they do. They are the result of the normal operation of conscious attention. Subjects with delusions are not more irrational than subjects who are self-deceived but rather the victims of the anomalous experiences that they have. At best, these subjects may be epistemically rational. Typically, though, if certain aspects of what we experience capture our attention and/or the epistemic reasons they provide are overweighted relative to other reasons we may have, then they may result in irrational beliefs. But, to the extent this is the case, it is an irrationality that all subjects suffer with respect to their conscious experience. It is a familiar fact of everyday life that we all find it difficult to arrive at more measured views on issues where our everyday experience very much favours a particular belief in conflict with the more measured view.[7]

Many have argued that to understand delusion we need to identify a second clinical factor to explain why some subjects form delusory beliefs on the basis of anomalous experiences and others do not (Langdon and Coltheart 2000: 201–6; Davies et al. 2001: 144). If a second factor is required, then this may be, or result in, significant irrationality justifying the claim that delusions are more irrational than self-deception both epistemically and procedurally. I have argued elsewhere, with Sullivan-Bissett, that there is no reason to look for a second clinical factor in

---

that there is a possible story in which the unlit lamp-post is relevant. Given that, there is no reason for supposing that the subject is any more confused than everyday cases in which people cite reasons that ostensibly fail to support a particular belief and are, similarly, inarticulate or unreflective about what else is needed for the support to be present. The basis of the claim that they take the lamp-post experience as presenting an epistemic reason for their jealous belief is not that they are possessed of a story about its relevance but that they, perhaps implicitly, believe that there is such a story.

[7] In their contribution to this volume Douglas Lavin and Lucy O'Brien suggest that delusions have a particular kind of non-literal content, which they seek to articulate independently of the issue of the kind of mental state that has this content (e.g., belief or imagining), expressing a subject's extreme disruption with respect to their relation to themselves. They take the expression of this content to be an affective phenomenon involving distress. In being the expression of an affective state, the contents are not taken to be produced with the aim of saying something true but rather expressing how the subject feels. So they would resist my claim that what subjects with delusions were saying was supported by the experiences they were undergoing. Their position doesn't seem sensitive to the way in which such subjects acknowledge the perplexing character of what they believe, the evidence against it, the way that they over time do respond to evidence, even in Cotard cases, and can show curiosity about the consequences of their hypotheses understood literally. This doesn't mean there isn't an affective element behind the delusion but emphasis on it shouldn't be at the expense of the cognitive aspect of the delusion which may be an explanation of distress as well as, potentially, caused by affective states (see Noordhof and Sullivan-Bissett 2021: 10302). The difference between the position I defend and theirs in part depends upon whether the emphasis is placed upon analogies with everyday experiences of extreme emotion (as they do) or on everyday responses to anomalous experiences (as I do). Everyday subjects who are undergoing experiences of extreme emotion equally tend not to say stuff like 'I have lost a part of me although I see that this is a weird thing to say because of all the medical evidence is that I'm intact'. They'd be more likely to say 'I'm describing what it feels like. Of course it is not literally true'.

IRRATIONALITY AND THE FAILURES OF CONSCIOUSNESS   297

seeking to explain monothematic delusions (Noordhof and Sullivan-Bissett 2021). Different responses to anomalous experience can be explained by individual differences between subjects in the normal range of responses to experience rather than anything clinically abnormal. There are many plausible individual differences that may give rise to different responses. For the present discussion, one interesting possibility is individual differences relating to different capacities of consciousness, specifically, conscious attention.[8]

Subjects may differ in the extent to which they give conscious attention to what is presented in experience, or fails to be presented in experience, as opposed to the content of other beliefs and judgements. These differences may ramify regarding the sensuous memories that result from experience. Experience is informationally rich and attention grabbing so contents of other beliefs and judgements are under a *prima facie* disadvantage. This *prima facie* disadvantage may be exacerbated by distinct mental styles and motivational differences. Some may be more inclined to attend to what they are experiencing and less inclined to focus on the beliefs that might throw that experience into question. For example, they don't focus on the belief that it is possible that the impostor-like quality of the loved one may be due to a failure to respond affectively as a result of damage to visual processing typical of Capgras as opposed to taking that experience at face value as indicating something is wrong with the person they took to be a loved one. We all know people in daily life who know what they experienced regardless of the other considerations we attempt to offer.

Might proponents of a two-factor theory of monothematic delusion reasonably argue that the different patterns I have adverted to are a clinically significant abnormality? There is no need to interpret the differences in this way to have an explanation of why delusory belief is formed. We may just differ in what we attend to, our motivational states may exacerbate this, and these result in differences in what beliefs we form. Such differences need not be the result of a deficit, or some generally characterized clinically significant bias. There is no reason to think that these different patterns of attention may constitute an abnormal performance failure (see e.g., Gerrans 2001; for detailed discussion of these options, see Noordhof and Sullivan-Bissett 2021).

---

[8] In his contribution to this volume, Garry Young argues that there is a second factor involved because there is neurological damage in Capgras subjects, although he acknowledges that the damage might not produce an abnormality in reasoning as opposed to a difference in the normal range of responses by a rational subject. There are a number of problems with this suggestion. The first is that it seems to conflict with his earlier recognition that the second factor has got to produce a clinically significant abnormality. The second is that if it is accepted that damage might just produce an alteration within the normal range of responses by a rational subject, then there will be Capgras cases amongst those with anomalous experiences but without the damage. This has, in fact, been found (Brighetti et al. 2007). The common explanation of Capgras cases will be the normal range difference they display rather than what, in particular, caused the difference in one case or another, e.g., neurological damage.

298   BELIEF, IMAGINATION, AND DELUSION

It may be helpful to compare the current approach with Brendan Maher's defence of the one-factor theory. Maher suggested that the difference between those who had delusions and those who did not is that the kinds of experience of those with delusions were 'much more intense and prolonged' and 'repeated or continue over an extended period' (Maher 1999: 566; Maher 2006: 182). I don't rule out this possibility but the difference can also be accounted for by the different strategies of attention I mentioned earlier or the amount of energy required to attend to one thing rather than another. Their attention may be more caught by experience and less by what they otherwise believe. This has an impact upon what is taken to be true.

To give an illustration of what I meant a moment ago about the energy required, a close relative of mine, previously of a sceptical and scientific orientation, found it increasingly difficult (due to old age and the effects of a stroke) to set his experiences in a context where immediate appearances are not necessarily taken on trust. For example, the fact that nurses were attending to people in distress was taken to be a sign that they were torturing the patients in question. This was not an invariable response. When the relative was tired, lacking in intellectual energy, and had a period of isolation, these kind of beliefs were manifested. However, when not tired and interacting, they showed a greater capacity to understand the nature of their surroundings and set things into context. This suggests that individual differences can arise rather like the mistakes of tiredness rather than because of something substantially abnormal. Our capacity to maintain contact with reality, balancing experience with background belief, is a hard won skill requiring mental energy and can be lost in the way that I have indicated.

Observations of this kind have been cited in favour of the so-called Spinozan theory of belief formation. The basic idea is that subjects default to believing what they perceive or, indeed, imagine and it takes additional mental energy, or resources, to reject what is immediately believed (Mandelbaum 2014: 69–75). We can allow for the possibility that we don't default to believing no matter what while explaining that, when we attend consciously to what is presented as true, we will believe that it is the case as a result of the overwhelming desire engendered. Mental energy and resources are required to reject to reject the belief for other reasons to which our conscious attention is not drawn without effort. When a subject persistently has anomalous experiences of a particular kind, this process will be ongoing and tiring.

In his contribution to this volume, Philip Gerrans sets out an account of the Cotard delusion that both explicitly rejects a two-factor account and centres the explanation of the delusion in terms of default thoughts that are the consequence of a breakdown of the default mode network that subserves imagination, dreaming, and memory and part of which constitutes our experience of ourselves. Loss of our experiences of ourselves gives rise to the distinctive default thoughts of

IRRATIONALITY AND THE FAILURES OF CONSCIOUSNESS   299

Cotard delusion like I don't exist. The tenacity of such default thoughts is explained by the breakdown coupled with a breakdown in decontextualized supervision (see also Gerrans 2014: 38, 83-6; Gerrans 2022: 14–15). Gerrans suggests that neither a second factor in the clinical sense is required (with this I agree) nor is it the case that there is any explanatory purchase to be obtained by reference to different patterns of attention or energy required.

The are two distinct issues raised by Gerrans approach. The first is that we are familiar with the fact that experiences we have, and thoughts that tenaciously come to us, need not result in belief. We may reject them, as opposed to endorse them, by bringing to bear other considerations. The question is why do subjects with delusions fail to do this? Talking about a particular kind of experience, or combination of experiences, giving rise to tenacious default thoughts is to label the thing that needs to be explained rather than explain it. Citing a lesion resulting in the breakdown of decontextualized supervision appeals to the same second deficit factor as Max Coltheart and co-workers do, shorn of its characterization in terms of belief evaluation (as Gerrans acknowledges 2014: 150–1). I have expressed my reservations with this elsewhere (Noordhof and Sullivan-Bissett 2021: 10292–4, and this chapter, fn. 6). But, even on its own terms, it does not explain how a subject can recognize the *relevance* of evidence against the delusory belief and yet retain it. Such a recognition would seem to indicate some form of decontextualization. My suggestion is that some subjects with delusions end up having delusions because of features of their conscious attention that are entirely normal but make them susceptible to delusion, perhaps at certain times (if the point about the energy required is well taken). The idea is that, while their attention may briefly be drawn to evidence against their delusion, they will invariably turn their attention to what their experience presents to be the case and so the delusory belief persists.

The second issue concerns the issue of distinct explanatory levels. Gerrans notes that his general characterization of delusion, as the result of

default cognitive processing, unsupervised by *decontextualised processing,* [that is] *monopolized* by *hypersalient information,*

may not map easily onto our everyday characterizations of delusion in terms of beliefs, attention, failures of rationality, and so on (Gerrans 2014: 38–41). This might be behind the thought that mention of attention and failures of rationality does not have anything explanatory to offer. Against this, the following points seem relevant. First, even if there is no easy mapping, the causal explanatory legitimacy of higher level states may be compatible with recognition of the causal explanatory significance of lower level states upon which the higher level states, at least partly, supervene. I have defended this elsewhere (e.g., Noordhof 1999; Noordhof 2006; Noordhof 2020: Ch. 9). Second, reference to higher level states raises different explanatory questions. For one thing, it raises the possibility that a

300 BELIEF, IMAGINATION, AND DELUSION

certain kind of delusion may be realized in more than one way in different individuals or creatures. We have already seen how some subjects don't seem to have lesions said to be behind deficits of various kinds or how there might be different ways in which decontextualization happens. For another, characterization in terms of higher level states can raise the question of why a phenomenon that typically has a certain kind of consequence at the personal level doesn't have it in the case of a certain kind of delusion, for example, some subjects don't take certain kinds of experience on trust so why do some subjects with delusions seem to do so?

A problem for two-factor theories is that their identification of a second clinically abnormal factor relating to belief formation and evaluation has the potential to have widespread ramifications. There is no reason to expect that the beliefs formed and retained should cluster round a certain theme as happens in the case of monothematic delusion. Recognizing that delusions may result from clinically insignificant differences in what we consciously attend to does not suffer from this problem. Most of what we attend to is quite normal. The problem is when a subject has anomalous, striking, or traumatic experiences. They can be overly inclined to attend to these experiences with the result that they form beliefs that are distinctive of monothematic delusions, or are otherwise distorting of their recognition of the way things are, or, simply, lack the energy to continually fight against the beliefs which naturally occur as a result of conscious attention. These beliefs become the basis for further beliefs that are confirmed by experiences interpreted in the light of the prior beliefs. Bayesian approaches to perception provide one model of this. As a result, delusory beliefs can entrench themselves. These differences explain why delusory subjects need not generally be more credulous with regard to experience (e.g., visual illusions) and yet struggle in the circumstances described (Davies and Coltheart 2000: 25–7).

We should be more wary than we are of anomalous, striking, or traumatic experiences. They can trap us in a system of beliefs that is increasingly unhelpful for us to understand the world in which we live and conscious attention, which is so often a means by which epistemic reasons have particular force over other motivational elements, can, in such cases, lead subjects astray.

References

Adler, Jonathan E. (2002). *Belief's Own Ethics* (Cambridge, MA: MIT Press).

American Psychiatric Association (2000). *Diagnostic and Statistical Manual of Mental Disorders* (Fourth edition) (Washington, DC: American Psychiatric Association).

American Psychiatric Association (2013). *Diagnostic and Statistical Manual of Mental Disorders* (Fourth edition, Text Revision (DSM-V-TR)) (Washington, DC: American Psychiatric Association).

IRRATIONALITY AND THE FAILURES OF CONSCIOUSNESS   301

Bayne, Tim and Fernández, Jordi (2009). 'Delusion and Self-Deception', in Tim Bayne and Jordi Fernández (eds.), *Delusion and Self-Deception* (New York: Psychology Press), 1–21.

Bayne, Tim and Pacherie, Elisabeth (2005). 'In Defence of the Doxastic Conception of Delusion', *Mind & Language*, 20/2: 163–88.

Brighetti, Gianni, Bonifacci, Paola, Borlimi, Rosita, and Ottaviani, Christina (2007). '"Far from the heart far from the eye": Evidence from the Capgras Delusion', *Cognitive Neuropsychiatry*, 12/3: 189–97.

Bykvist, Krister and Hattiangadi, Anandi (2007). 'Does thought Imply Ought?', *Analysis*, 67/4: 277–85.

da Costa, Newton C. A. and French, Steven (1990). 'Belief, Contradiction and the Logic of Self Deception', *American Philosophical Quarterly*, 27/3: 179–97.

Davies, Martin and Coltheart, Max (2000). 'Introduction: Pathologies of Belief', *Mind & Language*, 15/1: 1–46.

Davies, Martin, Coltheart, Max, Langdon, Robyn, and Breen, Nora (2001). 'Monothematic Delusions: Towards a Two-Factor Account', *Philosophy, Psychiatry and Psychology*, 8/2–3: 133–58.

De Brigard, Felipe and Prinz, Jesse (2010). 'Attention and Consciousness', *Wiley Interdisciplinary Reviews: Cognitive Science*, 1/1: 51–9.

Foley, Richard (1993). *Working Without a Net* (Oxford: Oxford University Press).

Frankish, Keith (2007). 'Deciding to Believe Again', *Mind*, 116/463: 523–47.

Funkhouser, Eric (2019). *Self-Deception* (London and New York: Routledge).

Gerrans, Philip (2001). 'Delusions as Performance Failures', *Cognitive Neuropsychiatry*, 6/3: 161–73.

Gerrans, Philip (2014). *The Measure of Madness* (Cambridge, MA: MIT Press).

Gerrans, Philip (2022). 'A Vessel Without a Pilot: Bodily and Affective Experience in the Cotard Delusion of Inexistence', *Mind and Language*, 1–22. https://doi-org. libproxy.york.ac.uk/10.1111/mila.12441.

Gilbert, Daniel T., Krull, Douglas S., and Malone, Patrick S. (1990). 'Unbelieving the Unbelievable: Some Problems in the Rejection of False Information', *Journal of Personality and Social Psychology*, 59/4: 601–13.

Graham, George (1986). 'Russell's Deceptive Desires', *The Philosophical Quarterly*, 36/143: 223–9.

Harman, Gilbert (1986). *Change in View* (Cambridge, MA: MIT Press).

Hieronymi, Pamela (2006). 'Controlling Attitudes', *Pacific Philosophical Quarterly*, 87: 45–74.

Hieronymi, Pamela (2009). 'Believing at Will', *Canadian Journal of Philosophy, Supplementary Volume*, 35: 149–87.

Hirstein, William (2006). *Brain Fiction* (Cambridge, MA: MIT Press).

James, William (1890). *The Principles of Psychology, Volume 1* (New York: Dover Publications).

Kentridge, R. W., Heywood, C. A., and Weiskrantz, L. (1999). 'Attention Without Awareness in Blindsight', *Proceedings of the Royal Society B: Biological Sciences*, 266/1430: 1805–11.

Lamme, Victor A. F. (2003). 'Why Visual Attention and Awareness Are Different', *Trends in Cognitive Sciences*, 7/1: 12–18.

Langdon, Robyn and Coltheart, Max (2000). 'The Cognitive Neuropsychology of Delusions', *Mind & Language*, 15/1: 184–218.

Leary, Stephanie (2017). 'In Defense of Practical Reasons for Belief', *Australasian Journal of Philosophy*, 95/3: 529–42.

Levy, Neil and Mandelbaum, Eric (2014). 'The Powers that Bind: Doxastic Voluntarism and Epistemic Obligation', in Jonathan Matheson and Rico Vitz (eds.), *The Ethics of Belief* (Oxford: Oxford University Press), 15–32.

Lucchelli, F. and Spinnler, H. (2007). 'The Case of Lost Wilma: A Clinical Report of Cagras Delusion', *Neurological Science*, 28: 188–95.

Lynch, Kevin (2012). 'On the "Tension" Inherent in Self-Deception', *Philosophical Psychology*, 25/3: 433–50.

Maher, Brendan (1999). 'Anomalous Experience in Everyday Life: Its Significance for Psychopathology', *The Monist*, 82/4: 547–70.

Maher, Brendan (2006). 'The Relationship Between Delusions and Hallucinations', *Current Psychiatry Reports*, 8: 179–83.

Mandelbaum, Eric (2014). 'Thinking Is Believing', *Inquiry*, 57/1: 55–96.

Mele, Alfred (1987a). 'Recent Work on Self-Deception', *American Philosophical Quarterly*, 24/1: 1–16.

Mele, Alfred (1987b). *Irrationality* (Oxford: Oxford University Press).

Mele, Alfred (2001). *Self-Deception Unmasked* (Princeton, NJ and Oxford: Princeton University Press).

Mele, Alfred (2009). 'Self-Deception and Delusions', in Tim Bayne and Jordi Fernández (eds.), *Delusion and Self-Deception* (New York: Psychology Press), 55–69.

Mele, Alfred R. and Moser, Paul K. (1994). 'Intentional Action', *Noûs*, 28/1: 39–68.

Millikan, Ruth (1984). *Language, Thought, and Other Biological Categories* (Cambridge, MA: MIT Press).

Moran, Richard (1994). 'Interpretation Theory and the First Person', *The Philosophical Quarterly*, 44: 154–73.

Moran, Richard (2001). *Authority and Estrangement* (Princeton, NJ: Princeton University Press).

Noordhof, Paul (1999). 'Causation by Content', *Mind & Language*, 14/3: 291–320.

Noordhof, Paul (2001). 'Believe What You Want', *Proceedings of the Aristotelian Society*, 101/3: 247–65.

Noordhof, Paul (2003). 'Self-Deception, Interpretation and Consciousness', *Philosophy and Phenomenological Research*, 57/1: 75–100.

Noordhof, Paul (2006). 'Environment-Dependent Content and the Virtues of Causal Explanation', *Synthese*, 149: 551–75.

Noordhof, Paul (2009). 'The Essential Instability of Self-Deception', *Social Theory and Practice*, 35/1: 45–71.

Noordhof, Paul (2018). 'Evaluative Perception as Response-Dependent Representation', in Anna Bergqvist and Robert Cowan (eds.), *Evaluative Perception* (Oxford: Oxford University Press), 80–108.

Noordhof, Paul (2020). *A Variety of Causes* (Oxford: Oxford University Press).

Noordhof, Paul and Sullivan-Bissett, Ema (2021). 'The Clinical Significance of Anomalous Experiences in the Explanation of Monothematic Delusion', *Synthese*, 199/3: 10277–309.

Noordhof, Paul and Sullivan-Bissett, Ema (2023). 'The Everyday Irrationality of Monothematic Delusion', in Paul Henne and Samuel Murray (eds.), *Advances in Experimental Philosophy of Action* (London: Bloomsbury), 87–112.

Owens, David (2003). 'Does Belief Have an Aim?' *Philosophical Studies*, 114: 283–305.

Peels, Rik (2015). 'Believing at Will Is Possible', *Australasian Journal of Philosophy*, 93/3: 524–41.

Radcliffe, Dana (1997). 'Scott-Kakures on Believing at Will', *Philosophy and Phenomenological Research*, 57/1: 145–51.

Ramachandran, V. S. (1996). 'The Evolutionary Biology of Self-Deception, Laughter, Dreaming and Depression: Some Clues from Anosognosia', *Medical Hypotheses*, 47: 347–62.

Rinard, Susanna (2015). 'Against the New Evidentialists', *Philosophical Issues*, 25: 208–23.

Rinard, Susanna (2017). 'No Exception for Belief', *Philosophy and Phenomenological Research*, 94/1: 121–43.

Rinard, Susanna (2019). 'Believing for Practical Reasons', *Noûs*, 53/4: 763–84.

Roeber, Blake (2019). 'Evidence, Judgment and Belief at Will', *Mind*, 128/511: 837–59.

Scanlon, T. M. (1998). *What We Owe to Each Other* (Cambridge, MA: Harvard University Press).

Scott-Kakures, Dion (1994). 'On Belief and the Captivity of the Will', *Philosophy and Phenomenological Research*, 54/1: 77–104.

Setiya, Kieran (2008a). 'Practical Knowledge', *Ethics*, 118: 388–409. Reprinted in his (2017) *Practical Knowledge* (Oxford: Oxford University Press), 39–61 [page references in text to latter].

Setiya, Kieran (2008b). 'Believing at Will', *Midwest Studies in Philosophy*, 32: 36–52.

Shah, Nishi (2003). 'How Truth Governs Belief', *The Philosophical Review*, 112/4: 447–82.

Shah, Nishi and Velleman, J. David (2005). 'Doxastic Deliberation', *The Philosophical Review*, 114/4: 497–534.

Steglich-Petersen, Asbjørn (2006). 'No Norm Needed: On the Aim of Belief', *Philosophical Quarterly*, 56/225: 499–516.

Steglich-Petersen, Asbjørn (2009). 'Weighing the Aim of Belief', *Philosophical Studies*, 145: 395–405.

Sullivan-Bissett, Ema (2018). 'Explaining Doxastic Transparency: Aim, Norm, or Function', *Synthese*, 195: 3453–76.

Sullivan-Bissett, Ema (2019). 'Biased by Our Imaginings'. *Mind & Language*, 34: 627–47.

Sullivan-Bissett, Ema and Noordhof, Paul (2013). 'A Defence of Owens' Exclusivity Objection to Beliefs Having Aims', *Philosophical Studies*, 163/2: 453–7.

Sullivan-Bissett, Ema and Noordhof, Paul (2017). 'Another Defence of Owens's Exclusivity Objection to Beliefs Having Aims', *Logos and Episteme*, 8/1: 147–53.

Szabados, Bela (1973). 'Wishful Thinking and Self-Deception', *Analysis*, 33/6: 201–5.

Trope, Yaacov, Gervey, Benjamin, and Liberman, Nira (1997). 'Wishful Thinking from a Pragmatic Hypothesis-Testing Perspective', in Michael S. Myslobodsky (ed.), *The Mythomanias: The Nature of Deception and Self-Deception* (Mahwah, NJ: Lawrence Erlbaum Associates), 105–31.

Tversky, Amos and Kahneman, Daniel (1982). 'Judgments of and by Representativeness', in Daniel Kahneman, Paul Slovic, and Amos Tversky (eds.), *Judgment Under Uncertainty: Heuristics and Biases* (Cambridge: Cambridge University Press), 84–98.

Velleman, J. David (2000). 'On the Aim of Belief', in J. David Velleman, *The Possibility of Practical Reason* (Oxford: Oxford University Press), 244–81.

Williams, Bernard (1970). 'Deciding to Believe', in Howard Evans Kiefer and Milton Karl Munitz (eds.), *Language, Belief, and Metaphysics* (Albany, NY: SUNY Press). Reprinted in his (1973) *Problems of the Self* (Cambridge: Cambridge University Press), 136–51.

Index

For the benefit of digital users, indexed terms that span two pages (e.g., 52–53) may, on occasion, appear on only one of those pages.

adaptive fitness 61, 64, 67, 113, 135–6, 142, 171, 191, 193, 247, 284, 285, 286
addiction 65
agency 5, 11, 35–6, 46, 86, 190, 192, 193, 234, 252
alief 57
Anton's syndrome 5, 70, 210
aphantasia 6, 11, 12, 108, 114, 118–19, 121, 122, 123, 124

belief
  aim of 1, 8, 15, 43, 44, 86, 208, 227, 232, 276–9, 287, 290, 292
  as behaviour guiding 1, 12, 29, 45, 48, 52, 54–55, 83, 94, 95–6, 129, 131, 137, 141, 236, 270–1, 272, 275, 278, 285
  biological account of 1, 9, 15, 275, 283–86, 293
  evidence for 1, 15, 45, 48, 55, 83–4, 86, 99, 240–1, 243, 245, 274, 276, 278, 280, 283, 289, 290, 292
  and inconsistency 55, 99, 129, 130, 137
  and inference 55, 83, 94
  justification of 116, 123, 133, 134, 266, 288
  normativity of 1, 2, 9, 15, 44, 45, 86, 87, 95, 171, 208, 240, 272, 275, 279–83, 284, 287, 291, 292
  occurrent 37, 56
  rationality of 3, 86, 234, 235, 240, 283, 290
  reasons for 14, 228, 230, 232–8, 266, 267, 271–3, 275, 276–9, 280–2, 286, 288–9, 290, 292, 294, 295
  spinozanism 275, 298
  teleological account of 1, 2, 9, 15, 275, 276–9, 284, 291
  and truth 1, 9, 15, 27–2, 44–5, 109, 208, 227, 232–3, 275, 277, 285, 287, 290, 293
  at will 9, 15, 83, 85, 267, 273–5, 276, 277, 279, 283, 286–7, 288–90, 292, 294, 295
  see also delusion, continuum thesis, religious attitudes
bimagining 3, 22, 23, 47, 55
blindsight 5, 70, 269
boxology 10, 28, 29, 39, 43, 51, 53, 57, 109–10, 113, 116, 117, 119–21, 122–4

capgras delusion 4, 7, 13, 22, 25, 26, 29, 30, 31, 33, 35–6, 46, 58, 129, 138–9, 151–78, 206, 210, 213, 222–3, 228, 255, 256, 271, 297
Charles-Bonnet syndrome 70–1
confabulation 29, 37, 100, 143
confirmation bias 86
conspiracy attitudes 7, 99, 130–1, 138, 139, 140, 141, 142, 143
consciousness, *see also* conscious attention 5, 7, 9, 15, 21, 37, 38, 61, 65, 68, 70, 85, 89, 153, 155, 156, 157–8, 160, 162, 163–4, 166, 167, 168, 169, 170, 173, 176, 177, 198, 216, 218, 219–20, 223, 230, 231, 235–6, 255, 276, 277, 279, 286–90, 292, 295–7
conscious attention 267–9, 270, 276, 290–4, 296, 297, 298, 299, 300
continuum theses
  belief/imagination 1, 3, 5, 10, 21, 42, 46, 47, 49–54, 56–7, 109
  delusional belief/other belief 26, 214, 227
cotard delusion 4, 7–8, 13, 47, 54, 58, 183–8, 194–6, 198–202, 206, 210–11, 213, 220, 240, 256, 296, 298–9
counterfactuals 7, 12, 69, 131, 133, 135, 136, 142

daydreaming 14, 81, 98, 102, 135
default mode network 135, 140, 185, 198, 199, 201, 298
delusion
  and abductive inference 7, 176, 254–5
  abnormal data 153, 159, 160–2, 163, 166, 167–9, 173, 177
  and attention 201–2, 255
  and avowal 82, 138, 139, 141, 208, 209, 216, 220–21, 223
  as behaviour guiding 3, 7, 10, 22–3, 25, 26–7, 29, 30, 54, 98, 99, 129–30, 139, 187, 271
  bayesian reasoning 153, 160–1, 167, 176, 201, 243
  belief evaluation 13, 155, 175, 176–7, 200, 255–6, 299, 300
  brain damage 13, 56, 60, 71, 130, 153–8, 162–3, 166, 167, 169, 172, 175–6, 185, 188, 189, 200, 206, 220, 249, 254, 256, 297, 299, 300

306 INDEX

delusion (*cont.*)
doxasticism about 1–2, 3–4, 8, 24, 26, 186,
206–8, 214, 217, 227–8, 241
evidence for 1, 3, 4, 8, 9, 13, 14, 25, 26, 27, 54,
151, 152, 153, 154, 161, 175, 177, 214,
221, 223, 240–1, 244, 248–51, 255, 257–8,
269–70, 299
and folk psychology 27, 201, 206, 217,
218, 221
as imaginings 3, 8, 22, 25, 35, 61, 98, 140, 206,
208–9
insight 13, 24, 186, 200–1, 217
hypothesis selection 160–2, 167–70,
176–7, 217
maintenance 152–3, 173, 175, 178, 201–2
monothematic 15, 71, 130, 140, 171,
206, 228, 254, 267, 294, 295–6,
297, 300
non-doxasticism about 2–4, 8, 9, 14, 25–6, 37,
130, 227–8, 238, 271
rationality of 4, 8, 9, 15, 155, 160–1, 169–170,
177, 184, 200, 201, 207–8, 214, 217, 227,
229, 266, 267, 268, 269, 270, 294, 296,
297, 299
reasoning bias 8, 9, 15, 177, 207, 244, 245,
248–52, 253, 254, 255–6, 297
reasoning abnormality 9, 154, 160–1, 168–9,
175–6, 184–5, 186, 187, 201, 202, 217,
252, 297
reasons for 3, 8, 14, 164, 227–33, 237–8, 240,
266, 295–6, 300
paranoia 68–9, 212, 246, 247, 252
performance error 169, 177, 178, 207, 297
polythematic 228
predictive processing 243, 246, 253, 257
therapeutic context 7, 9, 20, 138, 183, 194,
212, 214
delusional experience 1, 4, 7, 9, 13, 39, 138–9,
151, 153–9, 161–78, 184–5, 187–8,
199–202, 207–8, 212, 213, 217, 220,
253, 254–5, 256, 271, 295–300
depersonalization 7–8, 13, 183–6, 188–9, 193–6,
198, 199–200
dissociation between experiential and
propositional imagining 114–15, 116,
119–20, 121, 122–3
doxastic deliberation 9, 267, 268, 270, 271, 275,
276–8, 280, 281, 282, 284, 285, 286, 287,
290, 291, 293, 294
doxastic transparency 9, 15, 267, 271, 272, 273,
275, 276, 277, 278, 279, 280–2, 283,
284–6, 292–3, 294–5
dreaming, *see also* daydreaming 2, 198, 298
DSM 25, 270

emotion 13, 25, 45, 83, 98, 101, 116, 132–3, 136,
141, 142, 156, 190, 191–2 193, 194–5,
196, 209, 214, 216, 219, 256, 270, 296
epistemic innocence 169, 170–1, 173

fiction
and belief 133–4, 137
engagement with 132–6, 137, 142
and imagination 81, 98, 107
transportation 7, 133–4, 141

hallucination 2, 5, 11, 38, 60, 61, 62, 65–6, 67, 68,
69, 70–1, 72, 170, 198, 210–11, 240,
246–8, 252, 258
hypnosis 71

imagination
architecture of 6, 11, 107–14, 120, 122, 124
as behaviour guiding 2, 5, 12, 22, 45, 48, 51–2,
55, 83, 94–6, 98, 99, 140, 270
and evidence 2, 5, 45, 48, 83–7, 94, 99, 209
evolution of 111, 113
experiential imaginings 6, 11, 43, 107–24
and immersion 9, 10, 42, 47, 49, 50–3
and pretence 50, 52, 81, 91, 92, 107
see also aphantasia, continuum theses,
delusion as imagining, religious attitudes
as imaginings
imagining possibilities 5, 7, 64
propositional imaginings 6, 11, 43, 83,
107–24
rationality of 86
and quarantining 45, 92
and truth 2, 44–5, 50
at will 83, 85–6
implicit bias 2, 81, 98, 141
introspection 24, 28, 99, 116–17

learning
associative learning 60, 61, 62, 64
reinforcement learning 60, 61, 67, 68

magical thinking 14, 206, 214
metacognition
metacognitive capacities 5, 21, 30, 31, 197
metacognitive error 1, 4–5, 25, 35–7, 100–1,
103, 142
and delusion 5, 8, 23–4, 27, 29, 30, 31, 32,
33, 35–6, 38, 39, 140, 142, 184, 186,
201–2, 209
memory 28, 65, 67, 110, 113–14, 115–16, 117,
120, 135, 188, 198, 233, 234, 297, 298
mental imagery 6, 30–1, 118–19, 120,
121, 140

mental time travel 135, 136, 142, 192
mindreading 2, 107

narratives 7, 12, 46, 82, 89, 130, 131, 133, 134, 135–42

one-factor theory 154, 155, 186, 207, 217, 255, 297, 298

political belief 131, 273
predictive processing 60–4, 69, 71, 143
prediction error 5, 11, 62, 66, 71, 153, 157, 159–60, 166–7, 194, 195, 196, 242–3, 251, 253–4, 257, 258
principle of charity 151, 155
psychopathology 81, 119, 122, 123, 130, 131, 140, 143, 155, 166, 187, 189, 214, 216, 240, 242, 266
psychosis 60, 61, 62, 63, 64, 65–9, 70, 71, 240, 242, 245–8, 249, 251, 252, 253–4, 258

rationalism 221
reality monitoring 5, 6, 11, 12, 67, 70–1, 139
reality testing 5–6, 67, 201, 227
religious attitudes
  and avowal 6, 11, 23, 82–3, 92–4, 100–1, 103
  as behaviour guiding 94–9, 101
  doxasticism about 82–3, 85, 92, 99, 100
  and evidence 6, 11, 23, 82, 83, 84, 85, 86, 87, 92, 94, 99
  and evolution 86
  as imaginings 6, 11, 81–2, 83, 86, 87, 94, 98, 100–1, 103
  and inconsistency 85, 87–91, 99

and integration 82, 83, 84, 87, 90, 92, 99
and irrationality 86, 101, 103
non-doxasticism about 6, 11, 23, 81, 82, 83, 86, 87, 92, 94, 99, 101
and norms 86, 95, 97, 98
  see also religious faith
religious credence 11, 81, 94–5, 97, 103
  and quarantining 92, 93
  and the will 85–6
religious faith 11, 81, 101–3

salience 62, 63, 64, 165, 190, 191, 195, 253–4, 258, 299
schizophrenia 24, 35, 37, 38, 60, 63, 65–6, 69, 140, 187, 206, 240, 245–6, 248, 249–54, 258
self-awareness 183, 184, 185, 199, 220
self-representation 189, 190, 191
self-deception 2, 9, 15, 50, 81, 98, 130, 235, 236, 266–68, 269–70, 271, 272, 276, 277, 279, 286, 287, 294–5
self-knowledge, *see also* metacognitive error 5, 6, 8, 9, 10, 21, 22, 23, 28, 29, 30, 31, 32, 34, 36, 37, 39, 231
simulation 67, 72, 135–6, 140, 142
superstitious attitudes 2, 7, 9, 12, 55, 82, 99, 131–2, 136–7, 139, 141, 142

two-factor theory 6, 8, 11, 13, 71, 155, 174–7, 184–6, 188, 196, 199–201, 202, 207, 217, 254–6, 296–7, 298–9, 300

wishful thinking 94, 266, 268, 276, 277, 283, 286, 294